In Tandem—Pathways
towards a Postcolonial Anthropology |
Im Tandem – Wege zu einer
postkolonialen Ethnologie

Mirjam Lücking · Anna Meiser ·
Ingo Rohrer
(Hrsg.)

In Tandem—Pathways towards a Postcolonial Anthropology | Im Tandem – Wege zu einer postkolonialen Ethnologie

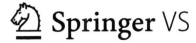

Hrsg.
Mirjam Lücking
The Hebrew University of Jerusalem
Jerusalem, Israel

Anna Meiser
Ludwig-Maximilians-Universität München
München, Deutschland

Ingo Rohrer
Albert-Ludwigs-Universität Freiburg
Freiburg, Deutschland

ISBN 978-3-658-38672-6   ISBN 978-3-658-38673-3 (eBook)
https://doi.org/10.1007/978-3-658-38673-3

Die Deutsche Nationalbibliothek verzeichnet diese Publikation in der Deutschen Nationalbibliografie; detaillierte bibliografische Daten sind im Internet über http://dnb.d-nb.de abrufbar.

© Der/die Herausgeber bzw. der/die Autor(en), exklusiv lizenziert an Springer Fachmedien Wiesbaden GmbH, ein Teil von Springer Nature 2023
Das Werk einschließlich aller seiner Teile ist urheberrechtlich geschützt. Jede Verwertung, die nicht ausdrücklich vom Urheberrechtsgesetz zugelassen ist, bedarf der vorherigen Zustimmung des Verlags. Das gilt insbesondere für Vervielfältigungen, Bearbeitungen, Übersetzungen, Mikroverfilmungen und die Einspeicherung und Verarbeitung in elektronischen Systemen.
Die Wiedergabe von allgemein beschreibenden Bezeichnungen, Marken, Unternehmensnamen etc. in diesem Werk bedeutet nicht, dass diese frei durch jedermann benutzt werden dürfen. Die Berechtigung zur Benutzung unterliegt, auch ohne gesonderten Hinweis hierzu, den Regeln des Markenrechts. Die Rechte des jeweiligen Zeicheninhabers sind zu beachten.
Der Verlag, die Autoren und die Herausgeber gehen davon aus, dass die Angaben und Informationen in diesem Werk zum Zeitpunkt der Veröffentlichung vollständig und korrekt sind. Weder der Verlag, noch die Autoren oder die Herausgeber übernehmen, ausdrücklich oder implizit, Gewähr für den Inhalt des Werkes, etwaige Fehler oder Äußerungen. Der Verlag bleibt im Hinblick auf geografische Zuordnungen und Gebietsbezeichnungen in veröffentlichten Karten und Institutionsadressen neutral.

Planung/Lektorat: Cori Antonia Mackrodt
Springer VS ist ein Imprint der eingetragenen Gesellschaft Springer Fachmedien Wiesbaden GmbH und ist ein Teil von Springer Nature.
Die Anschrift der Gesellschaft ist: Abraham-Lincoln-Str. 46, 65189 Wiesbaden, Germany

Danksagung

The contributions in this volume—dedicated to Judith Schlehe—illustrate the fruitful implications that a postcolonial impetus can provide for anthropological research, theory, and practice. Inspired by the "tandem" research developed by Judith Schlehe, the authors explore collaborative and culturally reciprocal processes in their own studies. They present alternate interpretations to "Western" perspectives and demonstrate their relevance to the discipline.

Introduction

Postcolonial approaches in anthropology are characterized by a critical reflection of the history of the discipline and, in doing so, rethink theoretical and methodological approaches. They encourage a critical examination of the discipline's involvement in colonial processes as well as the maintenance of unequal power structures. Postcolonial approaches question the authority of anthropological knowledge construction and the accompanying representation of the cultural "other" and "self". Furthermore, a postcolonial anthropology draws attention to transcultural entanglements, such as local interpretations of global symbols and practices. Thereby, it destabilizes supposedly "universal" concepts and patterns of explanation, locating them in time and space.

Inhaltsverzeichnis

In Tandem—Pathways towards a Postcolonial Anthropology | Im Tandem – Wege zu einer postkolonialen Ethnologie 1
Mirjam Lücking, Anna Meiser und Ingo Rohrer

Methods, Reciprocal Research, and Positionality

On Decolonizing Anthropology: Postcolonial Theorizing and Collaborative Methodologies 27
Primus M. Tazanu

Gemeinsames Beobachten als dekoloniale Praxis der ethnologischen Wissensgenerierung 43
Eveline Dürr

Ethnographie der Differenz jenseits binärer Ordnungen: Überlegungen zum Seitenwechsel anhand einer Beratungseinrichtung für Geflüchtete in Brasilien 69
Heike Drotbohm

Friendship and Camaraderie in Collaborative Anthropology 87
Sita Hidayah und Ingo Rohrer

Reflexivity, Engagement, Decoloniality: Shifting Emergences of Ethnography and Collaboration 103
Thomas Stodulka

What Can International Relations Learn from Anthropology? Reflections on an Interdisciplinary Student Research Project 127
Jürgen Rüland

Glocalized Religions, Revitalized Spirituality, and Plural Narratives of Modernity

Trans-Cultural Encounters, Positionalities, and Socio-Historical Burdens: A Reflection from a Muslim Anthropologist on Studying Christianity in Central Borneo 149
Imam Ardhianto

Spiritual Gifts and Material Exchanges in Four Palaces Mediumship 167
Kirsten W. Endres

Personal Encounters and Productive Engagement: A Vignette from the Continuing Effort at Understanding Rotenese Spiritual Representations 181
James J. Fox

Regulation of Muslim Marriage in Indonesia: Political Challenges Across the Public/Private Divide 189
Kathryn Robinson

Indonesian Selfie Tourism Abroad and at Home: Creating Images of a Cosmopolitan Self 209
Mirjam Lücking und Nuki Mayasari

Globalization, Migration, and Representation

Imagining Together: The Social Dimension of Imagination 231
Till Förster

A Javanese Conversation with Central Asia on Transitive Matters 259
Philipp Schröder

Faszination tsantsa? Interkulturelle Perspektiven auf die Schrumpfkopfpraxis bei den Shuar 273
Anna Meiser

Whom to Remember? An Outsider Perspective on the (Un)Making of Social Memory of the Holocaust through Stolpersteine in Freiburg, Germany 293
Vissia Ita Yulianto

Riding a Carousel Horse. REDD+ in West Kalimantan 313
Pujo Semedi und Carolina Astri

Herausgeber- und Autorenverzeichnis

Über die Herausgeber

Dr. Mirjam Lücking Martin Buber Society of Fellows, The Hebrew University of Jerusalem.

Prof. Dr. Anna Meiser Institut für Interkulturelle Kommunikation, LMU München. Institute for Intercultural Communication, LMU Munich.

PD Dr. Ingo Rohrer Institut für Ethnologie, Albert-Ludwigs-Universität Freiburg. Institute for Anthropology, Albert-Ludwigs-University Freiburg.

Autorenverzeichnis

Imam Ardhianto Department of Anthropology, Faculty of Social and Political Sciences, Universitas Indonesia, Depok, Indonesia

Carolina Astri WRI Indonesia, Jakarta, Indonesia

Heike Drotbohm Institut für Ethnologie und Afrikastudien, JGU Mainz, Mainz, Deutschland

Eveline Dürr Institut für Ethnologie, Ludwig-Maximilians-Universität München, München, Deutschland

Kirsten W. Endres Max-Planck-Institut für ethnologische Forschung, Halle, Deutschland

James J. Fox College of Asia and the Pacific, Australian National University, Canberra, Australia

Till Förster Ethnologisches Seminar, Universität Basel, Basel, Schweiz

Sita Hidayah Department of Anthropology, Faculty of Cultural Sciences, Gadjah Mada University, Yogyakarta, Indonesia

Mirjam Lücking Martin Buber Society of Fellows, The Hebrew University of Jerusalem, Jerusalem, Israel

Nuki Mayasari Yogyakarta, Indonesia

Anna Meiser Institut für Interkulturelle Kommunikation, Ludwig-Maximilians-Universität München, München, Deutschland

Kathryn Robinson College of Asia and the Pacific, Australian National University, Canberra, Australien

Ingo Rohrer Institut für Ethnologie, Albert-Ludwigs-Universität Freiburg, Freiburg, Deutschland

Jürgen Rüland Bonn, Deutschland

Philipp Schröder Nazarbayev University, Astana, Kazakhstan

Pujo Semedi Deparment of Anthropology, Faculty of Cultural Sciences, Gadjah Mada University, Yogyakarta, Indonesia

Thomas Stodulka Institut für Sozial- und Kulturanthropologie, Freie Universität Berlin, Berlin, Deutschland

Primus M. Tazanu Department of Sociology & Anthropology, Faculty of Social and Management Sciences, University of Buea, Buea, Cameroon

Vissia Ita Yulianto Southeast Asian Languages and Cultures, National Chengchi University, Taipei City, Taiwan

In Tandem—Pathways towards a Postcolonial Anthropology | Im Tandem – Wege zu einer postkolonialen Ethnologie

Mirjam Lücking, Anna Meiser und Ingo Rohrer

1 Introduction

Postcolonialism, as an intellectual movement that calls for a critical examination of imperialism and colonialism and draws attention to the persistence of imperialist structures, is not a new field of debate in the discipline of anthropology. Rather, we can look back on a history of discussions and debates that have been pursued in empirical work and theoretical elaborations and have been pushed forward by a vast number of thinkers and practitioners since at least the middle of the twentieth century in a grand variety of disciplines and contexts (Gandhi 1998; Young 2001; Loomba 2005; Go 2016). Far beyond the confines of the academic circle, postcolonial debates play an important role in the (re-)negotiation of local

M. Lücking (✉)
Martin Buber Society of Fellows, The Hebrew University of Jerusalem, Jerusalem, Israel
E-Mail: mirjam.luecking@mail.huji.ac.il

A. Meiser
Institut für Interkulturelle Kommunikation, Ludwig-Maximilians-Universität München, München, Deutschland
E-Mail: anna.meiser@ikk.lmu.de

I. Rohrer
Institut für Ethnologie, Albert-Ludwigs-Universität Freiburg, Freiburg, Deutschland
E-Mail: ingo.rohrer@ethno.uni-freiburg.de

© Der/die Autor(en), exklusiv lizenziert an Springer Fachmedien Wiesbaden GmbH, ein Teil von Springer Nature 2023
M. Lücking et al. (Hrsg.), *In Tandem—Pathways towards a Postcolonial Anthropology | Im Tandem – Wege zu einer postkolonialen Ethnologie*,
https://doi.org/10.1007/978-3-658-38673-3_1

and global challenges and in the overall orientation towards social change. Postcolonialism is thus not to be understood merely as a critical reflection of past events, but as an active, projective and progressive endeavour.

This is also reflected in the discipline of anthropology, where the postcolonial approach is not seen as concluded, but rather understood as a continuous process—as a pathway towards a new form of anthropology. It is the ongoing attempt to reflect the discipline's own involvement in the colonial process and its contributions to hegemonic Western knowledge. With it comes the impetus to reshape the epistemological foundations of the discipline, to criticize the taken-for-granted authority of anthropologists to speak about 'other' cultures, and to alter and overcome the conventional forms of describing cultural 'others' in an essentializing way.

Today, doing anthropological research with rather than about 'others' is a key feature of such postcolonial approaches. Instead of viewing and interpreting the world from the vantage point of Western hegemonic thinking, this means taking into account multiple perspectives and integrating so-called 'others' into the production, dissemination and discussion of knowledge, and indeed to consider the 'otherness' that one's own culture represents to its counterparts. Working in teams or in tandem significantly supports an understanding of how different viewpoints emerge from social contexts. Conscious reflection about positionality and the combination and diversification of different perspectives enhances a more holistic epistemology.

Judith Schlehe, to whom this book is dedicated on the occasion of her retirement, has contributed immensely to such a postcolonial approach. Throughout her career she has continuously engaged with the challenge of transferring postcolonial critique into new modes of practice, into new ways of doing anthropology. Judith Schlehe's creation of a tandem research model is probably the most innovative and outstanding result of her academic activities. At its core, the tandem model consists of the idea for anthropologists from the Global North and the Global South to work together in tandem teams to conduct reciprocal research in their respective own/foreign societies and constantly exchange ideas and perspectives in the process of researching, interpreting and writing up results. Judith Schlehe initiated the tandem project in cooperation with Gadjah Mada University in Yogyakarta, Indonesia, in 2004 as an international teaching research project. From the very onset, the tandem project emphasized the great value of reciprocal exchange within research constellations in one's own and 'other' societies and tremendously supported the South-North mobility of anthropologists from the Global South/Majority World. The tandem research project is a very successful endeavour, putting postcolonial critique into practice, and has proven to be a model beyond anthropology and beyond the initial tandem research student program between the anthropological departments of Freiburg and Yogyakarta.

Due to this success, we take the fruitful concept of the tandem as the point of departure for this book and as a guiding line for the critical reflection which runs through the various contributions in this volume. We will outline and explain this focus on the tandem model more clearly below, and in doing so we will also clarify where we see the line of connection to the other fields of postcolonial debates that are addressed in this book.

When researching in tandems, questions of representation and authority are critically unravelled. The approach enables reciprocal, transcultural understanding of social and cultural processes which ultimately also triggers reflection of positionality and expansion of knowledge construction. Postcolonial anthropology—and this is exemplified through the tandem approach—not only makes visible previously invisible practices of knowledge production and epistemologies, but it also further develops one's own tradition of knowledge production. Doing research in tandem not only means taking 'epistemologies from the South' seriously but engaging critically in the multitude of intersectional features that shape knowledge production. Instead of only writing back, which we indeed perceive as an essential step in challenging Western hegemony in academia, researching and writing together in a tandem format is a crucial second step in the creation of a more holistic understanding of social lifeworlds.

Tandem approaches thus have the potential to support the decentralization of knowledge production (cf. Schlehe 2013, p. 97) and to destabilise seeming Western 'universalisms'. In other words, tandem approaches provide opportunities to contribute to a 'World Anthropology' (cf. Lins Ribeiro and Escobar 2006). Tandem research blurs the dichotomy between anthropology abroad and anthropology at home, fostering awareness of numerous subcultures that shape social belonging and broadening the approach of multi-sited anthropology (Marcus 1995). Following Judith Schlehe's argumentation, approaches such as native anthropology and questions of insider and outsider are revisited through tandem perspectives.

Postcolonial debates often carry an understanding of cultures as moving and entangled in global space, which leads not only to cultural deterritorialization (Appadurai 1996), but also to a strengthening of the local. The tandem model allows these mechanisms to be analysed as being entangled, rendering attention to both microlevel and complementary insights.

Despite these very promising features of tandem research, there are numerous challenges when it comes to active collaboration. While language barriers and structural inequality in and between academic institutions might be considered to be minor issues, the ascriptions of research roles, power asymmetries and hierarchies between tandem researchers appear to be more complex tasks to discuss and resolve. Throughout the book, these aspects, challenges and difficulties will be addressed and discussed from different vantage points.

After all, we see the aim of this book as being to expand, broaden, enrich and revise debates and approaches as well as to lead to new pathways towards postcolonial anthropology. This also goes hand in hand with looking beyond the horizon of methodological approaches and acknowledging the tandem model as a close interweaving of theory and practice. As the above reveals, tandem approaches not only take up the issues raised in the course of the writing culture debate about the authority of anthropologists and the possibilities of representation of 'others'. Rather, such approaches refer in multiple ways to the dimensions of (re-)negotiation of local understandings of culture, of plural narratives of modernity, of debates on globalisation and of the overall impact of knowledge production on the contested interpretation of the world.

Judith Schlehe's oeuvre—and the discussions in this edited volume—reveal this intertwinement of practical and theoretical levels. In fact, Judith Schlehe's postcolonial positions have not only proven to be pioneering in the area of methodology. Her impulses for new readings of religion, spirituality, globalisation, migration and representation have left a lasting impact on the discussion and debates in the discipline and in interdisciplinary contexts. In her work one can clearly recognize this intertwining of theoretical considerations and practical methodological approaches. But she also puts a clear emphasis on the importance of grounded empirical insights. The combination of conceptual considerations and specific examples from ethnographic research lies at the core of Judith Schlehe's work and is honoured in the contributions to this book. Drawing on fieldwork, ethnographic examples, experiences with methodologies and theoretical considerations, the authors contribute to the broader discussion of promising pathways towards postcolonial anthropology. The book offers specific ideas for tandem research constellations and new viewpoints on religion, spirituality, globalisation and representation for students, researchers and lecturers of anthropology and related disciplines.

Connecting to the principal fields of Judith Schlehe's contributions and achievements, the volume is structured into three sections: 1) methodologies, 2) glocal religions, revitalized spirituality and plural narratives of modernity, and 3) globalisation, migration and representation. In the following, these three sections of the book will be introduced and each section's contributions will be briefly outlined.

We are very pleased that the fruits of collaborative and tandem approaches are also reflected in the authorship of this volume. Three contributions are co-authored, and several others resulted from tandem approaches and/or reflect on them. The variety of themes in this book furthermore exemplifies the intertwinement of methodology and theory, and the insights that result from grounded reflexive anthropological research. While the majority of contributions focus on Judith Schlehe's major region of expertise—Southeast Asia, in particular Indonesia—the others concern Latin America (Mexico, Brazil, Argentina, Ecuador), Central Asia, West Africa (Cameroon, Côte d'Ivoire) and Europe (Germany and Switzerland). In her research and teaching, Judith Schlehe always showed great curiosity in comparative perspectives and insights from other regions, which among other things led her to research visits to Mongolia, Cairo and Japan. The geographical breadth of the volume demonstrates that the discussed themes and questions are of global relevance and in fact are often transnationally connected. Nevertheless, postcolonial anthropology must be grounded in micro-perspectives from specific research contexts, and remain sceptical of global/universal explanatory patterns and challenge them. The following considerations for the three chapters of this book provide further questions and arguments on this.

2   Methodologies in Postcolonial Anthropology

The first chapter of this anthology addresses a central field of interest to which Judith Schlehe has devoted much attention in the course of her academic career, namely methodologies of doing research and representing research results. This focus stems from her close attention to postcolonial debates and her consideration of how to reorient not only the individual thinking of academics, but also the epistemological foundations of the discipline.

Postcolonial approaches in anthropology have to be understood as attempts to critically engage with the past and the present state of the discipline and with its historical involvement in the processes of colonization. Aware that anthropologists eagerly contributed to the objectification (and the implied degrading) of 'others', the postcolonial impulse aims to reconfigure a discipline which was and still is dominated by the contemporary centres of power, their academic cultures and epistemological principles. In order to do so, postcolonial scholarship seeks to make the cultural, political and linguistic experiences of formerly colonized societies comprehensible by including the voices, stories and images of people traditionally excluded from European/Western descriptions of the world.

This requires rethinking relationships with those people who have long been read as exotic 'others'.

At least since the reflexive turn (Asad 1973; Rabinow 1978) and the ensuing writing culture debate (Clifford and Marcus 1986), critical approaches have blossomed in anthropology that invite examination of the authority and power positions of anthropologists in the context of colonial legacies. While the reflexive turn instigated the development of an awareness of the positionality and situatedness of anthropologists as embedded in structures of inequality (cf. Venkatesh 2013, p. 4), the emphasis of the writing culture debate was focused on scholars' textual products and the conventions of representing 'others' (and objectifying them) in ethnographies.

However, it was not only the writing process that came under criticism in this context, but—more fundamentally—the methodological approach and the data collection done by anthropologists. The impetus to develop approaches that attempt to transfer the decolonial aspiration into adequate research practice is an ongoing process (see for instance Harrison 1991; Comaroff and Comaroff 2003; Faier and Rofel 2014; Chege 2015; Alonso Bejarano 2019; Reyes 2020), and anthropologists continue to struggle to overcome classic forms of field research in which a (usually male) researcher works alone and writes up the findings in an objectifying voice. Numerous efforts and experiments have been undertaken to decentre the production of knowledge and to propose a reverse anthropology that does not consider 'others' as mere objects of study, but invites people to study each other, to engage in dialogue and to explore new forms of collaboration and research that—among other things—question the categories of 'self' and 'other'. In particular, approaches that highlight collaboration in research have been embraced, explored and widely discussed (Lassiter 2005a,b ; Holmes and Markus 2008; Matsutake Worlds Research Group 2009; Konrad 2012; Boyer and Marcus 2020). The strong emphasis in these works on the relationships between anthropologists and their research participants, however, sometimes obscures the fact that anthropologists also work together with other academics in tandems, teams or larger units. Such academic teamwork or collaborative research is not only understood as an opportunity for triangulation, but also as a renegotiation of relationships, a reflexive practice and a starting point for avoiding biases. Especially when it comes to collaborations between researchers from the Global North and Global South, there is the opportunity to strengthen decolonial discussions and practices. This also holds true for collaboration with scholars from other disciplines, in which anthropologists are challenged to position and situate themselves in the interdisciplinary context.

Overall and in other words, collaboration in a postcolonial sense cannot be conceived solely as the relationship between anthropologists and their research participants but might encompass a larger set of individuals and entities and might take place in varying modes and forms (cf. Murphy 2020; Boyer and Marcus 2020).

This broader notion of a collaborative approach is the one that Judith Schlehe has made very strong in her work—especially through the tandem project she initiated and developed, and to which references are made in many of the contributions in the first chapter. At this point we only briefly outline this tandem project and invite further reading of the large number of publications Judith Schlehe and her collaborators have published (Schlehe 2006, 2013; Schlehe and Kutanegara 2006; Schlehe and Simatupang 2008; Schlehe and Hidayah 2013, 2014).

The tandem project started in 2004 when students from Germany and Indonesia were enabled for the first time to conduct collaborative research projects under the guidance of experienced anthropologists, first in Indonesia and then also in Germany. This project has been continued, modified, adapted and expanded over almost two decades—for example through interdisciplinary extension and the integration of cooperation partners from other universities. It has proven to be extremely successful and over the years has led to collaboration and discussion of postcolonial ideas and practices at various levels between students, senior scholars, administrative staff and academics from other disciplines, but especially between anthropologists and research participants.

We would also like to emphasize that the tandem project proposes an inverse anthropology in which the usual sites of research are also questioned and the Global North becomes a field of ethnographic inquiry. Unfortunately, this is still an exception and indicates that the locality or the spatial aspect of anthropological work must still be subjected to postcolonial critique.

The contributions gathered in the first chapter address these and further issues relating to the thematic fields of collaborative anthropology and postcolonial methodologies from different angles and with more or less direct reference to the work and ideas of Judith Schlehe. Indeed, some of the contributors have had personal experiences with the tandem project and were involved in it in one way or another. Others have developed ideas and gained insight in very different projects. All of them seek to contribute to a discussion of the dimensions of collaborative, inverse, reciprocal and decentering anthropological work.

The purpose of all these contributions is clear. It is not to suggest the one and only best practice, but to emphasize the diversity of approaches and ideas, and to explore the related limitations, challenges, opportunities and rewards. In other words, this chapter is about stimulating discussions that explore the potential and limits of postcolonial ethnographic practices.

The specific research techniques and survey methods that can support postcolonial approaches and collaborations, however, are largely excluded from these contributions. Here we point to the anthologies that have provided new proposals in recent years, either by developing approaches in (multi-)sensory anthropology (Pink 2009; Cox, Irving and Wright 2016; Culhane and Elliott 2017; Laplante, Gandsman and Scobie 2020) or by stressing feminist approaches (Neitz 2011; Lewin and Silverstein 2016).

In the first contribution to the chapter, **Primus Tazanu** argues that the discipline of anthropology is undoubtedly intertwined with colonial history and is still struggling to fully engage with decolonial approaches. Tazanu identifies the lingering colonial imprint in terms of epistemology and theorizing, and he briefly outlines the decolonial debates that have taken place in this regard. The focus of his article lies on his personal experience with a tandem research model. He shows how the categories of insider/outsider shift in the field situation, how positionality in the research context is altered and how this also has a direct influence on the results. Tazanu summarizes that such experiences, which destabilize self-perception and reveal new perspectives, are indispensable for decolonial reflection.

In her article, **Eveline Dürr** draws on experiences gained in the context of a project on tourism in precarious neighbourhoods. In this project, slum dwellers in Rio de Janeiro, Kingston and Mexico City were invited to become co-ethnographers and to travel (often for the first time) to visit a neighbourhood that was foreign to them together with the anthropologists. The article illustrates how the co-ethnographers experience, discuss and reflect on differences and commonalities and thus not only multiply the perspectives for the anthropologists conducting the research, but are also involved in a learning and exchange process that—back in their own neighbourhoods—proves to be useful or profitable for the co-ethnographers.

Instead of speaking of co-ethnographers, **Heike Drotbohm** employs the term para-ethnologist. Drawing on her work at a counselling centre for asylum seekers in Sao Paulo, she explains the multiple perspectives of employees on those seeking help. She traces which professional self-understandings and ethics underlie these perspectives and illustrates how these persons form an epistemological community, which can be understood as very heterogeneous despite common goals and clients. The implicit question raised by her work is to determine the extent to which the knowledge of such para-ethnologists can also be integrated into anthropological research.

In the article by **Sita Hidayah** and **Ingo Rohrer,** the focus lies on the question of relationships between collaborating academics. Starting from a critical reflection on the concept of friendship, which is also used as a combative term in postcolonial discussions, they postulate that it matters which terms are used to describe collaborative relations in postcolonial contexts. In arguing from their specific positionalities, they propose considering the concept of camaraderie for decolonial and collaborative approaches and expanding the discussion of academic relations.

Thomas Stodulka takes his encounters with Judith Schlehe as an opportunity to reflect on field research, collaboration with research participants and the related aspects of emotionality and affect. Starting from the impetus to show 'engagement' for and with research partners, he uses the example of his own field research with street children to explain what he understands by collaborative action anthropology and what meaning 'emotional talk' and affective relationships have not only during research, but beyond that, in academic work. He takes these considerations as the starting point to reflect on multimodal, artistic and digital approaches and the particular challenges that the Covid-19 pandemic poses for the future of a decolonial anthropology.

The chapter concludes with a contribution by **Jürgen Rüland** who takes his personal experiences in collaboration with Judith Schlehe's tandem project as a starting point from which to reflect on interdisciplinary collaborations. He outlines the differences in research approaches and methods between political science and anthropology, asking what political scientists—particularly scholars of international relations—might learn from interdisciplinary and collaborative research. Drawing on the example of the tandem project but arguing in more general terms, he concludes that scholars from international relations can benefit from the epistemological positions of anthropologists and might develop an awareness of their own positionality as well as the relational dimensions of methods. In doing so, however, he also points to the limits of such collaborations and the limitations to which not only interdisciplinary, but also collaborative and postcolonial approaches, are subject.

3   Glocalized Religions, Revitalized Spirituality and Plural Narratives of Modernity

As the section on methodology shows, postcolonial approaches in anthropology are characterized by a critical reflection of knowledge production and research methods as well as by decentring concepts and categories coined in the occidental hemisphere. They consider the role of power relations that underlie global asymmetries and intersectional entanglements. At the same time, postcolonial approaches also disclose the (subversive) agency of subaltern subjects who challenge the dichotomic division between powerful and powerless actors, between a dominating centre and a dominated periphery. For the study of religion and spirituality, this postcolonial perspective implies deconstructing allegedly universal categories such as 'religion' and 'modernity'. Talal Asad has already criticised an essentialist definition of 'religion'; he emphasized that the term, especially how it is understood by Clifford Geertz (Geertz 1973), has been deeply imprinted by a 'Western' and especially reformatory discourse on religion (Asad 1993). Jean and John Comaroff argue in a similar way in regards to the concept of 'modernity'; it needs to be contextualised, they claim, as it is 'profoundly ideological and profoundly historical' (Comaroff and Comaroff 1993, p. xi). Additionally, part of this 'Western' discourse is a rather dichotomous approach according to which modernity replaces religion and results in a disenchantment of the world. However, numerous ethnographic studies have demonstrated this is an assumption that hardly applies to the Euro-American context, at least not in this argumentative simplicity. Thus, Judith Schlehe and Evamaria Sandkühler state unambiguously: 'Religion should not necessarily be regarded as in opposition to modernity, but rather as closely intertwined in many cases' (Schlehe and Sandkühler 2014a, p. 9 f.).

Nevertheless, Khaleb Furani and Joel Robbins observe that the anthropology of religion is characterised by a secular constitution that is little considered among anthropologists: 'Anthropology has reflexively interrogated the influence of the colonial, post-colonial, and rhetorical conditions that have shaped its development; however, its growth within the decidedly secular academy has been largely ignored' (Furani and Robbins 2021, p. 501). In this sense, the anthropology that (allegedly) makes 'otherness' the object of its investigation should be more reflective of its own 'other', i.e., secular tradition when studying religions and spiritual practices (Furani and Robbins 2021, p. 505). Undoubtedly, this would also have implications for the methods of anthropological investigation in the religious field.

Furthermore, the postcolonial perspective reinforces the fact that religion and religious traditions are dynamic and plural. As Judith Schlehe has illustrated in various publications, they have to be analysed beyond Eurocentric perceptions and studied from a contextualized, holistic perspective (Schlehe 2009 and 2011; Schlehe and Nisa 2016; Schlehe and Sandkühler 2014a,b). Globally, new religious movements are emerging, characterized by a lack of institutionalized organization and individualized spiritualities. Revitalized indigenous traditions perceive themselves as counter-movements to hegemonic, historically established ontological discourses, religious norms and customs. So-called 'world religions' like Christianity and Islam are not monolithic, but adapt to political, economic and cultural developments in a given society; as a result, they undergo processes of syncretisation, hybridisation and popularisation. These can manifest, i.a., in emphasising national or cultural differentiations, as Judith Schlehe and Eva Nisa demonstrate in the concept of *Islam Nusantara* (Archipelagic Islam), which seeks to 'reconcile Islam with local cultures' in Indonesia (Schehe and Nisa 2016, p. 7).

Well-established conceptions within the 'Western' knowledge tradition have also strongly influenced the way relations between the natural and social environment are perceived. In light of the imminent human-made climate crisis, postcolonial discourses contest and seek to overcome their ideological foundations, namely the occidental philosophic dichotomies of 'nature' and 'culture', of 'subject' and 'object'. Instead, these approaches draw attention to indigenous cosmologies and worldviews wherein human and non-human beings are not considered to be separate entities but interact within a network of social relationships.

The authors in this second section exemplify these postcolonial phenomena and dynamics in the religious field. The case studies presented in the five articles discuss the methodological challenges of ethnological research of religion, illustrate the interplay between local spiritual traditions and global influences, and exemplify the negotiation of religious identities in a transnationally interconnected world. The articles by Ardhianto, Endres and Robinson, for example, demonstrate that it is necessary to critically question 'Western' categorization and patterns of understanding and to re-read them against the background of religious practices in the Southeast Asian region. However, Endres and Robinson also show how European narratives, such as 'modern', 'secular' and the 'emancipation' of women, have been locally appropriated and constructively reinterpreted in Vietnam and Indonesia. Fox explains how spiritual knowledge is revitalized in altered contexts, while Lücking and Mayasari elucidate the manner in which religious practices are represented in new media and thus charged with novel meanings. In both of these case studies, the performance of religious tradition in a changed context also creates innovative opportunities for cultural as well as social self-representation.

In detail, the five contributions are characterized by the following approaches and lines of argumentation: **Imam Ardhianto's** text ties in very well with the first section of this volume by relating methodological arguments to the anthropological study of religion and conversion. Ardhianto reflects upon his ethnographic research in a Christian indigenous community in Indonesia and Malaysia, discussing his own positionality as a male Muslim researcher from a suburban area of Jakarta among Kenyah Evangelical Christians in a remote region of Borneo. Similar to Primus Tazanu's ethnographic research in his home country of Cameroon (this volume), Ardhianto's research partners were also compatriots, not sharing, however, the same religious affiliation—and while the author belongs to the majority society in Indonesia, the Kenyah in Borneo are a minority with less power and political influence. As an Indonesian Muslim, Ardhianto was simultaneously an insider and an outsider in his field of research. He had to face the reservations and astonishment of his research partners as well as the transgression of his own norms. Still, he was able to acquire comprehensive, detailed knowledge and gradually achieve acceptance.

He notes that the researcher's positionality is not necessarily fixed but has the potential to be part of a learning process that goes hand in hand with the transformation of the researcher himself. Just as his presence changes the behaviour and discourse of the research subjects, the same holds true for the researcher himself. The 'other' becomes one's own and vice versa. Following Judith Schlehe and Sita Hidayah (2014), Ardhianto critically discusses the rigid dualistic categorization of being either an insider or an outsider in the study of culture, which especially in postcolonial societies of the Global South overlooks the multiple intersectional contexts the native anthropologist and his research partners are part of.

Another aspect highlighted by Ardhianto is the need to critically reflect on one's own attitude towards religion, religious belief and religious institutions. A Western liberal atheist (a common positionality in the anthropology of religion, as Furani and Robbins have also stated) is biased differently compared to a believer who studies religious phenomena and not in the sense of being an insider or outsider. Therefore, a postcolonial anthropology of religion necessitates diverse positionalities and thereby different approaches towards the study of religious communities, practices and beliefs.

Kirsten Endres deals with the indigenous religion of the Four Palaces, popular in Northern Vietnam: Mother Goddesses (Đạo Mẫu) govern a pantheon of four palaces with various female and male deities. Mediums play a crucial role during rituals by embodying particular deities and making contact with them. To become a medium, they have to undergo initial rituals and gain a regular ritual practice; the longer a woman or man works as a medium, the more their status is recognized. Endres' research is located in the urban setting of Hanoi in the first decade of the twenty-first century, around twenty years after the government of Nguyễn Văn Linh initiated a process of reforms named Đổi Mới ('Renovation') in 1986 oriented towards the liberalization of the socialist planned economy.

However, these reforms generated not only economic growth, but also a strengthening of religious traditions, including the religion of the Four Palaces. This development is at odds with Western modernization theories, which assume, in the Weberian sense, an ongoing process of secularization. As in her earlier works, Endres understands this process as an 'alternative modernity', wherein old and new ideas are creatively modified and wherein 'Western' modernity and religious traditions are actively negotiated (Endres 2011, p. 79 f.).

Endres starts from Marcel Mauss' concepts of gift exchange and reciprocity and demonstrates how gifts to the gods undergo ritual transformation and are passed on again to the believers. Social relations between gods, mediums and people are created by means of gift exchange. Against the backdrop of socio-economic changes, the ritualized exchange of gifts with the gods is also transformed and tendencies of social distinction gain importance.

Endres' research describes in a striking manner the constitution of a reciprocal network that overcomes the clear differentiation between human and non-human beings, market-oriented rationalities and religious potencies, as well as the material and spiritual worlds. The author applies Judith Schlehe's argument to her ethnological study of the Four Palaces by seeking to de-exoticize the Vietnamese 'other' and deepen understanding of the logic of gift exchange and mediumship. She shows that these logics do not simply obey the mechanisms of 'Western' modernity but rather draw selectively on its concepts and thus create a new and contemporary significance for religious ritual.

'Ethnography has always been a science of special encounters', **James Fox** states at the start of his article. His 'key informants' of these interactions were native poet masters from Rote Island in Eastern Indonesia. The creative oral ritual compositions of one of these, Hendrik Foeh, is the focus of his contribution. Hendrik Foeh was a participant in the Master Poets Project founded by Fox in 2006. Within the framework of the project, Fox brought together poets from varying Rote Island dialects for multi-day recording sessions in Bali. The aim was to transcribe, translate, archive and explain their recitations.

In Rotenese rituals, the human lifecycle is compared to the growth of plants: The forest represents society, the movement of the branches the interactions of its members—a metaphor expressed in multiple recitations. The poem Fox presents in the text narrates how the natural force of a cyclone ('the anger of the sea') hits the forest. Nowadays, the occasions for such recitations are not those of yesteryear; instead, Christian rituals dominate and traditional forms of performance have become less common. Hendrik Foeh now recites at meetings like those of the Master Poets Project. The context of the poems is thus different and alienated—nevertheless, the recitations and their content remain relevant. The poem presented in the text processes and interprets Rotenese lifeworld experiences with cyclones, then as now.

After a severe cyclone in April 2021, Fox sent a copy of Hendrik Foeh's composition about the natural disaster to his former students from Rote Island. By sharing the poem over the internet, they raised awareness among the population about both the dangers of the cyclone and their traditional knowledge. Its 'guardians', as the poets of Rote Island consider themselves, have become 'key informants' not only for ethnological researchers, but also for their own society. Fox's study carries several postcolonial dimensions: First of all, the Master Poets Project has created a space for the empowerment of indigenous knowledge and its holders. Moreover, it has been a 'learning experience' for researchers as well as indigenous knowledge holders who met as equals. Indigenous poetry is thereby understood as a source of knowledge taken seriously alongside other forms of knowledge. Finally, Hendrik Foeh's recitation is able to adapt to different and shifting contexts as well as forms of presentation, thereby generating new meanings.

In her contribution, **Kathryn Robinson** analyses historical changes in the regulation of marriage in Indonesia since colonial times; in particular, she focuses on women's marital rights. The author understands marriage as an 'institutionalized practice' that manages reproduction, represents contracts, establishes alliances and reproduces gender relations (here synonymous with power relations). In this sense, the regulation of marriage can be understood as a cultural debate that negotiates society's image of being a woman, her presence in the public and private spheres respectively, and gender roles. In a detailed overview, the author points out the ways in which different institutions and actors—the colonial and postcolonial state, customary law *(adat)* and Muslim law authorities—have adjusted and modified conjugal rules. During the colonial period, Indonesia experienced an emancipation of women's marital rights, inspired by Western education but pioneered, amongst others, by R. A. Kartini, a young Indonesian woman from the nineteenth century. The New Order regime (1966–1998) brought some reforms, but at the same time entrenched dichotomic, asymmetric gender roles between women and men. The Reformasi era (since 1998) is characterized by a more open and liberal policy, though it reinforces Islam as political power and thus Islamic discourse on gender issues. Robinson also highlights the role of the women's rights movements in Indonesia and analyses their positions and arguments across the historical epochs. Whereas advocates for women's rights drew from secular and liberal arguments in the colonial period, today's activists not only highlight that marrying should be a free, self-reflective choice; they (surprisingly) also adopt Islamic argumentation in order to assert their aspirations for female self-determination. In this way, they try to respond to the strengthening of Muslim positions by 'Islamising' their feminist discourse to some extent. Marriage and marriage policy are negotiated from different, sometimes conflicting cultural, political and religious positions and, in the case of Indonesia, are simultaneously embedded in both the country's colonial and postcolonial history, which is shaped by its own local traditions, as well as by Western and Muslim influences.

Mirjam Lücking and **Nuki Mayasari's** article on the creation of selfie images in the context of tourist activities forms the thematic transition between the second and third chapters of this volume—and thus between two of Judith Schlehe's main research interests: those of religious dynamics and those of popular cultural representations in a globally interconnected world. The selfies taken by Indonesian tourists posing in front of internationally recognized landmarks represent their participation in a transcultural and media-networked reality. The selfie-taking reflects the construction of a cosmopolitan identity; thus, the selfie-taker imitates and reinterprets global narratives, combining diverse cultural and religious traditions in the process.

The discussion starts with two case examples: the pilgrimages of Indonesian Muslims and Christians to Mecca and Jerusalem, as well as trips to domestic selfie parks with miniature replicas of famous tourist attractions from Indonesia and abroad. Theme parks and Muslim or Christian pilgrimage sites function as global spaces per se. The first enables international travel experiences at home, whrereas the other allows a religious experience in a transnational community. The pilgrimage portraits capture only a brief moment of a long journey. Nevertheless, they represent the transformed status of the pilgrims before, during and after their travel; the selfie from Mecca or Jerusalem testifies to the reason for the changed, higher social status of the pilgrims. On the other hand, family members and acquaintances entrust their photographs to *hajj* candidates and ask them to pray at the religious site for their own pilgrimages to come soon. In this case, the pictures are ascribed to a non-human agency.

Lücking and Mayasari interpret the creation of 'images of a cosmopolitan self' as an expression of postcolonial dynamics. The theme parks reflect processes of Indonesian 'nation-building' after the end of European colonization within a globalised world, displaying Dutch landmarks and at the same time illustrating the country's ethnically and culturally diverse society. The media representation of central religious sites abroad by Indonesian (and other) tourists, on the other hand, allows for their plural perception and interpretation. The religious pilgrimage sites captured and shared using the selfies (as well as the theme parks) thus become culturally hybrid places. In this way, the medium of selfies allows for a popular representation and interpretation of cultural and religious identities 'from below' that can subvert hegemonic narratives and discourses.

4 Globalisation, Migration and Representation

The third section of this volume discusses cultural representations in the context of globalisation, including experiences of transnational mobility/migration as well as representations among those who stay put, relating to mental mappings of the world and ways of positioning oneself within them.

In a colonial manner, early Western globalisation theories saw Europe as being at the forefront of globalisation. However, numerous historical studies have shown that globalised mobility and migration are not recent phenomena—for instance, the Mongol empire or the Chinese Silk Road created trans-regional mobility before European imperial expansion. Thus advancing the understanding of historical and contemporary representations of the world is a crucial postcolonial project that is entangled with a critique of Western hegemony in knowledge production.

From the last decades of the twentieth century onwards, neoliberal globalisation appears to have accelerated the circulation and entanglement of people, goods and money, as well as ideas and knowledge (see Appadurai 1996). A range of anthropological research has shown that globalisation involves significant shifts of cultural transformation and the development of new and hybrid forms of sociality (Hannerz 1996; Robertson 1998).

Even though globalisation was conceived by some as an opportunity for a more just world society, the globalised mobility of peoples and goods does not automatically imply greater understanding or equality among peoples. Physical mobility does not always entail social mobility in terms of improved welfare or social status, and while some privileged passport holders move freely, other peoples' mobility is precariously restricted. Biased representations of the world are often proof of such inequalities. The formal decolonization of countries in Latin America, Africa and Asia has not created greater equality between societies of the 'so-called' Global South/Majority World and the Global North or the 'West', including in knowledge production. In fact, the geographic terms are in themselves proof of Western hegemony, considering that geographically the terms only make sense from the perspective of European history. In socio-economic regards, the terms 'West', 'North' and 'South' do not describe geographical directions but mappings of the world into economically developed and less developed countries, the latter often former colonies (see Comaroff and Comaroff 2012). For people in

Southeast Asia, for instance, the 'West' is geographically not literally the 'Western world' but refers also to regions found west of Southeast Asia bordering the Indian Ocean, such as East Africa, the Middle East and South Asia. Australia is a 'Western' country even though it is located south of the equator. Thus global-local entanglements, the hybridisation of culture and its representation underlie complex processes and power relations (see Schlehe 2007, p. 454). Judith Schlehe (2017, p. 3) has emphasized the need 'to reflect upon the conditions of cultural production' and of representations of the world.

Consequently, transcultural encounters and the specific conditions of perceptions and representations of the world have been important pillars in Judith Schlehe's research and teaching. Among other things, Judith Schlehe has continuously stressed that evidence of the multi-directionality of North-South, South-North and South-South connections challenges theoretical conceptualizations in binary oppositions à la Huntington (like the 'West' and the 'rest' or the 'orient' and the 'occident' (cf. Huntington 1996)). Furthermore, she has shown that multiplicity does not necessarily imply cosmopolitan openness to the world, but that views and representations are often embedded in local social hierarchies.

Edward Said's *Orientalism* (1978) was a groundbreaking contribution to the disclosure of representations of culture as instruments of power in the context of colonial inequalities. As a continuation of *Orientalism* research, there has been complementary research on *Occidentalism,* or images of the West (see Carrier 1992; Coronil 1996). Yet rather than reversing the idea of *Orientalism,* Judith Schlehe and others pronounce the necessity to move beyond the dichotomies (Schlehe et al. 2013). In Freiburg's Southeast Asian Studies programme, insightful research about concepts of 'the West' in Asia has been accomplished under the leadership of Judith Schlehe and Jürgen Rüland in the framework of the programme 'Grounding Area Studies in Social Practice', under the programme pillar 'Beyond Occidentalism', in which considerations about *Occidentalism* have been reworked.

One of the research projects in the programme was titled 'Knowledge of the West in Indonesia: Anthropological Investigations in Urban and Rural Spaces on Java and Sulawesi'. Based on their work in Indonesia, Judith Schlehe, Melanie Nertz and Ita Yulianto (2013, p. 17) show that in contemporary Indonesia there is 'no coherent Occidentalist narrative' and that Indonesians orient themselves towards new imagined centres, among others in relation to Asian modernity such as Japan, Korea and China, and to the Arab World as the Holy Land of Islam. These multidirectional orientations are ambivalent. In her works, Schlehe gives room for these nuances and for micro-level ethnographic examples of specific conditions of such 'world making'.

The five contributions in the section 'Globalisation, migration and representation' relate to this and each analyses specific local phenomena in their global entanglement, providing examples of multicentric views of the world and indicating the relevant context of creating representations of 'self' and 'other'.

At first sight, it might seem as if the case studies have little in common: the Amazonian *tsantsa* (shrunken heads) in European museums. Indigenous representations and collective imaginations in West Africa; *Stolpersteine,* miniature Holocaust memorials; international REDD + policies; and popular commercialized religious practices. However, all five examples concern cultural or political representations within their social embeddedness and policies that are created in fields of tension and controversy, in negotiations between various actors and in a globalised, postcolonial context.

Till Förster's article 'Imagining Together' is a thought-provoking starting point for the overall discussion of representations of the world. As Förster aptly argues, any image or representation is preceded by imagination. Förster analyses imagination as a social practice of collective creativity. Against the backdrop of a general theory discussion on understandings of imagination, he shows that actors maintain or regain their agency through coherent images of complex social realities. This theoretical argument is illustrated with three empirical examples from West African societies: divination as a practice of creating meaning in the interaction between diviner and client; a charismatic movement wherein unmediated bodily and sensory participation generates images of an inclusive and undivided society; and the formation of 'greener pastures', wherein Europe is imagined as a promised land in the transnational exchange between migrants and their fellow citizens in West Africa. In all three examples, the collective imagination enables people to act.

That collective imaginings and subsequent cultural representations can be channelled by political and economic interests becomes obvious in **Philipp Schröder's** comparative analysis of Central Java and Indonesia, in particular for contexts where syncretic, vernacular spiritualities are made niche in times of an advancing script-oriented Islam. With reference to Judith Schlehe's (2019) work on paranormal practitioners, Schröder highlights the opportunities and limits for non-mainstream religious practices. Considering global and local hierarchies between religious and state actors, such subtle spheres of agency offer important insights into the agency of minorities and subaltern groups. Schröder points to changes of political regime in Central Asia and Indonesia as specific historical conditions under which public cultural performances take place, rendering them an arena of contested collective identity-making and nation-building in multi-ethnic societies. These observations on the similarities of the commercial and political use of popularized religious and cultural practices allows conclusions to be drawn about similar patterns of neoliberalization and power relations between authorities and individual practitioners.

The complex entanglements, hierarchies and conflicting interests in cultural representations are also relevant factors in **Anna Meiser's** analysis of Euro-American and Indigenous representations of Amazonian *tsantsa* (shrunken heads). Meiser gives numerous detailed examples which show that the *tsantsa* remain prominent and ambivalent intercultural artefacts among the ethnic group of the Shuar and within Ecuadorian society at large. As hybrid objects—being both socially constructed but also a product of murder—the *tsantsa* transcend dichotomies between nature and society, past and present, local and global. Controversies about exhibiting *tsantsa* in European and North American museums blur the seeming contrasts between negative and positive connotations of the objects and between museum exoticizations and everyday practices. Western exoticizations influence Indigenous representations of the *tsantsa* among the Shuar. Yet, even though the Western exoticizations are a form of ideational colonization, Shuar responses to this are by no means passive or subordinate. Despite unequal power structures, the meaning of the *tsantsa* is negotiated interculturally. Meiser's examples show that the Shuar do have creative agency in their engagement with foreign imaginations about their cultural traditions. Meiser argues in agreement with Bhabha (2007, p. 150) that such intercultural processes become a third space, allowing subversive practices and the questioning of colonial discourses.

Vissia Ita Yulianto discusses controversies about representation in a very different context. Her study offers different viewpoints on Holocaust commemoration through miniature memorials in Freiburg. The so-called *Stolpersteine,* literally meaning 'stumbling stones', are $10cm^2$ cobblestone-like blocks made of brass, which are embedded into the ground in front of the houses or workplaces of people who were deported, tortured or murdered by the Nazis. The stones usually show the names, dates of birth, deportation and death, and sometimes the professions of individuals, couples or families who were murdered by the Nazi regime. Yulianto specifically focuses on the commemoration of Sinti and Roma victims of the *Porajmos,* the genocide of the Sinti and Roma. She problematises a lack of awareness of non-Jewish genocide victims among the public in Freiburg. As one of the reasons for this lack of awareness, she discusses the information on the *Stolpersteine* memorials, which on the one hand is very personal but on the other hand does not give much information on the Nazi's racial categories, and therefore in the public perception many victims are subsumed under the Jewish majority of Holocaust victims, which means that Sinti and Roma, but also victims of Nazi euthanasia killings, or people who were killed because of their political or sexual orientations, tend to be overlooked in Freiburg's general social memory. Nevertheless, like Meiser's example of the *tsantsa*, Yulianto's study indicates that the *Stolpersteine* are not static but hybrid objects and that artists, families of victims and activists continue to shape their meaning.

Pujo Semedi and **Carolina Astri** shed light on the hybrid field of international development cooperation in Indonesia through an analysis of the failure of REDD + programmes in East Kalimantan. REDD + is a climate governance programme that was initiated by the UN in 2007, aiming at a reduction of emissions from deforestation and forest degradation. The programme is meant to offer economic incentives to local populations to engage in forest preservation, which means that local populations will not burn or cut down forests, won't engage in mining or palm oil plantations and, ideally, will support re-forestation so that forests continue to compensate for emissions. While several studies have shown the reasons for the failure of REDD + on a macro level, regarding laws, politics and economics, Semedi and Astri offer a micro perspective from the village and district levels, where only a small proportion of the enormous funding for REDD + has arrived. Obviously, neither international donors nor local farmers are passive implementors of the REDD + policy. The policy itself is not static, even if it appears as such in laws and regulations, but, just like the *tsantsa, Stolpersteine,* cultural performances and collective imagining, the REDD + policy is hybrid. Laws and policies are subject to implementation through an array of government officials, village elites and international donors who all follow their respective interests. Ultimately, the willingness of local elites appears to be a determining aspect for the success or failure of REDD + and competition with the economic appeals of palm oil plantations makes this a challenging undertaking. This example is a very strong indicator of the fact that local communities' agency matters for the future of the planet as climate change will ultimately affect all of us.

The *tsantsa, Stolpersteine* and cultural performances in Central Asia could be seen as representations resulting from the collective imaginings that are theorized by Förster. Like images of greener pastures in West Africa, they might appear as niches of cultural representation in globalised entanglements, but in fact they reveal much about social cohesion and collective practices, in short, about a society's agency. The example of REDD + policies underlines that the agency of communities on the ground can have a global impact. In this regard the study of cultural representations and people's agency in fields of powerful discourses fosters understanding of the conditions that trigger social change. These conditions consist of political power structures, economic dynamics, pragmatic interests and, as Judith Schlehe (2017, p. 19) shows, compromises. The relational negotiations within intercultural and interdependent settings may be 'subtle subversion'

(Schlehe 2017, p. 20) rather than open resistance. Postcolonial anthropology reveals the relevance of such subtle subversions, not romanticizing Indigenous (cultural) practices but scrutinizing the conditions under which they emerge and the ways in which they enable agency.

From this brief overview of the three sections of this book, it is clear that each contribution reveals fascinating insights into the specific case study and highlights aspects that stimulate dialogue and discussion in a broader framework. Precisely because the contributions are so diverse and have grown out of different contexts and collaborations, we are confident that readers will find inspiration to contemplate the current state of postcolonial debates and to think beyond the limits of present-day discussions.

In this we see the overall direction of the book. On the one hand, the contributions offer conclusions and lessons learned from tandem research, and comparative perspectives on religion and globalisation. These are viewpoints, so to speak, which take Judith Schlehe's engagement with postcolonial debates and her research interests as the starting point from which to draw retrospective conclusions. On the other hand, this book offers perspectives into the future by pointing out new questions, concerns and venues for further research, thus contributing to the ongoing discussions about pathways towards postcolonial anthropology.

Within these discussions, we have presented perspectives from tandem research as being particularly productive, even if the various contributions refer to this guiding theme to varying degrees and even if we see that ongoing structural inequalities still pose major challenges in the realisation of truly reciprocal research. We do not understand tandem research as a best practice or a strict model to follow. Rather, we see tandem research as a productive starting point to set thoughts in motion and to continue to open up new pathways to a postcolonial anthropology.

Acknowledgements The authors of the contributions shared Judith's pathways towards postcolonial anthropology as students and colleagues, and we sincerely thank them for their thought-provoking articles. Furthermore, we are grateful to the following individuals who significantly contributed to the completion of the edited volume: Margarete Brüll, Valentin Burgert, Graham von Carlowitz, Alec Crutchley, Gregor Dobler, Lisa Höhn, Cori Mackrodt, and Stefan Seitz.

References

Alonso Bejarano, C. 2019. *Decolonizing ethnography. Undocumented immigrants and new directions in social science.* Durham; London: Duke University Press.

Appadurai, A. 1996. *Modernity at large. Cultural dimensions of globalization.* Minneapolis, Minn.: University of Minnesota Press.

Asad, T. 1973. *Anthropology and the colonial encounter.* New York: Humanity Books.

Asad, T. 1993. *Genealogies of religion. Discipline and reasons of power in Christianity and Islam.* Baltimore: Johns Hopkins University Press.

Bhabha, H.K. 2007. *Die Verortung der Kultur.* Tübingen: Stauffenburg Verlag.

Boyer, D., and G.E. Marcus, Eds. 2020. *Collaborative anthropology today. A collection of exceptions.* Ithaca and London: Cornell University Press.

Carrier, J. 1992. Occidentalism. The world turned upside-down. *American Ethnologist* 19 (2): 195–212.

Chege, N. 2015. 'What's in it for me?' Negotiations of asymmetries, concerns, and interests between the researcher and research subjects. *Ethnography* 16 (4): 463–481.

Clifford, J., and G.E. Marcus. 1986. *Writing culture. The poetics and politics of ethnography.* Berkeley: University of California Press.

Comaroff, J., and J. Comaroff. 1993. Introduction. In *Modernity and its malcontents. Ritual and power in postcolonial Africa,* Eds. J. Comaroff and J. Comaroff, xi–xxxvii. Chicago: The University of Chicago Press.

Comaroff, J., and J. Comaroff. 2003. Ethnography on an awkward scale. Postcolonial anthropology and the violence of abstraction. *Ethnography* 4 (2): 147–179.

Comaroff, J., and J.L. Comaroff. 2012. *Theory from the South. Or, how Euro-America is evolving toward Africa.* Boulder, Colo.; London: Paradigm Publishers.

Coronil, F. 1996. Beyond Occidentalism. Toward nonimperial geohistorical categories. *Cultural Anthropology* 11(1): 51–87.

Cox, R., A. Irving, and C. Wright, Eds. 2016. *Beyond text? Critical practices and sensory anthropology.* Manchester: Manchester University Press.

Culhane, D., and D. Elliott, Eds. 2017. *A different kind of ethnography. Imaginative practices and creative methodologies.* Toronto: University of Toronto Press.

Endres, K.W. 2011. *Performing the divine. Mediums, markets and modernity in urban Vietnam.* Copenhagen: NIAS Press.

Faier, L., and L. Rofel. 2014. Ethnographies of encounter. *Annual Review of Anthropology* 43: 363–377.

Furani, K. and J. Robbins. 2021. Introduction. Anthropology within and without the secular condition. *Religion* 51(4): 501–517. https://doi.org/10.1080/0048721X.2021.1971495.

Gandhi, L. 1998. *Postcolonial Theory. An introduction.* New York: Columbia University Press.

Geertz, C. 1973. *The interpretation of cultures.* New York: Basic Books.

Go, J. 2016. *Postcolonial thought and social theory.* New York, Oxford: Oxford University Press.

Lins Ribeiro, G., and A. Escobar, Eds. 2006. *World anthropologies. Disciplinary transformations within systems of power.* London: Routledge.

Hannerz, U. 1996. *Transnational connections. Culture, people, places.* London and New York: Routledge.
Harrison, F.V., Ed. 1991. *Decolonizing anthropology. Moving further toward an anthropology for liberation.* Arlington: American Anthropological Association.
Holmes, D., and G.E. Markus. 2008. Collaboration today and the re-imagination of the classic scene of fieldwork encounter. *Collaborative Anthropologies* 1(1): 136–170.
Huntington, S.P. 1996. *The clash of civilizations and the remaking of world order.* Charlesbourg, Quebec: Braille Jymico Inc.
Konrad, M., Ed. 2012. *Collaborators collaborating. Counterparts in anthropological knowledge and international research relations.* New York: Berghahn.
Laplante, J., A. Gandsman, and W. Scobie, Eds. 2020. *Search after method. Sensing, moving, and imagining in anthropological fieldwork.* New York: Berghahn.
Lassiter, L.E. 2005a. *The Chicago guide to collaborative anthropology.* Chicago: University of Chicago Press.
Lassiter, L.E. 2005b. Collaborative ethnography and public anthropology. *Current Anthropology* 46(1): 83–106.
Lewin, E., and L.M. Silverstein, Eds. 2016. *Mapping feminist anthropology in the twenty-first century.* New Brunswick: Rutgers University Press.
Loomba, A. 2005. *Colonialism/Postcolonialism.* London: Routledge.
Marcus, G.E. 1995. Ethnography in/of the world system. The emergence of multi-sited ethnography. *Annual Review of Anthropology* 24: 95–117.
Matsutake Worlds Research Group. 2009. A new form of collaboration in cultural anthropology. Matsutake Worlds. *American Ethnologist* 36(2): 380–403.
Murphy, K.M. 2020. Imagination, improvisation, and letting go. In *Collaborative anthropology today. A collection of exceptions,* Eds. D. Boyer and G.E. Marcus, 40–53. Ithaca: Cornell University Press.
Neitz, M.J. 2011. Feminist methodologies. In *The routledge handbook of research methods in the study of religion,* Eds. M. Stausberg and S. Engler, 54–67. London, New York: Routledge.
Pink, S. 2009. *Doing sensory ethnography.* London: SAGE Publications.
Rabinow, P. 1978. *Reflections on fieldwork in Morocco.* Berkeley: University of California Press.
Reyes, V. 2020. Ethnographic toolkit. Strategic positionality and researchers' visible and invisible tools in field research. *Ethnography* 21(2): 220–240.
Robertson, R. 1998. Glokalisierung. Homogenität und Heterogenität in Raum und Zeit. In *Perspektiven Der Weltgesellschaft,* Ed. U. Beck, 192–221. Frankfurt am Main: Suhrkamp.
Said, E.W. 1978. *Orientalism.* New York: Pantheon Books.
Schlehe, J. 2006. Transnationale Wissensproduktion. Deutsch-indonesische Tandemforschung. In *Identitätspolitik und Interkulturalität in Asien,* Eds. B. Rehbein, J. Rüland and J. Schlehe, 167–190. Münster: LIT.
Schlehe, J. 2007. Kultureller Austausch und Globalisierung. In *Handbuch interkulturelle Kommunikation und Kompetenz. Grundbegriffe—Theorien—Anwendungsfelder,* Eds. J. Straub, A. Weidemann and D. Weidemann, 453–462. Stuttgart: J.B. Metzler.
Schlehe, J. 2009. Zur Inszenierung nationaler, lokaler und religiöser Identitäten in indonesischen Kulturparks. In *Form, Macht, Differenz. Motive und Felder ethnologischen*

Forschens, Eds. E. Hermann, K. Klenke and M. Dickhardt, 165–179. Göttingen: Universitätsverlag. https://doi.org/10.17875/gup2020-1282.

Schlehe, J. 2011. Cultural politics of representation in contemporary Indonesia. *European Journal of East Asian Studies* 10(2): 149–167. https://doi.org/10.1163/156805811X616093.

Schlehe, J. 2013. Wechselseitige Übersetzungen. Methodologische Neuerungen in transkulturellen Forschungskooperationen. In *Ethnologie im 21. Jahrhundert*, Eds. T. Bierschenk, M. Krings and C. Lentz, 97–110. Berlin: Reimer 2013.

Schlehe, J. 2017. Contesting Javanese traditions. The popularization of rituals between religion and tourism. *Indonesia and the Malay World* 45 (131): 3–23.

Schlehe, J. 2019. Cosmopolitanism, pluralism and self-orientalisation in the modern mystical world of Java. *Asian Journal of Social Science* 47 (3): 364–386.

Schlehe, J., and S. Hidayah. 2013. Transcultural ethnography in tandems. Collaboration and reciprocity combined and extended. *Freiburger Ethnologische Arbeitspapiere* Nr. 23. http://www.freidok.uni-freiburg.de/volltexte/9155/.

Schlehe, J., and S. Hidayah. 2014. Transcultural ethnography. Reciprocity in Indonesian-German tandem research. In *Methodology and research practice in Southeast Asian Studies*, Eds. M. Huotari, J. Rüland and J. Schlehe, 253–272. Houndmills: Palgrave Macmillan.

Schlehe, J., and P.M. Kutanegara, Eds. 2006. Budaya Barat dalam Kacamata Timur. *Pengalaman dan Hasil Penelitian Antropologis di sebuah kota di Jerman*. Yogyakarta: Pustaka Pelajar.

Schlehe, J., M.V. Nertz, and Y.V. Ita. 2013. Re-imagining 'The West' and performing 'Indonesian Modernities'. Muslims, Christians and paranormal practitioners. *Zeitschrift für Ethnologie* (138): 3–22.

Schlehe, J., and E.F. Nisa. 2016. The meanings of moderate Islam in Indonesia. Alignments and dealignments of Azharites. *Southeast Asian Studies at the University of Freiburg* (Occasional Paper No 31).

Schlehe, J., and E. Sandkühler, Eds. 2014a. *Religion, tradition and the popular. Transcultural views from Asia and Europe*. Bielefeld: Transcript.

Schlehe, J. and E. Sandkühler. 2014b. Introduction. Religion, tradition and the popular in Asia and Europe. In *Religion, tradition and the popular. Transcultural views from Asia and Europe*. Eds. J. Schlehe and E. Sandkühler, 7–25. Bielefeld: Transcript.

Schlehe, J., and G.R.L.L. Simatupang, Eds. 2008. *Towards global education? Indonesian and German academic cultures compared. Menuju pendidikan Global? Membandingkan budaya akademik Indonesia dan Jerman*. Yogyakarta: Kanisius.

Venkatesh, S.A. 2013. The reflexive turn. The rise of first-person ethnography. *The Sociological Quarterly* 54(1): 3–8.

Young, R.J.C. 2001. *Postcolonialism. An historical introduction*. London: Blackwell.

Methods, Reciprocal Research, and Positionality

On Decolonizing Anthropology: Postcolonial Theorizing and Collaborative Methodologies

Primus M. Tazanu

1 Introduction

Whether it is about acknowledging the ugly legacy of the discipline in colonial and imperialist ventures or the present call for decolonization, anthropology is constantly adapting to changing times. Arguments posit that anthropology (and other disciplines, for that matter) must decolonize, and, moreover, the theoretical literature on how to do so is vast, though it is rare to come across instances of anthropologists practically distancing the discipline from its colonial roots. One exception to this is Prof. Judith Schlehe of the Institute of Social and Cultural Anthropology, University of Freiburg, Germany. Schlehe has used her position as senior anthropologist to forge transnational collaboration between researchers who are positioned differently in relation to colonial legacies, believing that for anthropology to be a collective pursuit, all societies must be explorable by researchers from both the former colonizer and colonized groups. In this chapter, I draw from her insightful work on collaborative methodologies to demonstrate some of the ways in which anthropology is being decolonized. Decolonization, positionality, and reflexivity are some of the key features of anthropological theorizing and methodology that I take up as points of focus in this article.

Anthropology has had its fair share of challenges ever since it emerged as an academic discipline over a century ago. It has particularly been singled out for untold nasty legacies. First, though the field's alignment with colonial projects in

P. M. Tazanu (✉)
Department of Sociology & Anthropology, Faculty of Social and Management Sciences, University of Buea, Buea, Cameroon
E-Mail: tazanu@gmail.com; tazanu.primus@ubuea.cm

Asia, Africa, and the Americas might have appeared natural at the time, it quickly became evident that anthropologists were never neutral agents. Their uncritical support of colonial regimes in establishing control within the colonies has had lasting ramifications. For example, in places such as South Africa under apartheid, anthropology functioned as an apparatus for racist colonialists who were bent on justifying their claim that white people (white race) were biologically and culturally superior (Steyn 2001, p. 30 f.; Gordon 1988). Similarly, during the Vietnam War and the US-American imperial wars in South America, some American anthropologists wholeheartedly provided their anthropological knowledge to the aggressor, their nation (Borneman 1995). To many, anthropologists were not merely devoted to the study of human cultural diversity; they were untrustworthy, go-between tricksters who collected information about other cultures and subsequently sold or turned over their data to the conqueror/aggressor.

That anthropology was deeply involved in colonial and racial projects whereby people were classified scientifically as different and separate (Pels 2008, p. 281) is just one element of the ugly baggage surrounding the discipline. Because they were originally devoted to the study of the "others", that is, members of the so-called primitive non-Western societies and cultures, anthropologists were, consciously or unconsciously, bent on building profiles of people they saw as exotic, simple, and accessible. It was always about "other" societies, "other" people, not 'us' (the anthropologists). The ethnographies written in this context of the "other" were troubling, sometimes offering a misrepresentation of the studied cultures/societies. There are many key points which arise from the colonial legacy and the implication of anthropology. In *Anthropology and Colonialism,* Diane Lewis (1973) summarizes some of these legacies, emphasizing that anthropologists working under colonial regimes belonged to a respected and powerful group; they were not the detached, objective observers they portrayed themselves to be; their points of view were necessarily biased; they objectified and dehumanized the "others"; and lastly, anthropology was built on the exploitation of non-white people, etc. (see also Smith 1999; Said 1989).

The shameful history—some of it surrounding ethics, informed consent, respect for the natives and their institutions—arising out of this unholy union still haunts the discipline in ways that cannot be fully unravelled. Anthropologists are all too aware of this baggage, which is the reason many of them may not hesitate when asked to contribute to decolonizing the discipline. This is done either in debates or in practical ways. Among other things, decolonizing anthropology basically means acknowledging and distancing the discipline from its colonial roots as well as admitting that there are various "other" knowledges and ways of knowing. It is thus about epistemology and methodology. Back in the 1970s, critical scholars started wondering if outsiders are best positioned to understand and represent "other" cultures. It was a question that still informs the core debates on insider–outsider positionalities today, one that also grapples with the power dynamics between the anthropologists and those they study. Later in this chapter, I will partly reflect on my research among those I consider my people, unveiling the dilemmas of insider status but more importantly, revealing complexities that arise from collaborating in the field with an apparent outsider. But first, what is decolonization and what does it mean to decolonize anthropology?

2 Decolonizing Anthropology

The extensive and growing literature on decolonization cuts through the humanities, the social sciences as well as science disciplines to the extent that one can talk of decolonizing everything. Specific questions on decolonization target curricula (Mbembe 2016), language and mind (Ngugi 1986), methodology (Smith 1999; Schlehe 2008; Schlehe and Hidayah 2013), diversity in faculties (Nyamnjoh 2016), the dismantling of infrastructures (Mbembe 2016), etc. Central to all these is the call to distance the discipline from its colonial roots such that, for example, an African anthropologist sees the *Africanness* of the discipline. My goal in this chapter is to outline decolonizing anthropology from three fronts: knowledge, theory, and methods.

2.1 On Knowledge

Most academic disciplines, including anthropology, developed either during the European enlightenment period or at a time when Europe was colonizing countries in Asia, Africa, and the Americas. One can hardly talk about anthropology and most other disciplines without referring to this monumental period in European history. It is an era when European modernity and expansion were contrasted by an underside which scholars now describe as coloniality (Dussel 1993). Stemming mainly from Latin American scholars, coloniality emphasizes the long-standing impact and continuity of colonialism in non-Western societies right up to the present day. These scholars reveal how Euro-modernity and coloniality depended upon, influenced, and co-constructed each other in the sense that European modernity was achieved at the same time they colonized and subjugated "others". Coloniality is pervasive in all areas of our life—power, politics, economy, sexuality, knowledge, family, etc. (Maldonado-Torres 2007; see also Dussel 1993, 2002). The key question is how meaningful—at least to the colonized—is anthropology, a discipline that developed under conditions of colonial oppression? Voices have emerged within anthropological circles arguing that the discipline should be retained as a science and as a subject, but that the focus should be on the study of the coloniality of the subject so as to make evident the impact of colonialism (Escobar 1991).

Still, within the domain of epistemology, decolonizing also means making visible that which has been hidden. Aside from physically occupying other lands, part of the colonial project was to render the colonized invisible in all forms (Young 2012). The one thing with colonialism in the domain of knowledge production is that the conquerors projected their knowledge systems, presenting them as normal, correct, objective, and unquestionable (Lewis 1973). However, it did not end there. They also laid out schemes to erase, degrade, distort, and disqualify the knowledge systems of the colonized. Decolonial scholars have used the term *epistemicide* to describe this systematic destruction of the colonized knowledge systems (Mpofu and Steyn 2021). Epistemicide simply means destroying the sciences, philosophies, and histories of colonized or conquered people. Another vexing issue for some scholars who pin epistemicide on colonialism is precisely that Euro-modernity assigns reason and history to all things European (Gordon 2012), which is a way of degrading non-Europeans and rendering them invisible. It is a subject Franz Fanon dealt with in detail in *Black Skin, White Masks* (1967), wherein he explains how the European disassociates black people from reason, implying that they cannot produce any philosophical thought themselves (see also Mbembe 2001; Gordon 2012). All this leads to it being the non-Europeans whose epistemologies must be questioned, for they have not been identified as producers of knowledge. It is not surprising that this questioning of non-European knowledge systems is part of the fodder feeding conversations on decolonization.

Within this context whereby Western thought is normalized, another anthropological debate on decolonization looks more deeply at the difficulties of dismantling Western epistemological hegemony and its resilience within academic discourse and practices (Ngeh 2021; Williams 2018). The troubling thing is that disciplines such as anthropology have shaped the world and the ways in which we respond to this world in the postcolonial period. Scholars have generally agreed that decolonization ideally means exploring African worlds from within, on terms that critique established Western theory and practice. It is about people being curious about the world they live in from their own perspectives

(White 2019, p. 153). In fact, to talk about decolonization is to constantly critique the West as an assumed centre of the world or to 'provincialize' Europe as Dipesh Chakrabarty (2009) puts it. What is often neglected by Western science is that its constructed knowledge is embedded in a particular European context of time and space. The European experience is sometimes erroneously thought to be universal partly because Europeans exported their knowledge systems to the colonies. Thus, decolorizing would mean people reclaiming their space and looking at their own authenticity (George 2018, p. 108). This would lead to questions about how people understand the world around them when it concerns research, research methodology, and the types of knowledge that reflect their lived realities.

2.2 Theorizing in Anthropology, the Theorist

The work of non-Western researchers has entered the decolonization debate from many angles, one of which being that it should be taken seriously. There has been a general tendency in the academic world to de-intellectualize, say, African scholars, treating them as those who provide raw materials for Western academics to churn into theory. Anthropology has not arrived at this point by mistake; it is a tradition that has colonial roots whereby anthropologists working for the colonial regimes saw themselves as those who could write authoritatively about the colonized, with a few people selected within the colonized functioning as interpreters or research assistants. This scenario invented the figure of the theorist, of those who can write abstractly.

By the very nature of their work, researchers are key authority figures. They have the final say on what to write and what to publish, and this grants them enormous symbolic and political power. For example, anthropologists have long been accused of positioning the West as the centre of knowledge production. Such Eurocentrism has provoked many negative comments, one of the most stinging being that scholars apply Western knowledge, theories, and methods to every research situation irrespective of where the researchers find themselves. Some of the first anthropologists and writers in Africa such as Archie Mafeje (1976) and Ngugi wa Thiongo (1986) did not hesitate to identify the Eurocentricity of anthropology's theorizing and epistemology. They pointed out, with disappointment, that Europe is presented as a model from which every other studied society deviates in varying degrees. This is an awakening comment for anthropology: for the discipline to be truly international in terms of theorizing, it must embrace the varying national and regional perspectives on knowledge production.

Furthermore, it is obvious that because of socialization, how people perceive the world is dependent on their individual experiences and social identities such as race, gender, and geopolitical location. Anthropology, emerging from the colonial encounter, is based on the premise that the objective (usually white male) observer's experience and social identity must be ignored as though he is a god. One must reiterate that the idea of a neutral observer is a myth that has lingered in anthropology for a very long time (Mignolo 2009). In line with this all-knowing anthropologist, Francis Nyamnjoh (2012, pp. 68–71) has challenged anthropologists, arguing that an all-inclusive anthropology must cut across race and privilege. He further asks about as well as doubts the future of a discipline where power is concentrated in the hands of those who belong to the anthropological tribe. By 'tribe' he means a close-knit society in which those who belong jealously protect their territory and are hesitant to accept perceived outsiders. Nyamnjoh (2012) uses the metaphor of three blind men exploring an elephant to show that anthropology is enriched through diversity. Each blind man offers his own account of the elephant depending on which part of the animal he touches. Each version is immediately contested by the other blind men, even though their description of the elephant is not necessarily wrong. Nyamnjoh's message hits the point that no single telling of a story is complete and that our narratives are strongly influenced by who we are and where we are located. This urgent call for diversity in anthropology could further be expanded along gender and racial lines.

By diversity, I am referring to the changing configuration of the anthropological landscape wherein anthropologists are positioned differently and wherein those who feel marginalized in the discipline claim the right to be visible. Anthropology has slowly moved beyond a lonely male pursuit undergirded by normativities such as patriarchy and whiteness. Anthropological theory would be enriched if we had, for example, an increase in female researchers as well as researchers from groups of people who have otherwise/previously been the subjects of anthropological inquiry. This is especially true because anthropology is no longer preoccupied with studying the exotic "others" (Ortner 1998, p. 433). Rather, anthropologists are now conducting fieldwork in their own communities, as insiders. In the next section, I will demonstrate some of the methodological challenges one encounters when carrying out fieldwork as an apparent insider.

2.3 On Methodology

Judith Schlehe's response to the call to decolonize anthropology is revolutionary and radical precisely because she is unapologetic in allowing anthropology students—irrespective of their relation to colonial histories—to experience the strange and the familiar. The core of anthropological research is making the familiar strange while making the strange familiar to the researcher. According to Schlehe, the exotic lens works in both directions, stimulating researchers to reflect more on the taken-for-granted aspects of their culture. In this portion of the chapter, I will draw on my experiences to demonstrate how my work has benefitted from Judith Schlehe's decolonial collaborative research methodology (Fig. 1).

My reading of Schlehe's contribution to anthropology is that she wants anthropologists to constantly question who they are when they conduct fieldwork. When researchers speak from and are challenged by, for example, their racial, national,

Fig. 1 Bettina, Judith and Primus at Chapman's Peak, South Africa, July 2011 (Primus Tazanu)

ethnic, gender, and socioeconomic locations, they may see and write about the world around them more critically. This is not to claim that anthropologists never had an inkling that our different identities influence the type of data we access in the field. The innovative part of her contribution to the discipline is seen through her arduous task of facilitating research for people (Indonesian/Asian students) who would normally find it hard to conduct fieldwork in Germany/Europe. My focus on Indonesian students by no means downplays the support she offers to the German students (located within a more powerful geopolitical space) who travel to Indonesia to conduct research. Secondly, the collaborative work between these students from different parts of the world makes Schlehe's contribution all the more profound. Such collaboration enriches anthropology, making the discipline a collective pursuit and reaffirming that no individuals have "a monopoly on insights and truths" (Nyamnjoh 2012, p. 65).

For Schlehe, conducting fieldwork with another researcher—not just comparing individual findings achieved through individual fieldwork—can be a challenge, but the learning process, the methodological reflections, and (if necessary) the findings could stimulate the researcher in unexpected ways (see Schlehe 2008).

What is this model, really? In one of our very first meetings when I started my PhD at the Institute of Social and Cultural Anthropology, University of Freiburg in November 2008, Professor Schlehe thought it would be wonderful to conduct fieldwork together with another colleague who was also working on the meaning and uses of new media technologies among Cameroonians. Schlehe had started the model four years earlier with Indonesian and German students as an academic exchange and collaboration whereby the participating students could conduct joint fieldwork (in tandem) both in Germany and Indonesia. To combine their various perspectives, these students continue to alternately host each other as 'native' and 'foreign' researchers. This is a reciprocal process that paves the way for the students to see things, to see more, and to see differently through "comparative ethnographies in international settings" (Schlehe and Hidayah 2013, p. 17).

Judith Schlehe's tandem collaborative fieldwork approach is meticulous and well thought out, especially for anthropologists who are ready to challenge and be challenged by the intricacies of fieldwork. In conceiving this method, she likely looked back at her own personal experiences of conducting fieldwork over the decades and then concluded that there was more that could be done to decolonize anthropology. Schlehe admits that postcolonial "approaches are strong in respect to theory, [but] relatively few efforts have been undertaken to decolonize the social science methodologies in order to work out approaches based on equality and exchange" (Schlehe and Hidayah 2013, p. 3). Some of her key points are that this approach is not restricted to methods but also covers the conditions of the research that significantly influence anthropologists and their ethnographies. Furthermore the goal of collaborative fieldwork is not necessarily consensus but productive conversation, shared debate, dialogue, and enhanced self-reflexivity. It is another form of knowledge production that does not claim to be fixed or complete; it is open to transgressions depending on what the researchers encounter in the field. Doing collaborative fieldwork both exposes researchers and widens their horizons, and ideally, they should take advantage of the exposure to reflect on their positions—in the case of the Indonesian-German tandems—as assigned insiders or outsiders (Schlehe 2008; Schlehe and Hidayah 2013).

Much of what I have focused on so far has addressed the theoretical and practical benefits of the collaborative research between Indonesia and German students. I would now like to turn to how my collaboration with another researcher enriched my PhD when I studied under Professor Schlehe. As mentioned earlier, during my PhD, I partly conducted fieldwork with my tandem partner, a female Swiss researcher. We were both working on similar topics related to the meaning and uses of new communication technologies among Cameroonians. I was based at the University of Freiburg while Bettina Frei was studying at the University of Basel. Frei's field site in Cameroon was in Bamenda and mine was in Buea. These two cities are found in the anglophone part of the country.[1]

By late October 2009, we had spent a month in our various field sites, and I was battling with some challenges centred around who the research participants thought I was and what I was doing in Buea. Oftentimes, no matter how well we think we have revealed who we are to our research participants, there may still be lingering questions in their minds about our identities—even when we conduct research among our own people. These identities may be linked to the theme of our research, our personality, socioeconomic status, and importantly (in my case) migration history/status. How do you navigate these identities? How do you stay authentic to your research amidst ethical challenges that emerge in the field? Some of these dilemmas gradually subsided when I visited my tandem partner in her field site in Bamenda. Most of the research participants tended to ignore my presence and focused their attention on Bettina Frei. One of the lessons I learnt at this point was that I was not profiling myself enough, specifically as a Cameroonian who left the country many years back when the mobile phone and internet were in their inchoative stages. I had not provided satisfactory answers to the question of who I really was, which led the research participants to not take me seriously. Most of them believed and expected me to behave like a *bushfaller*

---

[1] Due to its colonial legacy, Cameroon is made up of former British and French territories.

enjoying his holidays.² This was my first lesson in the collaborative fieldwork, but there were many more to come.

Through our collaborative fieldwork, we realised that race, nationality, and gender played huge roles in determining the types of information we accessed as well as defining how we were perceived in the field. For example, my Swiss tandem partner was seen as educated and competent and it was assumed that she was pursuing her research interests with my assistance, a perceived 'native interpreter'. Before going into detail on how our collaboration affected our work, I will quickly point out that our research participants' age, level of education, degree of exposure to the media, expectations, and imaginations took our research into unexpected territory (Tazanu 2012, p. 50).

Race played out in our joint fieldwork in very intriguing ways. In part, it boiled down to whom our research participants perceived as the researcher. During our routine conversations in the field, my fellow Cameroonians tended to respond to Bettina Frei, providing her with 'answers' even when I was the one who had posed the question. They thought she was the (main) researcher whom I assisted to either facilitate communication between herself and the interlocutors or to help her access research participants more easily. Their belief that my tandem partner was an educated and competent researcher, unlike me (her assumed research assistant) drew from a long history between Africans and Europeans/Westerners, a history which projects the West and Westerners as those who carry out research. I would like to categorically state here that the bodies which conduct research do matter. Race here is not restricted to human physical appearance but also comprises an index of what the body represents. Malcolm X and James Baldwin describe race aptly when they say it is about power. Franz Fanon also wrote about this subject, critiquing the views of people who attribute knowledge, thought, and intelligence to Europeans while simultaneously creating the impression that "other" people (in this case, Africans) are less likely to contribute to knowledge (Fanon 1967; Ndlovu-Gatsheni 2019; Gordon 2012). Placing Europe at the centre of thought is a Kantian ghost that positions humans in terms of intelligence, begging the question as to who should produce knowledge, whose knowledge should be valued and appreciated, etc. As mentioned before in the case of colonial anthropologists, Europeans and people of European descent have for so long been linked to knowledge production. The fact of the matter is that race was never an

---

² *Bushfaller* is the term used to describe transnational migrants in Anglophone Cameroon. To capture this vividly, think of someone going to the bush where there is greener pasture and game and then coming back later with the booty/harvest.

issue when I conducted my fieldwork alone. It was only in the presence of my tandem partner that race-relevant practices (and narrative) revealed themselves.

In this scenario, one in which we were hierarchically placed in relation to what we were (or should have been) doing, questions emerged regarding who was expected to assist whom, who deserved more attention, who should have been taken more seriously, whose research process counted more, etc.[3] Whether it was because she was a foreigner, a white person, a woman, a researcher by default or an apparent (and more trusted) outsider, Bettina Frei was treated more kindly than me. In fact, her opinion was seldom challenged with passion. For example, when she insisted that life is hard for Cameroonians in Switzerland, our interlocutors, who hardly believed her at all, did not challenge her too much and were kind in their responses. This was unlike similar situations with me when they talked forcefully to the extent that I felt personally attacked. Most of them addressed me directly, saying 'you *bushfallers* do (not do)' this or that when they conveyed messages of transnational relationships. In fact, the interlocutors in my research particularly concentrated on family and friend relationships mediated by the mobile phone. This was a direct appeal that mainly drew from their unmet expectations—that the mediated relationships were not as good as they had wished. Most of them expected to use mobile phones for socioeconomic benefits—regular calls and using the phone to request remittances (Tazanu 2015). In other words, they were channelling their frustration through me, unlike with my tandem partner, to whom they extolled the welcoming nature of Cameroonians/Africans. In this regard, they talked of "African sociality—characterized by strong family ties, solidarity, and mutual support—which is opposed to counter images of decadent morality in the West" where migrants reside and have "declining consideration of values such as redistribution and responsibility" (Tazanu and Frei 2017, p. 82; Frei 2013). Thus, even as they talked about relationships and Cameroonians being welcoming, the underlying message conveyed to us was different. When talking to me, they were more concerned about their socioeconomic position in the relationship. With Bettina Frei, they essentialized what was believed to be African welcoming values and strong family ties.

Further interesting observations also emerged during the fieldwork. Because my tandem partner was not a Cameroonian, she in fact had access to certain information that was concealed from me, paving the way for us to critically examine the insider–outsider debate in social science research. To be more concrete, even

---

[3] Further addressing the topic of attention in this patriarchal setting, it could be emasculating for a black man if a restaurant bill were given directly to a white woman (in some cases, these bills were hesitantly offered to me, albeit with close watch on my tandem partner to see if she would take the bill instead).

though I considered myself a Cameroonian, an insider, those research participants who used the internet to scam people and to seek online relationships preferred to reveal this to Bettina Frei. Their thinking was that if I were truly a Cameroonian, I would know these activities; thus, they would not tell me what they thought I already knew. Secondly, some of them (young men) believed that revealing the secrets of scamming to me would be giving me tips that I could in turn use to improve my own scamming prowess. This is what they told Bettina Frei in my absence. They did not entirely believe that I was a researcher and were not convinced at all that I was not a fellow scammer.

To understand their position, one may need to delve into the cultural nuances concerning scamming and the practice of seeking out anonymous online relationships. When they conveyed to my tandem partner that they used the internet to expand their opportunities, to connect with (un)known "others", they were also demonstrating that they had not been left behind with regards to the use of the internet. In other words, they were insisting on their online competencies. At another level, revealing to Bettina Frei that they sought random online relationships was in a way imbricated in what some of the participants expected from her. For example, some of the female participants wanted her to help them navigate the online world from her position as a white woman. These participants would not admit to me that they were seeking online relationships because Cameroonians classify this as decadent online behaviour. Put differently, it would be embarrassing to admit that they were seeking online relationships with unknown people (usually white people). My tandem partner was thus an outsider who could be trusted as someone who would not pass judgment on those who sought online partners. Moreover, she was less likely to gossip about their 'unwelcome' online behaviour. It was partly for this reason that our research, which started on the same premises, took divergent turns. Her data led her to write more about the internet while mine pushed me to write more about the mobile phone and transnational sociality between friends and families (Frei 2013; Tazanu 2012).

Furthermore, within some circles, the relationship between my tandem partner and me was scrutinized, with some participants concluding that she was my online 'catch' that I had convinced to visit me in Cameroon. Returning to the field several months later, one of the participants admitted that his responses to our questions were intended to make my 'catch' trust me, a Cameroonian. During our joint fieldwork, some of them (men) begged me to connect them with Bettina Frei after realizing that she was not my girlfriend. Most of them believed marrying her would facilitate their migration to Europe.

To say the least, all these positionalities of race, gender, nationality, geopolitical location, personality, etc. influenced our data in significant ways. The field experiences described above would not be that surprising if we had not visited each other's field sites. Conducting joint fieldwork expanded our opportunities, exposed us to a wider world, and challenged what we would have otherwise taken for granted. My tandem partner, an apparent outsider, had access to information that was concealed from me, an assumed insider. These reflections on our joint fieldwork experiences reveal how tricky and perhaps how misleading the insider–outsider divide may be when doing fieldwork. The unexpected findings are some of the nuances that Schlehe talks about when she calls for collaborative tandem fieldwork.

Undoubtedly, the intricacies of collaborative anthropological fieldwork that I have described here constitute some of the ways in which anthropology is being decolonized, that is, how innovative practices are working towards distancing the discipline from its colonial roots and repertoires. Decolonizing anthropology entails many aspects, amongst which is the need for researchers to speak from their position. Furthermore, as seen in the case presented here, decolonizing anthropology also means acknowledging as well as demonstrating the ways in which our ethnographies are influenced by how we are perceived by the research participants. Influential contributions in decolonializing anthropological methods have come from those who experience the world differently because of their gender, race, or geopolitical location. Schlehe's insightful model, I suspect, can be traced to her unique position as a female and feminist researcher who sees the world differently. Moreover, she belongs to a marginalized category of researchers, being a female faculty leader in a discipline dominated by men in powerful positions. This further confirms that adding diversity to the anthropological research community truly does enrich the discipline because this diverse pool of people sees and experiences the world differently. In other words, a diversity of researchers is indicative that anthropology is slowly breaking away from its colonial roots.

3 Conclusion

Anthropology started off as a discipline dedicated to the study of "others" (non-Europeans) and its involvement in the colonial projects partly stems from this original orientation. Over time, the discipline has worked hard to overcome challenges ranging from the crisis of representation and the present debate about its colonial roots. In this chapter, I have joined the debate centred around decolonizing anthropology by drawing on the contribution of Judith Schlehe. She has demonstrated that tandem fieldwork between apparent insiders and outsiders, especially between collaborators from the former colonizing and colonized countries may yield interesting results. Conducting my own fieldwork with a white female researcher as my tandem partner, I realized that the prevailing ideas of white people as those who conduct research led Cameroonians to easily conclude I was my partner's research assistant. It is vital to reiterate here what race researchers have long known: white people become white people only when, for example, black people are on the scene and vice versa (Gordon 2012; Fanon 1967). Interestingly, though I was an apparent insider, the research participants mistrusted me and did not take me seriously. As demonstrated in my case, conducting fieldwork with another researcher is just one of the myriad ways in which the anthropological research process can distance itself from its colonial roots characterized by lonely yet adventurous pursuits of mostly white men writing about exotic "others". Much more needs to be done to decolonize anthropology, but in this chapter, I have concentrated on the work of one specific scholar who is working on decolonizing fieldwork in the discipline. Hopefully, Schlehe's collaborative methodology will become popular and normalized in the future such that anthropological fieldwork and research findings are products of collective pursuits.

References

Borneman, J. 1995. American anthropology as foreign policy. *American Anthropologist* 97 (4): 663–672.
Chakrabarty, D. 2009. *Provincializing Europe*. Princeton: Princeton University Press.
Dussel, E. 1993. Eurocentrism and modernity (Introduction to the Frankfurt lectures). *Boundary 2*, 20 (3): 65–76.
Dussel, E. 2002. World-system and "trans"-modernity. *Nepantla: Views from South* 3(2): 221–244.
Escobar, A. 1991. Anthropology and the development encounter. The making and marketing of development anthropology. *American Ethnologist* 18(4): 658–682.
Fanon, F. 1967. *Black skin, White masks*. New York: Grove Press.
Frei, B. 2013. *Sociality revisited? The use of the internet and mobile phones in urban Cameroon*. Bamenda: Langaa RPCIG.
George, L. 2018. Stirring up silence. What does decolonising anthropology in Aotearoa New Zealand really mean? *Commoning Ethnography* 1(1): 107–112.
Gordon, L. 2012. Black existence in philosophy of culture. *Diogenes* 59(3–4): 96–105.
Gordon, R. 1988. Apartheid's anthropologists: The genealogy of Afrikaner anthropology. *American Ethnologist* 15 (3): 535–553.
Lewis, D. 1973. Anthropology and Colonialism. *Current Anthropology* 14(5): 581–602.

Mafeje, A. 1976. The Problem of anthropology in historical perspective. An inquiry into the growth of the social sciences. *Canadian Journal of African Studies/Revue Canadienne Des Études Africaines* 10(2): 307–333.

Maldonado-Torres, N. 2007. On the Coloniality of Being, *Cultural Studies* 21(2–3): 240–270. https://doi.org/10.1080/09502380601162548.

Mbembe, A. 2001. *On the postcolony*. Berkeley, CA: University of California Press.

Mbembe, A. 2016. Decolonizing the university. New directions. *Arts and Humanities in Higher Education* 15(1): 29–45.

Mignolo, Walter. 2009. Epistemic disobedience, independent thought and decolonial freedom, theory. *Culture & Society* 26 (7–8), 159–181.

Mpofu, W., and M. Steyn. 2021. The trouble with the human. In *Decolonising the human. Reflections from Africa on difference and oppression,* Eds. M. Steyn and W. Mpofu, 1–24. Johannesburg: Wits University Press.

Ndlovu-Gatsheni, S. 2019. Provisional notes on decolonizing research methodology and undoing its dirty history. *Journal of Developing Societies* 35(4): 481–492.

Ngeh, J. 202 . Inclusion and exclusion of postcolonial subjects in knowledge production. Academic experience in Sweden, Cameroon, and Germany. In *Global South scholars in the western academy. Harnessing unique experiences, knowledges, and positionality in the Third Space,* Eds. S.B. Martin and D. Dandekar, 65–76. New York: Routledge.

Nyamnjoh, F. 2012. Blinded by sight. Divining the future of anthropology in Africa. *Africa Spectrum* 63–92.

Nyamnjoh, Francis. 2016. *#RhodesMustFall. Nibbling at resilient colonialism in South Africa.* Bamenda. Langaa RPCIG.

Ortner, S. 1998. Generation X. Anthropology in a media-saturated world. *Cultural Anthropology* 13(3): 414–440.

Pels, P. 2008 What has anthropology learned from the anthropology of colonialism? *Social Anthropology* 16(3): 280–299.

Said, E. 1989. Representing the colonized. Anthropology's interlocutors. *Critical Inquiry* 15 (2): 205–225.

Schlehe, J., and S. Hidayah. 2013. Transcultural ethnography in tandems. Collaboration and reciprocity combined and extended. *Freiburger Ethnologische Arbeitspapiere* 23.

Schlehe, Judith. 2008. Introduction. Multidirectional research practice in anthropology. In *Towards global education? Indonesian and German academic cultures compared,* Eds. J. Schlehe and L.L. Simatupang, 13–22. Yogyakarta: Kanisius.

Smith, L. 1999. *Decolonizing methodologies. Research and indigenous peoples.* London: Zed Books.

Steyn, M. 2001. *Whiteness just isn't what it used to be. White identity in a changing South Africa.* Albany, NY: State University of New York Press.

Tazanu, P. 2012. *Being available and reachable. New media and Cameroonian transnational sociality.* African Books Collective.

Tazanu, P. 2015. On the liveness of mobile phone mediation. Youth expectations of remittances and narratives of discontent in the Cameroonian transnational family. *Mobile Media and Communication* 3(1): 20–35.

Tazanu, P., and B. Frei. 2017. Closeness, distance and disappearances in Cameroonian mediated transnational social ties. Uses of mobile phones and narratives of transformed identities. *Journal of African Media Studies* 9 (1): 77–90.

Thiong'o, wa Ngũgĩ. 1986. *Decolonising the mind. The politics of language in African literature.* Nairobi: Heinemann Educational.
White, H. 2019. What is anthropology that decolonising scholarship should be mindful of it? *Anthropology Southern Africa 42*(2): 149–160.
Williams, C. 2018. Decolonising knowledge. Reflections on colonial anthropology and a humanities seminar at the university of the free state. *Strategic Review for Southern Africa 40*(1): 82–103.
Young, R. 2012. Postcolonial remains. *New Literary History 43*(1): 19–42.

Gemeinsames Beobachten als dekoloniale Praxis der ethnologischen Wissensgenerierung

Eveline Dürr

1 Einleitung

Die Freiburger Tandem-Lehrforschung des Instituts für Ethnologie, die von Judith Schlehe initiiert und seit 2004 gemeinsam mit der Gadjah Mada Universität in Yogyakarta, Indonesien, durchgeführt wird, zählt zu den Vorreitern in der Anwendung postkolonialer Forschungsmethoden in der wissenschaftlichen Lehre. Der Ruf nach partizipativer, stärker symmetrisch ausgerichteter Forschung ist zwar kein Novum, allerdings werden entsprechende Ansätze in der ethnologischen Ausbildung bis heute eher theoretisch diskutiert als praktisch vermittelt. Zu Recht bemerkt Lebrato (2020, S. 186): „[…] the discipline does little to train, foster, or evaluate participatory research as a core element". Auch wenn einige Anleitungen für das Erlernen des partizipativen Forschens existieren (siehe z. B. Parker et al. 2018) und *best practice* Beispiele bzw. sogar Prototypen vorliegen, die als Inspiration für verschiedene Formen der Zusammenarbeit in der Forschung dienen sollen (Boyer und Marcus 2021), stellt die Freiburger Tandem-Lehrforschung mit Blick auf die konkrete Anwendung partizipativer Methoden eher die Ausnahme als die Regel dar. Die Pionierleistung dieses Tandems besteht darin, dass es sich eben nicht wie bei einer klassischen Lehrforschung um einen einseitigen Forschungsaufenthalt deutscher Studierender im Ausland handelt, sondern dass wechselseitig zu spezifischen Themen in beiden Ländern gemeinsam geforscht und publiziert wird. Das Projekt geht von einem interkulturellen Ansatz aus und nutzt die verschiedenen Perspektiven aller Beteiligten gezielt für den

E. Dürr (✉)
Institut für Ethnologie, Ludwig-Maximilians-Universität München, München, Deutschland
E-Mail: eveline.duerr@ethnologie.lmu.de

Erkenntnisgewinn, ohne Ungleichheiten und Machtdifferenzen zu verschleiern. Als fester Bestandteil des Studiums in Freiburg etabliert dieser methodische Zugang damit einen Forschungsrahmen, der Multiperspektivität ermöglicht und flexible Forschungskonstellationen befördert (Schlehe und Hidayah 2013, 2014; Schlehe 2013). Ausgehend vom beidseitigen Verstehen geht es bei diesem Projekt auch um die Weiterentwicklung der ethnologischen Methoden generell – weg von der „einsamen Feldforschung" hin zu transkulturellen, multiperspektivischen und reziproken Kooperationen (Schlehe 2013, S. 97).

Auch in meinem Beitrag geht es darum, uneinheitliche Forschungsteams zu erproben und Heterogenität in vielfältigen Bereichen (kulturell, sprachlich, sozio-ökonomisch, bildungstechnisch etc.) sowohl als Ausgangspunkt als auch als Quelle der Perspektiven- und Wissensvielfalt und damit der Erkenntnisgenerierung zu betrachten. Ziel dieses experimentellen methodischen Ansatzes ist die Erschließung von neuen Räumen der kreativen und unkonventionellen Wissensgenerierung, die sich aus dem lokalen Kontext speist. Durch diese epistemische Praxis soll das Bedingungsgefüge der Wissensproduktion dynamisiert und die Architektur von Ethnographien neu ausgerichtet werden. Holmes und Marcus (2008) schlagen dafür Szenarien vor, die sie mit synchronisierten Ensemble-Inszenierungen im Theater oder auch mit Filmmontagen vergleichen, in denen Beziehungen zwischen disparaten und scheinbar unverbundenen Einheiten hergestellt werden. In diesen Konstellationen steht weniger die konkrete Planung einzelner, methodisch aufeinander abgestimmter Schritte im Zentrum als vielmehr das Zulassen des Ungeplanten, Irritierenden und Spontanen – damit sollen die der Feldforschung inhärente Flexibilität und Offenheit nicht nur stärker akzentuiert, sondern ganz bewusst zur (Ko)Produktion von Wissen eingesetzt werden. Mit Blick auf die beabsichtigte Heterogenität der Forschungskonstellation kann diese Form der Feldforschung in Anlehnung an De la Cadena (2015) als eine gemeinsame Arbeit *(co-labor)* verstanden werden, die nicht darauf abzielt Differenzen einzuebnen, sondern im Gegenteil versucht, Unterschiede und *frictions* produktiv zu nutzen (vgl. auch Tsing 2005, S. 246, in Schlehe und Hidayah 2014, S. 258).[1]

Die gegenwärtigen lebhaften Diskussionen über die Wissensgenerierung in der Ethnologie sind vor dem Hintergrund einer kritischen Methodenreflexion zu verstehen, die insbesondere im Nachhall der *writing culture*-Debatte der 1980er Jahre an Bedeutung gewann. Unter verschiedenen Vorzeichen differenzierte sich

---

[1] Weiterführend und inspirierend können hierzu auch konzeptionelle Überlegungen sein, die über menschliche Akteure hinausweisen und „Zusammenarbeit" im Zeichen der *multispecies*-Debatte in einen neuen Kontext stellen. Derartige Aufmerksamkeitsregime verstehen *collaboration* als „work across difference" (Tsing 2015, S. 29; vgl. auch Tsing et al. 2017).

die Diskussion über Macht und Binarität zwischen „weißen" EthnologInnen und „Indigenen" in den Feldforschungskontexten immer stärker aus. Es folgten methodische Neuausrichtungen, die von eher aktivistischen Ansätzen über eine *engaged anthropology* (Low und Merry 2010; vgl. auch Hale 2008) hin zu Debatten über Partnerschaftlichkeit versus Hierarchie reichten und im Zuge einer neuen Forschungsethik die Partizipation aller Beteiligter einforderten (Lassiter 2005; Fluehr-Lobban 2008; Rappaport 2008). Darüber hinaus wurde die Einbeziehung einer breiteren Leserschaft ebenso wie die Herstellung von verschiedenen Öffentlichkeiten *(publics)* erwogen und ein entsprechender Schreibstil diskutiert (Hale 2007; Rappaport 2008).

Besonderes Gewicht in diesen Auseinandersetzungen erhielten indigene Stimmen, die fundamentale Kritik an der Feldforschungspraxis übten und sie als kolonialistisch, eurozentrisch und hierarchisierend attackierten (Smith 1999, 2005; Bishop 2005; Morgensen 2012). Sie wandten sich dezidiert gegen die oft rassifizierte Logik der „westlichen" Wissensproduktion und forderten eine Neubewertung des lokalen Wissens, stellten Fragen nach Reziprozitätsleistungen und nach dem konkreten Nutzen von ethnologischen Forschungen für die lokalen Gemeinschaften. Diese Kritik verbindet sich mit gegenwärtigen Reflexionen über die Bewertung unterschiedlicher Wissensbestände und Evidenzpraktiken sowie über Formen der Erkenntnisgenerierung. Im Zuge dieser Diskussion wird „Wissen" als umstrittene Kategorie adressiert, die viel zu lange im Zeichen der westlichen Hegemonie stand und die es nun im Kontext von Dekolonisierungsbestrebungen in ein neues Licht zu rücken gilt. Um nicht nur für die Pluralität des Wissens im Sinne eines nicht-hierarchisierten Nebeneinanders zu werben, sondern Wissensbestände zueinander in Beziehung zu setzen und auch Reibungen, Überschneidungen und Abgrenzungen zuzulassen, propagieren insbesondere Intellektuelle aus Lateinamerika ein Denken entlang von epistemischen Differenzen und „Grenzen". Ausgehend von diesem *border thinking* (Anzaldúa 1987) etablierte sich eine Debatte über „anderes Wissen" als gelebte Erfahrung („otros saberes", vgl. auch *knowing otherwise*), die die „Kolonialität der Macht" (Quijano 2000, 2007) herausfordert. Als ein weit verzweigtes Strukturelement durchzieht Kolonialität nicht nur lokale und alltägliche Lebenswelten, sondern sie dominiert auch global ausgetragene Verteilungskämpfe und reproduziert hegemoniale Wissensstrukturen – auch in der Wissenschaft (Mignolo 2001; Lander 2000; Walsh 2012; Mignolo und Walsh 2018). Allerdings wird diesen Dekolonisierungstheorien selbst ein elitäres Potenzial vorgehalten, da sie die Strukturen des internen Kolonialismus nicht aufzulösen vermögen, sondern ganz im Gegenteil einen privilegierten akademischen Status aufrechterhalten – denn Formen des

Kolonialismus können sich auch im akademischen, dekolonialen Gewand zeigen (Rivera Cusicanqui 2012; vgl. auch Rivera Cusicanqui 2010).

Im Zuge dieser prominenten Diskussion über „Dekolonisierung" und „Wissen" zeigt sich ferner, dass die Diskurse über die „richtigen" Methoden eng verwoben sind mit spezifischen Anliegen in den jeweiligen Forschungskontexten. Die Frage, wer „Wissen" oder das Recht, es zu verwalten, besitzt, ist ebenso unterschiedlich zu beantworten wie die Frage, was unter „Partnerschaft" oder „Partizipation" zu verstehen ist. Dies ist umso bedeutender, da zunehmend seitens von Regierungen „Partizipation" als Instrument zur Durchsetzung spezifischer Interessen angeeignet wird und dadurch Ausschlüsse und Essentialisierungen entstehen, die der Intention von dekolonialen Projekten eher entgegenwirken als sie fördern (Kennemore und Postero 2020, S. 45).

Nicht zuletzt deshalb kann die Methodendiskussion in der Ethnologie nach meiner Einschätzung nicht losgelöst vom lokalen Bedingungsgefüge geführt werden. Die Einbeziehung von spezifischen Parametern des Lokalen ist auch deshalb von zentraler Bedeutung, weil es nicht nur den Forschenden obliegt, über ihre Methoden quasi autonom zu verfügen, sondern es sind vermehrt die AkteurInnen und Autoritäten vor Ort, die erst nach sorgfältiger Prüfung über die Durchführung eines Projekts entscheiden. Sie erstellen detaillierte, umfassende Leitlinien über den Ablauf und Nutzen von Forschungen aus ihrer Sicht und treffen Vereinbarungen über die Publikationsmodalitäten von „Wissen".[2] Das heißt, dass viele indigene Gemeinschaften längst selbst Prämissen und Prinzipien etabliert haben, die ihren Vorstellungen von Reziprozität, Respekt und verantwortungsvoller Zusammenarbeit entsprechen und damit eigene Forschungsethiken formulieren – in der Regel unabhängig von Ethikkommissionen an „westlichen" Institutionen (vgl. auch Peltier 2018), wodurch kritische Fragen nach deren Legitimation und Richtlinienkompetenz aufgeworfen werden.

Diese Entwicklung lässt vermuten, dass der Ruf nach der Dekolonisierung der Forschungsmethoden wohl auch der Macht der AkteurInnen vor Ort und nicht nur der Selbstreflexion und Einsicht „westlicher" ForscherInnen geschuldet ist. Denn wenn auch nicht in allen, so gewiss aber in vielen Forschungskontexten bezweifle ich, dass eine solitäre *top-down*-Feldforschung ohne das Einverständnis der zu untersuchenden Personen durchsetzbar wäre. Vielmehr bedingen und verstärken sich Dekolonisierungsbestrebungen der Wissenschaft sowie selbstbewusstes

---

[2] Vgl. Te Ara Tika Guidlines for Māori Research and Ethics, https://www.hrc.govt.nz/resources/te-ara-tika-guidelines-maori-research-ethics, das auch Hinweise für Ethikkommissionen enthält (aufgerufen am 11.05.2021); siehe als Beispiel die *Guidelines for Research in Heiltsuk Traditional Territory* (https://www.hirmd.ca/uploads/9/8/3/9/9839335/hirmd_research_application_2015new.pdf, aufgerufen am 07.06.2021).

Auftreten der lokalen AkteurInnen gegenseitig. Diese Prozesse sind wiederum rückgebunden an die Frage nach den Praktiken der Wissensgenerierung.

Ausgehend von diesen Überlegungen stelle ich im Folgenden zunächst ein Forschungsszenario vor, das durch die Beteiligung von extrem marginalisierten AkteurInnen am Forschungsprozess selbst gekennzeichnet ist. Den Schwerpunkt lege ich auf die Organisation und Operationalisierung dieses Vorhabens und bespreche sodann die konkreten Erfahrungen und Beobachtungen der gemeinsamen Feldforschung. Aufzeigen werde ich auch die Herausforderungen und Grenzen dieser Form des experimentellen Forschens, dessen Ziel die Erschließung neuer Wege in der Praxis der Wissensgenerierung ist. Abschließend lege ich dar, welche Schlussfolgerungen aus diesen Forschungskonstellationen gezogen werden können.

2 Experimentelles Forschen und gemeinsames Lernen organisieren

Im Rahmen eines multilokalen, interdisziplinären Forschungsprojekts der Universität Amsterdam, der London School of Economics and Political Sciences und der Ludwig-Maximilians-Universität München über die Touristifizierung und Kommodifizierung von städtischer Armut („Slumtourismus") in Kingston (Trench Town, Jamaika), Mexiko-Stadt (Tepito), New Orleans (Lower Nine Warth) und Rio de Janeiro (u. a. Favela Vigidal, Santa Marta, Complexo do Alemão, Morro da Providência, Rocinha) haben wir die BewohnerInnen der betreffenden Stadtviertel nicht nur als zu untersuchende AkteurInnen verstanden, deren Diskurse und Praktiken für unsere Forschungsfragen zentral sind, sondern wir haben sie darüber hinaus während eines ungefähr zehn Tage umfassenden Feldforschungssegments in den Prozess der Forschung als Forschende inkludiert – und zwar in ihnen jeweils fremden Städten.[3] Das heißt, dass beispielsweise BewohnerInnen des gewaltbeladenen Stadtviertels Tepito aus Mexiko-Stadt quasi als

---

[3] Die Aufenthaltsdauer war zwar je nach Verfügbarkeit der Beteiligten unterschiedlich, belief sich aber im Kern auf ca. zehn Tage, die wir vor Ort gemeinsam verbrachten. Bereits im Vorfeld der Antragstellung führten wir mit lokalen AkteurInnen Gespräche und diskutierten die Konzeption eines möglichen Projekts. In dieser ersten Phase des Projektdesigns entstand die methodische Idee, unsere Forschungsgruppe zumindest für eine begrenzte Zeitspanne im Feld um TeilnehmerInnen aus den verschiedenen Städten zu erweitern. Diesen Gedanken integrierten wir in unseren methodischen Ansatz im Zeichen eines experimentellen, offenen Forschens, womit wir die Finanzierung der Reise- und Aufenthaltskosten sowie der ÜbersetzerInnen sicherten. Gefördert wurde das Projekt im Rahmen der *Open Research Area*

„Ko-EthnographInnen"⁴ gemeinsam mit „uns" als Team in den Favelas von Rio de Janeiro unterwegs waren, während wiederum Personen aus dem berüchtigten Stadtviertel Trench Town in Kingston mit uns in Mexiko-Stadt Beobachtungen durchführten. Wir hatten beabsichtigt, pro Stadtviertel zwei bis maximal vier Personen aus anderen Städten in die Forschung zu inkludieren. Die Auswahl der Ko-EthnographInnen erfolgte durch die Projektmitarbeitenden im Laufe der Feldforschung. Sie fragten zunächst ihre engsten GesprächspartnerInnen an, aber auch andere Schlüsselpersonen, die in den Prozess der Touristifizierung involviert waren. Für den Fall, dass es mehr InteressentInnen als Plätze gegeben hätte, hätten wir das Los entscheiden lassen – dieser Fall ist allerdings nicht eingetreten. Das akademische Projektteam umfasste drei *principal investigators* von den beteiligten Universitäten, einen Postdoc und zwei Doktorandinnen. Auch diese Gruppe zeichnete sich durch kulturelle Mehrfachzugehörigkeiten und unterschiedliche Nationalitäten (Belgien, Deutschland, Großbritannien, Jamaika, Niederlande, Slowenien, USA) und Disziplinen (Sozialanthropologie, Geographie) aus – hinzu traten verschiedene Alters- und Karrierestufen und damit auch unterschiedlich ausgeprägte Feldforschungserfahrungen.

Stigmatisierte Stadtviertel mögen auf den ersten Blick homogen wirken, allerdings sind es ihre EinwohnerInnen keinesfalls. Zwar verfügen bei Weitem nicht alle über eine abgeschlossene Schulbildung, aber dennoch sind einige AkteurInnen beispielsweise NGO-affin, ökonomisch relativ gut aufgestellt und durchaus eloquent und schriftgewandt. Da unsere Schlüsselpersonen jedoch größtenteils aus der ersten Gruppe stammten und sich das Interesse an Schrifttum in Grenzen hielt, haben wir uns entschieden, von einer gemeinsamen Vertextlichung der Forschungsergebnisse abzusehen und uns lediglich auf den Feldforschungsprozess und Erfahrungsaustausch zu konzentrieren. Ko-AutorInnenschaft verstehe ich nicht per se als Signum für ethische Forschung, sondern zunächst als eine Praxis, die primär aus der akademischen Welt stammt und daher von Fall zu Fall verhandelt werden sollte. In diesem Punkt unterscheidet sich unser Vorhaben von anderen Projekten, die ebenfalls in stark marginalisierten Kontexten operieren und sich als dekoloniale Ansätze verstehen, und gerade deshalb großen Wert auf Ko-AutorInnenschaften und gemeinsames Schreiben legen. Als Beispiel dafür kann

---

(ORA) von der DFG, NWO und ESRC, wofür ich mich an dieser Stelle bedanke. Außerdem danke ich dem SFB 1369 Vigilanzkulturen der LMU München für die weiterführenden Diskussionen zum Thema des Beobachtens und dekolonialen Forschens.

⁴ Ko-EthnographInnen scheint mir als Begriff angemessener zu sein als Para-EthnographInnen (Holmes und Marcus 2006; siehe auch Beek und Bierschenk 2020), da es in meinem Fall um das systematische *gemeinsame* Beobachten und Forschen geht.

die Studie von Alonso Bejarano et al. (2019) zu nicht-dokumentierten MigrantInnen in den USA dienen. Allerdings verfügen die beiden Ko-Autorinnen Lucia López Juárez und Mirian Mijangos García als Aktivistinnen nicht nur über Redegewandtheit, sondern auch über eine wissenschaftliche Ausbildung und berufliche Erfahrung (vgl. auch Haenn 2020).

Die gemeinsame Feldphase war als experimentelles Forschen angelegt und primär als wechselseitige Lernerfahrung geplant *(co-learning experience)*, um darauf aufbauend neue Formen des gemeinsamen Forschens und der Wissensgenerierung auszuloten. Gleichzeitig wollten wir mit diesem Forschungsdesign Mehrfaches erreichen: Es ging uns nicht lediglich um ein partizipativ angelegtes „Experiment" zur Wissensgenerierung, sondern auch um eine Politisierung der Methoden durch die Relativierung von Mobilität für privilegierte Forschende. Ferner hofften wir auf eine Ermächtigung von marginalisierten AkteurInnen, die nur selten miteinander in Kontakt treten und von einer Süd-Süd-Vernetzung einschließlich eines Erfahrungsaustausches über die Touristifizierung ihrer Stadtviertel profitieren könnten. Durch die intersubjektive Forschung und Einbeziehung von ExpertInnenwissen, das sich aus nicht-akademischen Wissensbeständen speist, wollten wir benachteiligte Perspektiven systematisch inkludieren und ihre Sichtbarkeit erhöhen. Es war ein offenes Unterfangen, dessen Verlauf wir weniger mechanisch steuern als situativ moderieren wollten.

Ebenso wie die Auswahl der Ko-EthnographInnen oblag auch die Beschreibung der Ziele der gemeinsamen Unternehmung weitgehend den Projektmitarbeitenden in Absprache mit den Projektleitenden. Diese Beschreibungen sollten anschaulich sein, aber auch bewusst offen, um nicht von vornherein durch zu enge Vorgaben das Beobachtungsspektrum der AkteurInnen einzuengen. Außerdem diskutierten wir, welchen Gewinn sie selbst aus diesem Unterfangen ziehen könnten, wobei hier der städteübergreifende Erfahrungsaustausch über die unterschiedlichen Formen der Touristifizierung sowie das Kennenlernen einer anderen Stadt wesentliche Aspekte darstellten. Wir erklärten, dass wir in den jeweils anderen Stadtvierteln gemeinsam Beobachtungen durchführen wollten, um uns über Ähnlichkeiten und Unterschiede auszutauschen – eben mit ihnen als Personen, die selbst aus prekären urbanen Lebenswelten stammten und daher eine Expertise besäßen, über die wir selbst nicht verfügten. In diesem Sinne muss der Begriff der „Teilnehmenden Beobachtung" relativiert werden – es ging stärker um Beobachtung und sensorische Erfahrung, während sich die „Teilnahme" im Wesentlichen auf die geführten Touren vor Ort beschränkte. Die „Beobachtung" impliziert eine gewisse Distanz zum Geschehen, anders als das „Eintauchen" in die lokale Szene. Eine intensive Teilnahme am Alltagsgeschehen wurde durch die begrenzte Zeit sowie durch die Sprachbarrieren erschwert – auch wenn uns

SimultanübersetzerInnen begleiteten, die individuell für die Ko-EthnographInnen sowohl tagsüber durchgängig als auch bei den abendlichen Reflexionsrunden zur Verfügung standen.

Abgesehen von Praktiken wie „forschen" oder „beobachten" war auch „reisen" nicht allen Ko-EthnographInnen ein vertrautes Unterfangen. Mehrheitlich hatten sie keine Erfahrung mit Aufenthalten in nicht-eigenen Kontexten, teilweise auch nur begrenzt außerhalb ihrer jeweiligen Stadtviertel. Die Reisevorbereitungen, einschließlich der Beantragung der Reisedokumente, führten weitgehend die Projektmitarbeitenden vor Ort durch, ebenso wie die Organisation der Feldforschungssegmente, was aufgrund der damit verbundenen Hürden zu einer einschlägigen Feldforschungserfahrung wurde. Die Bürokratie und Hierarchie von Pässen, Visaanträgen und Reisebeschränkungen vermittelte das konkrete Erleben von Mobilitäts- und Grenzregimen, von Vorschriften, Stereotypisierungen und Benachteiligungen aufgrund von Phänotypus und Nationalität. Nicht nur bei den Reisevorbereitungen, sondern auch auf den Reisen selbst traten Divergenzen sehr deutlich hervor. Geplant war, dass die Ko-EthnographInnen in Begleitung der ProjektmitarbeiterInnen die Reise antreten würden. Allerdings verkomplizierte sich dies selbst noch am Flughafenschalter als die Vorlage von Impfpässen gefordert wurde, welche beispielsweise die Ko-EthnographInnen aus den Favelas nicht zur Verfügung hatten. Auch Reiserouten mussten kurzfristig geändert werden, als die Mexikaner ihren Flug nach Kingston nicht wie geplant antreten konnten, weil sie trotz aller Bemühungen kein Transitvisum für die USA erhielten und schließlich über Panama fliegen mussten. Allerdings konnte die Projektmitarbeiterin mit slowenischem Pass wiederum diesen Flug wegen Impfbestimmungen nicht wahrnehmen, weshalb sich die Gruppe am Flughafen spontan trennen musste.

Diese Formen der ungleichen Behandlung von Reisenden wurde innerhalb der gesamten Gruppe im Rahmen unserer regelmäßig stattfindenden Reflexionsrunden ausführlich diskutiert, zumal die Mehrzahl der Ko-EthnographInnen zum ersten Mal eine Reise angetreten hatte und sich dieser diskriminierenden Unterschiede bis dato nicht bewusst war. Bereits in diesen Gesprächen stellte sich eine intensive Reflexion über die jeweils eigene Situation ein, und vor allem über die Frage, wie diese Differenzierungen begründet wurden. Dadurch gelang eine Thematisierung von übergeordneten Strukturen und Machtverhältnissen, die über individuelle Lebenswelten hinauswiesen, diese aber auch prägten und einen gemeinsamen Referenzrahmen für die Gruppe herstellten.

Unsere Teams vor Ort hätten wohl kaum heterogener sein können mit Blick auf Herkunft, Status und Ausbildung, einschließlich der Hierarchiestufen an den Universitäten. Die Tatsache, dass die beteiligten Ko-EthnographInnen allesamt aus stigmatisierten und gewaltbeladenen Stadtvierteln stammten, war ihr kleinster gemeinsamer Nenner. Ansonsten waren sie sehr unterschiedlich mit Blick auf die Skalierung von Armut, Schulabschluss und Reiseerfahrung. So war auch die Unterbringung in Hotels für einige ebenso erstmalig wie die Benutzung der damit verbundenen Infrastruktur, beispielweise Aufzug oder Schlüsselsystem. „Fremd" erschienen auch einige Spezifika in den jeweiligen Städten, wie Straßenbahnen oder Gondeln in Rio de Janeiro, ganz abgesehen von teilweise ungewohnten klimatischen Verhältnissen, Währungen, Speisen und Tagesrhythmen.

Auch wenn diese Beschreibung als eine Auflistung von Defiziten gelesen werden könnte, spiegeln sich darin vor allem unsere eigenen Unsicherheiten und Befürchtungen wider. Schließlich war es für uns als AkademikerInnen das erste Mal, aus unserer Sicht nicht-erfahrene, nicht-reisegewandte Personen in einen gänzlich anderen Kontext zu integrieren. Jedoch lösten die von uns gesehenen Hürden keine gravierenden Unsicherheiten aufseiten der Ko-EthnographInnen aus. Selbst die erste Flugreise empfand eine Person zu unserer Überraschung nicht als sonderlich aufregend. Entgegen unseren Befürchtungen traten die AkteurInnen weitgehend selbstbewusst und mutig auf, getrieben von Neugier und Interesse, sich mit der lokalen Umgebung vertraut zu machen und diese mit allen Sinnen zu erfahren – Nicht-Wissen konterten sie häufig mit Humor und verbuchten dieses weniger als ein Defizit auf ihrer Seite, sondern eher als Merkwürdigkeit auf der anderen Seite.

Mit diesem Forschungsdesign verbindet sich eine Multiplizierung, Überkreuzung und damit eine Auflösung von klar konturierten Rollen im Forschungsprozess. Alle Beteiligten nehmen mehrere Rollen und Positionen wechselseitig ein – die Ko-EthnographInnen sind sowohl „Gegenstand" der Forschung als auch Forschende. Sie beobachten und erleben in ihnen fremden Städten spezifische soziale Welten, die ihnen mehr oder weniger vertraut sind – gekennzeichnet von Benachteiligung, Stereotypisierung und Diskriminierung sowie auch von Gewalt, internen Machtkonflikten und NGO-Initiativen, die es „gut" mit den BewohnerInnen meinen. Außerdem verfügen sie über eine gewisse Expertise mit Blick auf die Touristifizierung ihrer eigenen Lebenswelten, was eine weitere, letztlich vertraute Dimension darstellt. Nichts davon hingegen traf auf uns als AkademikerInnen zu – wodurch sich auch unsere Rollen im Team veränderten. Während wir beispielweise bei den Vorbereitungen der Reise und der Artikulation des Forschungsdesigns dominiert hatten, wurden wir nun zu „Lernenden", da wir über keine eigenen lebensweltlichen Erfahrungen in sogenannten „Slums"[5] verfügten. Diese Verschiebung der Rollen und die Anerkennung ihrer Expertisen wurde deutlich wahrgenommen und stimulierte die Ko-EthnographInnen, ihr Wissen zu artikulieren und mit uns zu teilen.

Durch die Destabilisierung der vorgegebenen Rollen in diesem methodischen Ansatz zeigt sich einmal mehr, dass die Abgrenzung von einer Ethnologie „at home" und „of the other" fragwürdig ist. Die Rollen und Positionen im Feldforschungsprozess sind immer aufeinander bezogen und miteinander verbunden, außerdem kann das „Zuhause" und das „Feld" nicht klar voneinander abgegrenzt werden. Dies gilt vor dem Hintergrund der globalen Vernetzung in mehrfacher Hinsicht, wie Gupta und Ferguson schon vor Jahrzehnten feststellten: „[…] in an interconnected world, we are never really ‚out of the field'" (Gupta und Ferguson 1997, S. 35). Vielmehr nehmen wir unser „Zuhause" zwangsläufig mit ins Feld – selbst dann, wenn wir es sogar als hinderlich empfinden mögen, können wir unsere eigenen sozialen Zusammenhänge und die damit verbundenen Positionen nicht einfach abstreifen (Dürr und Sökefeld 2017). Dies gilt auch für meine eigene Positionalität – ich schreibe diesen Beitrag aus der privilegierten Perspektive einer Professorin, auch wenn ich versuche, weniger privilegierten Positionen besondere Aufmerksamkeit zu schenken und gerade diese im Feldforschungsprozess zu beleuchten.

3 Gemeinsames Erforschen der Kommerzialisierung von Armut in den urbanen Amerikas

Unser Forschungsprojekt fokussierte primär auf Städte des globalen Südens in den Amerikas, wo unter dem Schlagwort „Slumtourismus" ganz unterschiedliche Formen der Inwertsetzung von Armut subsummiert werden. Die Bandbreite reicht von kommerziellen Anbietern, die TouristInnen mit Jeeps durch „Slums" fahren, über Motorrad- oder Fahrradtouren, die sich insbesondere an ein jüngeres Publikum richten, bis hin zu Besichtigungen zu Fuß mit lokalen Guides, die selbst aus den betreffenden Stadtvierteln stammen. Im Mittelpunkt unseres Interesses stand der gemeindebasierte Tourismus *(community based tourism)*, der häufig ein aktivistisches oder karitatives Anliegen vertritt und auf die prekäre Lebenssituation in „Slums" aufmerksam machen möchte (vgl. u. a. Dürr et al. 2021; Frenzel 2016;

---

[5] Der Begriff „Slum" ist umstritten, da es sich dabei in der Regel um eine Zuschreibung von außen handelt, die essentialisierend und homogenisierend auf völlig verschiedene lokale Kontexte angewandt wird (vgl. Dürr 2021).

Freire-Medeiros 2013; Vodopivec 2017; Vodopivec und Dürr 2019). In diesem Sinne verstehen sich die Führungen auch als eine Form der politischen Kritik und Ermächtigung, die eine selbstbestimmte Darstellung der eigenen Lebensform ermöglichen. Der thematische Schwerpunkt unseres städteübergreifenden Projekts lag auf den verschiedenen Formen der Selbstvermarktung und Repräsentationspolitik dieser Stadtviertel. Dabei spielten die Guides eine besondere Rolle, da sie als *broker* maßgeblich an der Transformation von „Armut" in ein touristisches Produkt beteiligt sind (Dürr et al. 2020; Jones et al. 2020).

Das Projekt inkludierte eine vielschichtige empirische Forschung, die in mehreren Phasen von 2015 bis 2016 durchgeführt wurde. Zu den Methoden zählte das konventionelle Repertoire einer stationären Feldforschung, wie Teilnehmende Beobachtung sowie formelle und informelle Interviews. Weitere Quellen, darunter eine Reihe populärer Medien (Filme, Musik, Videos, Blogs, soziale Medien, Romane) sowie schriftliche Dokumente, touristische Websites, Werbematerialien und Medienberichte, ergänzten die Beobachtungs- und Interviewdaten. Die Einbeziehung dieses breiten Quellenspektrums ermöglichte uns ein tieferes Verständnis der Repräsentationsstrategien und Ästhetisierungen, die bei der Vermarktung der Lebensweisen in stigmatisierten Vierteln zum Tragen kommen. In regelmäßig stattfindenden Teambesprechungen an den Universitäten in Amsterdam, London und München analysierten wir die Daten aus der Feldarbeit und verfassten in Schreibwerkstätten gemeinsam Texte. Gerade für diese vergleichenden Arbeitsschritte war es von immensem Vorteil, dass wir alle die Feldforschungsorte und maßgeblichen AkteurInnen des jeweils anderen Teams aus eigener Anschauung kannten.

Situationen und Orte mit allen Sinnen zu erfahren, zählt zum festen Bestand der ethnologischen Methoden und ist zentral für die Erschließung der Beziehungen von Menschen zu ihren soziomateriellen Umwelten (u. a. Pink 2009). In unserer Forschung spielte das körperliche Erleben auch deshalb eine wichtige Rolle, weil die Sensorik im Tourismus gezielt eingesetzt wird – denn Armut und Gewalt werden nicht nur visuell, sondern auch durch andere Sinne wahrgenommen (Jaffe et al. 2020). Darüber hinaus ist das Gehen als touristische Praxis sowie das Vertrauen in den Guide wichtig, der/die uns über mehrere Stunden in der Hitze über steile und verschlungene, aber vor allem auch „sichere" Wege führte, da die Gefahren in Slums nicht zu unterschätzen sind und in den touristischen Inszenierungen ebenfalls thematisiert werden.

Im Folgenden greife ich schwerpunktmäßig die Forschungskonstellation in Rio de Janeiro[6] heraus und fokussiere auf die Erfahrungen von Teresa aus Tepito in Mexiko-Stadt sowie von Luisa aus Trench Town in Kingston, Jamaika.[7] Beide Frauen ähneln sich darin, dass sie zum ersten Mal ins Ausland gereist sind, beide sprechen eine eher einfache Sprache und verfügen über einen niedrigen formellen Bildungsgrad. Teresa ist Mitte 50, arbeitet als Straßenhändlerin in Tepito und kennt das *barrio* ausgesprochen gut. Sie ist dort geboren und aufgewachsen, stammt aus einer großen Familie, zu der sie engen Kontakt pflegt, ist selbst unverheiratet und kinderlos. Teresa zeigt einen gewissen Stolz, aus dem *barrio bravo* in Mexiko-Stadt zu stammen und sieht die erst beginnende Touristifizierung ihres Stadtviertels weitgehend positiv. Luisa ist etwas jünger als Teresa und arbeitet im *culture yard* in Trench Town, der als Museum der Ikone Bob Marley dient. Sie gehört damit zu den wenigen Personen in ihrem Stadtviertel, die über eine feste Anstellung verfügen. Als alleinerziehende Mutter wohnt sie eher bescheiden in unmittelbarerer Nähe des *culture yard* und führt ihre Tätigkeit als Touristenführerin mal mit mehr, mal mit weniger Empathie aus. Luisa und Teresa unterscheiden sich auch durch ihre Sprache (Spanisch bzw. Patwa/Englisch), was die Kommunikation zwischen ihnen trotz der SimultanübersetzerInnen erschwerte. Beide Frauen zählten zu den Schlüsselfiguren für die Feldforschungen in Tepito bzw. in Trench Town.

3.1 Reden und Übersetzen

In Rio de Janeiro gehört der Besuch mindestens einer Favela zum Standardprogramm der Stadtbesichtigung. An Auswahl mangelt es wahrlich nicht, sondern ganz im Gegenteil eher an Entscheidungshilfen. Es existieren nicht nur unzählige Touren in den verschiedensten Varianten, sondern auch unterschiedliche Profile, mit denen sich die Favelas selbst vermarkten. Das Angebot reicht von den berühmten Sambaschulen über Drehorte ikonischer Filme bis hin zur Werbung mit einzigartiger Geschichte und Architektur. In Vigidal ist es vorrangig das

---

[6] Die Forschungskonstellation in Rio de Janeiro schloss eine weitere Person aus Kingston ein. Als Aktivist kooperiert Marc mit NGOs und ist in der Sozialarbeit engagiert.

[7] Leider war es mir trotz intensiven Bemühens vor Ort im September 2021 nicht möglich, das Einverständnis für die Verwendung des Klarnamens für diesen Beitrag einzuholen. Daher konnte ich auch den Inhalt dieses Textes nicht mit den Ko-EthnographInnen diskutieren. Es handelt sich bei dieser Darstellung also rein um meine Wahrnehmung und Interpretation des Geschehens.

Panorama, das TouristInnen anlocken soll, denn diese Favela bietet einen spektakulären Ausblick auf die ohnehin weltberühmten Strände und Buchten von Rio de Janeiro. Aufgrund der zunehmenden Präsenz von TouristInnen eröffneten in jüngerer Zeit einige Bars, B&Bs und Hostels für Backpacker, die von „oben" den Sonnenuntergang genießen können, ohne nachts durch die Favela absteigen zu müssen.

Diese Prozesse befördern jedoch nicht nur die Ökonomie, sondern auch die Gentrifizierung in Vigidal. Hinzu kommen Gerüchte, dass sich Fußballstars wie David Beckham oder Diego Maradona hier Grundstücke gekauft hätten. Die EinwohnerInnen in Vigidal bewerten diese Entwicklung unterschiedlich. Während einige Personen die neue Aufmerksamkeit als eine Form der Wertschätzung gutheißen und die ökonomischen Chancen wahrnehmen, formiert sich auch Widerstand gegen die steigenden Preise in der Favela.

Dies verdeutlichte unser Gespräch mit AktivistInnen aus Vigidal, die von einer NGO unterstützt wurden. Sie sahen die gegenwärtige Entwicklung der Favela kritisch und betrachteten es als ihre Aufgabe, das Bewusstsein der EinwohnerInnen für die negativen Auswirkungen des Tourismus in Vigidal zu schärfen und insbesondere gegen Gentrifizierung anzugehen. Den zunehmenden Einfluss von außenstehenden Personen, die die Favela für ihre Zwecke kapitalisierten und die Preise in die Höhe trieben, beklagten sie besonders. Ihre Ausführungen waren durchzogen von einer NGO-Sprache mit spezifischem Vokabular. Nahezu selbstverständlich fielen immer wieder Begriffe wie „Gentrifizierung", „Kapitalismus", „Neoliberalismus" und „Globalisierung". Weder Luisa noch Teresa waren mit dieser Sprache vertraut, geschweige denn zählten diese Begriffe zu ihrem Wortschatz. Dies verkomplizierte die simultane Übersetzung erheblich, da es eben nicht nur darum ging, Worte in eine andere Sprache zu übertragen, sondern auch darum, zwischen verschiedenen sozialen Welten zu übersetzen und damit verbundene Konzepte und Vorstellungen zu vermitteln. In dieser Situation wurde mir als Projektleiterin bewusst, dass ich meine Rolle als *broker* in dieser Konstellation unterschätzt hatte. „Übersetzung" hatte ich zu selbstverständlich den ÜbersetzerInnen überlassen, ohne der Multidimensionalität von Übersetzung genügend Rechnung zu tragen. Darüber hinaus offenbarte dieses Beispiel die starke Asymmetrie und Diversität der oft homogenisierten Kategorie „SlumbewohnerInnen", deren Kommunikation auch untereinander nicht unproblematisch ist.

Auf diese Übersetzungsprobleme reagierten Teresa und Luisa unterschiedlich. Während sich Luisa eher zurückzog und die Umgebung in Augenschein nahm, verfolgte Teresa ungeachtet der Kommunikationsprobleme das Gespräch aufmerksam und stellte einige Fragen. Sie wollte wissen, ob unsere GesprächspartnerInnen selbst aus der Favela und damit aus der hiesigen Gemeinschaft stammen würden. Denn nur dann könnte sie ihren Aussagen trauen. Schließlich zog sie Parallelen zu Tepito und kommentierte, dass auch dort „Auswärtige" für problematische Entwicklungen im „Inneren" verantwortlich seien und zwar an erster Stelle die „Koreaner" und „Narcos" – beide wollten sich in Tepito „einkaufen" mit dem Ziel, das Stadtviertel schlussendlich zu kontrollieren. Diese Entwicklung bezeichnete Teresa als Gentrifizierung – und übertrug den Begriff damit auf ihren eigenen Erfahrungshorizont. Es läge nun an den EinwohnerInnen der Favela selbst, den „Auswärtigen" Grenzen aufzuzeigen und in deutlicher Sprache klarzumachen: bis hierher und nicht weiter – womit sie auf ein in Tepito sehr präsentes Narrativ des Widerstands gegen nicht-lokale Kräfte rekurrierte, verdichtet in dem Ausspruch *Tepito existe porque resiste* – „Tepito gibt es nur, weil es Widerstand leistet". So habe sich Tepito beispielsweise immer wieder gegen die Stadtverwaltung durchgesetzt und dadurch u. a. den Abriss traditioneller Mietshäuser *(vecindades)* verhindert.

Indem Teresa die Stimme erhob, verschaffte sie sich nicht nur Gehör in der Gruppe, sondern sie beanspruchte eine spezifische Deutungshoheit aufgrund ihres lebensweltlichen Wissens, das sie auch für andere Kontexte und Personen für relevant erachtete und in dieser Situation weitergab. In diesem Personenkreis und an diesem Ort konnte Teresa eine akzeptierte Sprecherposition reklamieren und ihr Wissen durch ihre alltagsweltlichen Erfahrungen legitimieren – auch wenn sie ansonsten nur selten in der Öffentlichkeit zu Wort kam bzw. Gehör gefunden hätte. Durch die Anerkennung dieses situierten Wissens (Haraway 1988) verschoben sich die Rollen von Sprechenden hin zu ExpertInnen und von Zuhörenden hin zu Lernenden. Diese Transformation durch die Erzählung aus dem Alltag stellte sich im Laufe der Feldforschung mehrfach ein. Ausschlaggebend für die Kommentare der nicht-redegeübten Ko-EthnographInnen war das unverstellte und direkte Erfahrungswissen aus den eigenen Lebenswelten und den damit einhergehenden Positionalitäten. Dieses *knowing otherwise* speiste sich häufig aus implizitem Wissen. Die Verknüpfung von Beobachtung mit der Erzählung der eigenen (Lebens)Geschichte im Sinne eines *storytelling* rückte weniger die Faktizität als die Bedeutungsebene in den Mittelpunkt und offenbarte Annahmen, Erwartungen und Umgangsweisen mit bestimmten sozialen Situationen (vgl. Palmer 2014). Für uns als EthnologInnen verkomplizierte sich die Beobachtungssituation in dieser Forschungskonstellation enorm, denn es galt nun sowohl der lokalen Lebenswelt Aufmerksamkeit zu schenken als auch die Beobachtungen und Kommentare der Ko-EthnographInnen zu beobachten und zu dokumentieren. So stellte sich eine Gleichzeitigkeit beziehungsweise Überlagerung mehrerer Beobachtungsordnungen ein.

3.2 Erfahrung und Deutung

Auf dem Weg zu unserer Unterkunft in Vigidal wurde die Straße von einem umgestürzten Mast blockiert. Wir mussten das Auto verlassen und zu Fuß weiter, was aufgrund der Hitze und der sehr hügeligen, steinigen Favela mühsam war, zumal mit Reisegepäck. Hinzu kamen starke Gerüche, etwa von Kochstellen aus den Häusern oder von verfaulendem Müll. Teresa stöhnte zwar unter der Hitze, fühlte sich aber relativ „sicher" in unserer Gruppe, weil sie davon ausging, dass „wir" uns in der Favela auskennen würden. Daher vertraute sie darauf, dass wir wissen würden, wo und wann es gefährlich werden könnte. Denn in Tepito weiß sie genau, welche Straßenzüge sie wann besser meiden sollte. Dieses Wissen ist zentral für ihr Navigieren durch Tepito und bestimmt ihre Wege durch das *barrio*. Aufgrund ihrer lebensweltlichen Erfahrung weiß sie, dass Gefahr eben nicht überall lauert, sondern an spezifischen Orten und zu spezifischen Zeiten – und es z. B. tagsüber weniger gefährlich ist als in den Abend- und Nachtstunden.

Ganz anders hingegen Luisa, die in dem umgestürzten Mast eine Falle befürchtete und zögerte, das Auto zu verlassen. Zu Fuß durch eine Favela über schmale Treppen bergauf zu marschieren, zumal mit Gepäck, erschien ihr absurd und – aufgrund ihrer Erfahrungen in Trench Town – als keine gute Idee. Daran änderte weder die Gruppe noch die Tageszeit etwas, denn sie wusste, dass Gewalt unberechenbar ist. Wachsamkeit und Vorsicht sind zu jeder Stunde und unabhängig von der Begleitung geboten, auch aufgrund von möglichen Querschlägern bei Schießereien zwischen Gangs. Auch Luisa rekurrierte auf ihre lebensweltliche Erfahrung und auf ein eher implizites und unausgesprochenes Wissen, welches sie befürchten ließ, dass es sich bei dieser Situation um eine Falle handeln könnte. Verstärkt wurde ihr Unwohlsein durch die sensorischen Eindrücke, die sie als abstoßend empfand – das Gehen in ungewohnt steilem, unübersichtlichem Gelände, die Hitze, die starken Gerüche. Erst als wir unsere Unterkunft erreicht hatten, fühlte sie sich wieder „sicher" und entspannt.

Ausgehend vom unterschiedlichen Erleben dieser spezifischen Situation begann die gemeinsame Deutungsarbeit. Teresa und Luisa galten gleichermaßen als Expertinnen für Lebenswelten in gewaltbeladenen Stadtvierteln mit vergleichbar anmutenden sozialen Strukturen und normativen Ordnungen, rekurrierten allerdings auf differente Emotionen und Erfahrungswerte. Für beide Frauen stellten ihre Erfahrungen die Rahmung und auch die Legitimation ihrer Reaktionen dar und ließen eine uneinheitliche, kontroverse Deutung bestehen. Diese Differenzen galt es nicht zu glätten, sondern gemeinsam zu reflektieren und im Kontext unterschiedlicher gesellschaftlicher und politischer Zusammenhänge der jeweiligen Stadtviertel zu situieren. Auf diese Weise gelang im gesamten Team eine nuancierte und plastische Diskussion, die schließlich eine differenzierte Analyse der Gewaltwahrnehmung in sogenannten „Slums" ermöglichte.

3.3 Expertinnen und andere Geschlechterrollen

In Rio de Janeiro bietet die Stadtverwaltung den Guides aus den Favelas Schulungen an, um die Professionalisierung des Tourismussektors voranzutreiben. Diese Zertifizierung erlaubt es den TouristenführerInnen, auch in anderen Stadtvierteln Rio de Janeiros zum Einsatz zu kommen. Unser Guide Dalila berichtete uns, dass sich ihr Leben dadurch grundlegend verändert habe. Sie sei stolz darauf, nun selbst den TouristInnen das „wahre Leben" in den Favelas zeigen zu können – und dies in ihre eigenen Worte zu fassen. Schließlich spräche sie nicht nur als Guide, sondern vor allem als Einwohnerin einer Favela. Mit dem Hinweis auf ihre Zugehörigkeit zu der Gemeinschaft, über die sie spricht, legitimierte Dalila ihre Aussagen nicht nur, sondern sie verlieh ihnen darüber hinaus eine nahezu unantastbare Autorität.

Dalila berichtete uns mit Begeisterung von ihrem sozioökonomischen Aufstieg und fungierte auch für die Stadtverwaltung als Vorbild für soziale Mobilität und wirtschaftliches Vorankommen durch den Tourismus. Im Laufe der Feldforschung erfuhren wir jedoch auch von der Kehrseite dieser Medaille. Auf das Familienleben von Dalila, das durch konservative Rollen- und Geschlechtervorstellungen geprägt ist, hatte sich diese Entwicklung nicht nur positiv ausgewirkt. Ihr Ehemann sah die neue Mobilität seiner Frau kritisch und bewertete es eher negativ, dass sie in anderen Stadtvierteln von Rio de Janeiro unterwegs ist, viele Leute kennengelernt und ihr soziales Netzwerk enorm erweitert hatte. Dazu zählten auch wir, als internationales Forschungsteam, das Dalila nicht nur große Aufmerksamkeit schenkte, sondern sie auf eine Forschungsreise nach Mexiko einlud – die sie allerdings nur in Begleitung ihres Ehemannes antreten konnte. Durch den Aufenthalt von Dalila in Mexiko gewann unser ethnographisches Material an Dichte und Differenziertheit, da wir dort noch mehr über den Zusammenhang von Tourismus, Gender und Familie lernten.

Dalila und Teresa, die sich auf der Tour durch die Favela Santa Marta in Rio de Janeiro zum ersten Mal begegnet waren, trafen sich später in Tepito in Mexiko-Stadt wieder. Als wir dort vor dem Wandgemälde der „siete cabronas" saßen (Abb. 1), das „starke Frauen" aus Tepito abbildet – wovon uns einige in Person als Gesprächspartnerinnen zur Verfügung standen, darunter auch Teresa, verfolgte Dalila die Erzählungen dieser Frauen sehr aufmerksam.

Abb. 1 Wandbild der cabronas in Tepito, Mexiko-Stadt. (Foto: E. Dürr)

Während wir mit Bier und Softdrinks bewirtet wurden, berichteten uns die Frauen ausführlich über ihre individuellen Lebensumstände, Probleme und Errungenschaften. Sie beschrieben ihre Arbeit als Händlerinnen auf dem Straßenmarkt, ihren Einfluss als politische Akteurinnen im Dienste spezifischer Parteien, ihre Aufgaben als alleinerziehende Mütter und als wirtschaftlich verlässliche Partnerinnen in den Familien. Gleichzeitig aber erzählten sie auch von der oft sexualisierten Gewalt in Tepito. Sie berichteten von ihren Ängsten, von Bedrohungen durch die Drogenkartelle und von ihren Sorgen um die Zukunft der Jugend in Tepito. Teresa nahm in dieser Runde eine herausgehobene Stellung ein, da sie sowohl als Expertin über Tepito galt, sich aber auch als Kennerin der Favelas von Rio de Janeiro im weiteren Kreis der ZuhörerInnen präsentieren konnte. Teresa und Dalila tauschten sich nach dieser Gesprächsrunde über die unterschiedlichen Geschlechterbeziehungen weiter aus, wobei es von großem Vorteil war, dass sie den Wohnort der jeweils anderen aus eigener Anschauung kannten und somit auf einen geteilten Wissensbestand rekurrieren konnten.

Erst durch die Verschränkung ihrer alltäglichen Lebensräume konnte diese enge Vertrautheit zwischen den beiden Frauen erzeugt werden.

3.4 Transnationale Begegnungen

Eine gänzlich andere Form der Begegnung und des Austausches erlebten wir in der Favela Santa Marta in Rio de Janeiro. Dort ist der Tourismus fester Bestandteil des sozialen und ökonomischen Gefüges und spielt eine tragende Rolle in der Repräsentationspolitik der EinwohnerInnen.[8] In dieser Favela gilt neben der Fahrt mit einer Standseilbahn und imposanten Aussicht auf die Buchten der Stadt die Statue des Musikers Michael Jackson als herausragende Attraktion. In den steilen Gassen, die von zahlreichen Souvenirgeschäften gesäumt sind, befindet sich einer der Drehorte des Clips *They don't care about us* aus dem Jahr 1996. An dieser touristischen Inszenierung zeigt sich das Zusammenspiel unterschiedlicher Bezüge, die eine Favela zum Touristenmagnet transformieren. Ereignisse, Personen, Dinge oder auch Aussichtspunkte, die durch die TouristInnen Aufmerksamkeit erhalten, erlangen einen wichtigen Status für die BewohnerInnen – und diese Effekte werden durch die Narrative der Guides verstärkt. Santa Marta profitiert davon auf mehrfache Weise. Michael Jackson, ebenso wie andere Berühmtheiten, werden zu Vehikeln der Kommodifizierung und belegen die globalen Verbindungen benachteiligter, oft als isoliert wahrgenommener Stadtviertel – denn durch den Clip zirkuliert nicht nur die Musik, sondern auch die Favela weltweit. Ähnlich verhält es sich mit Trench Town, das durch die Musik und Texte von Bob Marley einen legendären Ruf erlangte. Diese Verbindungen materialisieren, ästhetisieren und kommerzialisieren sich in einer politischen Ökonomie von Armut, die ihren Ausdruck u. a. in Postkarten, Bildern, T-Shirts, pittoresken Mini-Favelas und unzähligen weiteren Souvenirs findet (Abb. 2).

---

[8] Im Jahr 2008 führte die brasilianische Regierung ein mehrstufiges, sogenanntes Pazifizierungsprogramm durch, in dem die Polizei versuchte, die gewaltbeladenen Favelas mit Spezialeinheiten (Unidades de Polícia Pacificadora, UPP) zu „befrieden". Im Vorfeld der Olympischen Spiele von 2016 waren diese oft extrem gewaltvollen Einsätze zwar stark umstritten, wurden jedoch von einigen unserer GesprächspartnerInnen begrüßt und als eine „Zäsur" in der Geschichte der Favela bezeichnet. Im Nachgang zu dieser staatlichen Intervention seien zahlreiche soziale Projekte entstanden und auch die massive, stark bewaffnete Polizeipräsenz, einschließlich der Überwachungstechnologie mit Kameras, hätte positive Effekte gezeigt. Endlich würde der Staat machtvoll durchgreifen und sich um die Belange der Favela kümmern. Nicht zuletzt hätte diese Maßnahme das Sicherheitsgefühl erhöht, was sich auch förderlich auf den Tourismus ausgewirkt hätte.

Abb. 2 Verkauf von Souvenirs aus Santa Marta, Rio de Janeiro. (Foto: E. Dürr)

Michael Jackson und seine Tanzmusik waren allen Beteiligten auf unserer Tour bekannt. Luisa sah darin Parallelen zur Ikone von Bob Marley und stellte die positiven Seiten einer Musik heraus, die mit benachteiligten Vierteln assoziiert würde. Marc, der ebenfalls aus Kingston stammte und mit einer NGO zusammenarbeitete, sah in der Musik eine Möglichkeit, Jugendliche von Gewalt und Drogen abzuhalten – eben solche Projekte würden in Kingston erfolgreich durchgeführt. Während wir auf der Aussichtsplattform standen, diskutierten wir die Gemeinsamkeiten von Samba und Reggae, wobei die Verbreitung der Musik von Bob Marley einhellig als die noch größere Erfolgsgeschichte gesehen wurde. Die Präsenz von Bob Marley in der Favela manifestierte sich auch im Graffiti seines Konterfeis auf einer Hauswand und diente Luisa nicht nur als willkommenes Fotomotiv (Abb. 3). Vielmehr wurde ihr durch diese überraschende Begegnung mit Bob Marley in den Favelas von Rio de Janeiro die transnationale Einbindung und globale Präsenz „ihrer" Musik deutlich und sie fragte sich, warum diese ausgerechnet in marginalisierten Stadtvierteln entstanden ist.

Abb. 3 Wandgemälde von Bob Marley in Santa Marta, Rio de Janeiro. (Foto: E. Dürr)

In diese Diskussion mischte sich Dalila, unsere Führerin in Santa Marta, ein. Sie berichtete ausführlich über den Besuch von Michael Jackson und betonte immer wieder, dass nahezu alle TouristInnen diese Musik kennen würden – und war sichtlich stolz, dass dieser Clip in „ihrer" Favela gedreht worden war.

Auch dieser gemeinsame Erfahrungsaustausch wirkte bei späteren Begegnungen nach – etwa in Jamaika, als Luisa unsere Gastgeberin in Trench Town war und uns durch den *culture yard* von Bob Marley führte. Im Unterschied zu Santa Marta steht die Touristifizierung von Trench Town erst am Anfang. Luisa verstand ihre Rolle als Guide anders als Dalila in Santa Marta – Luisa fühlte sich nicht für den Ruf von Trench Town verantwortlich und es war schon gar nicht ihr größtes Anliegen, diesen zu ändern. Sie legte mindestens so viel Wert auf unsere Verköstigung mit selbstgekochten Speisen wie darauf, uns den Musiker Bob Marley und das Stadtviertel näher zu bringen. Dennoch trat sie bei unserer Feldforschung in

Trench Town als Expertin hervor – auch weil sie durch den gemeinsamen Aufenthalt in Rio de Janeiro besser verstehen konnte, was die Interessen, Fragen und Belange unserer Gruppe waren. Wir bemerkten deutlich, dass unsere sozialen Beziehungen sowie der Ablauf unserer Feldforschung in Trench Town durch den Aufenthalt in Rio de Janeiro bereits vorstrukturiert waren. Geteilte Erfahrungen und Erinnerungen dienten oft als Ausgangspunkte für Gespräche, zumal die Reise- und Auslandserfahrung für die Mehrzahl der Ko-EthnographInnen einzigartig war. Außerdem entwickelten sich durch die gemeinsame Wissensproduktion in jeweils „fremden" Städten intensivere Verbindungen auf persönlicher Ebene (vgl. auch Schlehe 2013, S. 103), wovon schlussendlich die Arbeit der gesamten Gruppe profitierte. Allerdings gilt dies auch für das umgekehrte Vorzeichen: Konflikte zwischen einigen Personen führten zur Belastung und Fragmentierung der gesamten Gruppe, die diese Spannungen aushalten musste. Diese Reibungen waren unterschiedlicher Art und reichten von kritischen Kommentaren darüber, dass nicht alle Teammitglieder bei den Touren aufmerksam genug wären bis hin zu Missstimmungen wegen Speisen, die zwar reichlich bestellt, aber dann mit abfälligem Kommentar nicht bzw. nur zögerlich verzehrt wurden. Hier erlebten wir die Feldforschung als gemeinsame „Arbeit", einschließlich von *frictions,* die eben nicht nur produktiv durch die Artikulation von Differenzen, sondern auch hemmend durch nicht aufgelöste Spannungen wirken konnten.

4 Ausblick: Räume öffnen und Wege einer dekolonialen Forschung gemeinsam erkunden

Im Unterschied zum eingangs umrissenen Tandemprojekt an der Universität Freiburg handelte es sich bei meinem Beispiel nicht um ein Lehrprojekt für Studierende, sondern um ein Forschungsprojekt, das vorrangig auf den urbanen globalen Süden fokussierte. Damit verfolgte es per se andere Ziele. Außerdem wurden die Fragestellung und das Forschungsdesgin nicht im Zuge eines *wechselseitigen* Forschens entwickelt. Dennoch sind beide Vorhaben bewusst experimentell und offen angelegt. Sie gehen von sich überkreuzenden, instabilen Rollen sowie stärker von Positionalitäten aus als von kulturellen Zugehörigkeiten. Es geht weniger um die Frage, wie wir als akademisch ausgebildete ForscherInnen Teil der Gemeinschaft werden können, die wir erforschen, sondern vielmehr um das Überschreiten, Infrage stellen und Auflösen von Grenzen und Eindeutigkeiten. Mit den fluiden und sich ständig ändernden Rollen verbindet sich ein transformatives Potenzial, das schließlich zu einer neuen Form des „wir" im Forschungsprozess führen kann (vgl. Siry et al. 2011). Gleichzeitig entstehen mit diesem Ansatz weitere Beobachtungsperspektiven, da die Beobachtung der Beobachtung inkludiert wird. Diese Dopplung und Verschränkung gilt es noch weiter systematisch auszuloten und methodisch fruchtbar zu machen.

Im Verlauf unserer Gespräche gewannen wir alle neue Einsichten. Wir verstanden viel differenzierter, was Arm-Sein und Stigmatisiert-Sein für andere bedeuten kann. Selbst wenn Armut auf den ersten Blick in jeder Stadt Ähnlichkeiten aufweisen mag, lernten wir die Spezifika kennen und stellten Bezüge zu nationalen und globalen Kräften her. Auch in diesem Sinne diskutierten wir Strukturmerkmale, die in den jeweiligen Städten vergleichbar sind, aber die individuellen Lebenswelten wiederum unterschiedlich prägen.

Dennoch will ich weder diesen Ansatz noch das dynamische Beziehungsgeflecht nachträglich idealisieren – denn auch unsere Feldforschung verlief nicht immer spannungsfrei. Allerdings konnte durch dieses offene Forschen ein Raum für neue Positionen und Subjektformierungen geschaffen werden, wobei die Wissenszusammenhänge, Erfahrungen und Selbstzeugnisse der Ko-EthnographInnen von besonderer Relevanz waren. Ihr Wissen kam in vielfältiger Weise durch eine spezifische Art der emphatischen Erzählung bzw. performativen Rede zur Geltung und ihre Interpretationen erfuhren durch dieses Forschungsarrangement eine Aufwertung. Durch die internen Gespräche in der Gruppe entstand ein kommunikativer und interaktiver Rahmen, der die gemeinsame Wissensgenerierung förderte, auch wenn nicht immer Einigkeit über die konkrete Deutung von Situationen herrschte. Auch diese Differenzen galt es durch gemeinsame Arbeit nicht zu verwischen, sondern im Kontext unterschiedlicher lebensweltlicher Erfahrungen, aber auch verschiedener gesellschaftlicher und politischer Zusammenhänge zu betrachten.

Dieser Ansatz hin zu einer gemeinsamen, kreativen Deutungsarbeit im Sinne einer „reflexive team ethnography" (Turunen et al. 2020) kann sicherlich ausgebaut werden. Beispielsweise kann das methodische Potenzial, das sich mit der Begegnung von extrem marginalisierten Personen verbindet, noch weiter ausgeschöpft werden und darauf zielen, dauerhafte Netzwerke zu etablieren, um heterogene, aber doch auch vergleichbare Lebenswelten in Dialog miteinander zu bringen und damit die Süd-Süd-Achse noch mehr zu stärken als uns dies in diesem Vorhaben gelungen ist. Weitgehend offen geblieben ist in unserem Projekt auch die Frage nach der gemeinsamen analytischen Bearbeitung der Feldforschungsdaten – auch hier sind noch weitere Wege zu erproben, die nicht durch Lese- und Schreibfähigkeiten begrenzt werden und die Rolle der Ko-EthnographInnen in einer für sie ansprechenden Weise noch stärker konturieren.

Zumindest wäre das aus meiner Sicht für unser Projekt wünschenswert gewesen – wobei ich mir nicht ganz sicher bin, ob das nicht vor allem ein Anliegen der akademischen Welt ist.

Literatur

Alonso Bejarano, C., L. López Juárez, M. A. Mijangos García, und D. M. Goldstein. 2019. *Decolonizing ethnography. Undocumented immigrants and new directions in social science.* Durham: Duke University Press.

Anzaldúa, G. 1987. *Borderlands/La frontera: The new mestiza.* San Francisco: Aunt Lute Books.

Beek, J. und T. Bierschenk. 2020. „Bureaucrats as para-ethnologists: The use of culture in state practices". *Sociologus – Journal for Social Anthropology* 70(1): 1–17.

Bishop, R. 2005. „Freeing ourselves from neo-colonial domination in research. A kaupapa Māori approach to creating knowledge". In *The SAGE handbook of qualitative research* (3. Aufl.), Hrsg. N. K. Denzin, und Y. S. Lincoln, 109–138. Thousand Oaks, CA: Sage.

Boyer, D., und G. E. Marcus, Hrsg. 2021. *Collaborative anthropology today: A collection of exceptions.* Ithaca: Cornell University Press.

De la Cadena, M. 2015. *Earth Beings. Ecologies of practice across Andean worlds.* Durham, NC: Duke University Press.

Dürr, E. 2021 „Slum". In *Staatslexikon der Görres-Gesellschaft,* Bd. 5, 8. Aufl., 137–139. Freiburg: Herder Verlag.

Dürr, E., R. Acosta, und B. Vodopivec. 2021. „Recasting urban imaginaries: Politicized temporalities and the touristification of a notorious Mexico City barrio". *International Journal of Tourism Cities* 7(3): 783–798.

Dürr, E., R. Jaffe, und G. A. Jones. 2020. „Brokers and tours: Selling urban poverty and violence in Latin America and the Caribbean". *Space and Culture* 23(1): 4–14.

Dürr, E., und M. Sökefeld. 2017. „Zeit im Feld: Feldforschung als Paradigma und Praxis". In *Soziale Ästhetik, Atmosphäre, Medialität: Beiträge aus der Ethnologie,* Hrsg. C. Lang, U. Münster, P. Zehmisch, und J. Zickgraf, 229–238. Münster: LIT.

Fluehr-Lobban, C. 2008. „Collaborative anthropology as twenty-first-century ethical anthropology". *Collaborative Anthropologies* 1(1): 175–182.

Freire-Medeiros, B. 2013. *Touring poverty.* London: Routledge.

Frenzel, F. 2016. *Slumming it: The tourist valorization of urban poverty.* London: Zed Books.

Gupta, A., und J. Ferguson. 1997. „Discipline and practice. „The field" as site, method and location in anthropology". In *Anthropological locations. Boundaries and grounds of a field science,* Hrsg. A. Gupta, und J. Ferguson, 1–46. Berkeley: University of California Press.

Haenn, N. 2020. „Review of decolonizing ethnography. Undocumented immigrants and new directions in social science, by Alonso Bejarano, C., L. López Juárez, M. A. Mijangos García, und D. M. Goldstein". *Anthropos* 115(2): 545–546.

Hale, C. R. 2007. „In praise of „reckless minds": Making a case for activist anthropology". In *Anthropology put to work,* Hrsg. L. W. Field, und R. Fox, 103–127. Oxford: Berg.

Hale, C. R., Hrsg. 2008. *Engaging contradictions: Theory, politics, and methods of activist scholarship*. Berkeley, Los Angeles: University of California Press.

Haraway, D. 1988. „Situated knowledges: the science question in feminism and the privilege of partial perspective". *Feminist Studies* 14(3): 575–599.

Holmes, D. R., und G. E. Marcus. 2006. „Fast capitalism: Para-ethnography and the rise of the symbolic analyst". In *Frontiers of capital: Ethnographic reflections on the new economy,* Hrsg. M. S. Fisher und G. Downey, 33–57. Durham: Duke University Press.

Holmes, D. R., und G. E. Marcus. 2008. „Collaboration today and the re-imagination of the classic scene of fieldwork encounter". *Collaborative Anthropologies* 1(1): 81–101.

Jaffe, R., E. Dürr, G. Jones, A. Angelini, A. Osbourne und B. Vodopivec. 2020. „What does poverty feel like? Urban inequality and the politics of sensation". *Urban Studies* 57(5): 1015–1031.

Jones, G., R. Jaffe, und E. Dürr, Hrsg. 2020. Brokers and tours: Selling urban poverty and violence in Latin American and the Caribbean. Special Issue: *Space and Culture* 23(1): 4–76.

Kennemore, A., und N. Postero. 2020. „Reflections on collaborative ethnography and decolonization in Latin America, Aotearoa, and beyond". *Commoning Ethnography* 3(1): 25–58.

Lander, E., Hrsg. 2000. *La colonialidad del saber: eurocentrismo y ciencias sociales. Perspectivas latinoamericanas*. Buenos Aires: CLACSO.

Lassiter, L. E. 2005. *The Chicago guide to collaborative ethnography*. Chicago: University of Chicago Press.

Lebrato, M. 2020. „Disciplinary potential and individual choice: Reflections from participatory research on Oaxacan intercultural education". *Annals of Anthropological Practice* 44(2): 186–191.

Low, S. M., und S. E. Merry. 2010. „Engaged anthropology: Diversity and dilemmas". *Current Anthropology* 51(S2): S203–S226.

Mignolo, W. 2001. *Local histories, global designs*. Princeton: Princeton University Press.

Mignolo, W., und C. Walsh. 2018. *On decoloniality. Concepts, analytics, praxis*. Durham, London: Duke University Press.

Morgensen, S. L. 2012. „Destabilizing the settler academy: The decolonial effects of Indigenous methodologies". *American Quarterly* 64(4): 805–808.

Palmer, J. 2014. „Past remarkable: Using life stories to trace alternative futures". *Futures* 64 (2014) 29–37.

Parker, P., D. Holland, J. Dennison, S. H. Smith, und M. Jackson. 2018. „Decolonizing the academy: Lessons from the graduate certificate in participatory research at the University of North Carolina at Chapel Hill". *Qualitative Inquiry* 24(7): 464–477.

Peltier, C. 2018. An Application of Two-Eyed Seeing: Indigenous Research Methods With Participatory Action Research. *International Journal of Qualitative Methods*, (17)1 : 1–12. https://doi.org/10.1177/1609406918812346.

Pink, S. 2009. *Doing sensory ethnography*. London, New Delhi, Thousand Oaks: Sage.

Quijano, A. 2000. „Colonialidad del poder y clasificación social". *Journal of World Systems Research* 6(2): 342–386.

Quijano, A. 2007. „Coloniality and modernity/rationality". *Cultural Studies* 21(2): 168–178.

Rappaport, J. 2008. „Beyond participant observation: Collaborative ethnography as theoretical innovation". *Collaborative Anthropologies* 1(1): 1–31.

Rivera Cusicanqui, S. 2010. *Violencias (re)encubiertas en Bolivia*. La Paz: La Mirada Salvaje/Editorial Piedra Rota.
Rivera Cusicanqui, S. 2012. „Ch'ixinakax utxiwa: A reflection on the practices and discourses of decolonization". *The South Atlantic Quarterly* 111(1): 95–109.
Schlehe, J. 2013. „Wechselseitige Übersetzungen: Methodologische Neuerungen in transkulturellen Forschungskooperationen". In *Ethnologie im 21. Jahrhundert*, Hrsg. T. Bierschenk, M. Krings, und C. Lentz, 97–110. Berlin: Reimer.
Schlehe, J., und S. Hidayah. 2013. „Transcultural ethnography in tandems: collaboration and reciprocity combined and extended". In *Freiburger Ethnologische Arbeitspapiere Nr. 23*, http://www.freidok.uni-freiburg.de/volltexte/9155/.
Schlehe, J., und S. Hidayah. 2014. „Transcultural ethnography: Reciprocity in Indonesian-German tandem research". In *Methodology and research practice in Southeast Asian studies*, Hrsg. M. Huotari, J. Rüland, und J. Schlehe, 253–272. London: Palgrave Macmillan.
Siry, C., C. Ali-Khan, und M. Zuss. 2011. „Cultures in the making: An examination of the ethical and methodological implications of collaborative research". *Forum: Qualitative Social Research* 12(2): 1–24.
Smith, L. T. 1999. *Decolonizing methodologies: Research and Indigenous peoples*. London: Zed Books.
Smith, L. T. 2005. „On tricky ground. Researching the native in an age of uncertainty". In *The Sage handbook of qualitative research*, Hrsg. N. K. Denzin, und Y. S. Lincoln, 85–107. Thousand Oaks: Sage Publications.
Tsing, A. L. 2005. *Friction, an ethnography of global connection*. Princeton, NJ: Princeton University Press.
Tsing, A. L. 2015. *The mushroom at the end of the world: On the possibility of life in capitalist ruins*. Princeton: Princeton University Press.
Tsing, A. L., N. Bubandt, E. Gan, und H. A. Swanson, Hrsg. 2017. *Arts of living on a damaged planet: Ghosts and monsters of the Anthropocene*. Minneapolis: University of Minnesota Press.
Turunen, J., Čeginskas, V. L., Kaasik-Krogerus, S., Lähdesmäki, T., & Mäkinen, K. 2020. „Poly-space: Creating new concepts through reflexive team ethnography". In *Challenges and solutions in ethnographic research: Ethnography with a twist*, Hrsg. T. Lähdesmäki, E. Koskinen-Koivisto, V. L. Čeginskas, und A.-K. Koistinen, 3–20. London: Routledge.
Vodopivec, B. 2017. *Made in Tepito: Urban tourism and inequality in Mexico City*. Dissertation, LMU München: Fakultät für Kulturwissenschaften.
Vodopivec, Barbara and Eveline Dürr. 2019. „Barrio bravo transformed: Tourism, cultural politics, and image making in Mexico City". *The Journal of Latin American and Caribbean Anthropology* 24(2): 313–330.
Walsh, C. 2012. „„Other" knowledges, „other" critiques: Reflections on the politics and practices of philosophy and decoloniality in the „other" America". *Transmodernity: Journal of Peripheral Cultural Production of the Luso-Hispanic World* 1(3): 11–27.

Ethnographie der Differenz jenseits binärer Ordnungen: Überlegungen zum Seitenwechsel anhand einer Beratungseinrichtung für Geflüchtete in Brasilien

Heike Drotbohm

1 Einleitung: Die Kunst des Seitenwechsels

Ein besonders starkes und viel beachtetes Plädoyer von Judith Schlehe zielt auf den kritischen Umgang mit kultureller Differenz anhand der methodischen Innovationen einer kollaborativen Wissensproduktion. Das Herzstück dieses Vorhabens ist die transkulturelle Lehrforschung, die Judith seit 2004 in Freiburg mit einem außergewöhnlich hohen Maß an Kreativität und Energie leitet und begleitet: Jährlich arbeiten abwechselnd Ethnologie-Studierende der Universität Freiburg und der Gadjah Mada University in Yogyakarta für vier bis sechs Wochen in Tandems an gemeinsam entwickelten Forschungsprojekten und führen diese abwechselnd in Deutschland und in Indonesien durch (Schlehe 2006, 2013). Neben den an diese Arbeitsweise gerichteten Erwartungen, wie etwa die Nutzbarmachung von wechselseitigen Deutungen, faszinierte mich stets ganz besonders der methodisch in das Projekt eingelagerte intellektuelle Seitenwechsel.

Grundsätzlich gehört die Distanzierung von sozialisationsbedingt mitgebrachten Selbstverständlichkeiten und die Einnahme anderer, vormals unvertrauter Deutungsperspektiven zu den Grundprämissen der ethnologischen Feldforschung im Allgemeinen und der teilnehmenden Beobachtung im Besonderen. Da die Annahme, ein Verstehen Lebenswelten Anderer könne schlichtweg durch einen

H. Drotbohm (✉)
Institut für Ethnologie und Afrikastudien, JGU Mainz, Mainz, Deutschland
E-Mail: drotbohm@uni-mainz.de

Ortswechsel erreicht werden, längst verworfen wurde, erscheint die Identifikation zweier ‚Seiten' als eine zentrale epistemologische, methodologische und auch ethische Herausforderung. Die Idee einer Seite taucht im ethnologischen Forschungszusammenhang auch dann auf, wenn gefragt wird, auf wessen Seite man steht (Armbruster und Laerke 2010) oder wenn darauf verwiesen wird, dass ‚field', ‚site' und ‚location' zentrale ‚common-sense' Begriffe der Disziplin sind, die sich gleichermaßen störend wie hemmend auf den Forschungsprozess auswirken können (Fog Olwig und Hastrup 1997; Gupta und Ferguson 1997). Allerdings können nur wenige EthnologInnen[1] das Privileg einer Tandem-Forschung genießen, in die der Vergleich bzw. die Gegenüberstellung zweier komplementärer Perspektiven unmittelbar integriert ist, und daher stellt sich die Frage: Wie findet ein Seitenwechsel konkret statt, wenn die Forschung von einer einzelnen Person durchgeführt wird? Wie und in welchen Momenten konstituiert sich der Unterschied zwischen Eigenem und Anderem?

In der brasilianischen Stadt São Paulo galt die Beratungseinrichtung für Geflüchtete, in der ich meine ethnographische Forschung durchführte, schon seit der Zeit der Militärdiktatur (1964–1985) als wichtiger Adressat für die Belange von ExilantInnen und Geflüchteten. Hier, so meinte ich, würde ich dem Anspruch an eine ethnografische Forschung gerecht werden können, indem ich mich in den Arbeitsalltag der Einrichtung integrieren würde, um deren Binnenperspektive einzunehmen. An kaum einem anderen Ort sollte der antizipierte ethnologische Seitenwechsel leichter fallen als in einer derartigen Einrichtung. Es ist das Eingangstor, das Außen und Innen trennt, der Pförtner, der die Schwelle zum Gebäude kontrolliert, die unbestuhlte Wartezone, von deren Zwielicht die Wartenden übergehen in die Büros der Angestellten. Und es sind die routinierten, zügigen Bewegungen durch den Raum, vielleicht zum Kopierer, vielleicht zur Kaffeemaschine, die die Mitarbeitenden von den gelangweilt sitzenden oder verunsichert suchenden KlientInnen unterscheiden.

Die Zweiteilung der Forschungseinheit scheint in diesem Fall also durch die Außengrenzen einer Organisation, ihre Räumlichkeiten, materielle Infrastruktur, alltägliche Routinen und sozialen Interaktionen bestimmt. Dominic Boyer und George Marcus, deren Namen wohl mehr als andere für die methodologische Innovationskraft unseres Faches stehen, forderten jüngst, die ‚konventionelle' Ethnograph-Informant-Beziehung zu ersetzen, indem das theoriebildende Potenzial von ExpertInnen in die analytische Entwicklung der Forschung integriert würde. Erst über die Zusammenarbeit mit diesen ExpertInnen, die ihnen zufolge

---

[1] In diesem Beitrag vermeide ich das generische Maskulinum, alle anderen Gender-Varianten werden willkürlich oder wie passend verwendet.

als eine Art ‚Para-EthnologInnen' zu verstehen seien, werde identifizierbar, was diese ExpertInnen verstehen bzw. als verstehenswert ansehen: „The corrective is, again to integrate fully our subjects' analytical acumen and insights to define the issues at stake in our project as well as the means by which we explore them" (Boyer und Marcus 2020, 14). Diesen Umgang mit ‚Para-EthnologInnen' veranschaulichen sie anhand ganz unterschiedlicher „epistemic communities", wie den MitarbeiterInnen einer Bank oder den Mitgliedern der extremen, also faschistischen, politischen Rechten. Ihr Ansatz orientiert sich also zwar nach wie vor daran, den ‚native's point of view' nachzuvollziehen, er geht jedoch zugleich weit darüber hinaus, weil diese AkteurInnen in ihrem anekdotenhaften Räsonieren über die Gegenwart und den Zustand der Welt quasi-ethnologisch denken und argumentieren (Boyer und Marcus 2020, 30 ff.).

Im folgenden Beitrag unternehme ich den Versuch, die von mir ausgewählte brasilianische Organisationseinheit ebenfalls als eine ‚epistemische Gemeinschaft' zu verstehen. Ich orientiere mich hier an einer Begriffsannäherung des Politikwissenschaftlers Peter M. Haas, der folgende Charakteristika für epistemische Gemeinschaften benannte: eine geteilte normative Grundhaltung (1), eine geteilte Vorstellung von maßgeblichen Kausalitäten (2), eine geteilte Vorstellung im Hinblick auf die Validität spezifischen Wissens (3) und eine geteilte Vorstellung von der politischen Nützlichkeit des gemeinschaftlichen Handelns (4) (Haas 1992). Auf das Beratungszentrum in São Paulo, das in etwa gleichen Anteilen durch die katholische Kirche, den UNHCR und den brasilianischen Staat finanziert wird, treffen diese Merkmale zu: An fünf Tagen der Woche kümmern sich hier SozialarbeiterInnen und JuristInnen, PsychologInnen, FinanzverwalterInnen und zahlreiche VolontärInnen gemeinsam auf zwei Etagen von morgens bis abends in den vier Arbeitsbereichen ‚Assistenz', ‚Integration', ‚Schutz' und ‚mentale Gesundheit' um die Anliegen ihrer KlientInnen. Es handelt sich bei den MitarbeiterInnen der Einrichtung also um eine Gruppe von SpezialistInnen, die mit ihrem geteilten Wissen auf ein öffentliches Interesse, die Dokumentation, Beratung und Unterstützung von nicht-brasilianischen Neuankömmlingen in der Stadt, hinarbeiten. Die folgenden Überlegungen stammen aus der Anfangszeit der Forschungsphase vor Ort (2014), als ich versuchte herauszufinden, welche Art des Wissens und welche Ziele in dieser Einrichtung kultiviert werden. „Worum geht es den AkteurInnen, was ist ihr Anliegen?" war in dieser Zeit meine tägliche Orientierungsfrage.[2]

---

[2] Eine zentrale Akteursgruppe innerhalb der Einrichtung, nämlich die Geflüchteten, Migrant:inner oder Klient:innen, wird in diesem Text außen vor gelassen. Dies entspricht meiner Vorgehensweise in dieser frühen Forschungsphase, da ich Loyalitätskonflikte

Mein Text folgt meiner eigenen Suchbewegung im Feld. Nachdem ich kurz einige Eckdaten des spezifischen historischen Moments in Brasilien zusammengefasst habe, erläutere ich anhand einzelner zentraler Individuen deren Deutung und Einfluss auf die Entwicklung meiner Forschungsperspektive. Die Direktorin, der Padre, der Anwalt, die Psychologin und die Sozialarbeiterin stehen im Folgenden stellvertretend für einzelne Berufsgruppen, deren Zusammenspiel als konstitutiv für die epistemische Gemeinschaft verstanden wird und deren Haltungen sowohl Komplementarität als auch Widersprüchlichkeit zu erkennen geben.

2 Forschen in Zeiten der „Krise"

In den Monaten der Sondierung meiner Forschung (2014) wirkten ausgeprägte politische Transformationsprozesse in den alltäglichen Arbeitszusammenhang der Einrichtung hinein, stellten Routinen und Prozeduren infrage und bereiteten den MitarbeiterInnen besonderen Stress. Zum einen war Brasilien nach einer wirtschaftlich besonders erfolgreichen Dekade (bis ca. 2010) in eine schwere Finanzkrise geraten; zum anderen verschärfte ein beispielsloser Korruptionsskandal (Operação Lava Jato; dt: ‚Operation Hochdruckreiniger'), der sich bis in die Reihen der damals noch linksgerichteten Regierung der Arbeiterpartei zog, ab März 2014 die politischen Spannungen im Land. Während Hunderttausende regelmäßig auf Streiks und Massendemonstrationen gegen wachsende Staatsschulden, Preiserhöhungen, Arbeitslosigkeit, aber auch gegen den Vertrauensverlust in das politische System protestierten (Costa 2018), wurde der Eindruck einer politischen Lagerbildung auch im Alltag, in den Begegnungen zwischen Familienangehörigen, NachbarInnen und ArbeitskollegInnen, deutlich spürbar.

Schon wenige Monate nach Einsetzen der politischen und ökonomischen Krise machte sich dies auch auf der operativen Ebene der Alltagsarbeit bemerkbar. Sowohl der brasilianische Staat als auch der UNHCR hatten ihre Budgetüberweisungen im Jahr 2014 extrem verspätet. „Die Kassen des Staates sind leer und der UNHCR braucht sein Geld für die Krise in Europa", erläuterte mir eine seit über 20 Jahren dort arbeitende Sozialarbeiterin. Informelle Begegnungen, in der Teeküche oder nach Dienstschluss, in denen über die jüngsten politischen Entwicklungen diskutiert wurde, endeten mitunter mit dem Appell, im Angesicht der Krise zusammenzuhalten. Anders jedoch gestaltete sich die Einschätzung der

---

vermeiden wollte und darum zunächst versuchte, die Perspektive der Berater:innen zu verstehen, ohne sie mit der Perspektive der Klient:innen zu vermischen.

Lage in Einzelgesprächen, in denen mir wiederholt erklärt wurde, dass die Angst vor einem möglichen Arbeitsplatzverlust auch in Form eines bislang unbekannten Konkurrenzverhaltens unter den KollegInnen spürbar werde.

Darüber hinaus hatte diese nationale Krise auch Folgen für die Arbeit in der Einrichtung da es angesichts der genannten Veränderungen zu einem ungewöhnlich hohen Beratungsaufkommen gekommen war. Der Grund hierfür lag ebenfalls in der vorausgegangenen ökonomisch prosperierenden Ära, als die brasilianische Regierung unter Luiz Inácio Lula da Silva (2003–2010) in der Außen- und Grenzpolitik auf Süd-Süd-Solidarität und eine offene Grenzpolitik gesetzt hatte. Die Hochkonjunktur in der Rohstoff-, Textil- und Bauindustrie, vor allem aber die Vorbereitungen der Fußballweltmeisterschaft (2014) und der Olympischen Sommerspiele (2016) hatten Brasilien zu einem Ziel transkontinentaler Migrationsdynamiken werden lassen (Gato und Salazar 2018). Darüber hinaus galt das Land auch für jene, die ihre Herkunftsländer aufgrund extremer Notlagen verlassen mussten und irgendwie das Geld für einen Fernflug aufbringen konnten, als vielversprechende Alternative gegenüber Europa, dessen Grenzen nach einer kurzen Phase der Entspannung erneut restriktiven Kontrollen unterlagen (Faria und Paradis 2013).

Die einsetzende Rezession traf die genannten ökonomischen Bereiche besonders schwer, was vor allem im Sektor der informellen Beschäftigung mit sofortigen Kündigungen einherging. Viele MigrantInnen wurden arbeitslos und verloren dadurch ihren regulären Aufenthaltstitel. Insbesondere Migranten, die sich nicht auf ein tragfähiges verwandtschaftliches oder ethnisches Beziehungsnetz stützen konnten, suchten daher in dieser Zeit Rat bei humanitären Einrichtungen und entschieden sich aus der rechtlichen Bredouille heraus nicht selten für eine Beantragung von politischem Asyl. Brasilien gehört seit dem Ende der Militärdiktatur (1985) zu den führenden Mitgliedern der Vereinten Nationen und seine Asylpolitik gilt bis dato im internationalen Vergleich als vorbildlich (Jubilut 2006; Fischel de Andrade 2015). Zwar argumentieren KritikerInnen, dass die Ablehnungsquoten zu hoch seien, die Bearbeitungszeiten ewig dauerten und dass sich Asylsuchende darum häufig eine lange Zeit in einem legalen Schwebezustand befänden. Allerdings bietet diese lange, sich oft über mehrere Jahre erstreckende Verfahrensdauer einen entscheidenden Vorteil: In der Phase der Antragsbearbeitung ist der Aufenthalt der Asylsuchenden dokumentiert, was ihnen den Zugang zur Basis-Gesundheitsversorgung und zum Arbeitsmarkt ebenso wie zu weiteren sozialen Rechten ermöglicht. Darüber hinaus bieten humanitäre Einrichtungen eine Vielzahl an Beratungsleistungen an, wie etwa bei Wohnungslosigkeit, psychologischen und rechtlichen Problemen, oder aber beim Umgang mit den brasilianischen Behörden.

3 Die Direktorin: Kultivierung der professionellen Kohärenz

"War heute das erste Mal dort [in der Einrichtung im alten Stadtzentrum São Paulos]. Die Direktorin war begeistert, eine Ethnologin dabei zu haben. Sie kannte sogar die T.B. So einfach hätte ich mir den Zugang nicht vorgestellt. Ab nächster Woche kann ich mitarbeiten, angeblich in allen Abteilungen!"

(Feldtagebuch, März 2014)

Meine Kontaktaufnahme hatte funktioniert. Der telefonisch vereinbarte Termin fand statt, die etwa 40-jährige Direktorin wirkte entgegenkommend und das etwa 30-minütige, bei offener Bürotür geführte Gespräch zeugte von gegenseitigem Interesse. Innerhalb der Einrichtung war sie die verantwortliche Leiterin – mitunter täglich kommunizierte sie sowohl mit den Unterabteilungen innerhalb der Organisation als auch mit verschiedenen VertreterInnen des UNHCR und des Comitê Nacional para os Refugiados (CONARE), dem nationalen Komitee für Geflüchtete der brasilianischen Regierung. In diesem ersten Gespräch präsentierte sie mir das gemeinsame Hauptanliegen der Einrichtung: Die Organisation von Unterstützung für Neuzugewanderte – entweder über die Bereitstellung eigener Ressourcen oder über Kontakte in andere Einrichtungen innerhalb der Stadt. Sie machte deutlich, dass eben dieser Erwartungshorizont sie alle zusammenband: Die MitarbeiterInnen hätten zwar durchaus Respekt vor den mitunter stark unterschiedlichen Arbeitsweisen in den verschiedenen Unterabteilungen, arbeiteten aber auf der Grundlage ihrer jeweiligen professionellen Spezialisierungen auf dieses gemeinsames Ziel hin. Anschließend skizzierte sie in wenigen Sätzen die Geschichte der Einrichtung, die räumliche Anordnung innerhalb des Gebäudes und die wöchentlichen Arbeitsroutinen. Sie endete ihren Überblick mit der Formulierung: „Wir sind hier wie die verlängerte Hand der freundlichen Seite des Staates. Wenn möglich, versuchen wir, fremdenfeindliche Haltungen abzuwehren und Ausländern eine Hand zu reichen, um die gastfreundliche Seite Brasiliens zu erleben."

In ihrer Funktion brachte die Direktorin eine starke Fürsprache zum Ausdruck – nicht nur für die KlientInnen und deren spezifische Bedürfnislagen, sondern auch für die MitarbeiterInnen der Organisation: Sie unterstrich das Engagement, die spezifischen Belastungen dieses historischen Moments, das angespannte politische Klima in Brasilien und das Gefühl der Ohnmacht angesichts stetig steigender Zahlen von Neuzugewanderten, deren Bedürfnissen sie mitunter nur unzureichend entsprechen konnten. In dieser frühen Phase meiner Kontaktaufnahme war mir die Haltung der Direktorin leicht nachvollziehbar: Sie sah damals zunächst davon ab, mir die Details der unterschiedlichen Abteilungen und die Spezifika der Beratung von Asylsuchenden zu erläutern. Ihr Hauptanliegen war es, mir, der Forscherin, die ‚Einheit' der Organisation als einen Zusammenhang von Interessen zu vermitteln. Meiner Ansicht nach generierte sie auf diese Weise auch das Bild eines ‚schützenswerten' Kollektivs, auf das die Forschung Rücksicht nehmen sollte.

Nachdem ich ihr meine Ideen und mein Forschungsanliegen erläutert hatte, meinte sie, dass sie die Ethnologie und ihre besondere Arbeitsweise gut kenne. Gerne werde sie mir den Zugang zu sämtlichen Arbeitsschritten und Entscheidungsmomenten verschaffen. Sie sei gespannt auf meine Ergebnisse. Und, während sie mich nach unten zum Ausgang begleitete: ich dürfe gerne einmal in der Woche zu ihr kommen, um Unklarheiten zu diskutieren. Auf diese Weise werde es für sie möglich, meine Außensicht auf die Dinge zu hören. Ohne dass ich es einforderte, formulierte sie einen hohen Anspruch an Vertrauen, Egalität und wechselseitige Offenheit. Mich irritierte die Einfachheit des sogenannten ‚Feld'-zugangs. Die Direktorin war mir schnell vertraut, sie hatte Jura und Soziologie studiert, wir teilten zentrale Perspektiven der Sozialwissenschaften; die Ethnologie und vor allem deren Arbeitsweise (T.B. ist die zentrale ethnologische Methode – die ‚teilnehmende Beobachtung') waren ihr – was in Brasilien nicht untypisch ist – gut bekannt. Einerseits war sie vermutlich die entscheidende Gate-Keeperin, andererseits schienen ihre Perspektiven, ihr biographischer und akademischer Hintergrund ebenso wie ihre ethischen Anliegen meinen eigenen nur allzu sehr zu ähneln. War sie ‚ich' auf der anderen Seite?

4   Der Padre: Kultivierung der Güte

> *„Das Gespräch mit dem Padre war anstrengend. Erst ständig verschoben, dann ließ er mich ewig warten, dann war er distanziert, skeptisch und wollte mir diktieren, wie human die [Einrichtung] sei. Ich hatte das Gefühl, dass er jeden Satz schon x-mal gesagt hatte. Es wirkte alles irgendwie vorgetanzt. War mir nicht sicher, wie viel er vom eigentlichen Arbeitsalltag überhaupt mitbekommt. Er scheint über den Dingen zu schweben. Vielleicht werde ich ihm nicht gerecht, vielleicht arbeitet er an anderen Fronten. Ich sollte ihn nochmal treffen."*

(Feldtagebuch, August 2015).

Das vergleichsweise kurze und einmalige Gespräch mit dem geistigen Vorstand der Einrichtung fand in einem der großen Besprechungsräume statt. An einem großen ovalen Holztisch saßen wir einander gegenüber, um uns herum die Bibliothek. Von Beginn an konzentrierte er sich auf ein Detail in der Formulierung meines Anliegens. „Irgendwie gefällt mir das Wort nicht, ja, es stört mich sogar," sagte er als ich ihm erläuterte, dass ich zu ‚humanitären Bürokratien' arbeitete. ‚Humanitär' – das Menschenzugewandte – und ‚Bürokratie' – die kalte Ordnung des anonymen Sortierens und Entscheidens – verstehe er als zwei unvereinbare Gegensätze. In dieser Einrichtung arbeitet man nur für den Menschen, nicht für das Papier. „Es ist nicht das Gesetz, das wir retten wollen," untermauerte er emphatisch seine Kritik an dem Begriff.

Mich erstaunte, dass der Padre die Regelhaftigkeit und das Prozedere des Entscheidungsprozederes der Einrichtung, die ja nicht nur von der Kirche, sondern auch durch den brasilianischen Staat und internationale GeberInnen finanziert war, derart in den Hintergrund stellte. Deutlich wurde, dass sein Verständnis von Hilfe und Unterstützung auf einem umfassend(er)en Gebot der christlichen Nächstenliebe basierte, das dezidiert *keinen* Unterschied zwischen unterschiedlichen Veranlassungen und Motiven der Flucht, bzw. Nationalitäten, Altersgruppen, Geschlechtern, etc. machen sollte oder wollte. Sein Fokus war auf den menschlichen Dienst am bedürftigen, schutzlosen Menschen gerichtet, der mit Milde und Güte adressiert werden sollte.

Die Haltungen der anderen MitarbeiterInnen schienen diesem Dogma der christlichen Toleranz und des Mitgefühls zu folgen, was sich nicht nur in den expliziten Ansagen des Geistlichen, sondern auch in der materiellen Umgebung mit katholischem Ambiente vermittelte, wie etwa den Kruzifixen und den Sinnsprüchen auf den Postern und anderem Bildmaterial wie Flyern und Informationsbroschüren. Volontäre, AnwältInnen und PsychologInnen, SozialarbeiterInnen und JournalistInnen – sie alle unterstrichen bei unterschiedlichen Gelegenheiten die emotionale Identifikation mit ihrer Arbeit ebenso wie die ethische Verantwortung, die sie gegenüber ihren KlientInnen empfanden. Auffällig war bei diesen Positionierungen, dass die MitarbeiterInnen die katholische Rahmung mehrmals in schon fast defensiver Manier explizit in den Hintergrund stellten, indem sie hervorhoben, dass die Religionszugehörigkeit dezidiert keine Voraussetzung für ein Anstellungsverhältnis in der Einrichtung darstelle, dass die religiöse Zugehörigkeit der KlientInnen bei der Fallentscheidung keinesfalls eine Rolle spiele und dass das Handeln der Einrichtung ganz selbstlos ausgerichtet sei. „Wir arbeiten quasi-buddhistisch", sagte eine Mitarbeiterin und unterstrich auf diese Weise den Anspruch an Toleranz, Offenheit und Hierarchieferne, den sie mit ihrer Arbeit verband.

Das Religiöse – als Topos – wurde mir in diesen Konstellationen in möglichst verallgemeinerter Form als Kommunikationsgrundlage angeboten, um die Trennlinien, die im Zuge der für Förderorganisationen typischen Differenzierungsarbeit gezogen werden, zu verwischen. Indem Religion – und dabei vor allem die religiöse Grundhaltung der Offenheit und der Nächstenliebe – und nicht die Konfession in den Vordergrund gestellt wurde, teilten die MitarbeiterInnen die Selbsterzählung eines organisationsspezifischen, gemeinschaftsstiftenden Ethos, der dem kühl-rationalen Räsonieren von staatlichen Bürokratien gegenübergestellt wurde. Auch die Frage meiner eigenen Religionszugehörigkeit wurde auf diese Weise irrelevant gemacht. Im Hinblick auf dieses Arbeiten an einer kollektiven, oder kollektivierenden Grundlage, war die Position des Padres mit der der Direktorin vergleichbar. Beiden war, wenn auch in jeweils unterschiedlicher Weise, daran gelegen, das Bild einer funktionierenden organisatorischen Einheit zu zeichnen, das gegenüber einem als möglicherweise kritisch antizipierten Außen abgegrenzt wurde. Meine Abwehr hatte vermutlich mit seiner belehrenden, korrigierenden und distanzierten Kommunikationshaltung zu tun, die ich als Repräsentanz einer überholten, männlichen und – im Gegensatz zu den Inhalten seiner Erläuterungen – hierarchischen und unzugänglichen Seite empfand.

5 Der Anwalt: Kultivierung der ordnungsgemäßen Regelbefolgung

„Die Arbeit mit den Anwälten ist sehr spannend. Heute, bei Fernando, fielen mir die Unterschiede auf, die schon in der ersten Minute des Gesprächs gemacht werden. Bei manchen Klienten braucht er drei Minuten und dann sie sind schon wieder draußen. Bei den anderen nimmt er sich wirklich viel Zeit, fragt immer wieder nach, will jene Informationen rausfinden, die für die Entscheidung wichtig sind. Er betont, wie verantwortungsvoll seine Arbeit ist, zumindest bei diesen Fällen".

(Feldtagebuch, März 2014)

Er war einer der vier Anwälte der Einrichtung und gehörte nicht zu jenen, die im Anschluss an einen langen Arbeitstag noch gemeinsam mit den KollegInnen auf eine der abendlichen Demos in die Innenstadt gingen. Als etwa 40-jähriger Vater von zwei Kindern, dessen Frau gerade das dritte erwartete, erschien er immer besonders früh zur Arbeit und ging gerne möglichst pünktlich wieder nach Hause. Manche seiner KollegInnen empfanden ihn aufgrund seiner Zurückhaltung als Sonderling, andere als unangemessen streng oder schlicht konservativ. Er selbst erläuterte mir seine Arbeitsweise als besonders pflichtbewusst, er verstehe das Recht im Allgemeinen und das Asylrecht im Besonderen als eine wichtige Größe, die es zu schützen gelte. Darüber hinaus betonte er häufig, dass er bei seiner Arbeit für Geflüchtete, so anstrengend sie auch sei, viel Leidenschaft (,paixão') empfinde. In den von mir begleiteten Beratungsgesprächen fiel auf, dass er auf eine besonders ordnungsgemäße, schon fast akribische Durchführung der Erfassung und Dokumentation der Personenmerkmale achtete, was unter anderem ein sorgfältiges Abwägen von sachlichen und humanitären Gesichtspunkten beinhaltete. Im Rahmen dieser Regelbefolgung verstand er es als seine Aufgabe, MigrantInnen von Geflüchteten zu unterscheiden. Darüber hinaus wollte er jene Asylsuchende ausmachen, die eine realistische Chance auf Asyl hatten und jene, deren Anliegen als unsachgemäß oder aussichtslos eingeordnet werden mussten. Beide Unterscheidungen wurden Teil seines Fragerepertoires.

Grundsätzlich orientiert sich die Beratungspraxis des Juristen in einem solchen Interaktionsmoment an der standardisierten Prozedur internationaler Asylverfahren, in der die Glaubwürdigkeit des individuellen Asylgesuchs im Zuge einer standardisierten Fragetechnik getestet wird, um ‚echte' von lediglich performten Geflüchteten – wie er sie nannte – zu unterscheiden. Er war angehalten, an seinem Computer in dem Freitextfeld einer Word-Datei Angaben zur Glaubwürdigkeit der individuellen Fluchtgeschichte einzutragen, die sich auf überprüfbare Fakten beziehen wie etwa konkrete Orte, historische Fakten oder medial dokumentierte Ereignisse. Belege, die das Anliegen der Antragstellenden unterstützen könnten, wie rechtliche Dokumente, medizinische Gutachten, Mitgliedsausweise, usw. konnten an dieser Stelle ebenfalls aufgelistet werden. Zwar führte er in diesem Moment de facto keine ordnungsgemäße Prozedur der ‚Refugee status determination' (RSD) durch – dies blieb den MitarbeiterInnen des nationalen Comités für Flüchtlinge (CONARE) vorbehalten – doch sah er es als wichtig an, offensichtliche Inkonsistenzen nicht einfach zu übergehen, sondern darauf mit explizit-kritischen Rückfragen zu reagieren. Auf diese Weise markierte er seine Orientierung an einem internationalen Wahrheitsregime, das auf eine Kultivierung des Zweifels ausgerichtet ist (Bohmer und Shuman 2008; Fassin und d'Halluin 2007) und dem er sich aufgrund seines beruflichen Ethos in besonderem Maße verpflichtet fühlte.

Als Mitarbeiter dieser katholischen Einrichtung sah sich der Anwalt zwei eigentlich unvereinbaren Referenzsystemen gegenüber: Einerseits sollte er den brasilianischen Staat vertreten, dessen Sortierarbeit vorbereiten und im Hinblick auf die Glaubwürdigkeit der Fluchtnarrative eine erste Empfehlung aussprechen; andererseits war er angehalten, AntragstellerInnen bei der Entwicklung einer Fluchterzählung zu *unterstützen*. Dazu kam die Einbettung in das organisationsspezifische Umfeld, das – wie zuvor erörtert – mit einem explizit humanistischen Ethos an ‚Fälle' herantrat. Die verschiedenen Seiten der Einrichtung, die sich mehreren, politisch und ethisch unterschiedlich aufgestellten, übergeordneten

Institutionen verpflichtet sahen, spiegelten sich also in der anstrengenden Sortierarbeit der AnwältInnen wider, die dazu diente, den falsifizierbaren Unterschied zwischen ‚wahr' und ‚falsch' zu identifizieren.

Darüber hinaus spielte vermutlich die Tatsache mit hinein, dass die Position dieses individuellen Anwalts innerhalb der Einrichtung nicht gefestigt war. Eine offensichtliche Fehlentscheidung hätte für ihn, dessen Arbeitshaltung mitunter allzu konservativ oder restriktiv wahrgenommen wurde, weitreichende Konsequenzen haben können und eine allzu strenge Handhabe eines Einzelfalls hätte ihn ggf. ins Zentrum der (Selbst-)Kritik der Organisation gebracht. Seine besonders ordnungsgemäße Abwicklung der fallbezogenen Sortierarbeit stellte daher möglicherweise auch einen Moment der kommunikativen Absicherung gegenüber lateralen KollegInnen und Vorgesetzten dar. Die Vorstellung einer Außenseite zerfiel aus dieser Perspektive in ganz unterschiedliche Positionen, die wahrgenommen, im Arbeitsprozess berücksichtigt, und deren Anliegen in die alltäglichen Prozeduren einbezogen werden mussten, um einer möglichen Vereinzelung und damit dem Herausfallen aus der Organisation entgegenzuwirken.

6 Die Psychologin: Kultivierung der diskreten Offenheit

„Schade. Der Zugang zu den Psychologinnen ist schwierig. Ihr Interesse an Transparenz ist explizit nicht gegeben. Sie sind zwar freundlich und irgendwie auch kooperativ, betonen aber die Schutzwürdigkeit ihrer Klienten mehr als andere Abteilungen. Ich konnte bei keinem Gespräch mit Klienten dabei sein und nur allgemeine Gespräche über die Aufgaben an sich führen."

(Feldtagebuch, August 2015)

Wenn die Anwälte während ihrer Rechtsberatungen besonders gravierende Inkonsistenzen in den Fluchtnarrativen oder schwere Kommunikationshürden feststellten, begleiteten sie die KlientInnen gerne unmittelbar im Anschluss an das jeweilige Gespräch zu den PsychologInnen, wo ihnen weitere Beratung zukommen soll. Nicht nur die besonders diskrete Kommunikation, sondern auch die Räumlichkeiten und die anstellungsrechtliche Position der PsychologInnen innerhalb der Organisation unterschieden sich deutlich von den Arbeitsroutinen der anderen Abteilungen. Die in einem gesonderten Gebäudetrakt arbeitende Gruppe war über ein extra und temporär finanziertes Forschungsprojekt, das regelmäßig neu beantragt und bewilligt werden musste, separat angestellt. Dementsprechend schienen die PsychologInnen sich den internen Abläufen der Organisation kaum verpflichtet zu fühlen, sondern grenzten sich dezidiert ab. Ihre Arbeit war auf die Kontaktherstellung und enge therapeutische Zusammenarbeit mit den Geflüchteten ausgerichtet. „Im Grunde versuchen wir, die zahlreichen schwerwiegenden Irritationen, die diese Menschen aus ihren Herkunftsländern mitbringen und die sich auf dem Weg hierhin und im Kontakt mit den brasilianischen Behörden fortsetzen, auszugleichen. Wir versuchen, möglichst wenig neue Irritationen hinzuzufügen, sondern den Menschen einen angemessenen Raum zu geben, ihnen Offenheit zu signalisieren. Wenn nötig, können wir auch schweigen. Wir müssen nichts erfahren, herausfinden, tun, ordnen, erfassen. Wir arbeiten anders."

An dieser ausgeprägten Performanz der Selbstseparierung und der Diskretion war den PsychologInnen im Umgang mit ihren KlientInnen besonders gelegen – und auch die explizite Abgrenzung von meiner forschenden Praxis konnte ich so einordnen. Möglicherweise war zentral, den Abstand gegenüber den anderen Abteilungen zu markieren, um das Vertrauen der Geflüchteten zu gewinnen oder aufrecht zu erhalten. Vor allem die an investigative Techniken erinnernde Frageweise der JuristInnen wirkten auf zahlreiche Asylsuchende irritierend und die PsychologInnen achteten daher, im Kontrast, auf einen dezidiert anderen, offenen, weniger suchenden Fragemodus. Innerhalb der Organisation ergab sich aus Sicht der forschenden Praxis also eine neue Seite, ein nicht vollständig integriertes Element, dessen paradoxe Besonderheit sich über das Verhältnis von kultivierter Offenheit bei gleichzeitiger Geschlossenheit artikulierte. Die Existenz dieser Seite konstituierte sich nicht über eine möglichst gelungene Integration in den übergreifenden Arbeitszusammenhang der Organisation, sondern über eine dezidiert andere Beratungsarbeit, welche die Bedürfnislage des individuellen Gegenübers als besonders relevant setzte.

7 Die Sozialarbeiterin: Kultivierung der Verbindung nach außen

„Heute den ganzen Tag in der Abteilung ‚integraçao' gesessen. Die Sozialarbeiter arbeiten tagein tagaus an allem Möglichen. Kein Geld für den Bus? Antrag wird ausgefüllt. Keine Bleibe? Es wird mit den Unterkünften telefoniert. Keine Kleidung für das Neugeborene? Es findet sich was. Ein Blindenstock? Wird beschafft! Irgendwie geht es immer. Es ist wie ein Bienenstock, alles kommt und geht, andauernder Durchlauf. Anstrengend, irgendwie lustig auch, gute Stimmung."

(Feldtagebuch, März 2014)

Die Aufgaben der eine Etage tiefer arbeitenden SozialarbeiterInnen waren besonders vielfältig. Sie arbeiteten nicht in Einzelräumen, wie die AnwältInnen und die PsychologInnen, sondern in einem einzigen großen Raum mit brusthoch stehenden und häufig mit zahlreichen Fotos gespickten mobilen Trennwänden. Auf der ständig voll besetzten Stuhlreihe an der Wand warteten manche, die noch einen Schlafplatz suchten, weitere, die Unterstützung bei bürokratischen Dingen benötigten, oder wiederum andere, die vielleicht gehört hatten, dass neue Kleiderspenden eingetroffen waren. Vor allem die Unterbringung von Neuankömmlingen in einer der Unterkünfte São Paolos stellte hier eine der größten Herausforderungen dar. Ständig standen die SozialarbeiterInnen im Kontakt mit zahlreichen städtischen, kirchlichen oder philanthropischen Einrichtungen, die auf das gesamte Stadtgebiet verteilt etwa 10.000 Betten für obdachlose Personen anboten. Diese öffentlichen Unterkünfte unterschieden sich deutlich in ihrem technischen Standard, ihrer Größe, ihren Alltagsroutinen und -regeln, ebenso wie in ihrer Klientel: Manche waren tagsüber geschlossen, andere wiederum durften die BewohnerInnen nur mit Erlaubnis verlassen. Manche waren auf bestimmte religiöse, nationale oder ethnische Gruppen ausgerichtet, die einzelne Zuwanderungsphasen dominierten, manche zielten auf bestimmte Altersgruppen oder Geschlechter und nahmen sowohl AusländerInnen als auch BrasilianerInnen auf, wie beispielsweise jene für Waisen oder obdachlose Frauen.

Bei der Lösung spezifischer Anliegen war mitunter entscheidend, dass die SozialarbeiterInnen mit einer städtischen Versorgungsinfrastruktur konfrontiert waren, die in dieser Zeit der politischen und ökonomischen ‚Krise' an ihre Grenzen stieß. Einmal wurde mir erläutert, dass einige MitarbeiterInnen der Stadtverwaltung wenig Sympathie für die Anliegen von Geflüchteten hätten, im Gegenteil. Um diese Perspektive zu verstehen, folgte ich den Netzwerken der Beratungseinrichtung nach außen, indem ich die Stadtverwaltung als eine Art erweiterten Arm oder Antenne deutete. In den dort geführten Gesprächen wurde mir klar, dass der Umgang mit AusländerInnen für einige der dort arbeitenden Angestellten besonders fremd war. Der folgende Interviewausschnitt mit einer Mitarbeiterin, die sich im Rahmen ihrer früheren Anstellung als Streetworkerin vor allem für Sexarbeiterinnen eingesetzt hatte, veranschaulicht eine solche Haltung:

> Wir hatten immer Ausländer hier. Aber sie waren immer in der Minderheit. Jetzt ist es ein Drittel oder sogar mehr. In manchen Unterbringungen sind die Migranten die Mehrheit, sie nehmen den gesamten Raum. Das verursacht Probleme, das kannst du dir vorstellen. Viele sprechen nicht unsere Sprache, ich spreche kein Englisch oder Französisch oder (haitianisches) Kreolisch. Manche Probleme sind kulturell. Sie wollen dies, sie wollen das, dieses Essen geht nicht, und so weiter. Für uns Bürger ist es

schwierig, mit diesen Ausländern umzugehen. Es gibt so viele arme Brasilianer, die unsere Unterstützung brauchen. Diese Krise produziert täglich neue Arme. Es kann jedem passieren. Ich kann die nicht auf der Straße schlafen lassen. Diese Ausländer, manche von denen meinen, sie seien etwas Besseres. Sie sagen, dass sie eigentlich woanders hinwollen, dass sie keine Obdachlosen seien. Aber sie müssen lernen, dass sie ohne Obdach sind. Sie sind es einfach. (Interview, September 2015)

Diese Mitarbeiterin der Stadtverwaltung manövrierte zwischen zwei unterschiedlichen ethischen Referenzfeldern, indem sie zunächst auf die Spezifika der Bedürfnisse von AusländerInnen einging, um anschließend herauszustreichen, dass diese den armen oder wohnungslosen BrasilianerInnen gleichgestellt sein sollten. Zwar versuchte sie, über ethnische oder nationale Unterschiede hinwegzugehen; gleichzeitig rechtfertigte sie die ungleiche Verteilung von Empathie und Solidarität, indem sie ‚estrangeiros' (Ausländer) und cidadãos' (Einheimische, Staatsbürger) als zwei getrennte Einheiten beschrieb. Angelehnt an eine nationale Perspektive operierte die Mitarbeiterin mit der Unterscheidung zwischen einem stärker legitimierten und zu beschützenden Innen und einem demgegenüber als fragwürdig erscheinenden Außen.

Diese Hintergrundinformationen und die Haltungen von MitarbeiterInnen aus anderen Organisationen beeinflussten wiederum die Haltung der SozialarbeiterInnen in der Beratungseinrichtung für Geflüchtete, die wussten, dass sie es einerseits mit den Widerständen offen oder latent xenophober städtischer MitarbeiterInnen, aber auch mit zahlreichen pragmatischen Hindernissen zu tun haben würden. Ihnen ging es darum, individuelle Bedürfnislagen mit einem vorhandenen administrativen Deutungsraster in Einklang zu bringen, was im Idealfall eine reibungslose Kategorisierung und Versorgung nach sich ziehen würde. In ihrer Alltagsarbeit konzentrierten sich die SozialarbeiterInnen einerseits auf die Identifikation der Passgenauigkeit dieser Raster und andererseits auf einen möglichst klugen, flexiblen und geschickten Umgang mit den Zwischenräumen, wenn ‚Fall' und Raster nicht zusammenpassten. Die zügige Bearbeitung der Sonderfälle, wenn es hakte und keine vorgefertigte Lösung gefunden werden konnte – wie bei der Unterbringung einer besonders großen, mehrere Generationen umschließenden Familie oder der Beschaffung eines Blindenstocks – galt innerhalb dieser Gruppe als besonders befriedigend. „Dar um jeito", eine brasilianische Formulierung für „es hinbekommen, kreativ werden, sich etwas einfallen lassen", war eine von den Sozialarbeiterinnen gerne verwendete Formulierung, um anzuzeigen, dass sie bei der Verwischung der Differenzlinien einer kategorial ausgerichteten Sortierarbeit, der Herstellung der Verbindung zu Nachbarorganisationen oder anderen städtischen Einrichtungen und der Herbeiführung einer pragmatischen Lösung erfolgreich waren. Im Grunde arbeiteten die Sozialarbeiterinnen räumlich und inhaltlich gleichzeitig im Zentrum, oder im Herz der Organisation, da die meisten KlientInnen und MitarbeiterInnen irgendwie mit ihnen zu tun hatten. Gleichzeitig reichte ihre Arbeit in einer Art Brückenfunktion nach außen, wodurch ihre Kontakte und Kommunikationsroutinen für das Gelingen der allgemeinen Beratungsarbeit zentral wurde.

8 Fazit

Epistemische Gemeinschaften, wie FaschistInnen, Bankangestellte (Boyer und Marcus 2020) oder eben die die Mitarbeitenden einer Beratungseinrichtung für Geflüchtete, teilen zwar jeweils, innerhalb ihrer Arbeits- oder Denkeinheiten, eine gemeinsame epistemologische Orientierung, gleichzeitig ist ihre Sicht auf die Dinge jedoch keineswegs einheitlich. Je mehr sich die Forschung den Alltagsbegebenheiten aus einer intersubjektiven Perspektive näherte, umso mehr löste sich die zu Beginn dieses Beitrags skizzierte Projektion eines Seitenwechsels auf. Dabei wurde jedoch deutlich, dass ‚die Seite' nicht nur eine Einstiegsorientierung, sondern (in diesem Fall) ein Element des organisationsspezifischen Wissens darstellt, indem es an deren soziale Struktur und Arbeitskultur anschließt. Einzelne AkteurInnen, wie die Leiterin oder der Padre, streben zu einem Ideal der Versämtlichung, indem sie die Bedürfnislagen der Mitarbeitenden oder die spirituell-religiöse Grundlage eines einrichtungsweit geteilten Arbeitsethos in den Vordergrund stellen, um eine abteilungsübergreifende Wertehaltung auszumachen und so zur Konstituierung der Organisation als solcher beizutragen. Mitunter wandten sich die Mitarbeitenden anderen Seiten ihrer Beratungsarbeit zu, indem sie mit ‚außen', wie den übergeordneten oder den benachbarten Organisationen kommunizierten und deren Spezifika in ihre Arbeit einbezogen: Wenn die Direktorin mit dem Direktor des UNHCR, der Anwalt mit dem Flüchtlingskomitee oder die Sozialarbeiterin mit der städtischen Wohnheimkoordinatorin verhandelten, wurde die Seite der eigenen Organisation porös und die Zuständigkeiten, Einflussbereiche sowie die Arbeitsweisen dieser Anderen wirkmächtig.

Gleichzeitig arbeiteten die einzelnen Abteilungen mit unterschiedlichen und jeweils spezifischen beruflichen Standards und Orientierungen. Die Werte einer Juristin, die sich in ihrer asylorientierten Arbeit an einer möglichst genauen Befolgung von Regeln ausrichtete, unterschieden sich von dem Ethos des Psychologen, der sich mit Fragen der individuellen Traumabewältigung befasste, oder von dem der Sozialarbeiterin, die zu einem bestimmten Zeitpunkt etwa eine extrem geringe Anzahl von Nothilfepaketen zu verteilen hatte und eine pragmatische Lösung suchte, um trotz der Beschränkung ihrer Ressourcen möglichst Vielen eine angemessene Versorgung zukommen zu lassen. Im Allgemeinen gerieten diese unterschiedlichen professionellen Haltungen und Arbeitsweisen nur selten miteinander in Konflikt. In der Alltagsroutine blieben die Räume und Zuständigkeiten weitestgehend getrennt, die jeweiligen Tätigkeiten und Leistungsziele waren unterschiedlich definiert und die ungeschriebene Regel der Nichteinmischung wurde wechselseitig anerkannt. Letztlich ließ das Moment der Krise, das sowohl die Finanzierung einiger Segmente der Organisation und die dazugehörenden Arbeitsplätze als auch die nationale Ordnung zu gefährden schien, die Trennlinien zwischen den Abteilungen poröser werden. Die Krise fungierte dann auch als Erklärung oder Rechtfertigung für den Konkurrenzdruck, besonders unter den AnwältInnen, für das Abgrenzungsverhalten, besonders der PsychologInnen, oder auch für andere Konflikte, die dem übergeordneten humanistischen Ideal zu widersprechen schienen.

Der Seitenwechsel erwies sich letzten Endes im Laufe dieser Sondierungsphase der Forschung nur noch als impulsgebende Idee. Es ließen sich damit zwar die flexiblen schematischen Ordnungen der teilnehmenden AkteurInnen nachvollziehen, gleichzeitig löste sich die Erwartung eines epistemologischen ‚Anderen' zugunsten einer „multirelationalen" Wissensproduktion, wie Judith Schlehe es nennt, (Schlehe 2013, 101) auf. Deutlich wurde auch, dass das Konzept der Seite jeweils mit professionellen Haltungen verbunden ist, die im Hinblick auf einen spezifischen beruflichen Ethos entschlüsselt werden können bzw. sollten. Die ethnologische Forschung wird an einem solchen Ort, im Idealfall, zu einem inter- bzw. transdisziplinären Unterfangen, das anschließt an rechtswissenschaftliche, psychologische, theologische oder sozialpädagogische Zugangs- und Arbeitsweisen, um nur einige zu nennen. Eine derartige Beratungseinrichtung kann somit als intersubjektive, und vor allem auch als transdisziplinäre und transkulturelle Kontaktzone verstanden werden. Darin werden Binarismen wie z. B. ich – sie, innen – außen, religiös-humanitär – bürokratisch, Angestellte – Klienten nicht nur (re-)produziert, sondern reflektiert, nutzbar gemacht, gebrochen oder, wenn möglich, überwunden, wie Judith Schlehe es kürzlich in einer Bilanzierung ihres Tandem-Forschungsprojekts forderte (ebd.).

Literatur

Armbruster, H., und A. Laerke, Hrsg. 2010. *Taking sides. Ethics, politics, and fieldwork in anthropology.* New York/Oxford: Berghahn.
Bohmer, C., und A. Shuman, Hrsg. 2008. Rejecting refugees: Political asylum in the 21st century. London/New York: Routledge.
Boyer, D., und G. Marcus, Hrsg. 2020. *Collaborative anthropology today. A collection of exceptions.* Ithaka/New York: Cornell University Press.
Costa, S. 2018. „Estrutura social e crise política no Brasil". *DADOS – Revista de Ciências Sociais,* Rio de Janeiro 61(4): 499–533.
Faria, C. A. P. de, und C. Goulart Paradis. 2013. „Humanism and solidarity in Brazilian foreign policy under Lula (2003–2010): theory and practice". *Brazilian Political Science Review* 7(2): 8–36.
Fassin, D. and E. D'Halluin. 2007. „Critical evidence. The politics of trauma in French asylum policies". *Ethos,* Vol. 35 (3): 300–329.
Fischel de Andrade, J. H. 2015. „Refugee protection in Brazil (1921–2014): an analytical narrative of changing policies". In *A liberal tide? Immigration and asylum law and policy in Latin America,* Hrsg. David James Cantor, Luisa Feline Freier and Jean-Pierre Gauci, 153–184. School of Advanced Study, University of London, London.
Gato, L. G., und N. B. Salazar. 2018. „Constructing a city, building a life: Brazilian construction workers' continuous mobility as a permanent life strategy". *Mobilities* 13(5): 733–745. https://doi.org/10.1080/17450101.2018.1466504.
Gupta, A., und J. Ferguson. 1997. „Discipline and practice. The field as site, method, and location in anthropology". In *Anthropological locations: Boundaries and grounds of a field science,* Hrsg. Akhil Gupta und James Ferguson, 1–46. Berkeley: University of California Press.
Haas, P. M. 1992. „Introduction: epistemic communities and international policy coordination". *International Organization* 46(1): 1–35.
Jubilut, L. 2006. „Refugee law and protection in Brazil. A model in South America?" *Journal of Refugee Studies* 19(1): 22–44.
Olwig, K. F., und K. Hastrup, Hrsg. 1997. Siting culture. The shifting anthropological object. London/New York: Routledge.
Schlehe, J. 2006. „Transnationale Wissensproduktion. Deutsch-indonesische Tandemforschung". In *Identitätspolitik und Interkulturalität in Asien,* Hrsg. Boike Rehbein, Jürgen Rüland und Judith Schlehe, 167–190. Münster: LIT.
Schlehe, J. 2013. Wechselseitige Übersetzungen. Methodologische Neuerungen in transkulturellen Forschungskooperationen. In *Ethnologie im 21. Jahrhundert,* Hrsg. Thomas Bierschenk, Matthias Krings und Carola Lentz, 97–110. Berlin: Reimer.

Friendship and Camaraderie in Collaborative Anthropology

Sita Hidayah und Ingo Rohrer

1 Introduction

The Argentinian anthropologist Rita Segato has had a tremendous impact in Latin America and is also recognized as an influential academic in other parts of the world thanks to translations of her various works. Segato can rightly be regarded as an important contemporary decolonial thinker, whose goals and agenda have undoubtedly resonated with scholars who question the current scientific system and its perpetuation of unequal power relations, and who make practical proposals to try to break through the conventional production and dissemination of knowledge. Although Segato's work is primarily concerned with feminist analyses of violence (2003, 2013, 2017), she also frequently engages—most notably in her contribution to the anthology *Des/Colonizar la Universidad* (2015) and more recently in *Contrapedagogias contra la Crueldad* (2018)—with decolonial approaches to the university system and knowledge production.

Here we see a link to Judith Schlehe's collaborative, reciprocal anthropological research approaches, which she has developed and refined over many years of practical experience (Schlehe 2006; Schlehe and Kutanegara 2006; Schlehe and Simatupang 2008; Schlehe 2013; Schlehe and Hidayah 2013, 2014; Huotari, Rüland and Schlehe 2014). In this paper, we would like to focus on one aspect of decolonial and collaborative anthropology that has been touched upon

---

S. Hidayah (✉)
Department of Anthropology, Faculty of Cultural Sciences, Gadjah Mada University, Yogyakarta, Indonesia
E-Mail: sita.fib@ugm.ac.id

I. Rohrer
Institut für Ethnologie, Albert-Ludwigs-Universität Freiburg, Freiburg, Deutschland
E-Mail: ingo.rohrer@ethno.uni-freiburg.de

and emphasized both by Segato and Schlehe: friendship. Despite the centrality of friendship in the title of Segato's *Before the Mirror of the Evil Queen: Teaching, Friendship, and Empowerment as Decolonial Breaches in the University* and the emphasis Schlehe has repeatedly placed on friendship as a product of practical collaboration, we believe that a more thorough discussion of friendship as part of collaborative and decolonial anthropology processes is required. Friendship is mobilized in debates on decolonizing academia and beyond (cf. Gandhi 2005) to provide an alternative relationship model to competitive, calculating logics that perpetuate power imbalances and dependencies. Friendship is portrayed as a 'dissident relationality'—to borrow a concept from Gandhi (2005)—to university corporatism and neoliberal metrics of meritocracy because the values attached to ideas of friendship, such as mutual trust, selflessness, affection or loyalty, go beyond pragmatic goals of completing research projects and fieldwork.

Although decolonial thinkers and activists use the term and concept of friendship, we want to point out that friendship is linked to a set of ideas and conceptions that we find problematic, particularly because friendship—including in these decolonial contexts—is generally conceptualized from a Western point of view. In this paper we will therefore analyse and criticise the term friendship. We propose considering the idea of camaraderie as an alternative relationship model for collaborative anthropology, as we see it as explicitly political and determined by engagement in a common project. But the purpose of this paper is not exclusively to insist on new terminology. Rather, we would like to use the discussions and ideas we have taken from Argentina, Germany, and Indonesia to critically examine the relational dimensions of academic partnerships and to highlight aspects that can be overlooked if the concept of friendship is used carelessly.

2   Starting Points

We examine friendships in academic partnership against the backdrop of the anthropological study of friendship that Ingo Rohrer and other scholars have undertaken under Judith Schlehe's supervision as part of their research in the graduate school project *Freunde, Gönner und Getreue* (Friends, Benefactors and Loyalists) (Descharmes et al. 2011; Brandt and Heuser 2011; Heuser 2012; Brandt 2013; Rohrer 2014a, b; Feickert, Haut and Sharaf 2014; Müller, Edinger and Alvarado Leyton 2017).

More importantly, this article seeks to reflect on academic friendship and the practice of anthropology within collaborative anthropology in general from the perspective of two anthropologists who as students participated in the Tandem Research model initiated by Judith Schlehe. We were both part of the first cohort of students to participate in collaborative fieldwork exercises, first in Yogyakarta, Indonesia, in 2004, and then in Freiburg, Germany, in 2005. Our argument is based on our similar experiences as participants of the ALU and UGM tandem research, even though we were not on the same tandem team. By 2022, hundreds of students, lecturers, project officers, and partners from different universities, disciplines, and agencies will have taken part in the tandem projects (Schlehe and Hidayah 2013). Both of us followed the development of the projects over the years in various roles (as coordinator, lecturer, project collaborator). Our long-term friendships, like those of other members of the tandem program, extend beyond and over professional collaboration and fieldwork situations.

Sita Hidayah has primarily supported the program as a coordinator, while Ingo Rohrer has occasionally assisted with teaching and advising. At the end of 2020, we were able to facilitate the exchange of students and the exploration of collaborative anthropological work even during a pandemic thanks to the support of the German Academic Exchange Service, when we moved the tandem program to the digital space. The project was also opened for cooperation with another partner, the Universidad Nacional de San Martín in Buenos Aires, Argentina, during this phase.

In short, our two academic careers have been shaped and intertwined by the collaborative tandem research project initiated by Judith Schlehe. Thus in this paper we discuss friendship and close social relations in collaborative anthropology against the backdrop of academic engagement with friendship and the very personal experience of collaboration. Furthermore, we hope to bring together various decolonial perspectives, comments and experiences from around the world—primarily from Indonesia, Germany and, last but not least, Argentina, which also explains the initial reference to Segato.

After a brief review of the tandem research project and its aim of collaborative anthropology, we would like to expand on the emphasis on friendship in subsequent sections. The following section will explain why we are sceptical about the concept of friendship and why we propose the concept of camaraderie to broaden the discussion of collaboration and decolonial approaches in anthropology. We will conclude the article with closing remarks.

3   Tandem Research and Collaborative Anthropology

In 2004, Judith Schlehe first introduced the tandem project between Albert-Ludwigs University (ALU) and Gadjah Mada University (UGM) as a reciprocal partnership that challenges the notion that anthropological research is primarily conducted by Western anthropologists in the Global South, with anthropologists from the Global South serving primarily as field research assistants. Over the course of eighteen years of collaboration, the tandem project has covered different topics and formats and has included six universities in various forms: Albert-Ludwigs University (Freiburg, Germany), Gadjah Mada University (Yogyakarta Indonesia), Universitas Hasanuddin (Makassar, Indonesia), Universitas Indonesia (Jakarta, Indonesia), University of Basel (Basel, Switzerland) and Universidad Nacional San Martín (Buenos Aires, Argentina). In short, the tandem project driven by Judith Schlehe has thus evolved and changed several times, and the formats, topics, and forms of funding have all changed significantly over time. However, one main goal has remained consistent: to bring together people who want to benefit from discussion of their points of view and positionalities, and who want to pursue collaborative anthropology with a decolonial orientation.

The tandem project as a whole seeks to counteract inequalities and privileges resulting from colonial structures in the academic field and from conventional anthropological fieldwork by proposing collaborative and reciprocal research not only in the Global South but also in the Global North. This approach, the methods involved, and its ethics translate into partnerships to reposition the relationship between researchers (and the researched) in knowledge production. It is also a mode of engagement in doing and writing collaborative ethnographies. The equal partnership implies that the collaborative project will include everyone involved, from research conceptualization, decision making, and in principle autonomous yet parallel research administrations. The partner universities—first of all ALU and UGM—share benefits and responsibilities in roughly equal proportions. Overall, the collaborative model seeks to 'overcome categorical divisions such as "native" or "foreign" anthropologists' (Schlehe and Hidayah 2014).

In terms of methodology, the collaborative project stands for inventive experimentation. Unlike traditional ethnographic group projects in which individual researchers work independently toward a common goal, the tandem project conditions collaborative work and co-presence in the field of (at least two) researchers with different positionalities and different methodological approaches, as well as different academic and cultural backgrounds. Based on the collaborative project of fieldwork and data acquisition, the joint analysis of the material and the writing process in co-authorship must be highlighted as distinctive research practices for the tandem projects.

However, there are significant differences in capabilities and sources, both tangible and intangible, such as financial resources, language skills, and academic management on a practical level. There are also different structural hierarchies in decision making between Germany and Indonesia. Regardless of the many differences and challenges arising from them, the long duration and permanence of multiple collaborative projects demonstrate that the many parties involved respect the principle of cooperation and follow through on commitments to work on joint decolonial projects.

It goes without saying that over the years close social relationships have developed between the collaborators, whether they are between academics, students who participated in the tandem projects, research participants or other associates. The university networks bring interdisciplinary studies and actors together into these collaborative relationships. Hundreds of people have been brought together and have formed relationships that have often persisted over time and despite (physical) distance.

Beyond limited, subjective views, these relationships have always aided in broadening horizons and the possibilities for seeing problems and situations as well as in developing new questions and perspectives. These non-quantified, informal assessments of problems and ideas provide a variety of solutions for overcoming differences and imbalances in resources and abilities. We have learned from nearly two decades of collaboration that flexible ways of doing things and making use of connections and relationships can also be used to dismantle structural and administrative barriers as well as the logistics of academia. This option supplants the standardised university bureaucracies as well as the traditional ways of conducting research and disseminating knowledge. Flexibility, on the other hand, allows us to balance out inequalities and unattainable quality standards. Reciprocity is important, but flexibility is too. Not everyone can participate the same way, with the same achievement of standards. Often, this is because structural inequalities and bureaucratic barriers prevent students (even graduates and researchers) from participating equally.

We, the authors, can add that the initial collaboration and project work may pave the way for a long bond that is not necessarily limited by joint research projects or academic collaboration, but by (sometimes interrupted) communication and exchange in which academic and private topics are intertwined. This is the starting point for thinking about how projects like the collaborative tandem projects on the one hand allow space for academic cooperation and deeper learning about changes of perspective, postcolonial exchange, and triangulation in relation to specific questions and research objectives. On the other hand, it fosters intimacy and exchange, shaping perspectives in dealing with academic culture and a globally intertwined anthropology in the long run.

In retrospect, it will come down to the strong relationships that have developed among the members of these collaborative projects over the course of 18 years of tandem projects. We have naturally referred to these relationships that we experience, feel, and maintain as friendships, emphasizing mutual trust above all else. The belief that friendships form the foundation of the project, and that friendship can grow out of collaborative tandem research experience is undeniably correct, as we both have experienced. Why, then, are we still hesitant to acknowledge the concept of friendship as central for such a decolonial approach?

This will become clear in the following section, in which we will critically question the concept of friendship and clarify the imperative connotations it carries, which are not adequately reflected in the work of Segato, for example. Although we criticize her in this regard, we want to emphasize that in line with Schlehe's thinking, we share Segato's impetus to create another form of academic connectedness that on the one hand resists the conventional division of the West as producer and the South as consumer of academic knowledge and on the other hand opposes the neo-liberalisation of the scientific system. In other words, we believe that the relationships that form the basis of the collaboration between people and universities goes beyond friendly relations and is driven overall by mutual commitments and goals. In fact, we believe that the idea of friendship not only falls short of describing the dimensions of relations that the collaborative tandem project entails, but it is also problematic when understood solely from a Western point of view. We will therefore propose an additional concept, collegial camaraderie, that we believe is appropriate for describing and thinking about collaborative anthropology and the decolonial impetus behind it.

4 Friendship

Only in the last few decades has there been anthropological engagement with friendship. According to Stevenson and Lawthon (2017), the anthropological study of friendship has previously been overshadowed by the study of kinship or focus on economic and political relations (Friese 2010, p. 25). Pitt-River (1973) recognized that studies of friendship are closely related to studies of kinship because the 'nature' of the relationship is similar due to their affective and intimate characterizations. Nonetheless, despite this insight and the long discussion of friendship in neighbouring disciplines such as philosophy, political science, and sociology (cf. Rohrer 2014a, p. 48 f.), anthropological engagement with friendship only recently gained traction in the context of new approaches in kinship studies that recognized the flexibility and diversity of relationships. The concept of relatedness drew researchers' attention to questions about the boundaries and overlaps of various forms of social relations and it brought an interest in friendship (Carsten 2000). Without reproducing the entire corpus of the anthropological work on friendship here, it can be stated that scholars agree that friendship must be recognized for its diversity regarding conceptualization and practices (Grätz, Meier and Pelican 2004, p. 11).

The anthropological study of friendship conducted in Freiburg under the direction of Judith Schlehe as part of the research training group *Freunde, Gönner und Getreue* (Friends, Benefactors, and Loyalists), supports this viewpoint and reminds us that in historical and cross-cultural comparison friendship differs significantly in semantics, practices, and normative expectations (Brandt and Heuser 2011; Brandt 2013; Rohrer 2014; Feickert, Haut and Sharaf 2014; Müller, Edinger and Alvarado Leyton 2017). Despite the empirical evidence of variations and the subsequent discussions that worked towards a deconstruction and diversification of perspectives (Bell and Coleman 1999; Schmidt et al. 2007; Desai and Killick 2010), we see that friendship as it is conceptualized in the Western sense remains a very influential and dominant idea on a global level. And we believe that it is precisely this Western idea of friendship, with its implied normative ideas, that is mobilized as a combative term in decolonial debates. In the following, we will briefly highlight these normative ideas to provide a better understanding of why we believe that decolonial relationships should extend beyond friendship.

Public/Private
The distinction between a public and a private sphere is central to the Western concept of friendship. Friendship is associated with the private sphere and regarded as largely inappropriate in the public sphere, where informal, private, and affective relations supposedly undermine professionalism. Despite empirical studies casting doubt on ideal–typical separation, the idea that friendships may serve as a breeding ground for nepotism in professional contexts is highly influential. As a result, we believe that the use of the concept of friendship is particularly problematic in the Global South, where the focal point of corrupt practices is supposedly located—at least from a Western perspective.

Eye Level
The image of a relationship on equal footing is another idea strongly associated with the Western concept of friendship. Equal footing is a buzzword and a recurring theme in decolonial thinking and it is regarded as a desirable goal of collaborative work. Therefore, the concept of friendship appears to fit within the debates. We would like to emphasize that in the conceptualization of friendship, equal footing is considered a prerequisite rather than a desirable goal. Similarity, be it regarding common interests, values, or social markers as well as balanced encounters at eye level, is understood to be the foundation of friendship, whereas difference is understood to be potentially disruptive. As a result, we believe that the concept of friendship sets the wrong accents and perpetuates an image of difference as being problematic rather than being a positive and beneficial feature.

Obscuring Inequalities
Overall, we believe that the prevalent concept of friendship not only denies the potentiality of difference, but also tends to conceal imbalances and inequalities. To demonstrate this point, consider the ethnographic example of the region of Yogyakarta in Indonesia, where friends are considered to be equals and can converse on eye level. However, there are traditional hierarchies in interpersonal relationships based on age, status, and closeness between two or more people. According to this hierarchical matrix, people in the Javanese region speak on six levels of speech (six levels of diction, not tenses), whereas the Indonesian national language has only one level of speech. Friends talk at the lowest level of speech (Jawa Ngoko) while elders and superiors are addressed using the highest level (Kromo Inggil) in the Javanese language. We believe that emphasizing friendship relations may obscure such hierarchies and the associated imbalances and inequalities, which are of course also effective in the academic field and not just in a specific institute or a culturally specific region, but in the entire transnational relational network of academia.

Gender Relations
One may observe that hierarchies in academia are established primarily on the basis of seniority, merit, and scientific success, but we would like to address the issue of gender here as well. This is not only because we believe it to be a crucial differentiation in academia but also because it is perceived as a sticking point for friendship insofar as cross-gender friendships are considered complicated and fuelled by desire. Academic engagements prefer passion for one's study, the amount of energy devoted to fieldwork and other works to ensure 'maximum academic functioning' of scholars.

Furthermore, the dimension of gender has been conceptualized in the dichotomous pair of face-to-face and side-by-side relations, with friendships between men viewed as focusing on a third object (side-by-side), whereas friendships between women have been considered to be based on communication and mutual interest (face-to-face) (Wright 1969, 1982). We think that such a dichotomous division exists in collaborative research or academic work, where researchers focus on the same research object (side-by-side). In our opinion, the principle of masculine friendship as the basis of collaboration risks leaving little room for the face-to-face aspect, in which collaborators are primarily in conversation with and care for each other.

Dyadic Relations
Another central element that is dominant in conceptions of friendship is the emphasis on relationships between two people. This perspective, often referred to in the vocabulary of dyadic relations, is emphasized heavily by sociological studies but also maintained in anthropology. We believe that such a disregard for the embeddedness of dyadic relations in a broader context of social groups and networks remains a strong feature of concepts and ideas of friendship and is rooted in the overall emphasis on individuality within Western thought. We believe that it is misleading to speak of friendship as the ideal form of relationship, particularly in an academic context, because it ignores the contextual situation surrounding people and their relationships and, furthermore, emphasizes primarily direct relationships. We are convinced that in academic work, however, indirect relationships and a broader network of social contacts play important roles.

Voluntarism and Necessities
Scholars have emphasized the voluntary nature of friendships as a key feature in distinguishing them from other social relationships. Relationships with kin or neighbours, for example, are thought to be characterized by obligations and necessities rather than by voluntary association. Although anthropological work has deconstructed this strict demarcation and both the flexibility of kinship relationships as well as the utilitarian dimensions of friendships have been emphasized, we still see a continuation of the attribution of friendship to voluntariness. Again, we believe that using the Western concept of friendship in the context of academic collaboration is problematic because the obligations or necessities, as well as implied dependencies, may be overlooked.

In conclusion, we are convinced that using friendship as a positively connoted idea for academic collaboration risks obscuring these other aspects that distinguish academic relationships. By employing an unreflected concept of friendship, we see a way of undermining rather than strengthening the necessity of decolonial critique. In our opinion, when utilizing the idea of friendship it is a particularly Western concept of friend that is mobilized, which has to be understood as a predominantly male, close social relationship between two individuals who focus on a third object—for instance a joint leisure activity—and who harmonize best with each other when there is similarity in terms of interests, values and social markers, and when differences can be eliminated.

This serves as a reminder to continue critically engaging with the ideas and practices of collaborative and decolonial anthropology, not only to highlight their merits and possibilities but also to recognize their flaws and areas for improvement. We believe that reflecting on the close (and not so close) relationships and bonds that emerge from such collaborations is critical to moving the discussion forward. This is because, of course, anthropologists believe that small scale and on-the-ground experiences have an impact on larger structures.

5   Camaraderie

From an Indonesian point of view, Sita Hidayah initially suggested moving away from the term friendship, which emphasizes 'equality' and 'similarity' (such as class, thereby dissolving other differences) in Western but apparently also Argentine contexts. She suggests considering the term camaraderie because it does not hide the existing inequalities and provides an alternative mode of relationship in the process of the decolonization of academia. Although 'camaraderie' is not a less Western term than friendship, we believe it is important to discuss and consider the notions connected to it.

Before we go into greater detail, it should be noted that we understand that camaraderie and the practices, ideals, and conceptions associated with it appear problematic, particularly from a German perspective. Germany's war-hungry as well as war-glorifying history and the exaggeration and glorification of *kameradschaft* as part of the *'völkische'* project and German National Socialism cannot and should not be ignored (Kühne 1998, 2006, 2017; Grüneisen 2010), particularly since the term *kameradschaft* is still used by political right-wing groups in contemporary Germany and still carries an overemphasis on masculinity.

Camaraderie, however, does not have the same historical weight elsewhere and is instead associated with left-wing politics and solidarity relations. This is true, for example, in English-speaking contexts, where the word 'camaraderie' is borrowed from the French 'camarade'—a term that can also be translated as 'comrade'. Pivotal for this left-leaning connotation of camaraderie is the poem *The Dear Love of Comrades* (1891) by the American author Walt Whitman. According to Kristen Harris (2016) Whitman's global promises and conceptualization of camaraderie lay at the heart of many socialists in England and beyond. In her reading of Whitman's poem, Harris suggests that camaraderie evokes the bond that is developed when a common cause is fought for side by side, like in a brotherhood. But camaraderie implies something more: the idea of community or a group devoted to a cause that far exceeds any one person. John Mathias also had this dimension of relationships in mind when he ascertained that the term camaraderie is explicitly political, expressing a focus on engagement in a common project (Mathias 2010, p. 118).

In Indonesia, camaraderie is commonly translated as *persahabatan* (friendship) while the term comrade translates to *kamerad* in Bahasa Indonesia. This indicates that friendship and camaraderie can be conceptualized as intertwined relationships (cf. Nevarez, Yee and Waldinger 2017). The term *kamerad*, however, has acquired a negative connotation as result of the 1965 Indonesian 'communist' coup-d'état. The acquired connotation of the term comrade with communism is shown in *Comrade! History of Communism* by Robert Service (2007).

As these brief examples illustrate, the use and meaning of camaraderie are diverse and even current academic works that make use of the term do not provide a precise definition (Lerum 2004; Kearsey 2020; Ransom 2020). These works, however, point out that aspects of solidarity and care beyond the realm of personal affection and in contexts of hierarchical order in larger groups are the defining features of camaraderie.

Drawing on the cited literature, we believe that the term camaraderie, in comparison to friendship, emphasizes a shared interest and places far less emphasis on the private sphere, allowing for the establishment of relations that are free of cronyism and private collusion. Although military history as well as the current use of the term by right-wing groups is probably worrying to some, we consider that the emphasis that' is placed on hierarchical order and chains of command corresponds thoroughly with the management and structures of academia.

In other words, we consider that camaraderie makes power imbalances in the academic field far more transparent; it questions the idea of eye-level collaboration, and it does not obscure existing inequalities. We think camaraderie rather invokes a sentiment of cohesion and solidarity while also acknowledging hierarchical structures and recognizing differences without viewing them as problematic obstacles. Instead of aiming for the same level for all involved individuals, camaraderie, as defined, for instance, by Harris (2016) and Mathias (2010), promotes the idea of unreserved solidarity, regardless of and while acknowledging differences in respect to age, gender, ethnicity, and so forth.

This solidaristic character of camaraderie, in our opinion and experience from the tandem research project, is true despite the masculine connotation, which, as previously stated, is rooted primarily in the military tradition. We consider that the concept of camaraderie places a strong emphasis on common endeavours and commitments to accomplish goals, to which individual needs and sociological differences—including gender—must be levelled. Camaraderie subverts the notions of voluntarism and individual necessities that are central to the concept of friendship. Common objectives, on the other hand, come to the fore. We do not see these objectives, missions, or endeavours solely as joint research projects in which individual scientists collaborate in dyadic ensembles, but rather as pointing to the common goal of decolonizing the scientific system in its current form. In this respect, camaraderie can go beyond the framework of tandem teams or small groups that work together on specific projects. It rather calls for awareness of one's own situatedness in larger group contexts and invites one to identify with a solidaristic position. It is not only close social relationships that are central to academic collaboration and the impetus to decolonize academia. Speaking of camaraderie reminds us of the value of rather impersonal ties of larger groups and a shared image of a solidarity community which develops despite hierarchies, imbalances, and differences.

We believe that camaraderie is a much more appropriate term for the decolonial relationships we want to develop between academics, disciplines, universities, and countries. However, it is important to emphasize that we do not just want to introduce new terminology, but to invite further reflection and discussion on the forms of relationships that encourage the decolonization of the scientific system.

6 Conclusion

In this paper, we aimed to reflect on the relationships that form the basis of collaborative research approaches in anthropology and critically engaged with the concept of friendship, which is often pronounced in such contexts and in attempts to decolonize the discipline and academia. We have argued that the idea of friendship is not considered in its cultural plurality but that when using the term friendship in decolonial contexts, predominantly Western perspectives on friendships are invoked. We agree with the assertion that the meanings of friendships vary by culture based on our own experience with the tandem project introduced by Judith Schlehe and refined and altered over the years. We recognize that despite academic and cultural differences, mutual trust and friendship develop over time and provide foundations for other ways of doing collaborative anthropology.

Still, we argue that pronouncing friendship places an emphasis on eye-level relationships, dyadic relationships and voluntarism that is not quite appropriate for what we see as the core of the collaborative tandem research that was initiated by Judith Schlehe. We have discussed friendship as a positively connoted ideal that is strongly linked to dominant Western ideas but nonetheless pronounced as an ideal relationship model in attempts to decolonize academia and anthropological research. With this brief discussion we hope to spark debate about unequal power relations in the current knowledge production and dissemination system and to develop practical proposals. In collaboration and decolonizing approaches, we propose an alternative relationship model to friendship that seeks to recognize the importance of people's situatedness in larger group contexts and the solidarity required to achieve common goals while also promoting the levelling of unequal power relations and bureaucratic barriers.

Camaraderie was presented as a dissident rationality to academic corporatism and neoliberal standards of meritocracy as well as a relational mode that must be understood as complementary to personalized friendships. Even though the term camaraderie has its own set of meanings and plural connotations, we believe it is a useful concept for the debate because it reminds us to value larger networks of collaborations as well as more impersonal relations. It also implies—far more than friendship—common goals and joint projects as core ideas of relational networks, evoking a shared image of a solidarity community that develops despite the currently existing hierarchies, imbalances, and differences.

References

Bell, S. and S. Coleman, Eds. 1999. The anthropology of friendship. Enduring themes and future possibilities. In *The Anthropology of Friendship,* 1–21. Oxford; New York: Berg.

Brandt, A., and E. A. Heuser. 2011. Friendship and socio-cultural context. Experiences from New Zealand and Indonesia. In *Varieties of friendship,* Eds. B. Descharmes, E. A. Heuser, C. Krüger and T. Loy, 145–74. Göttingen: V&R Unipress.

Brandt, A. 2013. *Among friends? On the dynamics of Māori-Pākehā relationships in Aotearoa New Zealand.* Göttingen: V&R Unipress.

Carsten, J., Ed. 2000. *Cultures of relatedness. New approaches to the study of kinship.* Cambridge; New York: Cambridge University Press.

Desai, A., and E. Killick, Eds. 2010. *The ways of friendship. Anthropological perspectives.* New York: Berghahn Books.

Descharmes, B., E. A. Heuser, C. Krüger, and T. Loy, Eds. 2011. *Varieties of friendship. Interdisciplinary perspectives on social relationships.* Göttingen: V&R Unipress.

Feickert, S., A. Haut, and K. Sharaf, Eds. 2014. *Faces of communities. Social ties between trust, loyalty and conflict.* Göttingen: V&R Unipress.

Friese, H. 2010. Freundschaft. Leerstellen and Spannungen eines Begriffs. In *Strong Ties/Weak Ties,* Eds. N. Binczek and G. Stanitzek, 17–38. Heidelberg: Universitätsverlag Winter.

Gandhi, L. 2005. *Affective communities. Anti-colonial thought, fin-de-siecle radicalism, and the politics of friendship.* Durham: Duke University Press.

Grätz, T., B. Meier, and M. Pelican. 2004. Freundschaftsprozesse in Afrika aus sozialanthropologischer Perspektive. *Africa Spectrum* 39(1): 9–39.

Grüneisen, S. 2010. *Kameradschaft in Militärorganisationen. Kameradschaft in Extremsituationen.* Working Paper. Bielefeld: Universität Bielefeld.

Harris, K. 2016. *Walt Whitman and British Socialism. The love of comrades.* New York: Routledge.

Heuser, E. A. 2012. Befriending the field. Culture and friendships in development worlds. *Third World Quarterly* 33 (8): 1423–37.

Huotari, M., J. Rüland and J. Schlehe, Eds. 2014. *Methodology and research practice in Southeast Asian studies.* Houndmills: Palgrave Macmillan.

Kearsey, J. 2020. Control, camaraderie and resistance. Precarious work and organisation in hospitality. *Capital & Class* 44(4): 503–511.

Kühne, T. 1998. Zwischen Männerbund und Volksgemeinschaft. Hitlers Soldaten und der Mythos der Kameradschaft. *Archiv für Sozialgeschichte* 38: 165–189.

Kühne, T. 2006. *Kameradschaft. Die Soldaten des nationalsozialistischen Krieges und das 20. Jahrhundert.* Göttingen: Vandenhoeck & Ruprecht.

Kühne, T. 2017. *The rise and fall of comradeship. Hitler's soldiers, male bonding and mass violence in the twentieth century.* Cambridge: Cambridge University Press.

Lerum, K. 2004. Sexuality, power, and camaraderie in service work. *Gender and Society* 18 (6): 756–776.

Mathias, J. 2010. Of contract and camaraderie. Thoughts on what relationships in the field could be. *Collaborative Anthropologies* 3: 110–120.

Müller, C., S. Edinger, and C. Alvarado Leyton, Eds. 2017. *Nahbeziehungen zwischen Freundschaft und Patronage. Zur Politik Und Typologie Affektiver Vergemeinschaftung.* Göttingen: V&R Unipress.

Nevarez, M. D., H. M. Yee and R. J. Waldinger. 2017. Friendship in war. Camaraderie and prevention of posttraumatic stress disorder prevention. *Journal of Traumatic Stress* 30: 512–520.

Pitt-Rivers, J. 1973. The Kith and the Kin. In *The Character of Kinship* ed. J. Goody, 89–106. Cambridge: Cambridge University Press.

Ransom, J. C. 2020. Love, trust, and camaraderie. Teachers' perspectives of care in urban high school. *Education and Urban Society* 52(6): 904–926.

Rohrer, I. 2014a. *Cohesion and dissolution. Friendship in the globalized punk and hardcore scene of Buenos Aires.* Wiesbaden: Springer VS.

Rohrer, I. 2014b. Zusammenhalt und Auflösung. Zu Freundschaft in der globalisierten Punk- und Hardcore-Szene von Buenos Aires. In *Faces of communities. Social ties between trust, loyalty and conflict,* Eds. S. Feickert, A. Haut and K. Sharaf, 193–208. V&R Unipress: Göttingen.

Schlehe, J. 2006. Transnationale Wissensproduktion. Deutsch-indonesische Tandemforschung. In *Identitätspolitik und Interkulturalität in Asien,* Eds. B. Rehbein, J. Rüland and J. Schlehe, 167–190. Münster: LIT.

Schlehe, J. 20 3. Wechselseitige Übersetzungen. Methodologische Neuerungen in transkulturellen Forschungskooperationen. In *Ethnologie im 21. Jahrhundert,* Eds. T. Bierschenk, M. Krings and C. Lentz, 97–110. Berlin: Reimer.

Schlehe, J., and S. Hidayah. 2013. Transcultural ethnography in tandems. Collaboration and reciprocity combined and extended. *Freiburger Ethnologische Arbeitspapiere* 23. http://www.freidck.uni-freiburg.de/volltexte/9155/.

Schlehe, J., and S. Hidayah. 2014. Transcultural ethnography. Reciprocity in Indonesian-German tandem research. In *Methodology and research practice in Southeast Asian studies,* Eds. M. Huotari, J. Rüland and J. Schlehe, 253–272. Houndmills: Palgrave Macmillan.

Schlehe J. and P. M. Kutanegara, Eds. 2006. *Budaya Barat dalam kacamata Timur: pengalaman dan hasil penelitian Antropologis di sebuah kota di Jerman.* (Westliche Kultur durch eine östliche Brille gesehen. Erfahrung und Ergebnisse ethnologischer Forschung in einer deutschen Stadt). Yogyakarta: Pustaka Pelajar.

Schlehe, J., and G.R.L.L. Simatupang. 2008. *Towards global education? Indonesian and German academic cultures compared. Menuju pendidikan global? Membandingkan budaya akademik Indonesia dan Jerman.* Yogyakarta: Kanisius.

Schmidt, J. F. E., M. Guichard, P. Schuster, and F. Trillmich, Eds. 2007. *Freundschaft und Verwandtschaft. Zur Unterscheidung und Verflechtung zweier Beziehungssysteme.* Konstanz: UVK.

Segato, R. L. 2003. *Las estructuras elementales de la violencia. Ensayos sobre género entre la antropología, el psicoanálisis y los derechos humanos.* Buenos Aires: Prometeo.

Segato, R. L. 2013. *La escritura en el cuerpo de las mujeres asesinadas en Ciudad Juárez.* Buenos Aires: Tinta Limón.

Segato, R. L. 2015. Brechas descoloniales para una universidad nuestroamericana. In *Des/Decolonizar la universidad,* Eds. Z. Palermo and W. Mignolo, 121–141. Buenos Aires: Del Signo.

Segato, R. L. 2017. *La guerra contra las mujeres.* Buenos Aires: Tinta Limón.

Segato, R. L. 2018. *Contrapedagogías de la crueldad.* Buenos Aires: Prometeo.

Service, R. 2007. *Comrades! A history of world communism.* Massachusetts: Harvard University Press.

Stevenson, A., and R. Lawthom. 2017. How we know each other. Exploring the bonds of friendship using friendship ethnography and visual ethnography. *Anthrovision* 5.1: 1–20.

Wright, P. H. 1969. A model and a technique for studies of friendship. *Journal of Experimental Social Psychology* 5(3): 295–309.

Wright, P. H. 1982. Men's friendships, women's friendships and the alleged inferiority of the latter. *Sex Roles* 8 (1): 1–20.

Reflexivity, Engagement, Decoloniality: Shifting Emergences of Ethnography and Collaboration

Thomas Stodulka

1   Prologue

'Thomas, I strongly advise you to leave the field now. You are too involved and tired. It is time for you to take a step back and try to see the bigger picture again. Don't forget you can always come back,' Judith Schlehe advised me in early 2008 during a conversation in Yogyakarta, Indonesia. She looked concerned. I had realized previously that my involvement in the lives and deaths of interlocutors and friends had started to substantially affect my own health, but Judith's worried face seeped differently, more tangibly, into my mind. I started to reflect and take a step back. Slowly at first, sustainably since then.

Prior to this encounter, I had been involved in collaborative and applied research with street-related communities for almost two consecutive years without a break. Many friends had died in those two years, many of them as a result of HIV and AIDS and other chronic illnesses. The research group I was involved in had established a community shelter for chronically ill persons at the urban margins the year before and the team's voluntary work, commitment and care had increasingly consumed everyone's energy. There were too many of our friends that had

---

Passages of this article have previously been published in Stodulka, T. 2021. Methods and the construction of knowledge. Fieldwork and ethnography. In *The SAGE handbook for cultural anthropology,* Eds. L. Pedersen and L. Cligett, 85–104. Thousand Oaks: Sage.

T. Stodulka (✉)
Institut für Sozial- und Kulturanthropologie, Freie Universität Berlin, Berlin, Deutschland
E-Mail: thomas.stodulka@fu-berlin.de

© Der/die Autor(en), exklusiv lizenziert an Springer Fachmedien Wiesbaden GmbH, ein Teil von Springer Nature 2023
M. Lücking et al. (Hrsg.), *In Tandem—Pathways towards a Postcolonial Anthropology | Im Tandem – Wege zu einer postkolonialen Ethnologie,*
https://doi.org/10.1007/978-3-658-38673-3_6

started to become severely ill and many of them never recovered. We all needed more support and, ultimately, to take a step back, reflect and recover.

I remember Judith's advice vividly. She was never my supervisor or professor during graduate studies or my doctoral research, but we had many mutual friends and people we cared about in Yogyakarta. Coincidentally, I even ran into 'Mbak Judith' during my first fieldwork as a master's student in my mid-20 s in 2001 at the beachside town of Parangtritis, where she had conducted long-term fieldwork, and where I was taking my first fieldwork steps at a small bamboo hut that served as a hideout and recreation refuge for so-called 'street kids' *(anak jalanan)*. Her advice mattered. And, indeed, I returned to Yogyakarta many more times to continue learning from my interlocutors and friends.

A few years ago, I started devoting my research time and focus to the role of affect and emotion in ethnographic knowledge construction, a continuous attempt to understand how to balance fieldwork immersion with stepping back, seeing the bigger picture—and how to teach this essential ethnographic practice to students and early-career anthropologists. This article contributes to this bigger methodological picture and zeroes in on ethnographic trajectories of research collaboration, long-term immersion, and shifting formats of knowledge construction. I will start with a historicized introduction on reflexive and engaged ethnography before I draw on some lessons learned from fieldwork in Yogyakarta. The second part of the chapter attends to emerging ethnographic methods and reflects on contemporary shifts in collaborative research designs and methodologies referred to as multimodal, digital, artistic, and decolonial.

2   Emerging Collaborative Ethnographies

2.1   Reflexive Ethnography

Explicit critique of fieldwork and ethnography as politically and socially embedded endeavours has been formulated by Talal Asad (1973) on the discipline's colonialist pathways, and by Michelle Rosaldo and Louise Lamphere (1974), who highlighted the discipline's gender bias and 'white male supremacy-ism'. During the 1980 s, anthropology went through what has often been described as a 'catharsis' where fieldworkers' (post-)colonial complicity, ethnographic authority and the raison d'être of ethnographic research were radically deconstructed. The objectivity paradigm was rejected along with the ethnographer's authority over the production of data about society, culture and experience.

Whatever one's perspective and retrospective on this literary turn (Behar and Gordon 1995; Clifford and Marcus 1986), ethnographic fieldwork and writing significantly changed in the aftermath. This was obviously not just a consequence of shifting scholarly discourse. Rather, the discipline's epistemology has changed fundamentally since the 1980s due to significant shifts in globalized transnational communication, mobility, and labour regimes, all with their consequences (Appadurai 1996; Hannerz 1996). Another result tied to epistemological debates ever since then is that anthropologists (though not only them) almost unanimously agree that ethnographic knowledge is always situated, positioned and constructed (Haraway 1988; Schlehe 2020). The literary turn has taught anthropologists that narratives, stories and observations emerging from fieldwork are always 'particular' and 'partial'. As such, they must constantly be juxtaposed with data constructed from other fieldwork encounters, by including various interlocutors' perspectives on a particular phenomenon, or by drawing on other dimensions to the data—an approach that grounded theorists call 'methodological triangulation' (Rothbauer 2008). Only after such long-term involvement can a retrospective detachment and critical deconstruction of biases be achieved, so that scientifically grounded statements can be formulated and translated into a text. 'Positionality' has been extended to the discussion of fieldwork ethics, yet little attention has been paid to the question of how ethnographers deal with their ascribed positionalities in methodological and emotional terms (Sakti and Reynaud 2017) beyond psychoanalytical concepts of transference and countertransference (Devereux 1967; Nadig 2004) or sociological discourses of research as 'emotional labour' (McQueeney and Lavelle 2017; Pollard 2009).

2.2 Engaged Ethnography

In addition to substantial debates on the poetics and politics of ethnographic knowledge production, anthropologists started increasingly calling for a 'primacy of the ethical' (Scheper-Hughes 1995) that called for ethnographers as activists that acted alongside the communities they studied with. In this 'compassionate turn' (Sluka and Robben 2012), burgeoning fieldwork trajectories included action and engaged research components on the grassroots level, expanding on the ethos of applied anthropology, advocacy anthropology and solidarity (Bourgois 2002; Tsing 2005). Such engaged projects are encouraged by some yet denigrated by other research departments and national academic landscapes (Antweiler 1998; Klocke-Daffa 2019). I remember my own attempt at placing an article which argued for a combination of what was then still a division between 'academic' and 'applied anthropology' in a German-language anthropology journal, only for the editor-in-chief to berate me for 'talking nonsense'. Realizing that many of Germany's white male anthropology at that time was the global exception and not the convention, I felt relieved when I encountered the work of Indonesian anthropologists Bambang Ertanto, Maya Pravitta, Pande Made Kutanegara, Kusen Alipah Hadi, Yustinus Trisubagya, Ani Himawati, Baskara T. Wardaya or Pujo Semedi. Although they had other issues to resolve (such as underpayment, a lack of department positions, overburdening teaching assignments, overly rigid bureaucracy, or feudalistic campus hierarchies), all anthropologists—both those employed in academic positions and those working in activist collectives—participated in community-building projects aside from writing their theses, essays and books. Philippine anthropology is a similar intellectual activist project, honouring engaged and action-oriented anthropology based on ethnographic fieldwork, as are the many examples from South Asia, Africa, Australia, and the Americas (García Palacios and Castorina 2014; Reynaud 2017; Robinson 2005; Stodulka 2019).

Today, interlocutors and research partners are manifestly aware of what anthropology is, what harm it can do in terms of epistemic violence (in terms of Gayatri Spivak's reading of Michel Foucault and their thoughts on the relationships between knowledge, power and social control in academics' refusal to listen closely and co-theorize with interlocutors and research participants) or how it can open up job opportunities within collaborative fieldwork practice. Far from being represented as passive respondents, those we live and study with today know from media reports or experience with other anthropologists how ethnographers are supposed to behave and compensate them for their time and hospitality in the field. Today, former interlocutors are anthropologists or experts themselves, work for NGOs or are hired by international corporate social responsibility projects as experts. Taking contemporary societal conditions of doing ethnography into consideration, the following exemplification expands on the chapter's intention to elaborate that fieldwork does not only imply the flexible shifting of research questions or theoretical perspectives. First and foremost, it is a careful tuning of methods used to ethically, responsibly, respectfully and scientifically relate to the lives of "others" with whom we intend to study (Mattes and Dinkelaker 2019). Most importantly, it highlights how crucial it is to allow oneself to constantly learn from "others" while probing, failing and improving in different methods. I want to share my way of learning from the field by drawing on long-term involvement with street-related communities and their lifeworlds in and around Yogyakarta. The article will then illustrate the shift in ethnographic methods and will ultimately reflect on diversified postcolonial methodologies that aim at the decolonization of curricula, practices and infrastructures of knowledge production.

3 Doing Collaborative Ethnography: Coming of Age in the Streets of Java

Fieldwork with street-related children, adolescents and young adults has to take their spatial mobilities and extensive fields of social interaction and encounters into account, while at the same time providing the researched, collaborators and researcher with enough reasons for such time-intensive, psychologically and physically challenging endeavours (Stodulka 2017). In trying to understand how the protagonists deal with marginality, stigma and illness, a systematic focus on affect and emotions offers gateways to mutual understanding. Long-term involvement with street-related communities is a process that requires empathy, the communication of respect and a flexibility that allows the ethnographer to participate in their sophisticated lives. As a unique way of observing, witnessing and trying to understand and explain what matters most to the persons and communities ethnographers study with, ethnography might be best described as a 'theoretically informed practice' (Comaroff and Comaroff 1992, 27) that is personal, intimate and affective on the one hand, and analytical, detached and scientific on the other (Wolf 1996).

3.1 Collaborative Action Research

After getting involved in the lives of street-related communities in particularly emotive and emotional ways, I was almost coerced to engage in what I then defined as 'collaborative action research.' The term can be traced back to the social psychologist Kurt Lewin in the 1950s and can be briefly defined as an open-ended spiral of posing questions, gathering data, reflection and collectively deciding on a course of appropriate and ethical action on behalf of and with the protagonists. The primary target was the enhanced accessibility of the constructed knowledge for those persons and communities I lived alongside.

My collaborators and I set up a support and care network for street-related communities after we experienced shared feelings of frustration over the rise in prevalence of HIV on the streets and had lost many friends to the disease. The group consisted of volunteers from various social and professional backgrounds and our primary concerns were that our network function on a voluntary basis and closely collaborate with street-related communities. Within this loosely structured framework, we jointly organized workshops in various formats, on the streets, in open spaces offered by NGOs—particularly the eco-social collective *Milas*—or in squatter communities on the city's margins. In the face of AIDS-related deaths and severe social suffering, this informal network gained a certain stability without the support of international funding agencies and finally took the form of a shelter and community-based counselling centre for chronically ill street-related persons between 2008 and 2013. Operating on private donations, the network focused on care and support for HIV-positive friends, facilitated HIV/AIDS prevention workshops, and served as a link between communities, hospitals and the bureaucracies of the local government's healthcare apparatus.

From an ethnographic perspective, the collaboration provided insights into the affectivity of key interlocutors, not least because we shared frustration and despair when yet another friend died, but also small-scale victories once we had managed to provide ill friends with cost-free medication and medical treatment. From a methodological perspective, the collaboration facilitated access to various research sites and fostered an understanding of their connections from the various protagonists' perspectives. When the shelter team became the primary caretaker of hospitalized friends, the scope of our tasks was beyond that of a hospital room (e.g. the provision of food, clothes, medication, supportive care). In those cases where our friends died, the shelter team arranged burial permits, organized funerals, persuaded local clerics to perform last rites, built and maintained graves, and scheduled rituals of remembering the deceased according to local traditions. I learned from these experiences that stigmatization and marginalization did not necessarily end with the young persons' deaths. They lingered on through authorities' refusal to allow graveyard burials except from in those empty land slots at the urban margins defined as 'social welfare cemeteries' that could also be mistaken for urban gardens or neglected grassland for grazing sheep.

So as to fight further suffering and the deaths of more people with in-depth knowledge of the protagonists' health risk behaviours, we conducted focus group discussions with street-related communities that were jointly administered after the workshops. Alongside the sometimes-more, sometimes-less participatory activities, which helped to create a relaxed atmosphere, the late-night conversations after the workshops were not only very pleasant, but also turned out to be illuminating in better understanding reproductive health and consumption practices on the streets. In addition to providing stories, these workshops and conversations were very helpful in creating an atmosphere of mutual trust by taking collective action against the spread of HIV/AIDS and other immediate threats to life. Whereas the focus group discussions elicited insights into health issues, help-seeking behaviour and perceptions of HIV/AIDS and STDs among street-related communities, facilitating and participating in voluntary counselling and testing fostered my awareness of stigma-related emotions and triggered collective actions seeking to challenge discriminatory local discourses by organizing public discussions and outreach events.

Participation in and observation of theatre workshops and public performances that staged the life histories of so-called 'street children' offered insights into the dynamics of the street-related communities' hierarchical ways of constructing a community ethos and identities, and revealed protagonists' perspectives on their notions of the ideal life course, how 'things should be', and what hindered them in achieving better lives (Boal 1985). Similarly, collective viewing of video material that the young protagonists and I had produced during the early years of our research became a welcome break from everyday life in the backyard of an open house, a break that transformed into quick-witted get-togethers full of collective evaluations and the humorous mocking of on-screen actions, conversations and appearances. Other ethnographers have worked with similar visual techniques such as, for example, photovoice, or the collective analysis of children's drawings and stories (Nolas et al. 2019; Röttger-Rössler et al. 2019). Such fieldwork methods might be mistaken as mere 'hanging out' by less informed colleagues or bystanders, yet they relate to ethnography's art of situated oscillation between fieldwork immersion and systematic documentation in careful and ethically responsible ways at the same time.

In addition to the above-mentioned methods, which aimed at playful integration into the everyday activities and lives of the protagonists, the team also engaged in more disruptive methodologies, such as audio-visually recorded semi-structured interviews in order to better understand local concepts of chronic illness and intervention strategies from the perspectives of professional NGO workers, doctors, nurses and bureaucratic elites. A long-term critical discourse-based analysis of local newspaper article clippings proved effective in understanding social, cultural and political elites' public articulations on 'street children' and the stigma related to HIV/AIDS. In addition, I documented and interpreted public signs, street banners and statements by religious, political and cultural authorities in relation to stigmatizing public rhetoric.

The collaborative approach proved beneficial in various ways: it helped me gain access to many different research sites; negotiate my positionalities as social activist, anthropologist and friend; obtain deeper knowledge concerning the social dynamics within and between street communities; and acquire data on expert discourses among the city's stakeholders involved in public healthcare, plus governmental and non-governmental support strategies. But in order to learn about the protagonists' emotional experiences beyond collective and participatory encounters, I felt that I had to spend not only days, but also nights at the street junctions and that I could no longer reject the protagonists' requests to engage in 'emotion talk' with me that I had initially avoided for fear of getting emotionally too closely involved.

3.2 Actor-centred Ethnography and Emotion Talk

The actor-centred conversations with key protagonists, which they described as either 'psikologi' (psychology) or '*curhat* sessions' (a common expression, *curahan hati*—pouring one's heart out), provided personal stories on past and present turning points in the protagonists' coming of age on the streets. Protagonists would recount past events and social dramas through their *curhat* narratives.

When compared to the refined, psychoanalytically influenced method of person-centred interviewing (Hollan 1997; Spradley 1979), my conversations were less scheduled, more situational and contingent. The technique of open narrative interviewing had to be adjusted to the research setting, where the use of audio recorders and the setting up of interview situations were difficult due to the lack of an interview as a concept and discursive space.

When considering the emotionality and the intimacy of life story and *curhat* narratives, it is important to take both ethical and epistemological issues seriously. They require positional scrutiny and reflection. James Peacock and Dorothy Holland (1993) classify life story epistemologies as either 'life-focused approaches', which define self-narratives as mirrors of reality or 'story-focused approaches', which are more interested in the structure of the story. The former perceive the person as the source and object of narration, the latter argue that it is the narration that defines and constructs the person. Stories of hardship and suffering can be told for various reasons: as reflection and personal meaning-making; as emotional relief; as a way to impress the interlocutor; gain respect; evoke appreciation; enhance social esteem; or as a strategy and tactic to emote others and motivate them to identify with and take action on their behalf. Moreover, getting involved in persons' emotional life stories during fieldwork is based on mutual trust, exhaustive language proficiency and long-term commitment by the ethnographer. It is important to highlight that with established trust comes ethical responsibility: not every story is to be shared publicly. Hence the decision of which stories were to be kept and which were to be told for scientific and political reasons was always taken together with the protagonists of the research in feedback rounds before publishing my monographs and related articles.

4 Stepping Back: Affective Scholarship and Field-desk Enmeshments

Michael Fischer (2018) reminds us that ethnographic knowledge construction does not end at the moment when anthropologists decide to step outside of whatever they have defined as their field. Raymond Madden's definition of the field seems helpful here in understanding its liquid and dynamic quality: 'Ethnography turns someone's everyday place into a thing called a "field" (Madden 2010, 54). Ethnographers then themselves become place makers and fieldwork transpires as a form of place making. The ethnographic field can be seen as 'the synthesis of concrete space and investigative space', and as an 'interrogative boundary' (ibid., 38 f.) where certain questions about geographic, social or emotional landscapes can be asked. Hence involvement in and communication with host or epistemic communities sometimes continue for years after the initial fieldwork despite long geographic distances or other divides. With regards to diversified publication formats in blogs and online forums that provide opportunities to comment on, respond to, or reorganize written, visual or other multimodal forms of representation, ethnographic knowledge construction can expand into almost unbounded spaces and temporalities. Coming up with a convincing and readable story that is ethically and scientifically sound, resonates with contemporary fieldwork standards, and lends an ear to shifting and increasingly short-term academic and political trends, styles and turns, is a tough and emotionally challenging job. At the time of my last transition back to academia from five periods of altogether five years of fieldwork, I wondered whether the fieldworker's ethics and methods, biography and personality, professional and personal experience, as well as training and motivation, senses, positionalities and subjectivities could all be included when constructing and representing fieldwork experiences and aspiring to thick descriptions.

I wondered how one could translate this into methodological practice in constructing adequate representations of the lives and experiences that the protagonists had so generously shared with me over the years. I felt uneasy vis-à-vis the demand to limit and control my subjectivity for the sake of an acknowledged 'traditional empiricism' that ultimately targeted 'objectified data' on the "other". Ethnography works differently. Instead of separating tacit from formative theory, or isolating 'bias' from 'truth', anthropologists work through—not against—their subjectivities and emotions (Davies and Spencer 2010; Jackson 1998) until they puzzle out through long-term engagement what matters to those they research and live alongside. Ethnographic knowledge construction follows particular context- and training-related paths of systematic reasoning that combine the intellectual with the emotional (Gottlieb 2012), the epistemic with the ethical (Rappaport 2008), and the political with the personal (Okely 2012). My own particular path worked along methodological, epistemological and theoretical discussions of the ethnographer's affects, feelings and emotions by taking them seriously as ethnographic data. The documentation of ethnographers' affects, i.e. taking them seriously as relational scientific data and juxtaposing them with more detached 'traditional' data sets, is a way of not only acknowledging tacit knowledge, but of working through it in ethnographic terms.

Anthropologists have addressed the methodological significance of emotions as embodied social communicators acting between ethnographers and their interlocutors (Davies 2010; Spencer 2010; Svašek 2010). It feels important to underline that emotional reflexivity does not begin at the desk but starts during ethnographers' encounters in the field and their documentation. Indeed, anthropology's disciplinary rationale calls for researchers to immerse themselves in the lives of "others" and to affectively relate to those lifeworlds as empathetic and compassionate fieldworkers. Only in so doing can anthropologists 'blend in' enough to grasp the protagonists' ways of feeling-thinking, narrating and navigating through their local worlds. It therefore seems only logical to pay careful attention to affective and emotional practices during fieldwork. Since fieldwork produces positionalities that can be particularly affective, a methodologically informed documentation of and reflection on researchers' affective and emotional positionalities promises to open up complementary and candid pathways to ethnographic data construction. Enhanced emotional literacy (Davies and Stodulka 2019; Thajib et al. 2019) and a methodology taking ethnographers' affects and emotions epistemologically into account helps in translating field experiences based on observations, participation, conversations and imagination into a language that speaks to those who have not 'been there', and who have not directly 'witnessed', or 'immersed' themselves. As some colleagues have pointed out, all this requires strong writing skills in order to create fair and thick descriptions of contemporary lifeworlds.

Paying attention to affect and emotions and documenting them systematically enriched my ethical awareness in establishing and maintaining field rapport vis-à-vis power asymmetries between researcher and collaborators and contributed to the formation of anthropological theory. I was aware that identities, subjectivities, behaviour and speech are relational, contextual and contested phenomena, and yet it took me years to make sense of the protagonists' dramatic switching of language, attuning body performance and postures, dress, style and speech when encountering "others". In places that they had carved out of the city scape as their own they publicly articulated a community pride in their 'deviant' cultural practices, particularly when expat activists, travellers, journalists, artists, students and young women were present, only to reveal flawless Javanese displays of the culturally appropriate respect and deferent propriety according to the cultural etiquette in encounters with policemen, food stall and shop owners, or doctors and nurses in community care centres and hospitals, sometimes only a few moments later. I became sceptical of 'the truth' behind their stories whenever I was drawn into emotion talk that concluded with a subtle yet coercively concerted plea to take action on their behalf, especially once I found out a few days later that some emotive speeches were twisted again in conversations with "others". At times, it was painful feeling used or finding out that stories of extreme hardship and suffering might have been fabricated. Not knowing where to put recurring emotions of disappointment and deception, I jotted them down in my emotion diary that I kept separate from my analytical, descriptive and methodological field notes. Years later, when again trying to make sense of the protagonists' behaviour at my desk, a qualitative content analysis of my emotion diary triggered surprising insights.

The analysis produced an emotional landscape that was almost identical to those that I had mapped out in the interviews and narratives of the protagonists' most prominent interaction partners. The recognition, reflection and analysis of my own emotions as related to encounters with the protagonists and their comparison with the narratives of NGO activists, expatriate social workers, artists, doctors, nurses and others helped me to develop a theoretical framework that attended to the social, emotive and affective practices in these encounters. A more affectively aware attention to what was at stake in street encounters could only emerge after I had compared my own emotions as they emerged in encounters with the young men to NGO activists', street workers' and "others" narratives about their involvements with those young men. I realized that my emotions were not an exclusively subjective experience, but a social fact that related me to both the protagonists and their interaction partners. Documenting and analysing emotions as they emerged in encounters with the young men and juxtaposing them with those articulated by other interaction partners in interviews and conversations triggered new questions for the ethnographic material and helped me formulate a theory that I later defined as 'emotional economies'. It helped me comprehend the young men's ways of coping with scarce material, economic and kinship resources. I realized that emoting to particular persons rhetorically and involving them in their lives and concerns affectively by attuning emotional displays to the context of particular social encounters according to their motivations and urgencies contributed to expanding their social networks, and social and economic capital. For example, whereas activists, researchers, backpackers, artists, or journalists could be useful for their economic potential, students could be moved to support them with shelter, doctors and nurses with care and medical support free of charge, food stall owners and artists with snacks, drinks and goods, street-related women, tourists, or expatriates with comfort or sex. Systematically putting my emotions into the ethnographic picturing of "others" encounters helped explain the young men's empathy and their unrivalled emotive and social skills of transforming scarce material, economic, and kinship resources, marginality and stigmatization into affective bonds and vital socioeconomic cooperation. By relating to, affectively bonding with and emotively addressing particular persons who could provide them with resources they needed not only to survive, but also to lead a 'good life', the young men managed to transform social ties into material goods, money and wellbeing. While coming of age on the streets, most young men learned and continuously refined their social skills, empathic and transcultural competences of assessing and framing encounters with various interaction partners according to their own needs and desires. The social, cognitive, and emotional knowledge immanent to their art of perspective-taking significantly distinguished them from their peers who were not living on the streets. Their capability to relate and interact in highly diverse social fields was amplified by their permanent exposure to "others", where the refinement of social encounters, adequate display of emotions, and placement of emotives was important for survival.

In addition, analysis of my emotion diary triggered an understanding of the activists', artists', researchers' or students' imaginations and motivations to remain involved with the young men and women over years, sometimes decades, despite complaints about them that were ceaselessly articulated in interviews and conversations. Similar to me, they did not empathize, listen, care and engage without reason. They were not merely 'exploited'. NGO activists, journalists, travellers, anthropologists, young women or shop owners pursued their own motivations in their encounters with the young men. They equally engaged in emotional economies but benefited in different terms. Whereas the young men translated emerging affective bonds into economic and other capital on the spot, others profited in the long run. Travelers and expatriate residents became involved in exciting, romantic, and adventurous affairs, or long-term and fulfilling relationships, sometimes marriages. Activists, volunteers, and researchers could profit from the 'vocational expertise' acquired during their internships and research, enabling them to secure further funding for their respective projects, or to produce documentaries, dossiers, journal articles and ethnographies. In my case, for example, the affective bonds and related subsequent artifacts like this chapter, documentaries or books transformed from social capital from 'the field' into cultural capital materializing in the form of educational qualifications and, subsequently, into economic capital by means of my employment at the university. In the context of knowledge construction, empathy and affectively relating to "others" are not only ethnographic skills to generate scientific knowledge, but—not unlike the street-related protagonists—they are also practices in the pursuit of other more personal and human goals of leading a 'good enough life'.

This sustained interest in systematically engaging with ethnographer subjectivities, affects and emotions during and after fieldwork resonates with the burgeoning new literature on multimodal ethnography and arts-based methods since the 2010s. These connect different modes of knowledge construction based on phenomenology, constructivism and fieldwork collaboration (Holmes and Marcus 2008; Varvantakis and Nolas 2019).

5 Emergent Collaborations: Multimodality, Digitality and the Arts

Multimodal, digital, and artistic scholarships have flourished over the last decade for a variety of reasons. These range from significant technological developments in communication to increased awareness that ethnography is a collaborative endeavour between researchers and participants in their aspiration to influence scientific and public discourses (Dicks et al. 2006; Pink 2011). In an extension to the 'compassionate turn' of the 1990s, wherein anthropologists sided with marginalized communities, multimodal ethnographies predominantly 'study up' (Nader 1972) and collaborate with urban designers, architects, political stakeholders, media gatekeepers, and data scientists. If we consider how the ever-growing flood of digital media affects our understanding of the world, methods in digital ethnography become steadily more important. The 'digital turn' has changed ethnographers' perceptions of their field from connected spaces to mixed and virtual realities calling for the combination of both on- and offline methods and modes of knowledge construction. Digital media and communication technologies have substantially shaped the ways ethnographers communicate and stay in touch with their interlocutors and research protagonists. These technological advances have created new possibilities for multi-temporal fieldwork over extended periods of time with both large numbers of online participants or small sets of persons in terms of collaborative, multivocal, and multimedia ethnographies. With regards to shifting styles of ethnographic representation, the last ten years have witnessed a mushrooming of open access formats, blog writing and living online documents. In times of limited funding and restricted mobilities paired with increasing ecological awareness that limit fieldwork travel, new formats of knowledge construction are necessary. Limits to actual face-to-face and in-situ fieldwork, which have long been the backbone of ethnographic research, also create new collaborations between the arts and the sciences online and in the public spaces of museums, galleries, libraries and community centres.

Besides attuning to these everyday pragmatics, multimodal ethnographies aim to create and combine methods that can be purposefully integrated into the daily routines of research participants. Instead of setting up artificial interview situations, asking interlocutors to tick boxes of questionnaires, or summoning them into laboratory experiments, ethnographers focus on developing methodologies from which participants can benefit instead of disrupting their everyday flows of life. Multimodal ethnographies engage in the usage of different media and artifacts (e.g. producing photographs, drawings, animated models and simulations of future societal or political scenarios) and embed them in participant observation as 'natural experiments'. As an extension to ethnographic methodologies that strictly adhere to grounded theory, proponents of this emerging trend aim at bringing different modes and media of learning through the field together in creative ways (Kohrs 2018; Stodulka et al. 2018; Stoller 1997). In reference to sensuous and affective scholarship, Varvantakis and Nolas remind us that 'sense-making in the field and after is a multisensory practice that is at once an intellectual and visceral process. Such sense-making implies various forms of entanglement: of body and mind, field and desk, past and present, to name a few of these enmeshments' (2019, 368). Although grounded in face-to-face research, multimodal ethnography shares challenges of combining existing and yet-to-be-explored methods with digital ethnography (Coleman 2010; Pink et al. 2018). The latter is a bustling endeavour that continues in its resourceful attempts to combine classic close reading with novel technologically assisted statistical methods (e.g. natural language processing, data mining, or programming algorithms) for the analysis of language and image-based (big) online data alongside continuous technological advancements in both our everyday lives and fieldwork documentation methods.

Another burgeoning area of fieldwork and ethnography is the critical study of (big) data and datafication (Boellstorff and Maurer 2015). Within this interdisciplinary research field, a growing number of anthropologists are studying humans' ways of living with data, data power and the pragmatic impact of data management plans, data protection laws and data ethics. Ruckenstein and Schüll, two authors who combine FGDs and interviews with technologically assisted programming and algorithms, highlight that a 'related strain of scholarship that might be characterized as "data activism" explores how the capacities of data technology might be harnessed to promote social justice, equality, new forms of agency, political participation, and collective action—and to challenge accepted norms and ideological projects' (2017, 272). Ultimately, data activism extends to anthropological practice itself, since ethnographers start to directly feel the impact of fundamental revisions of national and transnational jurisdictions and laws on digital data protection, copyright and personal rights. Doing research alongside vulnerable or politically controversial communities both on- and offline creates new ethical responsibilities towards our interlocutors, their online personae and e-communication.

Whereas some ethnographers have always maintained close ties to the arts, arts-based methods of knowledge construction (Schneider 2016) are increasingly thriving in anthropology classrooms. In addition to collaborative visual anthropologies (Walter 2018) and experimental collaborations between artists and anthropologists (Kusumaryati and Karel 2020), contemporary forms of artistically inspired ethnography also utilize the arts as theoretically informed fieldwork practice (Fig. 1).

Fig. 1 Performance Art—World AIDS Day 2007, Resistance walk and demonstration of the key protagonist and the author against stigmatization and discrimination of marginalized communities living with HIV and AIDS in Yogyakarta. (Photo: Agung Prihartono)

Similar to Ingold's ethnographic walking and drawing (2011), Causey (2016) and Taussig (2011) remind anthropologists of the epistemological power of sketching and drawing, in contrast to snapshot photography and smartphone video, when attending to the field. Lowe, for example, teaches a combination of different methods (Schnegg and Lowe 2020) and makes use of theory and practice from still painting to attune the ethnographer's perception and senses to the field in graduate courses. In a collaboration between graphic illustrators, anthropologists and refugees, Martínez (2019) and colleagues created (ethno-)graphic short stories of forced migration trajectories that were exhibited in public libraries. Recently, Rohleder and Kessner (2021) have merged art and anthropology to explore the thin lines between trauma and resilience with regards to past experiences of sexual and slow violence. Anthropologists have underscored that arts-based methods can 'generate deep insight by going beyond rational-cognitive ways of knowing and providing new ways of understanding people's real lived experiences and views; [...] offer ways to "give back" and contribute to a community' (van der Vaart et al. 2018). This aligns with anthropology's longstanding discussion of fieldwork ethics, reciprocity and giving back appropriately to host communities and non-academic audiences (Faubion 2011; von Vacano 2019).

Collaborations between civil society stakeholders, artists and ethnographers in the context of political participation or the transformation of health and illness regimes reify anthropologists' longstanding tradition of engagement, advocacy and activism. Pollmann (2019) and her team of artists, designers, architects, anthropologists, psychiatrists and patients, comprises an outstanding collective and multimodal effort in attempting to create new psychiatric spaces from not only affected, but involved patients' perspectives. Byron Good's and Mary-Jo Del Vecchio-Good's (2019) transcultural collaborations on mental health and illness in Indonesia illustrate ethnographers' political commitment and aim their critique at expert discourses in order to shape realities on the ground.

6 Ultimate Challenges: Decolonizing Collaboration 'after' COVID-19

The COVID-19 pandemic substantially affects anthropology as a discipline. Fieldwork cannot be conducted or has changed significantly, the mobility of researchers is limited, presence on-site is replaced by online contact, planning security gives way to uncertainty. The current situation is particularly challenging for early-career researchers who cannot carry out their fieldwork as planned and who often cannot draw on the connectivities of professional contacts and trustful friendships from previous fieldwork collaboration. Lacking close social bonds and affective relationships that can be activated for online discussion groups, conversations and interviews, or employed for proxy-fieldwork teams, the pandemic challenges supervisors and graduate students to address important questions that go beyond the pandemic moment. Early-career researchers have to find new ways to conduct their research in contemporary data-saturated and digitalized lifeworlds beyond exclusively drawing on online surveys, interviewing and virtually modelled online realities. How can ethnographers be present in their field without being there? Against the background of these complex developments, digitalization and its ethical, sociopolitical and epistemological implications shift into anthropological focus as research questions and knowledge construction trajectories. Whatever happens in the decades to come, it seems crucial that anthropologists remain open-minded to other disciplines that traditionally work with texts and media while sticking to anthropology's genuine processes of interpreting contemporary lives.

Another, more continued and historically driven epistemological endeavour, an extension to reflexive, action- and arts-based, multimodal or engaged ethnography, is the ethnographers' engagements in postcolonial methods through collaboration and aspiring decolonization of research infrastructure and project designs. It seems timely yet again to remind ourselves of Walter Mignolo's (2011) statement that nobody escapes the wounds and abuses of coloniality, not even those who have never been colonized. In contemporary political landscapes where social movements for equal rights and resistance to alt-right currents are gaining social and epistemological momentum around the globe, it seems consequential that ethnographers contribute their share from their personal and scholarly positionalities and entanglements. In a climate of increased eco-anxiety, political disillusionment, decreased trust in scientific facts and cancel cultures, listening to each other, no matter what our positionalities might be, or how contradictory they might be perceived at a first glance, seems paramount. 'Postcolonial theories', 'decolonizing methods', 'theories from the South' or 'decoloniality' have become the ultimate aspirations of ethnographic practice during the last twenty years, if not longer. Important and previously suppressed debates on equal pay, ethics of collaboration, brain drain, intellectual extractivism, cultural and other appropriation are finally rhetorically out in social media and public discourses. Sometimes it even seems, as Louis Yako (2021) has written, that the term 'decolonizing' is used in such wide and broad arrays that it becomes a buzzword for anyone who wants to draw attention to their work without substantial contribution, experience, or knowledge on the issue. Moreover, language shifts do not always imply shifts of mind and action. It takes concrete decolonial forms of collaboration to illustrate how more transparent, diversified and balanced knowledge production practices might be possible now and in the future (Allen and Jobson 2016). How do we translate tandem and team research (Schlehe and Simatupang 2008; Schlehe and Hidayah 2014) into (post-)pandemic digitality? What role will local and language expertise play in the future? How can these be collaboratively garnered and shared? And what new forms of gatekeeping will these new forms of translocal collaboration produce in terms of data sharing, provision, access and archiving? Drawing on Michel Trouillot's *Silencing the Past*, I follow Yako (2021) again, who writes that the process of history production, very much like ethnographic knowledge production, is full of silences. Silences enter the process of historical production at four crucial moments: the moment of fact creation (making sources), the moment of fact assembly (making archives), the moment of fact retrieval (making narratives) and the moment of retrospective significance (making history in the final instance). What remains crucial in anthropologists' endeavours of reflexive, engaged, multimodal, digital, artistic or decolonial research collaboration is to always critically ask how data, narratives, stories or materials were collected and why certain facts were collected while others were ignored or omitted. And, once they are presented to us as 'legitimate' knowledge, we must question whether they are indeed legitimate. Legitimate for whom? Who is being served and who is being disadvantaged by any given version of knowledge? In fact, using these moments as a constant way to evaluate any knowledge at hand will allow us not only to decolonize knowledge production, but also to constantly evaluate power itself. This includes measuring of those who gave themselves the task of measuring everyone else with little or no accountability when it comes to measuring themselves.

7 Conclusion

In anthropology's continuous pursuit of collaborative methodologies and aspiration to decolonize research practices and infrastructure, the practice of inclusive epistemologies, for example, has demonstrated how collaborative teaching, researching and supervising can slowly transform longstanding epistemic power asymmetries through transcultural tandem fieldwork and ethnography. Only time can tell whether tandem, team, or multimodal ethnography, mixed methods, or various configurations of newly emerging scholarships will keep anthropology close to the heartbeat of mundane or extraordinary lived experiences, or whether they will become neat footnotes in the discipline's diverse kaleidoscope of theories and methodologies. In the early 21st century, where not only natural and cultural landscapes are changing dramatically and rapidly before our eyes, but where previous centres of concentrated epistemic and academic power in the hands of a few are gradually dispersing into global networks of knowledge production and exchange, one all-encompassing question continues to be crucial for our discipline to remain intellectually and ethically instructive: Will future anthropologies manage to continuously decolonize their practices of teaching, studying, practicing and representing constructed knowledge, or will newly emerging infrastructures of translocal and digitized collaboration and global sharing be only substitutes for the older hegemonies?

References

Allen, J.S., and R.C. Jobson. 2016. The decolonizing generation. (Race and) theory in anthropology since the eighties. *Current Anthropology* 57(2): 129–148.
Antweiler, C. 1998. Ethnologie als gesellschaftlich relevante Humanwissenschaft. Eine Systematisierung praxisorientierter Richtungen und eine Position. *Zeitschrift für Ethnologie* 123(2): 215–255.
Appadurai, A 1996. *Modernity at large. Cultural dimensions of globalization*. Minneapolis: University of Minnesota Press.
Asad, T., Ed. 1973. *Anthropology and the colonial encounter*. London: Ithaca Press.
Behar, R., and D.A. Gordon, Eds. 1995. *Women writing culture*. Berkeley, CA: University of California Press.
Boal, A. 1985. *Theatre of the oppressed*. New York: Theatre Communications Group.
Boellstorff, T., and B. Maurer, Eds. 2015. *Data, now bigger and better!* Chicago, IL: Prickly Paradigm Press.
Bourgois, P. 2002. Understanding inner city poverty. Resistance and self-destruction under U.S. apartheid. In *Exotic no more. Anthropology on the front lines*, Ed. J. MacClancy, 15–32. Chicago, IL: University of Chicago Press.
Causey, A. 2016. *Drawn to see. Drawing as an ethnographic method*. Toronto: University of Toronto Press.
Clifford, J., and G.E. Marcus, Eds. 1986. *Writing culture. The poetics and politics of ethnography*. Berkeley, CA: University of California Press.
Coleman, E.C. 2010. Ethnographic approaches to digital media. *Annual Review of Anthropology* 39(1): 487–505.
Comaroff, J., and J. Comaroff. 1992. *Ethnography and the historical imagination*. Boulder, CO: Westview Press.
Crapanzano, V. 1980. *Tuhami. Portrait of a Moroccan*. Chicago, IL: University of Chicago Press.
Davies, J. 2010. Introduction. Emotions in the field. In *Emotions in the field. The anthropology and psychology of fieldwork experience*, Eds. J. Davies and D. Spencer, 1–31. Palo Alto, CA: Stanford University Press.

Davies, J., and D. Spencer, Eds. 2010. *Emotions in the field. The psychology and anthropology of fieldwork experience*. Palo Alto, CA: Stanford University Press.

Davies, J., and T. Stodulka. 2019. Emotions in fieldwork. In *Sage research methods foundations*, Eds. P. Atkinson, S. Delamont, A. Cernat, J.W. Sakshaug, and R.A. Williams. London: Sage. https://doi.org/10.4135/9781526421036783199.

Devereux, G. 1967. *From anxiety to method in the behavioral sciences*. The Hague: Mouton.

Dicks, B., B. Soyinka, and A. Coffey. 2006. Multimodal ethnography. *Qualitative Research* 6(1): 77–96.

Faubion, J.D. 2011. *An anthropology of ethics*. New York, NY: Cambridge University Press.

Fischer, M.M.J. 2018. *Anthropology in the meantime. Experimental ethnography, theory, and method for the twenty-first century*. Durham, NC: Duke University Press.

García Palacios, M., and J.A. Castorina. 2014. Studying children's religious knowledge. Contributions of ethnography and the clinical-critical method. *Integrative Psychological and Behavioral Science* 48(4): 462–478.

Good, B. J., C. R. Marchira, M.A. Subandi, F. Mediola, T.H. Tyas, and M.-J. DelVecchio-Good. 2019. Early psychosis in Indonesia. Reflections on illness and treatment. *International Review of Psychiatry* 31(5–6): 1–13.

Gottlieb, A. 2012. *The restless anthropologist. New fieldsites*. Chicago, IL: New Visions University of Chicago Press.

Hannerz, U. 1996. *Transnational connections. Culture, people, places*. London: Routledge.

Haraway, D. 1988. Situated knowledges. The science question in feminism and the privilege of partial perspective. *Feminist Studies* 14(3): 575–599.

Hollan, D. 1997. The relevance of person-centered ethnography to cross-cultural psychiatry. *Transcultural Psychiatry* 34(2): 219–234.

Holmes, D. R., and G.E. Marcus. 2008. Collaboration today and the re-imagination of the classic scene of fieldwork encounter. *Collaborative Anthropologies* 1(1): 81–101.

Ingold, T. 2011. *Being alive. Essays on movement, knowledge and description*. Abingdon: Routledge.

Jackson, M. 1998. *Minima ethnographica. Intersubjectivity and the anthropological project*. Chicago, IL: Chicago University Press.

Klocke-Daffa, S., Ed. 2019. *Angewandte Ethnologie. Perspektiven einer anwendungsorientierten Wissenschaft*. Wiesbaden: Springer Verlag.

Kohrs, K. 2018. Learning from linguistics. Rethinking multimodal enquiry. *International Journal of Social Research Methodology* 21(1): 49–61. https://doi.org/10.1080/13645579.2017.1321259.

Kusumaryati, V., and E. Karel. 2020. *Expedition content. Sensory ethnography lab*. Cambridge, USA. Film.

MacDougall, D. 1998. *Transcultural cinema*. Princeton, NJ: Princeton University Press.

Madden, R. 2010. *Being ethnographic. A guide to the theory and practice of ethnography*. London: Sage.

Martínez, A. 2019. Picturing encounters. A workshop for storytellers and illustrators! Encounter-Blog. https://www.encounter-blog.com/en/picturing-encounters/. Accessed 23 February 2022.

Mattes, D., and S. Dinkelaker. 2019. Failing and attuning in the field. Introduction. In *Affective Dimensions of Fieldwork and Ethnography*, Eds. T. Stodulka, S. Dinkelaker, and F. Thajib, 227–231. New York, NY: Springer.

McQueeney, K., and K. M. Lavelle. 2017. Emotional labor in critical ethnographic work. In the field and behind the desk. *Journal of Contemporary Ethnography* 46(1): 81–107.

Mignolo, W. 2011. *The darker side of western modernity. Global futures, decolonial options*. Durham, NC: Duke University Press.

Nader, L. 1972. Up the anthropologist. Perspective gained from studying up. In *Reinventing anthropology*, Ed. Dell Hymes, 284–311. New York, NY: Random House.

Nadig, M. 2004. Transculturality in process. Theoretical and methodological aspects drawn from cultural studies and psychoanalysis. In *Transculturality, epistemology, ethics and politics*, Eds. H.J. Sandkühler and H.-B. Lim, 9–21. Frankfurt am Main: Lang.

Narayan, K. 1993. How native is a native anthropologist? *American Anthropologist* 95(3): 671–687.

Nolas, S.M., V. Aruldoss, and C. Varvantakis. 2019. Learning to listen. Exploring the idioms of childhood. *Sociological Research Online* 24(3): 394–413. https://doi.org/10.1177/1360780418811972.

Okely, J. 2012. *Anthropological practice. Fieldwork and the ethnographic method*. London: Berg.

Peacock, J.L. and D.C. Holland. 1993. The narrated self. Life stories in process. *Ethos* 21(1): 367–383. https://doi.org/10.1525/eth.1993.21.4.02a00010.

Pink, S. 2011 Images, senses and applications. Engaging visual anthropology. *Visual Anthropology* 24(5): 437–454.

Pink, S., M. Ruckenstein, R. Willim, and M. Duque. 2018. Broken data. Conceptualising data in an emerging world. *Big Data & Society* 5(1): 1–13. https://doi.org/10.1177/2053951717753228.

Pollard, A. 2009. Field of screams. Difficulty and ethnographic fieldwork. *Anthropology Matters* 1 (2): 1–24.

Pollmann, T.C. 2019. *visions4people. Artistic research meets psychiatry*. Berlin: Jovis.

Pool, R. 1991. Postmodern ethnography? *Critique of Anthropology* 11(4): 309–331.

Rappaport, J. 2008. Beyond participant observation. Collaborative ethnography as theoretical innovation. *Collaborative Anthropologies* 1(1): 1–31. https://doi.org/10.1353/cla.0.0014.

Reynaud, A. 2017. *Emotions, remembering and feeling better. Dealing with the Indian residential schools settlement agreement in Canada*. Bielefeld: transcript.

Robben, A.C.G.M., and J. A. Sluka. 2015. Ethnography. In *International encyclopedia of the social & behavioral sciences*, Ed. J.D. Wright, 2nd ed., vol. 8, 178–183. https://doi.org/10.1016/B978-0-08-097086-8.12065-3.

Robinson, G. 2005. Anthropology, explanation and intervention. Risk and resilience in a parent and child-focused program. *Anthropological Forum* 15(1): 3–25.

Rohleder, J., and S. Kessner. 2021. Hear me to feel me—audio installation. Owdnegrin, http://owdnegrin.de. Accessed 23 February 2022.

Rosaldo, M.Z., and L. Lamphere, Eds. 1974. *Woman, culture, and society*. Palo Alto, CA: Stanford University Press.

Rosaldo, R. 1989. *Culture and truth. The remaking of social analysis*. Boston, MA: Beacon.

Rothbauer, P. 2008. Triangulation. In *The SAGE encyclopedia of qualitative research methods*, Ed. L.M. Given, 893–894. Thousand Oaks, CA: Sage.

Röttger-Rössler, B., G. Scheidecker, and A.T.A. Lam. 2019. Narrating visualized feelings. Photovoice as a tool for researching affects and emotions among school students. In *Analyzing affective societies. Methods and methodologies*, Ed. A. Kahl, 78–97. London: Routledge.

Ruckenstein, M., and N.D. Schüll. 2017. The datafication of health. *Annual Review of Anthropology* 46(1): 261–278.

Sakti, V. K., and A.-M. Reynaud. 2017. Understanding reconciliation through reflexive practice. Ethnographic examples from Canada and Timor Leste. In *Ethnographic peace research. Approaches and tensions*, Ed. G. Millar, 159–180. Cham: Palgrave Macmillan.

Scheper-Hughes, N. 1995. The primacy of the ethical. Propositions for a militant anthropology. *Current Anthropology* 36(3): 409–420.

Schlehe, J. 2020. Qualitative ethnographische Interviews. In *Methoden ethnologischer Feldforschung*, Eds. B. Beer and A. König, 91–111. Berlin: Reimer.

Schlehe, J., and S. Hidayah. 2014. Transcultural ethnography. Reciprocity in Indonesian-German tandem research. In *Methodology and research practice in Southeast Asian studies*, Eds. M. Huotari, J. Rüland and J. Schlehe, 252–273. London: Palgrave Macmillan.

Schlehe, J., and G.R. Lono Latoro Simatupang, eds. 2008. *Towards global education? Indonesian and German academic cultures compared. Menuju pendidikan global? Membandingkan budaya akademik Indonesia dan Jerman*. Yogyakarta: Kanisius.

Schnegg, M., and E.D. Lowe, eds. 2020. *Comparing cultures. Innovations in comparative ethnography*. Cambridge: Cambridge University Press.

Schneider, A. 2016. Appropriations across disciplines. The futures of art and anthropology collaborations. In *Beyond text? Critical practices and sensory anthropology*, Eds. R.A. Cox, A. Irving and C.J. Wright, 20–30. Manchester: Manchester University Press.

Sluka, J.A., and A.C.G.M. Robben. 2012. Fieldwork in cultural anthropology. An introduction. In *Ethnographic fieldwork. An anthropological reader*, Eds. A.C.G.M. Robben and J.A. Sluka, 1–45. Chichester: Wiley-Blackwell.

Spencer, D. 2010. Introduction. Emotional labour and relational observation in anthropological fieldwork. In *Anthropological fieldwork. A relational process*, Eds. D. Spencer and J. Davies, 1–34. Newcastle upon Tyne: Cambridge Scholars Publishing.

Spradley, J.P. 1979. *The ethnographic interview*. Belmont, CA: Wadsworth.

Stodulka, T. 2017. *Coming of age on the streets of Java. Coping with marginality, stigma and illness*. Bielefeld: transcript.

Stodulka, T. 2019. 'Is fieldwork funny?'—Navigating political anger, academic realism, and ethnographic comedies of error. An interview with Roderick Galam. In *Emotionen im Feld. Gespräche zur Ethnografie, Primatografie und Reiseliteratur*, Eds. K. Liebal, O. Lubrich, and T. Stodulka, 77–92. Bielefeld: transcript.

Stodulka, T., N. Selim, and D. Mattes. 2018. Affective scholarship. Doing anthropology with epistemic affects. *Ethos* 46(4): 519–536. https://doi.org/10.1111/etho.12219.

Stoller, P. 1997. *Sensuous scholarship*. Philadelphia: University of Pennsylvania Press.

Svašek, M. 2010. 'The field'. Intersubjectivity, empathy and the workings of internalised presence. In *Anthropological fieldwork. A relational process*, Eds. D. Spencer and J. Davies, 75–99. Newcastle: Cambridge Scholars Publishing.

Taussig, M. 2011. *I swear I saw this. Drawings in fieldwork notebooks, namely my own*. Chicago, IL: Chicago University Press.

Thajib, F., S. Dinkelaker, and T. Stodulka. 2019. Introduction. Advancing affective scholarship. In *Affective dimensions of fieldwork and ethnography,* Eds. T. Stodulka, F. Thajib and S. Dinkelaker, 8–23. New York: Springer. https://doi.org/10.1007/978-3-030-20831-8_2.

Trouillot, M.-R. 1995. *Silencing the past. Power and the production of history.* Boston, MA: Beacon.

Tsing, A.L. 2005. *Friction. An ethnography of global connection friction.* Princeton, NJ: Princeton University Press.

van der Vaart, G., B. van Hoven, and P. Huigen. 2018. Creative and arts-based research methods in academic research. Lessons from a participatory research project in the Netherlands. *Forum Qualitative Sozialforschung* 19(2). https://doi.org/10.17169/fqs-19.2.2961.

Varvantakis, C., and S.-M. Nolas. 2019. Metaphors we experiment with in multimodal ethnography. *International Journal of Social Research Methodology* 22(4): 365–378.

von Vacano, M. 2019. Reciprocity in research relationships. Introduction. In *Affective dimensions of fieldwork and ethnography*, Eds. T. Stodulka, S. Dinkelaker and F. Thajib, 79–86. New York, NY: Springer.

Walter, F. 2018. *On the Road with Maruch—Filming culture and collaboration as a transcultural partnership process.* Berlin: Weissensee Verlag.

Wolf, D. L., Ed. 1996. *Feminist dilemmas in fieldwork.* Boulder, CO: Westview Press.

Yako, L. 2021. Decolonizing knowledge production. A practical guide. CounterPunch. https://www.counterpunch.org/2021/04/09/decolonizing-knowledge-production-a-practical-guide/. Accessed Aug 25 2021.

What Can International Relations Learn from Anthropology? Reflections on an Interdisciplinary Student Research Project

Jürgen Rüland

1 Introduction

On first sight, the disciplines of International Relations (IR) and social and cultural anthropology do not seem to have much common ground. While IR is preoccupied with studying macro processes of global and regional order, institutional architectures and the interactions of states including war and peace, social and cultural anthropology are regarded as disciplines focusing on micro processes such as the cultural practices of Indigenous people, village customs and more recently—shedding the colonial legacy of studying pre-industrial societies in the non-Western world—the everyday life of a broad range of social groups in all parts of the world. Unsurprisingly, thus, not only in terms of themes but also in terms of epistemology and methodology, mainstream IR and anthropology seem to lie worlds apart.

Conventional IR is a positivist and nomothetic discipline (Brigden and Mainwaring 2021 p. 3) seeking to identify generalizable patterns of actor behavior. It seeks to establish causal relationships and searches for objective truths, thereby focusing on material processes and facts. Methodologically, it tends to prefer a deductive approach, by which research is organized as a rigorous and formalized

---

For valuable comments on a draft version of the chapter, I am indebted to Mirjam Lücking.

J. Rüland (✉)
Bonn, Deutschland
E-Mail: juergen.rueland@politik.uni-freiburg.de

© Der/die Autor(en), exklusiv lizenziert an Springer Fachmedien Wiesbaden GmbH, ein
Teil von Springer Nature 2023
M. Lücking et al. (Hrsg.), *In Tandem—Pathways towards a Postcolonial Anthropology | Im Tandem – Wege zu einer postkolonialen Ethnologie*,
https://doi.org/10.1007/978-3-658-38673-3_7

theory-testing process. Much of what is considered to be the standard epistemological and methodological state of the art of the discipline is summarized in the seminal volume by King, Keohane and Verba (KKV) (1994). By contrast, as an idiographic discipline (Wehrer 2019, p. 14) anthropological research tends to rest on a phenomenological and hermeneutic epistemology and an inductive methodology. The latter requires extensive fieldwork which paves the way for a reflexive relationship between researcher and reality. Anthropology is thus an interpretive discipline, which is critical of explanatory approaches and their inherent concern with causality. It thus implies critique when mainstream IR scholars denounce attempts to bridge these diverse premises of what is considered "good scholarship" as "ethnographic IR."

Despite these deep-rooted reservations, which are mutual between the two disciplines, a group of anthropologists and IR scholars joined hands in a highly innovative project of interdisciplinary and transcultural student research. Led by the social anthropologist Judith Schlehe and the Department of Social and Cultural Anthropology of the University of Freiburg, the project brought together scholars and students of anthropology and IR from the University of Freiburg and their counterparts at the Gadjah Mada University (GMU) in Yogyakarta, and later also at the Hasanuddin University (Unhas) in Makassar, Indonesia. Given the great differences between the two disciplines cursorily delineated above, the question inevitably emerges what IR scholars and students could learn from this "disciplinary boundary crossing" (Mandaville 2002, p. 199) exercise.

As an IR scholar I will trace this question in the subsequent sections from the IR perspective and will first discuss at a more general epistemological and methodological level where and in what way IR could benefit from anthropological scholarship, before in the next step focusing on the German-Indonesian student research project mentioned above. The last section concludes the insights gained and charts some preliminary ideas on how to proceed from here.

2 IR and Social and Cultural Anthropology: Strange Bedfellows?

In the last two decades, mainstream IR has come under increasing fire from critics who take issue with the profound Western-centeredness of its theorizing. For too long, IR was an "American social science" (Hoffmann 1977). Critics contend that theory-building mainly rested on Western historical experiences, ideas, norms, practices and institutions, while the drivers shaping political agency in societies of the Global South were largely ignored. The history of Indigenous political thought and intellectual history in countries of the Global South remained widely uncharted and unknown terrain, albeit that this is not something for which only Western scholarship can be held responsible. In many countries of the Global South political philosophy is virtually non-existent in the political science curricula or if it is present, it is limited to the classical Western canon of political thought from Aristotle to Marx. Over time, a division of labor evolved, by which scholarly institutions in developed Western countries became the locus for theoretical advancement, while research in and on the Global South was limited to the subaltern task of providing the empirical data to test theories of Western origin. Where Western and Southern scholars cooperated, the former were responsible for the research design, analytical framework and methodology, while the latter were needed due to their intimacy with the field and their privileged access to information and data.

With accelerating globalization and the rise of new powers in the Global South in the 2000s, research agendas in IR began to shift. Scholars as well as policy-makers in the West increasingly realized that Western-centric theories prevented them from properly understanding the political dynamics caused by these global changes. More expertise on the non-Western world was required. Paradigm shifts in the discipline aided this process.

The first and most tangible of these paradigmatic changes was the rise of *constructivist* scholarship. The "constructivist turn" in IR of the 1990s entailed a fundamental critique of the dominant positivist strand in IR with its rationalist epistemology. Instead of the pre-occupation with manifest materialist factors and the concomitant logic of social action based on consequentialism, constructivism posited a logic of appropriateness and ideas, norms, identity and knowledge as drivers of political agency (March and Olsen 1989). Preference building no longer rested on pre-given, exogenous interests, but was conceived as endogenous and, hence, an intersubjective and relational process. Constructivist analyses of international relations thus opened unprecedented avenues for *"longue durée"* perspectives, the conceptualization of history as collective memory (Assmann 1992; Scupin 2017, p. 176) and greater empathy towards culture and context, important prerequisites for understanding politics in non-Western settings. Yet a precondition for freeing IR research from the rigidities of positivist theorizing was that the new constructivist approaches steered clear of the liberal bias and the teleological tendencies in much of the global governance literature predicting a transformation of world politics towards accelerating legalization, contractualization and constitutionalization (Zangl and Zürn 2004).

In the 2000s, a second paradigm shift generated a new type of *area studies,* which—rather than dissociating itself from the mainstream discipline as in the past—consciously combined regional expertise with state-of-the-art knowledge of the theoretical and methodological progress in the mainstream discipline. This helped to make disciplinary knowledge better applicable to the analysis of political practices, processes and decisions in regions with cultures that differ markedly from Western thinking (Basedau and Köllner 2007; Huotari et al. 2014; Huotari and Rüland 2014; Ahram et al. 2018).

At approximately the same time, Peter Katzenstein's call to engage in *"analytic eclecticism"* constituted a third novelty in IR research (Katzenstein 2007; Hemmer and Katzenstein 2002; Katzenstein and Sil 2008). Analytic eclecticism takes issue with the inability of the dominant schools of thought in IR to cope for the sake of parsimony with the increasing complexity of world politics. Rather than concentrating on only one research tradition, "analytic eclecticism takes components of different research traditions and combines them to produce new analytical frameworks" (Katzenstein 2007, p. 397). However, rather than being only a "theoretical synthesis of existing research traditions" (ibid.: 398), "analytic eclecticism" selectively adopts and reinterprets "concepts, causal mechanisms, explanations and prescriptions from particular research traditions" (ibid., p. 398). Analytical components of competing theoretical schools are thus creatively reassembled and interconnected, giving rise to "novel frameworks" and enabling scholars "to capture a more nuanced understanding of a complex world" (ibid., p. 398). In a pragmatist philosophical tradition, Katzenstein and Sil qualified analytic eclecticism as "a problem driven rather than paradigm driven research" (Katzenstein and Sil 2008, p. 110).

All three innovations boosted inter- and transdisciplinarity: They opened IR avenues to neighboring disciplines such as sociology, history and anthropology. In particular, critical IR scholars working on non-Western regions eagerly tapped these disciplines for their analyses. Some of them even spoke of an "ethnographic turn" in IR (Vrasti 2008), arguing that by integrating ethnography, a key method used by anthropologists, into IR's methodological toolbox, the context sensitivity of studies would markedly increase. While speaking of an "ethnographic turn" in IR may have been exaggerated, a few IR scholars nevertheless consciously applied anthropological methods in their research (Neumann 2002) or at least propagated their use (*inter alia,* Vrasti 2008, 2010; Rancatore 2010; Wedeen 2010; Lie 2013; Schlichte 2013; Scupin 2017; Montsion 2018; Bridgen and Mainwaring 2021). A debate emerged on how anthropological approaches and methods could enrich IR. The most significant of these arguments will be discussed in subsequent paragraphs, subdivided into the epistemological, methodological and empirical impulses IR may receive from anthropology.

2.1 Epistemological Impulses

Bringing anthropology into IR strengthens approaches challenging IR's domination by positivist rational choice-based analyses. These rest on the assumption that maximizing utility is the key motivation of political actors. As *homines oeconomici* they calculate how they can realize the greatest possible benefit with the lowest costs. Positivist scholars influenced by this concept of man thus focus their analysis on material and manifest phenomena and their causality, implying a consequentialist logic of social action. They believe that such a prism represents an objective social reality. Bridgen and Mainwaring (2021, p. 5) found that 90% of the articles published in the top twelve IR journals in 2014 followed such a positivist orientation.

By contrast, anthropologists have great reservations about nomothetic scholarship, with its lean and parsimonious theories, causality and confining the logic of social action to rational choice (Scupin 2017, p. 160). Relying on a hermeneutic epistemology, anthropology pursues, as Jackson (2008, p. 92) points out, interpretative approaches which seek to explicate constitutive relations. For them, social relations are reflexive and intersubjective, and hence must be historicized. Anthropologists thus display deep skepticism towards the abstractions typical of (mainstream) IR (Vrasti 2010, p. 83; Montsion 2018, p. 11), which in their view obfuscate constitutive processes and by glossing over important empirical details easily ends up in the essentialism trap. Huntington's clash of civilizations is one of the most obvious examples in this respect (1993).

The interpretive hermeneutic approach also entails anthropologists questioning objective and singular truths (Brigden and Mainwaring 2021, p. 11). Instead, they regard social realities as "messy and complex" (Brigden and Mainwaring 2021, p. 13) and truths as multiple and only partial (Clifford 1986). While anthropologists share this view with constructivist IR scholars, in their interpretations more than the latter they take into account the position of the researcher in the process of research and her or his relations with the object(s) of study. The positionality of the researcher thus has a major bearing on the research findings (Rancatore 2010, p. 71). The lesson IR scholars can draw from this understanding of knowledge generation is that they also need "to understand themselves as situated observers within a (continually moving) 'field'" (Mandaville 2002, p. 200).

2.2 Methodological Inspirations

Anthropology's hermeneutic epistemology implies methodological choices that, while not unknown in IR, the discipline's mainstream usually avoids. Although there is a debate in anthropology about ethnography as the discipline's main method due to its infamous legacy as a tool of colonialist rule and its erstwhile Orientalist orientation (Vrasti 2008, pp. 281, 284; Schlehe and Hidayah 2014, p. 255 f.), it has not been thrown overboard. It has been redefined as a method with emancipative potential and the ability to give voice to marginalized and underprivileged social groups (Vrasti 2008, 2010). Ethnography is a fundamentally inductive method and the reason why anthropological scholarship normally rests on grounded theory (Pouliot 2007, p. 364). While—as Pouliot (2007, p. 374) rightly argues—"perfect induction is impossible," anthropological research can nevertheless serve as an inspiration for IR to include to a greater extent than hitherto induction into its repository of methods. This would include combining deductive and inductive methods (Rüland 2017) or working with abduction (Friedrichs and Kratochwil 2009). Integrating induction into IR helps to identify empirical blind spots that are overlooked by deductive approaches due to their rigidity. This is particularly helpful in research on non-Western foreign policy behavior where guidance by theories generated in the West may lead to false conclusions and misleading advice for (Western) policymakers.

While constructivist scholarship has made great inroads in IR over the last 25 years—especially in Europe, less in North America—as a science "in search of meaning" (Pouliot 2007, p. 364), methodologically it strongly relies on Foucauldian discourse analysis. The assumption behind this choice is that meaning is best expressed in language and texts. Yet, as Lie (2013, p. 202) argues, this "linguistic turn" in IR and its focus on rhetorical patterns entails the "problematic tendency to equate discourse with practice." Neumann (2002, p. 630) thus recommends that IR follow the example of anthropology and sociology and turn away from an analysis primarily "based on beliefs, ideas, norms and so in favor of a more concrete analysis," thereby reconciling meaning and materiality (ibid., p. 629; see also Pouliot 2007, p. 374; Adler and Pouliot 2011, p. 2). The emergence of practice theory, which Neumann and, more systematically, Adler and Pouliot (2011) propose, explicitly recommends anthropological field-based methods as a step complementing the lopsided focus on discourse and devoting greater attention to the agency and everyday behavior of political actors (see also Lie 2013, p. 202).

More than textual analysis, research on practices is strongly dependent on fieldwork. It is here where IR scholars can learn much from anthropology as ethnographic research is strongly reliant on fieldwork and participant observation

(Schlehe 2003), a data gathering technique defined as the practice of scholars "immersing themselves in the lives, material and social environment, and daily activities of a group of people for an extended period of time" (Brigden and Mainwaring 2021, p. 4). Serious anthropological research is thus unthinkable without long periods of data collection in the field (Lie 2013, p. 204). Vrasti (2008, p. 286) is probably right when she qualifies ethnography as the "most grounded" method in social sciences.

This contrasts markedly with mainstream IR research, where fieldwork plays only a subordinated role (Bridgen and Mainwaring 2021, p. 8), even in the study of international phenomena in non-Western regions. While IR themes revolving around diplomacy, state bureaucracies and security, to name a few examples, often do not easily lend themselves to the practice of participant observation (Lie 2013, pp. 203, 209 f.), fieldwork in the form of qualitative interviews nevertheless creates direct access to ministerial staff, employees of international organizations and foreign policy elites. Although expert interviews certainly cannot compensate for lengthy periods of working and living in the midst of informants who at the same time may be the objects of study, it creates valuable insights into their ways of thinking and acting (Pouliot 2007, p. 369).

As social scientists, IR scholars should have received ample interview training. Unfortunately, though, this is not necessarily the case. Even if conducting fieldwork and interviews is part of the IR curriculum, often researchers are not adequately prepared for fieldwork in culturally diverse settings. This increases the likelihood of committing mistakes in the field, which at the end of the day may result in biased and misleading research findings or in the worst case even a complete failure of the intended research (Kusic and Zahora 2020). Such errors include lack of cultural sensitivity, an absence of empathy for the sentiments of informants, naïve interview questions decoupled from the life world of the interviewees, using academic jargon unfamiliar to them, or inadvertently ignoring political divisions among the informant population.

Given the pivotal significance of fieldwork in ethnographic research, dialogue of IR scholars with anthropologists may not only teach them how to organize and conduct fieldwork in a way that it produces meaningful results. It also provides them important lessons about research ethics and etiquette in the interaction with informants (Vrasti 2010, p. 84). This includes the protection of sources, especially, if—as is often the case in IR and political science—research topics are politically sensitive because research is conducted in non-democratic political systems. Also a maximum of transparence concerning the research objectives vis-à-vis the informants is part and parcel of such research ethics.

As mentioned above, IR often focusses on "high" politics including security, power configurations, foreign policy grand strategies and the work of international organizations. This means that IR scholars often interact with elites. English is the *lingua franca* in exchanges with these elites. Although communication thus seems to work smoothly, it is an invaluable advantage if IR scholars—like anthropologists—are proficient in the local language of their informants. Often nuances of meaning are lost in translation if respondents express their thoughts in English, for them a foreign language. The English terminology thus tempts unwitting researchers to believe that there is ideational and conceptual congruence between them and their interviewees. Democracy, participation, human rights or multilateralism are treacherous because they are polyvalent concepts that can easily be misrepresented. Deconstructing their local connotation as inherent in vernacular language would help scholars grasp much better what their informants think and how they argue and why they behave as they do. The significance of "knowing the local tongue" (Vrasti 2010, p. 83) further increases when IR researchers interact with ordinary people, marginalized groups or persons affected by political action. Typical examples where this is inevitable are studies in the fields of migration, peace building and development or where research seeks to study actors' everyday practices.

The "constructivist turn" in IR and the intensified engagement with hermeneutic scholarship as practiced in anthropology has given qualitative research methods a strong boost in IR. It has overcome the aversion of mainstream IR to case studies and small-N comparisons, which it regarded as non-generalizable and hence largely worthless for theory building (Wehrer 2019, p. 14). In fact, the last two decades have seen a veritable outburst of publications refining qualitative methods including case study research and systematizing small-N comparison (George and Bennett 2005; Gerring 2008; Mahoney 2010; Brady and Collier 2010; Huotari and Rüland 2014; Ahram et al. 2018). In the process, anthropological methods such as "thick description" (Geertz 1973) became acceptable in IR.

Even more fruitful were attempts to bridge the hiatus between methodologies preferentially used by the rationalists and reflexivists. "Process tracing," for instance, is a method that reconciles rationalists' search for causality with the reflexivist penchant for identifying mechanisms constituting the behavior of (political) actors (Checkel 2006). Also, Lieberman's (2005) "nested analysis," Ragin's "Qualitative Comparative Analysis" (QCA) (1987) and the intensifying trend towards "mixed methods" (Creswell and Creswell 2017; Plano et al. 2008) are emblematic of this trend.

In sum, these are welcome developments as they increase the context sensitivity of IR, especially when it comes to research in the non-Western parts of the globe (Lie 2013, p. 217). In that sense, they also contribute to the emergence of a truly "Global IR" (Acharya 2014), which by consciously reflecting so far much neglected (historical) experiences and their path dependencies, as well as cultural peculiarities in regions of the Global South, are better able to capture the complexity, contingency, plurality and polycentric nature of contemporary world politics (Scholte 2005, p. 186).

2.3 Empirical Gains

Dialoguing with anthropology also helps IR open itself to new themes. As already mentioned above, much of mainstream IR research has an "elitist bias" (Björkdahl et al. 2019, p. 123). It is a discipline often focusing on themes that are beyond the life world of ordinary people and their routines (ibid., p. 123; Montsion 2018, p. 390). Introducing anthropology's emic perspectives (an insider identity position) (Lie 2013, p. 210 f.) through participant observation and other field-based research methods makes IR more perceptive of everyday processes by paying "specific attention to non-elite constructions, meanings and experiences" (Björkdahl et al. 2019, p. 123). "Studying down" (Stryker and Gonzalez 2014) enables IR to better comprehend how globalization and its pathologies, the ensuing cross-border interdependencies, arcane circles of technocratic experts in international organizations and struggles of states for global or regional hegemony, affect people's lives. This "turn to micropolitics" and "mundane practices" helps "emplacing the discipline in the lived space of the everyday" (ibid., p. 123 f.). Working with "enacting methods" (Aradau and Huysmans 2014), such a lens may facilitate critical scholarship that—like anthropology—gives voice to the losers of modernization (Björkdahl et al. 2019, p. 125; Mandaville 2002, p. 202), marginalized and underprivileged groups. These include Indigenous people, disabled persons, the rural and urban poor, victims of gender injustice or families whose settlements are demolished and living conditions destroyed for the sake of large-scale, often socially and environmentally unsustainable, infrastructure projects including dams, roads, railways, oil and gas pipelines, power plants or industrial estates. Such grassroots perspectives may not only document how globalization-induced neo-liberal modernization adversely affects social groups, but they also chart avenues for them to fight "domination and control" (ibid., p. 125). Research in fields such as (post-conflict) peace building (Lederach 1997; Mac Ginty and Richmond 2013; Mac Ginty 2014; Rüland et al. 2019), migrant attitudes and (political) behavior (Kessler and Rother 2016), refugee strategies, the response of local communities to the current (Asian) connectivity drive (Prakash 2016; Rüland 2020) or diffusion processes of ideas, norms and policies and the way they are appropriated in recipient societies (Acharya 2004; Risse 2016; Rüland 2017; Jetschke 2022 forthcoming) stand to benefit from anthropological approaches.

Transforming IR into a more fieldwork-affine discipline profoundly embedded in the life worlds of "real" people also promotes a better understanding of culture (Scupin 2017, p. 153). The nuancing effect of field experience protects IR scholars from homogenizing and thus essentializing and stereotyping culture. Instead, the historicizing element inherent in anthropological methods helps scholars to better grasp the inextricable contradiction between the *"longue durée"* and path dependent dimension of culture and the nature of culture as a process underlying change through persistent "reinterpreting, renegotiation and transforming meaning" (ibid., p. 157).

3 A German-Indonesian Student Research Project: From Tandem to Teamwork

After these more general reflections about the benefits emerging for IR in an inter- and transdisciplinary engagement with anthropology, the following section more concretely focuses on one of the rare cases in which anthropology and IR have intensively cooperated. The opportunity for this cooperation originated in a student research project jointly conducted by the University of Freiburg and the Gadjah Mada University (UGM) in Yogyakarta, Indonesia. The project was launched in 2004 by Judith Schlehe and the University of Freiburg's Department of Social and Cultural Anthropology in cooperation with the counterpart department at UGM. Until 2011 an exclusive project for anthropology undergraduates, the core of the activities were six-week fieldwork summer schools in Indonesia and Germany that took place in alternate years. German-Indonesian bi-national student teams (tandems) conducted fieldwork on self-defined topics under an umbrella theme. *"Academic Cultures"* or *"Popularizing Cultures"* are examples of such overarching themes. Lecturer teams from both universities supervised the carefully selected student tandems. Design, progress and findings of the research were closely guided and discussed in three workshops organized at the beginning, during and at the end of the fieldwork.

Yet the project was not limited to German students conducting fieldwork in Indonesia. In the following year Indonesian teaching personnel and students travelled to Germany, studying there the same umbrella theme as in the previous year in Indonesia together with their erstwhile German tandem partners. The project became an integral part of the curriculum of the two anthropology departments, which included compulsory participation in preparatory seminars on the respective country (Indonesia in the case of the German students), comprehensive training in qualitative research methods and development of research proposals. On the German side, it also included language training in *Bahasa Indonesia,* including a two-week intensive course after the students' arrival in Yogyakarta (Schlehe 2006; Schlehe and Hidayah 2014).[1] From 2007 to 2017, the project was funded by the German Academic Exchange Service (DAAD).

The novel aspects of the project were the bi-national student research tandems and the project's reciprocal structure. In the process, both student groups experienced the role of insider and outsider anthropologist. This means that the researcher who for one year was the native anthropologist (the host), in the following year became the visiting, foreign anthropologist (the guest) even though it transpired that a persons' cultural and national background is not always the major criterion to define who is an "insider" or "outsider" in the research situation (Schlehe and Hidayah 2014, p. 255). Apart from reflecting on the positionality of the researcher and the effect of context for research findings, the joint fieldwork highlighted the role of the team members as differently positioned equals (Schlehe and Hidayah 2014, p. 259). It thus broke up the usually asymmetric division of labor between researchers from developed and developing countries as described in the previous section (Schlehe 2006; Schlehe and Hidayah 2014). Later, the tandem approach was also successfully applied to PhD students who jointly organized their fieldwork (Schlehe and Hidayah 2014, p. 268; Lücking 2021).

In 2011 transcultural student research went into its next phase by adding to it an inter- and transdisciplinary dimension. It became conceptually embedded in a larger project sponsored by the German Federal Ministry of Education and Research (BMBF) between 2009 and 2016. Apart from anthropology, political science, economics and history were part of this project. Titled *"Grounding Area Studies in Social Practice,"* the project sought to overcome the limitations of textual and discourse analysis, which after the "linguistic turn" in social sciences also dominated methodology in area studies. Instead, inspired by practice theory, the project sought to empirically study everyday social behavior in Southeast Asia in its complex socio-cultural plurality and diversity through extended grassroots-based fieldwork.

---

[1] This was also the case for Indonesian students destined to travel to Freiburg, albeit to a lesser degree due to the lack of German language training facilities at UGM.

Subsequently, the political science departments of both universities, represented through the international relations sub-discipline, became new partners in the project. IR students joined the tandems, which subsequently became transcultural teams of three students. Three years later, in 2014, the project further expanded by incorporating anthropology and IR students from Universitas Hasanuddin (Unhas) in Makassar, an important center of tertiary education outside Java. In the process, several cohorts of IR undergraduates from the three universities had a chance to participate in the project. The participation of these students raises the question what—apart from extending their personal horizons by travelling, meeting Indonesian or German students and creating lasting friendships—was the value added for them. At least three major points can be highlighted.

First, students learned to comprehend what inter- and transdisciplinary work practically means. While in methodology courses, textbooks and research proposals interdisciplinarity is recurrently celebrated as a prime way to optimize research findings by complementing the approaches of one's own discipline with theoretical insights, specific methods or data gathering techniques from neighboring disciplines, few scholars, let alone students, have ever actively practiced interdisciplinary research under field conditions. In the project, students underwent an exercise in inter- and transdisciplinary research under the particularly challenging conditions of a transcultural setting, requiring them to effectively cope with the criteria another discipline and another academic culture define for themselves as good scholarly practice. In the process, IR students' initial confidence in the way their discipline and the pertinent academic culture address the research themes at hand was visibly shaken. The interdisciplinary and transcultural research teams continually found themselves locked in protracted negotiations and re-negotiations of the research design and the best access to informants and interlocutors in the field. IR students thereby frequently encountered profound skepticism among anthropologists towards deductive approaches mentioned in the previous section. Similarly great was their reservation, if not outright hostility, towards the "number-crunching" of statistics and quantitative methods. For IR students this inevitably implied a challenge to think more critically about the origin of such data, how they have been generated and gathered, what may be the biases inherent in them and to what extent these biases affect conclusions. They also had to cope with the more policy-oriented research perspective of their Indonesian IR colleagues, who were less interested in fancy theories than in contributing to their country's developmental effort, its security, the defense of its national sovereignty and its rise as a respected player in global and regional affairs. In sum, taken-for-granted disciplinary certitudes were subjected to serious questioning, had to be newly justified and often adjusted to the conditions prevailing in the field.

Second, participation in the project markedly shaped—or rather, reshaped— IR students' approach toward methodology. A key experience for them was the significance of fieldwork for empirical research and the testing of theories. With the rise of constructivism and the ensuing "linguistic turn" in IR, textual and discourse analysis also became highly popular among IR students who at home in Germany frequently used these methods in their term papers and theses. Yet the concrete fieldwork experience taught them that the analytical value of texts is limited. Texts may help to analyze how social actors frame social realities and thereby to identify the objectives they pursue, but often these accounts differ markedly from the situation prevailing on the ground. For instance, students analyzing Indonesian refugee policies found that on paper refugees from Iraq, Syria, Afghanistan and Somalia were confined with few rights to migration centers, but that in Makassar local authorities turned a blind eye to migrants' movements, allowing them to work in the urban informal economic sector and to mingle with local Indonesians. Although six weeks is by far too short a period to practice genuine participant observation, the fieldwork gave IR students at least some grasp of how direct face-to-face interaction with the respondents may nuance their understanding of the latter's real life worlds. It also highlighted the blessings of triangulation, the virtues of qualitative research, research designs based on mixed methods and the combination of deductive and inductive methods.

The fieldwork exercises with anthropologists also opened IR students' eyes to everyday processes of international relations. While—as stated in the previous section—IR tends to focus on "high politics" such as security policy, the international distribution of power or processes of international cooperation, the micro-dimension of international politics has largely been neglected. Joint research with anthropologists thus directed IR students' attention to "studying down,'' as anthropologists say. Exemplary cases in point are studies of the effects of international organizations and foreign policy decisions at the local level. The consequences of migration policies, religious or ethnic conflicts, peace building and post-conflict peace building or environmental policies such as coal mining on local communities and the activities of local NGOs and civil society groups as advocates of the losers of modernization (for instance, in the case of the ASEAN Economic Community), have become popular topics into which IR students participating in the project immersed themselves with great enthusiasm.

Another experience IR students had in the field was that the toolbox of methods with which they were equipped in their discipline's methodology courses was often inapplicable or in need of major revision. Standard methods widely used in the discipline had to be adjusted to the concrete (local) context. Students learned how abstract interview questions formulated in consonance with the theoretical or methodological requirements of the discipline came to nothing, especially if the respondents were persons with a low level of formal education. Slum dwellers or peasants confronted with a Likert scale have great difficulties in understanding this method for rating agreement or satisfaction levels with a given item. Finding ways to emphatically approach such respondents became a major challenge for (German) IR students who could witness the subtler methods their fellow students from anthropology employed to access target groups whose life worlds were far beyond their experiences and imagination. They learned to read "between the lines," that is, identifying the contextual and emotional subtext of responses to their queries (more on this important aspect from an anthropological perspective, see Lücking 2019, p. 113). Moreover, German IR students were sensitized to the fact that Indonesian respondents considered blunt and interrogative interview questions as impolite and therefore should be avoided in favor of a more casual way of interviewing. Conversely, Indonesian students realized that in Freiburg German respondents expected interviewers to economize on their scarce time and come quickly to the crucial points of their investigation. Also, social hierarchies have to be considered. For instance, in focus groups, leaders tend to speak for the group and their statements often reflect more their position than their opinion (Schlehe and Hidayah 2014, p. 266.). In some cases, respondents seek to impress the foreign researcher(s), but in other situations, where conformity is highly valued and critical views are socially sanctioned, they may be more open towards foreigners, at least as long as they interview them without local witnesses.

Third, while political science and, in particular, IR in Freiburg has always been open to non-Western themes, the project exposed students to Southeast Asia, a region which normally has no place in German IR curricula. It drove home the at first sight trivial message that even for German students IR does not end at the borders of the European Union or the North Atlantic orbit, but that in an age of globalization, worldwide interdependencies rapidly grow. In other words, what happens in Southeast Asia and Indonesia may also have effects on policy options and living conditions in Germany. The interruption of supply chains for many industrial products that originate in Southeast Asia's work banks during and after the Covid-19 pandemic is only one example, but is economically quite consequential (Rüland 2021). The exposure to non-Western life worlds is thus much less trivial in the light of the marginal role that these world regions enjoy in German media, politics and university curricula. Participation in the project in some cases reassured students of their interest in non-Western themes, with the result that they used their field research for their theses, later enrolled in internships and MA programs with an explicit non-Western focus and even envisaged a professional career in the field of development cooperation. But even those who will seek a career in more conventional professions—as journalists, teachers or public officials in Germany—have developed a feeling for cultural difference, the aspirations and motivations of people whose living conditions are still affected by centuries of colonial suppression, the situatedness of knowledge and the multiperspectivity of social phenomena. They learned that fieldwork is a relational process in a polycentric world and has to cope with intersecting differences including nationalities, ethnicity, religion, class, gender and different scientific disciplines (see also Scholte 2005).

4 Conclusion

The previous sections have demonstrated the benefits for IR that an intensified engagement with anthropology can generate on a more general epistemological and methodological level, as well as a more practical level through cooperation such as in the student research project discussed above. The learning effects that this cooperation generated for IR are particularly noticeable in non-Western settings. Engagement with the epistemological positions of Anthropologists helps IR scholars to increase the context sensitivity of their research and to become aware of their positionality as well as the relational dimensions of methods and the ensuing multiperspectivity of findings. It helps them to combat the Western-centeredness of the disciplinary mainstream's theoretical assumptions and methodological tool boxes and by "decolonizing social science methods" (Schlehe and Hidayah 2014: 253) gradually move towards a Global IR. It gives additional justification to the concept of analytic eclecticism, which proves particularly fertile in research contexts where scholars cannot rely on preexisting knowledge. For Indonesian IR students, the reciprocal fieldwork summer schools also markedly widened their disciplinary and cultural horizons by studying phenomena such as the rise of right-wing populism in Germany and Europe. It helped them to leave behind the unfortunate quasi-colonial division of labor, mentioned in the sections above, in which Indonesian scholars are confined to research in their home country and an auxiliary role in projects with international partners. Yet bringing anthropology into IR should not tempt IR scholars to romanticize anthropology or practice "pure anthropology" as demanded by Vrasti (2008, 2010). As many IR themes are not conducive to ethnographic methods, IR scholars should not try to be anthropologists and even though anthropologists may consider IR's engagement with their discipline as "patchwork ethnography" (Rancatore 2010), it is a gain for IR that markedly improves the understanding of cultural diversity. What has not been addressed in this essay is what anthropologists can learn from IR. This is another agenda that would include discussion of the extent to which anthropologists as interpretive scholars need "theoretical scaffolding" to structure findings, how case study research can contribute to theory building and how comparative methods in line with the concept of comparative area studies (CAS) (Ahram et al. 2018) can be better integrated into anthropological research.

References

Acharya, A. 2004. How ideas spread: Whose norms matter? Norm localization and institutional change in Asian regionalism. *International Organization* 58(2): 239–275.
Acharya, A. 2014. Global international relations (IR) and regional worlds. *International Studies Quarterly* 58(4): 647–659.
Adler, E., and V. Pouliot. 2011. International practices. *International Theory* 3(1): 1–36.
Ahram, A., P. Köllner and R. Sil, Eds. 2018. *Comparative area studies. Methodological rationales and cross-regional applications.* Oxford: Oxford University Press.
Aradau, C., and J. Huysmans. 2014. Critical methods in international relations. The politics of techniques, devices and acts. *European Journal of International Relations* 20(3): 596–619.
Assmann, J. 1992. *Das kulturelle Gedächtnis. Schrift, Erinnerung und politische Identität in frühen Hochkulturen.* München: Beck.
Basedau, M., and P. Köllner. 2007. Area studies, comparative area studies, and the study of politics. Context, substance, and methodological challenges. *Zeitschrift für Vergleichende Politikwissenschaft* 1(1): 105–124.
Björkdahl, A., M. Hall, and T. Svensson. 2019. Everyday international relations. Editors' introduction. *Cooperation and Conflict* 54(2): 123–130.
Brady, H.E., and D. Collier. 2010. *Rethinking social inquiry. Diverse tools, shared standards.* Plymouth: Rowman & Littlefield.
Brigden, N., and C. Mainwaring. 2021. Subversive knowledge in times of global political crisis. A Manifesto for ethnography in the study of international relations. *International Studies Perspectives.* https://doi.org/10.1093/isp/ekab003.
Checkel, J.T. 2006. Tracing causal mechanisms. *International Studies Review* 8(2): 362–370.
Clifford, J. 1986. Introduction. Partial truths. In *Writing culture. The poetics and politics of ethnography*, Ed. J. Clifford, 1–26. Berkeley: University of California Press.
Creswell, J.W., and J.D. Creswell. 2017. Research design: Qualitative, quantitative and mixed methods approaches. Los Angeles: Sage.
Friedrichs, J., and F. Kratochwil. 2009. On acting and knowing. How pragmatism can advance international relations research and methodology. *International Organization* 63(4): 701–731.

Geertz, C. 1973. Thick description. Toward an interpretative theory of culture. In *The interpretation of cultures. Selected essays*, Ed. C. Geertz, 310–323. New York: Basic Books.

George, A., and A. Bennett. 2005. *Case studies and theory development*. Cambridge, MA: MIT Press.

Gerring, J. 2008. *Case study research. Principles and practices*. Cambridge: Cambridge University Press.

Hemmer, C., and P. Katzenstein. 2002. Why is there no NATO in Asia? Collective identity, regionalism, and the origins of multilateralism. *International Organization* 56(3): 575–607.

Hoffmann, S. 1977. An american social science. International relations. *Daedalus* 106(3): 41–60.

Huntington, S.P. 1993. The clash of civilizations. *Foreign Affairs* 72(3): 22–49.

Huotari, M., and J. Rüland. 2014. Context, concepts and comparison in Southeast Asian studies—Introduction to the special issue. *Pacific Affairs* 87(3): 415–440.

Huotari, M., J. Rüland, and J. Schlehe, Eds. 2014. *Methodology and research practice in Southeast Asian studies*. Basingstoke: Palgrave Macmillan.

Jackson, P.T. 2008. Can ethnographic techniques tell us distinctive things about world politics? *International Political Sociology* 2(1): 91–93.

Jetschke, A. 2022 (forthcoming). The diffusion of institutions, norms, and policies. In *Edward Elgar handbook on regionalism and global governance*, Eds. J. Rüland and A. Carrapatoso. Cheltenham Edward Elgar.

Katzenstein, P. 2007. Regionalism reconsidered. *Journal of East Asian Studies* 7: 395–412.

Katzenstein, P., and R. Sil. 2008. Eclectic theorizing in the study and practice of international relations. In *The Oxford handbook of international relations*, Eds. C. Reus-Smit and D. Snidal, 109–130. Oxford: Oxford University Press.

King, G., R.C. Keohane, and S. Verba, Eds. 1994. *Designing social inquiry. scientific inference in qualitative research*. Princeton: Princeton University Press.

Kessler, C., and S. Rother. 2016. *Democratization through migration. Political remittances and participation of Philippine return migrants*. Lanham, MD: Lexington.

Kusic, K., and J. Zahora. 2020. Introduction. Fieldwork, failure, international relations. In *Fieldwork as failure. Living and knowing in the field of international relations*, Eds. K. Kusic and J. Zahora, 1–13. Bristol: E-International Relations.

Lederach, J.P. 1997. *Sustainable reconciliation in divided societies*. Washington DC: United States Institute of Peace Press.

Lie, J.H.S. 2013. Challenging anthropology. Anthropological reflections on the ethnographic turn in international relations. *Millennium* 41(2): 201–220.

Lieberman, E.S. 2005. Nested analysis as a mixed-method strategy for comparative research. *American Political Science Review* 99(3): 435–452.

Lücking, M. 2019. Reciprocity in research relationships. Learning from imbalances. In *Affective dimensions of fieldwork and ethnography*, Eds. T. Stodulka, S. Dinkelaker and F. Thajib, 109–121. Cham: Springer.

Lücking, M. 2021. *Indonesians and their Arab world. Guided mobility among labor migrants and Mecca pilgrims*. Ithaca, NY: Cornell University Press.

Mac Ginty, R. 2014. Everyday peace. Bottom-up and local agency in conflict-affected societies. *Security Dialogue* 45(6): 548–564.

Mac Ginty, R., and O. Richmond. 2013. The local turn in peace building. A critical agenda for peace. *Third World Quarterly* 34(5): 763–783.

Mahoney, J. 2010. After KKV. The new methodology of qualitative research. *World Politics* 62(1): 120–147.

Mandaville, P. 2002. Reading the state from elsewhere. Towards an anthropology of the postnational. *Review of International Studies* 28: 199–207.

March, J. G., and J. Olsen. 1989. *Rediscovering institutions. The organizational basis of politics*. New York and London: The Free Press.

Montsion, J. M. 2018. Ethnography and international relations. Situating recent trends, debates and limitations from an interdisciplinary perspective. *The Journal of Chinese Sociology* 5(9): 1–21.

Neumann, I. 2002. Returning practice to the linguistic turn. The case of diplomacy. *Millennium* 31(3): 58–78.

Plano Clark, V. L., and J.W. Creswell. 2008. *The mixed methods reader*. Los Angeles: Sage.

Pouliot, V. 2007. 'Sobjecitivism'. Towards a constructivist methodology. *International Studies Quarterly* 51: 359–384.

Prakash, A., Ed. 2016. *Asia-Europe connectivity vision 2025. Challenges and opportunities*. Jakarta: Economic Institute for ASEAN and East Asia (ERIA).

Ragin, C.C. 1987. *The comparative method. Moving beyond qualitative and quantitative strategies*. Berkeley: University of California Press.

Rancatore, J.P. 2010. It is strange. A reply to Vrasti. *Millennium* 39(1): 65–77.

Risse, T. 2016. The diffusion of regionalism. In *Oxford handbook of comparative regionalism*, Eds. T. A. Börzel and T. Risse, 87–108. Oxford: Oxford University Press.

Rüland, J. 2017. *The Indonesian way. ASEAN, Europeanization and foreign policy debates in a new democracy*. Stanford: Stanford University Press.

Rüland, J. (2020). Old wine in new bottles? How competitive connectivity revitalises an obsolete development agenda in Asia. *Journal of Contemporary Asia* 50(4): 653–665.

Rüland, J. 2021. Covid-19 and ASEAN. Strengthening state-centrism, eroding inclusiveness, testing cohesion. *The International Spectator*. doi: https://doi.org/10.1080/03932729.2021.1893058.

Rüland, J., C. von Lübke, and M.M. Baumann. 2019. *Religious actors and conflict transformation in Southeast Asia, Indonesia and the Philippines*. London: Routledge.

Schlehe, J. 2003. Formen qualitativer ethnographischer Interviews. In *Methoden und Techniken der Feldforschung*, Ed. B. Beer, 71–93. Berlin: Reimer.

Schlehe, J. 2006. Transnationale Wissensproduktion. Deutsch-indonesische Tandemforschung. In *Identitätspolitik und Interkulturalität in Asien. Ein multidisziplinäres Mosaik*, Eds. B. Rehbein, J. Rüland and J. Schlehe, 167–190. Münster: LIT.

Schlehe, J.-, and S. Hidayah. 2014. Transcultural ethnography. Reciprocity in Indonesian-German tandem research. In *Methodology and research practice in Southeast Asian studies*, Eds. M. Huotari, J. Rüland and J. Schlehe, 253–272. London: Palgrave Macmillan.

Schlichte, K. 2013. Was die Politikwissenschaft von der Ethnologie lernen kann. In *Ethnologie im 21. Jahrhundert*, Eds. T. Bierschenk, M. Krings and C. Lentz, 249–263. Berlin: Dietrich Reimer.

Scholte, J. A. 2005. *Globalization. A critical introduction*. Basingstoke: Palgrave Macmillan.

Scupin, R. 2017. Anthropology, conflict, and international relations. In *Advancing interdisciplinary approaches to international relations*, Eds. P. James and S. A. Yetiv, 153–187. Basingstoke: Palgrave Macmillan.

Stryker, R., and R. González, Eds. 2014. *Up, down and sideways. Anthropologists trace the pathways of power*. New York: Berghahn.

Vrasti, W. 2008. The strange case of ethnography and international relations. *Millennium* 37(2): 279–301.

Vrasti, W. 2010. Dr Strangelove, or how I learned to stop worrying about methodology and love writing. *Millennium* 39(1): 79–88.

Wedeen, L. 2010. Reflections on ethnographic work in political science. *Annual Review of Political Science* 13: 255–272.

Wehrer, M. 2019. Anthropology and international relations. Oxford research encyclopedia of international studies. https://oxfordre.com/internationalstudies/view/10.1093/acrefore/9780190846626.001.0001/acrefore-9780190846626-e-530. Accessed: 17 November 2021.

Zangl, B., and M. Zürn. 2004. Make law, not war. Internationale und transnationale Verrechtlichung als Baustein für Global Governance. In *Verrechtlichung – Baustein für Global Governance?*, Eds. B. Zangl and M. Zürn, 12–46. Bonn: Verlag J.H.W. Dietz Nachfolger.

Glocalized Religions, Revitalized Spirituality, and Plural Narratives of Modernity

Trans-Cultural Encounters, Positionalities, and Socio-Historical Burdens: A Reflection from a Muslim Anthropologist on Studying Christianity in Central Borneo

Imam Ardhianto

1 Introduction

This article explores lessons learned from studying an Indigenous Christian community, the Kenyah, by a young male Muslim anthropologist in two different countries which have differing Muslim-Christian relations, namely Malaysia and Indonesia, which border each other on the island of Borneo. In so doing, this approach elaborates on the implications of intersectionality of social class, ethnic identity, citizenship, and religious affiliation that in many ways shape the transcultural encounters between the author and many interlocutors in both the state of Sarawak in Malaysia and the Indonesian Province of North Kalimantan. I argue that an anthropologist who comes from a non-anglophone and Western institution, who is studying socially similar yet culturally foreign groups, needs to destabilize the notion of strict oppositional categories of "self" and "other" as a metaphor in doing and writing ethnography. Taking this into consideration, the task of a non-Western anthropologist is to reveal the problematics of how to navigate a more complex and shifting form of sociality when doing data collection and presenting ethnographic analysis. The task is to reveal the experience of crossing layers of identities and situations encountered in many stages of ethnography.

I. Ardhianto (✉)
Department of Anthropology, Faculty of Social and Political Sciences, Universitas Indonesia, Depok, Indonesia
E-Mail: imamardhianto@ui.ac.id

© Der/die Autor(en), exklusiv lizenziert an Springer Fachmedien Wiesbaden GmbH, ein Teil von Springer Nature 2023
M. Lücking et al. (Hrsg.), *In Tandem—Pathways towards a Postcolonial Anthropology | Im Tandem – Wege zu einer postkolonialen Ethnologie*,
https://doi.org/10.1007/978-3-658-38673-3_8

It is through this experience that ethnographic insights may appear in different forms, contrasting with a western scholar's experience of doing ethnography. In explaining this argument, this paper will elaborate on two aspects. The first is the problematic of doing participant observation when rapport requires the researcher to forego their beliefs and dietary restrictions. The second is the author's cultural and historical burden as a Muslim observing, elaborating, and understanding ethnohistorical accounts of how the Kenyah interpret and define the experience of becoming Christian within two different denominations.

The materials I use in this paper stem from my research projects on Kantu ethnic groups in the upper Kapuas and my study of the Evangelical church and *adat* transformation in upland central Borneo. As a prerequisite criterion for ethnography, participant observation is a way to immerse oneself in the fieldwork by systematically going back and forth between being a participant and an observer across a long duration of research. It is interesting that the issues of how the researcher's belief and identity are intertwined in the various encounters within long ethnographic fieldwork is rarely elaborated in handbooks on ethnography. This paper explores in more specific detail the methodological reflection of my project to study Christianity and landscape transformation among the Kenyah in upland Borneo. As a person born into a Javanese family, who grew up in a suburban part of Jakarta and was educated in a mix of puritan and traditionalist Islam, studying Christian Kenyah in Malaysia is a challenging opportunity to reveal the negotiations between my cultural-religious background and my research experiences in the field.

The specific intersectionality of my personality and identity brought me to the 'insider/outsider' problem and its relation to ethnographic authority in anthropological research, which became an important topic in the practice of ethnography after the emergence of the 'native anthropologist' concept (Narayan 1993). A similar topic emerged in the study of religion, with many processes required to understand a category, knowledge, and beliefs that the researcher does not have (McCutcheon 1999). As per discussions in the literature on these two issues, an ethnography of religious phenomena must address the burden of authenticity and representation emerging from the problematics of the insider/outsider issue. How is a liberal, atheist, male Westerner able to understand an esoteric feeling and meaning in Islamic mysticism? Or, in my case, how is an Indonesian, Muslim, male social scientist from the Indonesian capital able to start research on Christianity in innermost Borneo?

Several publications have already discussed the insider/outsider problem in anthropological research. Most of the literature has described the importance of moving beyond a romanticized and essentialized dualistic category of insider/outsider and has emphasized the dynamics of multiple categories of identity in fieldwork, or what Narayan called 'multiplex identity' (Narayan 1993, p. 673). This approach criticises the dichotomist stereotype of foreign and Indigenous anthropologists. In the same vein, Schlehe and Hidayah (2014) describe the problematical notion of these stereotypes, which usually view the category as follows: On the one hand, the 'outsider' or 'foreigner' is more aware of taken-for-granted aspects of the culture, less involved in internal power struggles, hierarchies, and dependencies, less obliged to meet various expectations and sensibilities, and less caught up in gender roles or religious affiliation. On the other hand, the 'insider anthropologist' allegedly has easier access to local modes of communication and narrative formats, better understanding of non-verbal cues, and better intuitive understanding (Schlehe and Hidayah 2014, p. 256). In reality, the dichotomy between insider and outsider is neither clear nor rigid. For anthropologists from the southern part of the world, educated in a post-colonial setting, the category of insider/outsider obscures a broad range of multiple intersecting social and political categories such as ethnicity, religion, class, majority-minority relations, gender, sub-culture, and academic training. Responding to this problematic dichotomy, a suggested alternative is to avoid essentializaton in categorizing someone as a native, an Indigenous, or an 'insider' anthropologist. On the contrary, we should consider how multiple affiliations and many more intersecting structural factors should be considered as being between the two categories (Schlehe and Hidayah 2014, p. 257). Narayan proposes the same approach in her influential essay regarding what comprises a native or a non-native anthropologist. Narayan suggests that anthropologists, whatever their background, should consider the process of shifting identities in relationship to the people and issues an anthropologist seeks to represent (Narayan 1993, p. 683).

In the process of ethnographic research, both researcher and research subjects continuously co-constitute their social categories to understand each other. Along with the process of social identification, each actor has expectations that are influenced by the intersecting categories of each other's identity. A member of the older generation of the Kenyah in upland Borneo being interviewed about religion by an anthropologist from the Western world with fancy gadgets and a contrasting physical appearance would probably provoke certain expectations related to his experiences. He would probably answer the anthropologist's questions about the change to Christianity with reference to interactions with missionaries. A different response might appear if he/she met a young Indonesian anthropologist. The religious sermon would probably change if a Western anthropologist were sitting in the pews. A young anthropologist would probably keep/maintain social distance from the elders of a particular longhouse community. Women may have a barrier to interviewing men at night, but probably would have a benefit in exploring women's perspectives in the community. By noting these conscious positionalities, an anthropologist can aim to explore the research subject with awareness of the possibilities and constraints that influence the kinds of insights and information he/she may gain from the fieldwork. Building rapport involves a constant struggle to overcome social distance and cultural differences. This chapter aims to provide my personal narratives on studying the problematics above by illustrating my sketch of experiences in the field regarding participant observation, the process of understanding the social scope of the research subject, as well as the issues of limitation and opportunities in the very process. One thing that undoubtedly marks the criteria of good anthropological research is participant observation. How should we do this? In the following section I discuss my experience of the problematics and the importance of bodily and sensorial experience of encountering culturally different "others".

2 Eating and Drinking in the Field: Rethinking Bodily Experience and Religious Conviction in Participant Observation

How should a Muslim anthropologist do participant observation? What are the limits and the opportunities to do so? What are the ethical and epistemological issues that we should consider in order to grasp cultural understanding and the social mechanisms of other religious practices? One thing I learned from several stages of my previous research is that the main limitation in doing so is related to our shifting and uncanny experience of bodily sensibilities over cultural difference regarding what can be seen, touched, and eaten. The problem is partly how we understand and accept with an open mind the different theological convictions of our research subject. However, it is mostly related to the way we deal with all our senses.

During my early years after graduating from my undergraduate degree (2006–2010), I had the chance to do six months of ethnographic research in Borneo. Influenced strongly by *'komunitas antropologi UI'*[1] ideas of a good anthropologist, I came to the field aiming to practice total immersion in a Kantu ethnic group's village in West Kalimantan. My first experience of foregoing dietary

---

[1] There is a popular opinion among the anthropology community in Universitas Indonesia regarding what an anthropology student or alumnae should be and how their identity should be defined. These include a kind of bohemian and free liberating process of withdrawing

restrictions to achieve a research goal was when I had the chance in 2011 to be a guest at the wedding of the *Kepala Adat's* daughter in the village of Nanga Pintas, Embaloh, Kapuas Hulu. I had the opportunity, after two months of fieldwork there, to join the marriage ceremony along with the family to take the groom from another village by canoe. The bride's older brother danced near the edge of the canoe and for the very first time I saw dozens of large cans containing Arak, a local alcohol, being passed to everybody while they rowed the canoe. As the *Kepala Adat* knew that I was a Javanese Muslim, he was reluctant to offer the alcohol to me, but his women relatives insisted that I drink it, and eventually I became drunk during the marriage celebration, along with one elementary school teacher from Malay ethnic background who drank with me despite the fact that he had been trying to avoid doing so. The event was chaotic and the sense of conviviality was really strong, as it is in many Iban and Kantu events that are marked by high pitched sounds as well as people giving each other alcohol. When we arrived at the groom's place, the people in the canoes were to go to greet the groom's family and at the same time drink the Arak that had been prepared by the groom's family (Fig. 1).

Though the father of the groom knew that I had already had a drink, he gave me a glass of Arak. After we finished the stage in the groom's village, we returned to the bride's village. The celebration took a full day. In the middle of feast, I was very drunk and fell over on the floor after throwing up. It looked like I was partially unconscious. All the villagers laughed at me. The next day, everywhere I went in the villages, people greeted me by name and asked what I wanted to do, they invited me into their houses or to hunt tortoise in the forest. The older people started to talk more informally and in detail about Bentian rituals to cure people. That process of drinking alcohol and participating in ritual dancing during the marriage celebration was a step to move beyond my cultural stereotypes. I became the Javanese Muslim that got drunk and humiliated himself by throwing up. The events helped to stop me being seen as a stranger wandering in and investigating their social life from a distance. At that time, I was happy to do so. It seems like I had passed what Clifford Geertz experienced when he ran away from a cockfight after a police raid. For the sake of my research goals, this was a practical way of being accepted and getting known in the village and among important *adat* leaders. However, an uneasy feeling lingered afterward. Was it right to do that? Had I gained a significant entry point by doing so? One thing that

---

from religious belief. In many important events, especially during the *'Inisiasi'* or the acceptance of new freshman undergraduates, this idea that most anthropologists have their own religion *'agama antrop'* is one of many popular topics often discussed during the event.

Fig. 1 The arrival of the bride and how she welcomed by the groom's family with Arak (strong alcoholic liquor). (Source: Yudhi Yanto, 2010)

struck me was that my research colleague in the neighbouring village, one of my juniors, was still fasting through the month of Ramadhan and never drank *arak*, yet was still able to gain the locals' trust to a similar extent that I did from my experience of drinking. He even was invited to participate in and closely observe *Petena,* a ritual conducted to settle disputes by inviting ancestors. Had I over-romanticized a Geertzian way of becoming an anthropologist? Looking back at that comparison today, I think I had. A few years later, I changed my mind during my PhD fieldwork. Despite the fact that in North Kalimantan the cultural divide between upland animists/Christians and lowland Muslims is represented by what we eat and drink, I decided not to drink alcohol or eat pork. Of course, sometimes there were lapses, as result of both my own sloppiness and unawareness, and my research subject forgetting my dietary restrictions, but once we got to know each other we knew that we could maintain those differences. Alas, at that stage I think that maybe we don't need to cross my own religious conviction to get ethnographical insights.

The importance of dietary restrictions not only influenced how I conducted participant observation, but the ambiguity and the feeling of uneasiness in relation to dietary restrictions also arose among my research subjects in the field regarding the experience of changing religion. When I visited the Kenyah village of Long Busang in Sarawak in 2013, Asan Lusat, one of the most respected Kenyah elders in upland central Borneo, told me of his experience of re-conversion to Christianity in 2012 after 34 years as a Muslim. He went to the head of the village, called *pala kampong'*, to give an important cultural possession, an inherited machete *(parang)*, as a sign of a peace-making ritual used when there is tension, quarrel and conflict between two people. The reason for this act was his decision to return to Christianity after more than 30 years practicing Islam. He believed that this act could bring trouble to his community and he presumed that the head of the village would question his decision. The head of the village rejected the gift, saying that the re-conversion would not cause disputes or problems in the village.

Asan told me that at first he was hesitant to reconvert to Christianity, yet he missed eating forest boar meat and had started to feel awkward eating deer after all of his children, who are Muslim and Christian, had started their own families and moved away. His story about his reconversion took me by surprise on the very first day of my visit. Contrary to my previous understanding of conversion as something serious, individual, and involving a deep-seated religious conviction, Asan Lusat recounted his understanding of conversion as something practical and socially related to other people, such as his intention to eat wild boar again and the experience of separation from his family after they had left the household and moved to the nearest city. This explanation bothered me and questions haunted me. Was his explanation only a merely superficial response or was it just that I didn't have enough time to probe the question? Are faith and religious identity not that 'serious'? Was my confusion related to my cultural bias as a Javanese Muslim with modern education? After my preliminary visits to this place, my colleague Dave Lumenta, a Menadonese Indonesian anthropologist who had already undertaken extensive research in Central Borneo, told me that this is just as typical of the upland people's understanding of religion. All religious convictions involve acts which relate to material things and in Borneo eating and drinking is the most crucial sign of people's religions transformation. My experience of foregoing my dietary restrictions in my early days of doing ethnography seems to support that assertion.

My experience of crossing dietary boundaries is one example that shows how eating/not eating and drinking/not drinking can open different ways of doing participant observation. In terms of how religious belief influences the process in the field, restrictions and also the religious sensibilities of the researcher are limiting, yet open different ways of mutually learning about and constituting what both the anthropologist and research subject understand about a particular subject.

3   Religious Positionality and Historical Burden

The problems I experienced during fieldwork in gaining trust and insights that brought me to my focus of my research in the initial stages mostly resulted from the historical burden of the Muslim-Christian relationship at the national, regional, and local levels in Indonesia. Concerning the national level, I was doing my fieldwork at a time when allegations had been brought against the first Christian governor of the Indonesian capital of Jakarta, Basuki Tjahaja Purnama (Ahok). An alliance of conservative and radical Islamist political groups accused him of religious blasphemy. Being loaded with multiple political interests related to the Jakarta gubernatorial election, the issues were becoming a national concern, as the Islamists' political move exposed racial and religious antagonism between Chinese Christians and the Muslim populist movement. That movement's ability to mobilize millions of people to push the Indonesian president to jail the incumbent governor for blasphemy was growing. People discussed the problem with me during my fieldwork; even a pastor from Sarawak, Malaysia, asked about it. On a few occasions, people asked me whether I supported the Islamic mass mobilization. Despite my easily answering 'no', the question indicates the problems present in inter-religious relations at the time.

On the regional level, the historical antagonism between the lowland Muslim sultanate and the upland animists that was common in the nineteenth- and twentieth centuries had transformed into the relation between the Christian community and coastal Muslims, resonating with the social differentiation maintained among the Kenyah in Apokayan. In this context, I was categorised by many of my informants as alok (stranger), a term referring to a spectrum of social markers that stand in contrast to the identities of the Kayan, Kenyah, and Punan social groups of central Borneo. People who do not belong to one of these three social groups are irrevocably labelled alok. However, the term has also come to refer to other, previously excluded groups such as the Iban, Lundayeh, and upriver communities in upper Mahakam River. In addition, the term indicates that members of those groups are not swidden farmers and, essentially, are coastal Muslims

(Lumenta 2008, p. 87). Every time I arrived at a new household, the children of my interlocutor called me 'om alok' (uncle alok). This language is a sign of social distance and at the same time implies people who are not Christian and do not eat pig/pork. During the preparation of food for a funeral for a relative of someone that offered me a place to stay during my fieldwork, a different dish was made for me. The historical explanation of the social differentiation between alok and the Kenyah goes further than a term of address and dietary contrast might imply. Even today, most of the ethnic groups from the uplands are collectors of forest products such as eaglewood (gaharu), which are sold to alok people, such as Malay Muslims, Arab middlemen, and the Chinese from Tanjung Selor, a downriver city in North Kalimantan.

At the local level, it was not long after my arrival that a few adherents of the fundamentalist Islamic movement Jamaat Tabligh[2] proposed to the village leader the building of a mosque in Apokayan, despite the fact that the Muslim population consisted of only a few foreigners working as public officials and a health facilitator. In contrast with other villages in the mid-river areas of many river basins in Kalimantan, Apokayan does not have a large enclave of Javanese and Buginese who had stayed there as merchants or lived nearby as migrants. During my stay, one Buginese who had a grocery store in the village even had to leave because of competition with the local Kenyah trader. Given this situation, the proposal to build a mosque was rejected by the adat committee and village leader, resulting in social tension and anxiety. Although I never heard any direct sentiments against Muslims, I could feel people's reluctance to meet with me during the initial stage of my research. In contrast to previous anthropologists' experience decades before, who were mostly non-religious and Western, in central Borneo at least, it was quite difficult for me to get a sense of full acceptance and to make people feel comfortable to tell about their socio-religious experience and allow me to be involved in their religious activities.

The first time I went to a GKII (Gereja Kemah Injil Indonesia/Indonesian Gospel Tabernacle Church). Sunday service, some members of the church committee asked for my identity card and interrogated me for quite a while because they

---

[2] Jamaat Tabligh is an Islamic organisation which has an 'evangelical version' of doctrine and focus. The name can be translated as 'The Outreach Society'. The movement was started in 1927 by Muhammad Ilyas al-Kandhlawi in India. Its stated primary aim is spiritual reformation of Islam by reaching out to Muslims across social and economic spectra and working at the grassroots level to bring them in line with the group's understanding of Islam. Besides the representative I heard in Apokayan, other members of the movement were also visiting Kenyah Badeng villages on the border of Indonesian Borneo and Sarawak in 2013, and even brought along a preacher from Egypt.

were afraid of foreigners and terrorists following the Samarinda church bombing in East Kalimantan in 2015. The interrogation stopped only with the arrival of Pak Made, a former Balinese police officer who had married a Kenyah and had been living in Long Nawang for decades, who had helped me with transportation from the nearest small airport. He explained my presence to the committee. This type of limitation to my immersion in the Christian community was the most significant barrier in my fieldwork. In addition, my gender limited my encounters with women, who predominantly have equal roles with men in church activity in the GPIB (Gereja Protestan Indonesia Barat). It was difficult for me to explore issues of hierarchy and autonomy in inter-gender topics, areas that I think would be an interesting focus for future research.

However, despite the limitations I experienced due to my Muslim background, I had a few advantages in studying Christianity in central Boneo. The first was my sensitivity to differences that existed among Christian denominations, despite my interlocutors telling me otherwise. Encountering an unfamiliar religious practice helped me to ask about details that probably would be not very important for a theology student, such as why those in the GKII prefer to confess their experience with God through healing and dreams, which is often not the case in the GPIB; or why a certain church uses a guitar and another does not. My awareness of this advantage came, interestingly, from a Calvinist pastor in one of the villages who told me that some of my questions were rather naïve, especially concerning the liturgy.

My other advantage involved learning details about the past, something I was able to do from the beginning of the research. People's orientation toward their early conversion narratives, which usually came from those in typical Evangelist Christian communities, helped me to get detailed ethno-historical information about tensions and debates during the early period of Christianity and the withdrawal of the adat system of taboo. This information led me in turn to ethnographically informed archival research about the early conversion period. Understanding the history of how the Kenyah became Christian in the first place was important information for my research. The last aspect of positionality, which also enmeshed with my identity as a Muslim and a male from the capital, was the identity of the ethnographer. While at first people were quite hesitant to discuss Christianity in detail with me, my knowledge of old religion and stories about my travel in Sarawak fascinated people in Long Nawang and Nawang Baru, and likewise in another villages in Sarawak. My extensive knowledge of stories that I had obtained from various villages provided me with an advantage. My interlocutors compared my knowledge to that of two previous anthropologists that studied the Kenyah, Dave Lumenta and Herbert Whittier from the United States.

Knowing that history would be significant in the forthcoming process of district splits as a source of cultural justification and also for the sake of identity, they accepted me as someone who could gather and document their history, despite the obstacles and social distance I brought to the field as a Muslim.

4 Overcoming Blurred Categories: Understanding the P-E Denomination in Central Borneo

Classifying varieties of church denomination within the Pentecostal and Evangelical movements is complicated because in order to do so, different measurements and understandings are required both from etic and emic points of view. For academics, who usually refer to the etic category, efforts to categorize the church face the challenge of the huge diversity of historical, liturgical, and institutional forms. On analysing this complexity, Anderson suggests that scholars studying Christianity need to be aware of the dynamics of the range of criteria that they use (Bergunder et al. 2010). In his elaboration, criteria for classifying and understanding church varieties are always subjective and arbitrary, and differences may not be perceived as significant by the movements being assessed by these criteria. Meanwhile, there is also the possibility of neglecting differences that may be quite important to church members. Emic and etic views always create such differences in viewpoint. The phenomenon of Pentecostalism and the Evangelical Church is, however, much more complex than any neat categorizing will allow (Bergunder et al. 2010, p. 15).

To address the complexity and sometimes diverging definitions of denomination, Anderson confirms the importance of analysing the various denominations as a wide variety of movements scattered throughout the world that can be described as having 'family resemblance'. By following that Wittgensteinian term, he argues that family resemblance in understanding varieties of Pentecostal and Evangelical church does not mean that there is a specific thing that they all have in common, but that they all have certain similarities and relations with each other. Describing or defining something must allow for 'blurred edges', so an imprecise definition can still be meaningful (Bergunder et al. 2010). Anderson's method is useful in this research as it leads me to understand the church-making process as a way for people to define their church in relation to their place in the diverse churches of Indonesia. Anderson's method also worked in dialogue with my etic point of view, which came from my exploration of archives about the historical context of the GKII and GPIB in Borneo, and from social science and Christianity studies literature.

As a researcher from an Islamic background, it was not easy for me to understand the various strands of Christian denominations, especially related to the classification of theological doctrine, liturgy, and the form of the church community itself. In the initial phase of this study, I could not see the differences among various sects of the Protestant Church, although I had previously encountered various Christian ethnic groups in Borneo during several years of research and consultancy work in identifying high conservation value in several parts of Borneo for a palm oil company between 2009 and 2014. My experience living in Tangerang, a suburb of Jakarta, between 1998 and 2002 had left me with the impression that Christianity had only two denominations: Catholicism and Protestantism. My limited knowledge of Christianity and my socio-cultural distance were perhaps influenced by aspects of my background in which Christianity was perceived as the culturally repugnant "other". This cultural-religious barrier began during my adolescence, related to my intense engagement with an Islamic youth organization, *Remaja Islam Masjid,* that at the time was influenced by the new and rising Tarbiyah[3] movement, which developed politically at the end of Soeharto dictatorship in 1998. The pretext of the prejudice was based on the movement in that period that created hostility against the Christian community, which was accused of proselytizing to the poor Muslim population in suburban Jakarta. In November 1998, exactly at the period of the Semanggi II riots, my religious mentor gave me a grotesque picture of Pam Swakarsa, a paramilitary group said to have been created by General Wiranto. The picture showed a gory slaughter, supposedly depicting the victims of Christian secular power infiltrating a student movement in Jakarta. Thus my aversion to Christianity did not arise from my status as a liberal, secular, or non-religious person, as perhaps most Western anthropologists identify themselves, but rather as a result of my experience and religious background as a Muslim who grew up in a particular place and time. My experience contrasts with that of many anthropologists of Christianity who address Christianity as a culturally repugnant phenomena representing the very opposite of liberal-secular conceptions of the world and social life (Robbins 2003). While my education in anthropology undoubtedly gave me the sensitivity and training to open my mind to cultural variation, my social background nonetheless influenced my pre-existing knowledge related to apprehending the varieties

---

[3] Tarbiyah is a revivalist Islamic movement in Indonesia that grew during the last decade of Soeharto's New Order regime. The ideology is basically puritan and was largely influenced by Ikhwanul Muslimin (the Muslim Brotherhood) in Egypt. Nowadays, it takes its political manifestation as Partai Keadilan Sejahtera (the Justice and Prosperity Party), which was influential in mobilizing its constituents to promote anti-China and anti-Christian sentiment during the DKI Jakarta gubernatorial election.

of Christianity in Indonesia and my cultural and personal proximity to the ideas, practices, and followers of this religion.

In the context of the fieldwork, my lack of knowledge became more problematic as I read material based on anthropology, church studies, and from archives. In that process, I encountered gaps in my knowledge. Jan Sihar Aritonang and Karel Steenbrink categorize the Christian & Missionary Alliance, a missionary group from the US that educated most of the GKII founders, as the pioneering Evangelical mission and churches in Indonesia (Aritonang and Steenbrink 2008). Considering that the GKII among the Kenyah originated from this mission, my first impression was that this church could be categorized as Evangelist. For example, the GKII replicates the C&MA's concept and method, as well as the role of the church cluster it founded/gathered under the so-called 'Alliance' or Gospel Tabernacle cluster *(Rumpun Kemah Injil).*

In addition, GKII teachings are similar to those of C&MA and can be summarized as four principles, usually called the 'four-fold Gospel': Christ saves, sanctifies, heals, and will return as the Lord. The hope and conviction of the Second Coming of Christ motivated C&MA missionaries to proclaim the gospel to people who had never heard or received it before. This evangelistic effort was conceived of as hastening the return of Jesus Christ. All of these beliefs are represented in a letter from Rev. Fisk explaining his experience and vision in establishing Christianity in the Kayan tributary (Fisk 1930). However, from my direct observation, the GKII Church showed not only evangelist characteristics but Pentecostal liturgical features and doctrines as well, such as the priority of the battle with diabolical spirits and its specific form of liturgy that emphasises healing. During my initial discussions about the liturgy, pastors and deacons in downriver Kenyah village settlements and in the Long Bia theological school emphasized the strong role of miracles and healing as the main activities of Sunday church services. Furthermore, and surprisingly, during my fieldwork in 2015, the GKII was incorporated into the Indonesian Church Alliance (Persekutuan Gereja-gereja di Indonesia) which is usually more closely related to the influence of the European Calvinist Church than to the Indonesian Pentecostal Church Alliance (Persekutuan Gereja-Gereja Pentekosta di Indonesia; PGPI). The Indonesian Church Alliance lists 89 churches and does not include the Pentecostal Church, which has its own alliance organization. This history of complicated affiliations made the process of defining denomination quite difficult.

However, my lack of knowledge about Christianity and the difficulty in defining denominations turned out to be a blessing in disguise. My questions to my interlocutors in the field and my reading of different kinds of Christian strands brought me to the finding that even the Kenyah themselves struggle to resolve this question, mainly engaging with it by thinking about what kind of Christian they are. Our conversations revealed that they primarily define their Christianity by contrasting themselves with other denominations in Apokayan. This ethnographic revelation brought me to their narrative of the history of conversion and schism in the villages, an issue which still mattered when I was doing my fieldwork. During my fieldwork, when I asked about what kind of church the GPIB or GKII was, most of my informants tended to hesitate, especially when I tried to probe by comparing their church with other churches in Indonesia. The GKII community proclaimed that it was just the same as other Protestant churches, such as those of the GPIB. However, they also agreed that the GKII has a different history in Indonesia and sees its fellow church in Sarawak as similar, especially concerning liturgy, in contrast to the neighbouring GPIB church. Nonetheless, it was also apparent that the GKII is different from the Borneo Evangelical Mission of Sarawak in doctrinal principles, since the former does not consider holy spirits or speaking in tongues to be the main features of the church.

By following what my interlocutors said and explained about the denominations and by tracing the historical narratives, I experienced a tension between my effort to simplify and classify the kinds of Christianity on the one hand and grasping the complexity and confusion on the other. This tension turned out to be productive, as the situation and my approach led me to critically engage with the varieties of Christian forms, practices, and interpretations. Hence I benefitted from the information in the narratives of how the Kenyah themselves classify and understand the socio-religious form of their church and its change in the course of history. Based on my interactions with my interlocutors, I was able during the last stage of my writing to find several categories that helped me to delineate what kind of Christianity they followed. Thus the socio-religious category delineated from the fieldwork is dialogic in nature.

By the end of the research, I had identified four aspects that are important as criteria for discussing what kind of Christianity I was studying and its relevance to the focus of my research, such as socio-religious form. These are: 1) liturgy, 2) institutional structure, 3) local people's role in the church, and 4) themes emphasized in Sunday services. While Calvinist Protestant churches such as the GPIB hold liturgy in solemn Sunday services through *'Kidung Jemaat'* (church hymns), gospel songs and sermons based on a top-down template from the central church organization in Jakarta, the GKII allows reverends or local parishes to create their sermons spontaneously and to choose gospel songs related to the current situation where they live. Furthermore, on a more substantive aspect of the sermon, the theme among the GKII consists of the preservation of dualism and the continuance of life before and after receiving Christ (infidel/animist/pagan and old traditional belief vs. Christian life). The churches established in the villages also provide a place for locals to be fully involved in the establishment and maintenance of the church as reverend, deacon, member of a local parish, or even lay church official. Most of the regional committee members of North Kalimantan GKII churches during my field visits were Kenyah, in contrast to the GPIB, which sent people from other regions, such as Toraja, Semarang, and Jakarta to become reverends in central Borneo, as in the case of Apokayan. From my observations during Sunday services and also through interviews, the emphasis of their doctrine on the importance of the tenets that Jesus saves, sanctifies, heals, and will return as the Lord was a message signalling the influence of the Pentecostal-Charismatic doctrine, which is now increasingly influenced by Christian popular culture from the US and many places in the world, as often mentioned in anthropological studies of Christianity.

As I collected narratives and observations in the field, I found that the elements of Christianity mentioned above resonate with almost all the criteria explained by one of the famous scholars of Christianity in Indonesia, Aritonang (Aritonang and Steenbrink 2008), who identifies a third stream of Christianity that he marks as Evangelical and Pentecostal. Aritonang positions the C&MA as the first church mission to be influential in the development of Pentecostal and Charismatic denominations in Indonesia. Aritonang's extensive study of Christianity in Indonesia, published at a time when the anthropology of Christianity was an emerging field, reveals the strong connection of Kenyah Christianity and the GKII Church with Pentecostal elements.

My inquiry to identify what kind of Christianity I encountered in the fieldwork brought me to questions regarding church differentiation and socio-religious categories. Both topics involve the history of locals being converted, the break from and church relation to older beliefs and metaphysical beings, the form of institutional structure and, later on, the liturgy. In these four criteria constructed from the fieldwork, the question of contested socio-religious forms of hierarchy was a primary feature in oral histories and archives, as well as in my observations. Hierarchy, autonomous egalitarianism, and the recombination of both socio-religious forms resonated in the discussion of religious authority over rituals, which is an issue also strongly connected to denominational schism. These experiences and reflections, the dialogue between my background and its limitations, previous studies that delineate the socio-religious scope of denomination and my encounters with the Kenyah themselves together brought me to the focus of this research.

5 Conclusion

This chapter is a follow-up elaboration to many existing elaborations of positionalities in textbooks on ethnographic methods. The notion that the ethnographic research process is situated and constructed in the field is present in many publications on methodologies. However, I believe that there is still a small number of publications that explain how ethnographical insights and also the researcher's self-identification are transformed along with the research subject. I think this entry point can be found among many people who have religious convictions and cultural identities that differ from liberal and white or Anglo-Saxon cultural backgrounds. I myself, despite that I cannot claim to be a good and strong believer, am still culturally attached to my Muslim background. It is this background that helped me shape and brought me to the focus of my research, as well as to the way my research subjects made sense of how they defined and delineated differences from each other in the field. It is exactly my lack of knowledge about Christianity and the difficulty of defining denominations that helped me to arrive at a specific subject that perhaps could not have been seen by an anthropologist from another background. Furthermore, the context of being someone that came from a 'centre' to what my research subjects called a remote area *(daerah terpencil)* also influenced the way people interacted with me. It is within this overlapping category that I have my own difficulties and limitations, as well, of course, as opportunities. This paper is only a starter, an invitation for anthropologists to reflect on and to be honest about the relationship of his/her religious trajectory to the ethnographic thinking process in the field. The overlap of religious education and enculturation, the structural political context related to it and the many layered identities could contribute to opening up a horizon of interreligious encounter that is vital to the development of ethnographic methodology. It is not just the reality of the field and the dynamics of ethnographic subject that shape how we imagine our methodology, but also our lives and our multiple professional and personal commitments – from childcare and health concerns to financial, environmental, political, and temporal constraints, to relationship commitments at 'home', (Günel et al. 2020), and of course included here are our religious commitments. Maybe we need more elaboration from a believing yet open minded anthropologist, which perhaps could solve what Joel Robbins called the problem of awkward relations between theology and anthropology (Robbins 2007). Only by doing that can anthropology provide different entry points for religious elaboration beyond a liberal starting point.

References

Aritonang, J. S., and K. A. Steenbrink, Eds. 2008. *A history of christianity in Indonesia.* Leiden: Brill.

Bergunder, M., A. F. Droogers, and A. Anderson, Eds. 2010. *Studying global pentecostalism. Theories and methods.* Berkeley: University of California Press.

Fisk, G. E. 1930. In contact with the Dyak in Dutch borneo (extracts of a letter). *Pioneer,* 1930.

Günel, Gökçe, S. Varma, and C. Watanabe. 2020. A manifesto for patchwork ethnography. *Member Voices, Fieldsights* 9.

Lumenta, D. 2008. *The Making of a Transnational Continuum: State Partitions and Mobility of the Apau Kayan Kenyah in Central Borneo, 1900–2007.* PhD Thesis, The Graduate School of Asian and African Studies, Kyoto University.

McCutcheon, R. T., Ed. 1999. *The insider/outsider problem in the study of religion. A reader. Controversies in the study of religion.* London: Cassell.

Narayan, K. 1993. How native is a 'native' anthropologist? *American Anthropologist* 95 (3): 671–86.

Robbins, J. 2003. On the paradoxes of global Pentecostalism and the dangers of continuity thinking. Religion 33 (3): 221–231.

Robbins, J. 2007. Anthropology and theology. An awkward relationship? *Anthropological Quarterly* 79 (2): 285–94. https://doi.org/10.1353/anq.2006.0025.

Schlehe, J., and S. Hidayah. 2014. Transcultural ethnography. Reciprocity in Indonesian-German tandem research. In *Methodology and research practice in Southeast Asian studies,* Ed. M. Huotari, J. Rüland and J. Schlehe, 253–72. Basingstoke; Houndsmill; Hampshire; New York: Palgrave Macmillan.

Spiritual Gifts and Material Exchanges in Four Palaces Mediumship

Kirsten W. Endres

1 Introduction

Hanoi in October 2006. The traffic on Giải Phóng Road is murderous and the air is thick with exhaust fumes. On the back of my scooter sits Mrs. Thiền, a stout woman in her fifties. She holds two huge plastic bags laden with cans of beer, soft drinks, biscuits, crackers, bags of candy, instant noodle packets, Ajino Moto (MSG), sugar, cigarettes, green tea, mangos, oranges, and some areca nuts. To an outside observer, it might seem as if we were driving home from a shopping spree. But this impression is deceptive. In actual fact we are on our way back from a *hầu đồng* ritual held at a private temple in Văn Điển on the southern edge of Hanoi, and the plastic bags cutting into Mrs. Thiền's hands are filled with 'divine gifts' *(lộc)* from the Four Palaces deities. As is customary in Four Palaces mediumship, the medium had prepared offerings *(đồ lễ)* for each deity embodied during the ritual and in a quantity sufficient enough to distribute one item of each set to everyone present. Just like the other ritual participants, we had happily placed our 'divine gifts' in a provided bag to take home for consumption and distribution among friends and family.[1]

K. W. Endres (✉)
Max-Planck-Institut für ethnologische Forschung, Halle, Deutschland
E-Mail: endres@eth.mpg.de

[1] This article is largely based on chapter four of my book *Performing the Divine. Mediums, Markets and Modernity in Urban Vietnam* (NIAS Press, 2011). Preliminary research was carried out between 2001 and 2004, followed by an intensive year of fieldwork in 2006 as part of a three-year DFG-funded research project hosted by the University of Freiburg. I am grateful to Judith Schlehe for her generous support and mentorship during that time, and to the Four Palaces mediums who shared with me their knowledge and insights.

© Der/die Autor(en), exklusiv lizenziert an Springer Fachmedien Wiesbaden GmbH, ein Teil von Springer Nature 2023
M. Lücking et al. (Hrsg.), *In Tandem—Pathways towards a Postcolonial Anthropology | Im Tandem – Wege zu einer postkolonialen Ethnologie*,
https://doi.org/10.1007/978-3-658-38673-3_9

Ritual offerings are of course not unique to Four Palaces mediumship, nor to Vietnam more generally. Gifts made to otherwordly entities, be they deities, ancestors, or spirits/ghosts, are a universal phenomenon common to humans throughout the ages that is best characterized as an 'exchange of material objects for supernatural returns' (Osborne 2004, p. 2). But my intention in this essay is neither to universalize nor to exoticize the (Vietnamese) cultural "other", as anthropologists have often been accused of doing (Lewis 1998; see also Schlehe 2014). Instead, I wish to contribute to deepening an understanding of the centrality and significance of spiritual gifts and material exchanges in Vietnamese ritual practice by approaching the religious gift economy of Four Palaces mediumship from a Maussian perspective. In his classic work, first published in 1924, Mauss viewed the gift as a total social phenomenon or fact that gives expression to the religious, legal, moral and economic institutions in society (see Mauss 1990). He identified three distinct obligations in the process of gift exchange: the obligation to give, the obligation to receive, and the obligation to reciprocate. Mauss also mentioned a fourth obligation—that is, the obligation of human beings to make gifts to the gods and to the persons who represent them (which, as in the example of the potlatch, may even compel the gods to give in return more than they were given). However, Mauss did not elaborate much further on the role that 'gifts to the gods' and 'gifts from the gods' play in the wider context of social relations and community building.

That is what I am attempting in this essay. In the following sections, I first review the Vietnamese concept of *lộc* and discuss its multiple meanings and manifestations. I then briefly recall some basic ideas about ritual possession in Four Palaces mediumship, before narrowing my focus down to the practice of making offerings to the Four Palaces deities and the rules and particularities of (re)distributing them as *lộc* in the course of the *hầu đồng* ritual. By way of conclusion, I argue that the intricacies of *lộc* distribution during ritual possession not only contribute to ensuring the flow of *lộc* between the human world and the supernatural realm, but also play a key role in negotiating social status and consolidating relationships within the ritual community.

2 The Vietnamese Concept of *lộc*

Whenever Vietnamese religious believers visit a shrine, temple or Buddhist pagoda in order to worship and make wishes, they present offerings to the deity (or deities) enshrined there. A basic set consists of some fruit, flowers, incense, and votive paper money. These items are carefully arranged on a little plate borrowed from the temple and then placed on the altar. When the worshipping ritual is complete, the devotees linger in the temple compound for a while and then reclaim the edible items, now transformed into *lộc*—'divine gifts' from the deities, for consumption.

The term *lộc* is a Sino-Vietnamese word that in ancient times referred to the salary of a mandarin official. This prestigious position in the imperial administration was a gateway to prestige and prosperity. *Lộc* (in Chinese: lu) is strongly connected with the terms *phúc* (fu), happiness, and *thọ* (shou), longevity, in both China and Vietnam. Taken together, this triad of concepts denotes the three attributes of a good life. Unlike a salary earned through hard work and effort, *lộc*—in the sense of a person's fate/fortune in life—is commonly regarded as granted by heaven *(lộc trời cho)*—which implies that wealth and prosperity are also seen as part of a person's fate cast down by heaven's decree. But human beings can also improve their fates, for example through self-cultivation, determination, and a virtuous lifestyle. As one ritual master *(thầy cúng)* explained to me in June 2006: 'We also have the proverb "morality wins over fate" *(đức năng thắng số)*, which means that if a person lives in a morally good way then this will conquer fate,' although women's fates are generally thought to be far more intractable and hence tougher to change than men's (Leshkowich 2006, p. 290). Furthermore, paying respect to and presenting offerings to a wide pantheon of deities and ancestors can have a positive impact on a person's destiny. According to Vietnamese belief, the latter are attentive to human needs and aspirations, and respond to worshippers' attention by bestowing upon them 'divine gifts'—that is, *lộc*.

There are two kinds of divine gifts. First, they can take the tangible shape of a talisman or lucky charm, such as a souvenir purchased during a pilgrimage to a religious site or, as mentioned earlier, a sacrificial object reclaimed after worshipping (Soucy 2006). Such an object imbued with *lộc's* potency may also be handed on to others, which is said to increase the giver's *lộc* even more. *Lộc* is thus transferable and as such part of larger social processes of care giving, reciprocal exchange, and relationship construction. Second, *lộc* may take the form of good luck in business, in achieving career goals, or in games of chance. Whatever the case, *lộc* is directed entirely towards worldly material concerns, in particular towards financial success and wealth accumulation. Wealth and prosperity are therefore also thought of as a material manifestation of divine benevolence.

Such divine benevolence may be further enhanced by proper moral conduct in the sphere of economic practice. My more recent research on social relations in the marketplace reveals that observing proper standards of commercial morality is seen by many traders as a means of securing *lộc* that can be passed on to one's offspring, whereas heaven may withdraw its favour from a trader who does not comply with the social norms and moral values that regulate trading relationships (Endres 2019, pp. 93 ff.). Material wealth, however, also obliges human beings to fulfil their ritual obligations with proper sumptuousness. An often-cited Vietnamese phrase says 'offerings depend on the financial means' *(tuỳ tiền biện lễ)*, which means that ritual expenditure depends on (and should correspond to) each person's economic means. A wealthy family who does not, for example, celebrate their lineage ancestor's death anniversary with appropriate lavishness would be looked upon as lacking filial piety and heart *(tâm)* (see Malarney 2002, Jellema 2005). Generosity in ritual spending is therefore an important part of the obligation to repay the (moral) debt one owes to ancestors and divinities.

To sum up, *lộc* may be safeguarded by moral virtue, enhanced by ritual practice, reciprocated in ritual exchange, distributed among kin, and transferred to future generations. *Lộc* is thus in constant circulation: from heaven to humans, from humans to deities and ancestors (in the form of lavish offerings), and from deities and ancestors back to humans.

3 *Hầu đ`ông* Ritual Practice

Lộc also plays an important role in Four Palaces mediumship. In post-Đổi Mới Vietnam, ritual possession associated with the worship of Mother Goddesses and their pantheon underwent an unprecedented upsurge and came to constitute a vital arena in which devotees could negotiate their identities and make sense of Vietnam's economic and social transformations under market socialism.[2] Four Palaces adherents generally perceive the world as divided into four distinct domains or palaces *(phủ)* governed by the Mother Goddesses: Heaven (Thiên Phủ), Earth (Địa Phủ), Water (Thủy Phủ), and Mountains and Forests (Nhạc Phủ). Associated with these 'palaces' is a pantheon of male and female deities ranked in a hierarchical order: Great Mandarins, Holy Ladies, Princes, Princesses, and Boy Attendants (Ngô Đức Thịnh 2006). The Four Palaces deities' legends and defining characteristics have been passed down orally through songs for the spirits

---

[2] During high socialism, the possession rituals were regarded as wasteful superstition and were thus prohibited. Starting from the mid-1990s, mediumship associated with the Mother Goddesses (Thánh Mẫu) and their pantheon was gradually reconceptualized as Mother Goddess Religion (Đạo Mẫu) or Four Palaces Religion (Đạo Tứ Phủ). The devoted efforts of Vietnamese social scientists to re-situate spirit mediumship within the category of folk belief *(tín ngưỡng dân gian)* recently culminated in the 2016 inscription of *hầu đồng* rituals on the Representative List of the Intangible Cultural Heritage of Humanity (see Lauser 2018).

known as *chầu văn* (Norton 2009). Even more importantly, they are re-enacted through ritual performance (referred to as *hầu đồng, lên đồng, hầu bóng*, or *hầu thánh*).

Like in many other possession religions, a person's calling into mediumship often becomes apparent in a critical period of life. A health condition that does not respond to medical treatment, a run of poor luck in business or personal matters, or haunting dreams may indicate that a person might be destined to enlist in the spirits' service. In this respect it is important to note that it is not a person's free decision to do so, but a matter of her or his fate, or more specifically, their 'spirit root' *(căn)* (Nguyễn Thị Hiền 2007). This spirit root is perceived as dating back to a previous life and usually implies the idea of a debt owed to one or several deities of the pantheon. This debt needs to be repaid by serving the spirits in this life and becoming a medium. As a minimum requirement, a medium has to hold one *hầu đồng* ritual per year. In principle, any medium with at least ten years of ritual practice, appropriate knowledge, and a private temple may call themselves *đồng thầy* (master). A lay practitioner who has completed the initiation ritual is referred to as a child of the spirits *(con nhà thánh)* and a master's follower or disciple *(con nhang đệ tử)*. Because the objective of a *hầu đồng* ritual is essentially self-therapeutic, lay practitioners are responsible for any expenditure associated with the ritual performances.

Most Four Palaces deities have a primary temple as well as several secondary temples. On many different occasions throughout the year, *hầu đồng* rituals are held at such temples as well as at private shrines. For each deity the medium plans to 'serve' (which is the literal meaning of *hầu*) during the ritual, offerings *(đồ lễ)* need to be prepared in sufficient quantity so that every ritual participant can receive a share during *lộc* distribution. The ritual performance usually unfolds with the embodiment of the Five Great Mandarins, followed by a variable number of Holy Ladies, Princes, Princesses, and Boy Attendants. When the medium senses a divine presence, he or she gives a signal indicating the deity's identity and throws off their crimson head scarf. The ritual assistants sitting to the left and right then change the medium into the appropriate attire. When the costume is complete, the medium gets up, bows respectfully in front of the altar and proceeds to perform a short ritual dance that reflects the deity's rank, gender, and personality. After the dance the medium sits down again and drinks a few sips of rice wine or water from a small cup. Male deities smoke cigarettes while listening to the music and reward the musicians with small sums of money. The deity then 'acknowledges' *(chứng)* the offerings by waving a lit stick of incense over them and allocates shares to the participants, a practice called *phát lộc*. During this phase, participants may also approach the deity embodied in the medium with a specific request for which they beg the deity's special favour *(xin lộc)*, such as a cup of 'incense water' infused with healing qualities, or a prediction (and counsel) about a specific issue in life. Finally, the medium signals the deity's departure by covering their head again with the crimson scarf, whereupon the musicians start inviting the next deity to mount the medium.

By offering flowers, votive paper objects, food offerings and divine entertainment, Four Palaces mediums repay their karmic debt and ask the deities to be benevolent to them. The deities respond to that attention by bestowing good fortune, health and prosperity as well as divine gifts *(lộc)*. Four Palaces mediumship may thus be conceived of as a gift exchange between deities and humans, with both parties engaged in cycles of giving, receiving, and repaying each other. However, in reality it is a bit more complicated than that. First of all, the deities do not physically take the offerings to their realm; they are instead redistributed to the ritual participants and taken home for consumption. The redistributive nature of gifts to deities thus reveals the existence of a different type of gifting relationship. In reciprocal gifting in the Maussian sense, the giver expects delayed reciprocity from the receiver. It is a dyadic relationship between the two parties only. In contrast, in the religious gift economy of the Four Palaces, the gift, although dedicated to a deity, is ultimately presented to another human. Yet something important is missing in this picture, namely that the gifts have been transformed through the ritual act of first offering them to the deities, as they are now no longer just a simple gift, but a divine gift, that is, *lộc*. One could perhaps argue that the medium actually represents the deity, which would render the medium-as-human irrelevant in this exchange. But as I shall discuss below, this is not the case.

4 The Art of Distributing *lộc*

Let me now elaborate a bit further on the practice of making offerings to the Four Palaces deities and (re)distributing them as *lộc*. First of all, before the start of the ritual, each participant is expected to hand an envelope with a monetary contribution to the medium. Mrs. Thiền, the woman mentioned in the introductory vignette, taught me the words to use when handing over the money envelope: 'Here is a tiny bit to ask for the deities' blessings *(đây là một ly một lai để xin lộc thánh).*' These contributions in no way cover the costs of the ritual, but, like at weddings and funerals, they are important for the consolidation of the relationship between host and invitees (Soucy 2014). Second, the (re)distribution of the offerings (as *lộc*) in Four Palaces mediumship follows a number of rules according to the hierarchical order within the ritual community and the hierarchy of functions or roles during the ritual.

The basic rules are as follows: First of all, the temple owner or caretaker *(đồng đền),* the ritual master *(thầy cúng,* a specialist who performs the necessary ritual acts preceding a *hầu đồng*), the musicians, the assistants, the kitchen staff in charge of preparing the festive meal *(cỗ)* that is shared communally after the ritual, and the 'deity's chair', that is the performing medium, all receive their due shares. To do so, the medium usually places the offerings on a little plate and hands it to one of the ritual assistants, who then takes the offerings and puts them into a cardboard box prepared for the recipients. Next, the medium allocates special shares to individual participants by pointing to the recipient who then has to come forward to receive the 'divine gift' (often accompanied by an extra) directly from the deity's hands (see Fig. 1). But, as Mrs. Thiền explained, the sequence to be observed during *phát lộc* is not a matter of sympathy or dislike. The performing medium first has to look around to see if there are any other master mediums *(đồng thầy)* or temple owners/caretakers who need to be addressed. Next, he or she must address other fellow mediums in the group, the oldest first, then down to the younger ones. Here it is important to note that it is not the actual age of the medium that counts, but the number of years that person has been a practicing medium. For example, if there is a woman who has been a medium for ten years, she needs to be addressed before a woman who has been a medium for only seven years. Moreover, the general social norms related to age are overruled by the distinction between mediums and non-mediums, which means that younger mediums in the group need to be addressed before older non-mediums among the ritual participants.

Next, the performing medium has to make sure that each of the remaining participants receives fair treatment. This means that the medium also has to consider how much each of the participants has contributed to the ritual. As mentioned above, the monetary contribution to the costs of the ritual is usually handed to the medium in an envelope before the start of the ritual. The amount is specified by each group and averaged 100,000 đồng in 2006 (approximately four euros). Some groups have imposed their own rules, for example that half of the amount presented in the envelope has to be returned to the invitee in the course of the entire ritual. This is easy if everyone sticks to the 100,000 đồng rule, as the medium can then in advance prepare small red lucky money envelopes with 50,000 đồng notes. If, however, a participant contributes more than the expected amount, then the medium has to keep track of how much he or she owes to each participant. The distribution of offerings is therefore a complicated matter that constitutes an important mechanism of building and consolidating relationships

Fig. 1 A medium allocates *lộc*. (Photo by author; Hanoi, February 2006)

between the performing medium and his or her invitees: friends, relatives, fellow mediums, followers (if the performer is a master medium), or between a follower and his or her master.

The same is true for the part of the ritual during which individual participants may approach the deity directly with a particular request. This practice is called *xin lộc,* asking for blessed gifts, and involves a direct exchange transaction between petitioner and deity. The petitioner kneels down beside the deity, politely presents some money bills spread out on a plate and puts forward his or her request in polite, ritualized speech. The deity (embodied in the medium) receives the plate, 'acknowledges' the offerings, then takes some of the bills away and puts in some smaller denominations, plus maybe a little extra back, such as a flower, a phoenix-shaped areca nut, or a cigarette. Sometimes, the petitioner receives a little bit more than he or she offered, but usually it is less. When these special treats have been passed out, the medium signals with a quick hand gesture that the remaining offerings may now be distributed communally. This task is taken over by one or two helpers who have to ensure that everyone present receives an item. If the offerings in kind are not sufficient, they must be replaced by the approximate equivalent in cash. Whereas the gifts received directly from the hands of the medium are the most prized and usually not shared with—or distributed further to—other people, the gifts received during the final redistribution phase may even enhance the *lộc* of the recipient if he or she passes it on to other people outside the ritual community.

More than anything else, the amount and quality of redistributed offerings—and, for that matter, the number of guests invited—in the course of a *hầu đồng* ritual are an index of a medium's prosperity and prestige. As objects that convey a sense of beauty and luxury, they are employed both to contribute to the overall sumptuousness and aesthetics of the ritual and to effectively assert a claim to a certain social status. They are thus instrumental in the 'strategies of distinction' (Bourdieu 1984) that wealthy mediums use to differentiate themselves from less affluent practitioners. Moving from the altars of the deities into the plastic bags of the ritual participants (see Fig. 2), the offerings take on a social life of their own (Appadurai 1986). They are scrutinized and commented upon, praised for their quality or sneered at for their cheapness and used as measures to set new or enhanced standards for the ritual community.

The socio-economic transformations that mark Vietnam's post-*Đổi Mới* era, along with its growing abundance of new and attractive consumer goods, have prompted an explosion of ritual expenditure and have significantly changed both the range and the number of sacrificial offerings in urban Four Palaces mediumship. According to contemporary ritual aesthetics, these items must, above all, have appealing packaging that matches the colour of the deity's costume. This new sense of ritual aesthetics makes the silvery cans of Diet Coke or Halida Beer a suitable offering for the Third Mandarin and the Third Prince associated with the Water Palace, whereas blue cans of Pepsi or Tiger Beer may be used as offerings for the Fifth Mandarin or the Seventh Prince. Colourful packets of instant noodle soup or biscuits are presented to several of the Lady and Princess deities. The Third Princess, dressed in white, may be offered bags of Ajino Moto (MSG) and sugar, or small boxes of milk. Non-processed goods such as areca nuts, fresh fruit such as mangos, apples, oranges, star fruit, and so on are frequently presented to ethnic female deities associated with the 'natural' environment of the Mountains and Forests. While some Four Palaces mediums dismiss modern consumer goods as being contrary to tradition, others point to the practical side of sacrificial practice: 'We have to choose tasty things as offerings,' a male master medium told me, 'things that can be taken home for consumption instead of being given away to outsiders' (conversation with author, 24 March 2005).

Fig. 2 *Lộc* taken home for consumption after a *hầu đồng* ritual. (Photo by author; Hanoi, February 2006)

Whether an object is considered valuable (in terms of utility or good taste) or trifling, the offerings distributed during a *hầu đồng* are intensely coveted must-haves even if the receiver will give them to their needy neighbours as soon as she returns home. As one master explained, this is because 'the jealousy of husband and wife cannot compare with the jealousy of mediums' *(ghen vợ ghen chồng không bằng ghen đồng ghen bóng)*. It is therefore imperative that a medium always prepares enough offerings to ensure that none of the ritual participants are left empty-handed (see Fig. 2).

All these elements of ritual transaction—who receives *lộc* directly from the hands of the deity, how many extras are given and to whom, how much is taken from the plate of the petitioner, how much is given back—are matters of close scrutiny, debate and gossip. Among the various skills that are required of an adept medium, the 'art of distributing *lộc*' *(nghệ thuật phát lộc)* is crucial to ritual mastery, and the act of distributing the offerings as blessed gifts among the devotees requires social and interpersonal competences that reach far beyond a lavish display of wealth and generosity. The complexity of ritual performance puts young and unskilled mediums under a lot of stress. On the one hand, they are expected to focus their hearts and minds on the deities in order to perform them into being. On the other hand, they must remember all of these social rules and keep track of the offerings and monetary matters in ritual exchange. Some mediums even complained to me that the issue of distributing blessed gifts has recently gained too much prominence, making it more difficult for a medium to concentrate on the *hầu đồng* ritual's spiritual aspects.

Some mediums therefore try to lessen the emphasis on *lộc* distribution. They may choose to prepare fewer offerings (i.e. not for each and every deity) or summon fewer devotees forward for individual blessings, both of which also save time. To keep participants from rummaging through their plastic bags and fussing over their *lộc* instead of focusing on the ritual performance, some mediums have started to spatially separate *lộc* distribution from the ritual 'stage' by having the plastic bags filled 'offstage' and handing each participant their share on their way out. Nevertheless, for the vast majority of Four Palaces adherents, the offerings remain their most important concern, as they are their primary 'investment' in the supernatural realm that earns them 'interest' in the human world—both in the sense that the deities are expected to reward them with *lộc* and bestow well-being and prosperity upon them, as well as in the sense that the distribution of offerings reinforces their bonds with other humans.

5   Conclusion

My discussion started out from the concept of *lộc,* a term that, taken in its abstract sense, refers to fate/fortune and prosperity and in a more concrete sense to an object that has, by way of ritual transformation, been imbued with the potency of the supernatural realm to bring wealth and good fortune to its receiver. This transformation happens through the act of making an offering to a deity. I have conceived of *lộc* as a gift and as Mauss and others have pointed out, gifts consolidate relations through understandings of obligatory reciprocation. In this light, as Alexander Soucy has cogently argued, *lộc* 'can be understood as a material representation of the bond between two agents, supernatural or otherwise' (2006, p. 115).

Exchange relations between the earthly world and its divine counterpart, the otherworld, have always been central elements of Vietnamese religious belief and ritual practice (Taylor 2004, p. 225). The supernatural realm is imagined as a reflection of the human world *('dương sao, âm vậy'),* which is why their inhabitants are thought of as having the same needs and desires as mortals. Transactional sacrificial practices are therefore understood as a constitutive part of the reciprocal relationship between people, ancestors, and deities that keeps the flow of wealth and prosperity in constant motion.

On a more mundane level, *lộc* also has important social functions: it generates obligations, strengthens the emotional bonds of relationships, and may elevate, yet also challenge, a person's status within the ritual community. In Four Palaces mediumship, sumptuous offerings expressing a medium's fate/fortune and wealth are presented to the many deities of the pantheon, reciprocated as divine gifts and redistributed among the ritual participants as potent tokens of the deities' benevolence. Mediums engaged in market activities, for example, often feel that they receive *lộc* in terms of increased business profits as a direct consequence of their ritual service to the deities. This, however, also seems to increase the pressure to spend more lavishly on rituals in order to secure the deities' unremitting benevolence. Many see this trend with critical eyes. Moreover, it is felt that lavish displays of ritual generosity are increasingly motivated by a desire to compete with other mediums in organizing ever more sumptuous *hầu đồng* rituals. Ritual ostentation and status competition among mediums were therefore at the heart of the debates regarding the commodification and commercialization of Four Palaces mediumship during my research in the early 2000s. The question of whether these trends show signs of intensification or decline in the current volatile economic climate would undoubtedly be an interesting starting point for further research into the vibrant and complex world of Four Palaces mediumship in contemporary urban Vietnam.

References

Appadurai, A., Ed. 1986. *The social life of things. Commodities in cultural perspective.* Cambridge, UK: Cambridge University Press.

Bourdieu, P. 1984. *Distinction. A social critique of the judgment of taste.* Cambridge, MA: Harvard University Press.

Endres, K.W. 2011. *Performing the divine. Mediums, markets and modernity in urban Vietnam.* Copenhagen: NIAS Press.

Endres, K. 2019. *Market frictions. Trade and urbanization at the Vietnam-China border.* New York: Berghahn.

Jellema, K. 2005. Making good on debt. The remoralisation of wealth in post-revolutionary Vietnam. *The Asia Pacific Journal of Anthropology* 6(3): 231–248.

Lauser, A. 2018. *Staging the spirits. Lên Đồng – cult – culture – spectacle. Performative contexts of a Vietnamese ritual from controlled possession to staged performance.* GISCA Occasional Papers No. 20. Göttingen: Institute for Social and Cultural Anthropology.

Leshkowich, A. M. 2006. Woman, Buddhist, Entrepreneur. Gender, moral values, and class anxiety in late socialist Vietnam. *Journal of Vietnamese Studies* 1: 277–313.

Lewis, H. S. 1998. The misrepresentation of anthropology and its consequences. *American Anthropologist* 100(3): 716–31.

Malarney, S. K. 2002. *Culture, ritual and revolution in Vietnam.* London: RoutledgeCurzon.

Mauss, M. 1990. *The gift. The form and reason for exchange in archaic societies.* New York, London: W. W. Norton.

Ngô, Đức T. 2006. The mother goddess religion. Its history, pantheon, and practices. In *Possessed by the spirits. Mediumship in contemporary Vietnamese communities,* Eds. K. Fjelstad and T.H. Nguyen, 19–30. Ithaca, New York: Cornell University Press.

Nguyễn, T. H 2007. 'Seats for the spirits to sit upon'. Becoming a spirit medium in contemporary Vietnam. *Journal of Southeast Asian Studies* 38: 541–558.

Norton, B. 2009. *Songs for the spirits. Music and mediums in modern Vietnam.* Urbana and Chicago: University of Illinois Press.

Osborne, R. 2004. Hoards, votives, offerings. The archaeology of the dedicated object. *World Archaeology* 36(1): 1–10.

Schlehe, J. 2014. Translating traditions and transcendence. Popularised religiosity and the paranormal practitioners' position in Indonesia. In *Religion, Tradition and the Popular,* Eds. J. Schlehe and E. Sandkühler, 185–201. Bielefeld: Transcript.

Soucy, A. 2006. Consuming *loc* – creating *on*. Women, offerings and symbolic capital in Northern Vietnam. *Studies in Religion/Sciences Religieuses* 35(1): 107–131.

Soucy, A. 2014. Wedding invitations and relationship management in Hanoi. *The Asia Pacific Journal of Anthropology* 15(2): 141–157.

Taylor, P. 2004. *Goddess on the rise. Pilgrimage and popular religion in Vietnam.* Honolulu: University of Hawaii Press.

Personal Encounters and Productive Engagement: A Vignette from the Continuing Effort at Understanding Rotenese Spiritual Representations

James J. Fox

1   Introduction

Ethnography has always been a science of special encounters. The often-used designation of the 'key informant' cited in ethnographic monographs has repeatedly pointed to these crucial relationships. In my own case, I have relied on a marvellous assortment of remarkable individuals in the course of my fieldwork since 1965 among the Rotenese of eastern Indonesia. I have described many of these personal encounters in different contexts. These remarkable individuals include Stefanus Adulanu, the Head of the Earth in Termanu, who told me that he was kept up at night wondering at why I had come to Rote and who became my ritual language teacher and confidant during most of my first fieldwork; Guru

---

Dedication: I am delighted to be able to contribute this vignette to honour Judith Schlehe whom I first met when she was at the beginning of her field research in Java. Throughout her career, Judith has contributed substantially to our understanding of Indonesia and of Java in particular. The character of her research based on decades of remarkable personal engagements with those whom she has encountered brims with insights into the complexity of representations that she has gained from her close involvement with her subjects. Among many exemplary papers, I would cite some of Judith's recent papers on Javanese conceptions of the self (Schlehe 2013, 2017, 2019), all of which reflect changes in Javanese traditions that she has documented in her research.

J. J. Fox (✉)
Red Hill, Australia
E-Mail: james.fox@anu.edu.au

N. D. Pah whose first question to me when I visited him in the domain of Thie (Ti) was why I had taken so long to search him out; Esau Pono, my Rotenese 'elder brother' and close colleague of many decades who twice visited Canberra to assist in translating filmed materials and other field documents; Peu Malesi who attached himself to me as my personal poet master and was always willing to guide a ritual for me; and Mias Kiuk, my Rotenese 'father' who offered me and my wife accommodation and sustenance at Ufa Len and set up a still to produce the lontar gin which drew a steady stream of local 'informants' to his house for daily discussions. All of these individuals and many more were personal friends and fundamental to my research.

In this paper, I want to focus on another remarkable individual, Hendrik Foeh from the domain of Oenale whom I met on Bali as one of the participants in my Master Poets Project. Although I admit that my acquaintance with him has been limited and I have never spent time with him on Rote, I regard him as an engaging individual, a talented poet and an innovative figure in the Rotenese tradition of oral composition. This paper will focus on him and on one of the products of his creative ability.

2 The Master Poets Project

The Master Poets Project was begun in 2006 as a research effort to record, transcribe, translate and eventually archive the ritual language compositions of leading oral poets from different dialect areas of the island of Rote. For decades, I had concentrated my study of ritual language on two domains of the island: the central domain of Termanu (or Pada) and the southwestern domain of Thie (Ti). In contemplating my forthcoming retirement, I had decided to try and understand ritual language recitation across the length of the island. Given that the languages of Rote form a dialect chain consisting in a number of related languages spoken in eighteen historical distinct polities (nusak: 'domain'), my two-domain perspective on an island-wide tradition was, I felt, too limited a view of complex linguistic practices.

Rotenese ritual language is a form of elevated poetic speech whose primary distinguishing feature is its strict and pervasive canonical parallelism. This canonical parallelism requires the pairing of all words—nouns, verbs and adverbials—in oral compositions. Many of the formal lexical pairs used in ritual language rely on distinct synonymous terms drawn from the chain of dialects that make up its related languages.

To achieve my goal, I decided to invite noted Rotenese poets from different dialect areas to the island of Bali for a succession of intensive recording sessions. Removed from restriction on recitation common on Rote and in a group to themselves I was confident that the poets would perform brilliantly and enthusiastically. It would be a learning experience for them as well as for me. This proved to be the case.

I travelled to Rote to gather my first group of just four poets: three from the domain of Termanu, Esau Pono, Joel Pellondou and Zet Apulugi and one noted poet, Ande Ruy, from the eastern domain of Ringgou whom I sought out and persuaded to join the group on Bali. We were joined by Dr Tom Therik, a former student of mine.

This 1st recording session went well and set the pattern for the ten subsequent sessions that followed. All our gatherings on Bali were lively affairs with occasional drumming and a great deal of *sesandu*-playing. At times poets would vie with each other in their performances but there was also among most participants, a keen interest in what other poets knew and how they performed. The number of poets at each session increased and many 'master poets' joined the group for several sessions, especially as recordings increased. Besides recording new recitations, a part of each subsequent session was spent in going over previous recordings, transcriptions and translations.

From the outset and for all subsequent sessions, Ande Ruy took the lead in seeking out new poets from different domains. His judgement of a poet's ability, knowledge and fluency were crucial in finding the best poets on Rote. By the time of our fourth year's recording session, we were joined by Dr Lintje Pellu, another of my former students, who knew Ande well and provided the arrangements for travel to Bali. Ande took part in all our recording sessions and invariably briefed new poets on what to expect.

It was for our 5th recording session, in October 2009, that Ande was able to recruit Hendrik Foeh from the domain of Oenale at the far western end of Rote. Hendrik presented himself differently from most Rotenese poets whom I had met. Most Rotenese poets are outgoing. As the custodians of traditional knowledge, they tend to expect a degree of social recognition and generally seek to display their special knowledge. They are performers, sometimes exuberant performers and speaking is their forte. By contrast, certainly among the eight other poets that had come with him to Bali from the domains of Ringgou, Bilba, Termanu, Korbaffo and Dengka, Hendrik was quiet, soft-spoken, almost self-effacing. His recitations, however, were beautiful and remarkable. What was remarkable was the compression of most of his recitations: each was clear and succinct but only offered a relative minimum of lines, far fewer than other poets generally provide.

In Rotenese (or more specifically in Termanu), there are recognized short poems *(bini keke'uk)* which may be drawn from longer recitations. In fact, however, there is no limit on how long (or short) a poem *(bini)* may be. In a ritual setting, a recitation can be extended to fit the situation. For example, a death chant *(bini mamates),* which recounts the formulaic life-course for the deceased and may be accompanied by circle dancing, would formerly continue for hours, slowly, steadily with the elaboration, alteration and repetition of lines.

When I spoke to him on his own, Hendrik was articulate in providing exegesis (in Indonesian) on his poems—in contrast to some poets—indeed some of the most fluent master poets –whose only comments on their recitations consist of further related recitation.

I was so impressed by the quality of Hendrik's recitations that I tried to invite him to rejoin the group in the following year. He declined this invitation because of family commitments but he was able to join the group again for our 7th recording session in October 2011 at which he recited a beautiful version of a poem well-known throughout Rote, *Suti Solo ma Bina Bane* (in the Oenale version: *Suti Sai ma Bina Liu:* 'Suti from the Sea and Bina from the Ocean' see Fox 2016: pp. 377–387). He also joined the group again at our 10th recording session in June 2017 at which time we had some of our best discussions.

3 The Rotenese Botanic Idiom and the Representation of Social Life

To understand this recitation requires crucial cultural explication. This recitation could possibly be adapted as a death chant *(bini mamates),* but its emphasis on renewal makes it similar to a variety of poems of regeneration that can be used in possible lifecycle rituals (see Fox 2014, pp. 138–141). The recitation is cast in a botanic idiom since many critical Rotenese rituals of the life cycle rely on this idiom. The idiom draws direct comparison of human life with the processes of the growth of different plants that are formulaically designated as specific human icons. Although similar botanic idioms are common among Austronesian-speaking populations, among the Rotenese, this idiom is pervasive and explicit (see Fox 1971).

Society (or a particular community) can be compared with an intact forest whose rubbing and scraping branches constitute the interaction of its members. This is the metaphoric basis that underlies Hendrik's recitation. Like most Rotenese traditional poetic statements, this recitation carries a moral message: that the creatures who are the progeny of the forest support its survival and integrity.

In Rotenese social parlance, the mother's brother, who is the representative of the life-giving wife-givers, is considered a person's *to'o-huk:* 'trunk mother's brother or mother's brother of origin' (Fox 1971). The idea of a 'trunk' implies an 'origin' and derivation from this base. One's progeny (in this context: *ana/boa*) are one's living successors. Their support maintains the continuity of life.

As a poetic composition in canonical parallelism, the fifty lines of this recitation rely on exactly twenty-seven dyadic sets. Most lines are paired but interspersed among them are several single lines comprised of double sets. (Line 3 is an 'orphan' line which Hendrik introduces prematurely and then discontinues, only to take it up again in line 8.)[1]

Pua Rulis//No Sanggu
Hendrik Feoh

1. Ina leo Pua Rulis	A mother like Cyclone Areca
2. Te'o leo No Sanggu.	An aunt like Storm Coconut
3. Ruli fo'a ma sain rala...	A cyclone wakes the sea...
4. Ara bebengga lasi okan	They speak of the forest's roots
5. Boe ma ara fafade nura hun,	They tell of the wood's trunks,.
6. Lasi nenci tetende	A well-tended forest
7. Ma nura nendi hahandek.	And a well-watched over wood.
8. Sanggu ana fo'a ma liun	A storm wakes the ocean
9. Ma ruli ana fela ma sain	A cyclone strikes the sea
10. Ana heheli lasi okan	It aims at the forest's roots
11. Ma ana alae nura hun.	And it targets the wood's trunks.
12. Ana kali su'u nura hun	It tears at the wood's trunks
13. Ma ana te'a foi lasi okan.	And it pulls at the forest's roots.
14. Lasi mana bonggi sio	The forest that gives birth ninefold
15. Ma nura mana rae falu,	And the wood that brings forth eightfold,
16. Nura anan nara no'uk	The wood's numerous progeny
17. Lasi anar nara heta	The forest's many progeny
18. Ana mba'a feo lasi okan	Set a wall around the forest roots
19. Ma ana latu eko nura hun.	And set a ring round the wood's trunks.
20. Sanggu ana kali su'u	The storm tears fiercely
21. Te nura ta nata-nggengge	But the wood does not tremble

---

[1] I have discussed Rotenese poetic performance art in various publications (see Fox 2014; 2016 and in specific detail, Fox 2022).

22. Ma lasi ta naka-riti.	And the forest does not waver.
23. Ona ana boe-boe fe'a foi	Ever harder it pulls and lifts.
24. Ana nda keko ma nda lali	It moves and shifts
25. Ana boe-boe kali su'u.	It tears ever more fiercely.
26. Fai esa ma ledo esa	On that day and at that time
27. Nura hun neu seri	The wood's trunks begin to totter
28. Ma lasi okan neu rae.	And the forest's roots begin to loosen.
29. Nura anan nara nouk	The wood's numerous progeny
30. Ma lasi boan nara hetar	The forest's many creatures
31. Manu lasi, lasi anan	Forest hens, the forest's child
32. Kuku nura, nura boan	The wood's cuckoos, the wood's creature
33. Ara lutu eko lasi oka	Set a ring round the forest's roots
34. Ma mba'a feo nura hun,	And set a wall round the wood's trunks.
35. Nura hun neu rae	The wood's roots begin to loosen
36. Lasi okan neu seri.	The forest's trunks begin to totter.
37. Mbilas mengge-mea lasi	The red snake of the forest
38. Fo lasi boan	A creature of the forest
39. Modo kai-sao nura	The green snake of the wood
40. Fo nura anan-na	Progeny of the wood
41. Ana huru here lasi dale	Binds tightly in the depths of the forest
42. Ma ana tengga here nura dale.	And grasps tightly in the depths of the wood.
43. Nura foi neu hun	The wood lifts its trunks
44. Ma lasi foi neu okan.	And the forest lifts its roots.
45. Tehu ana ta nata-nggengge	It no longer trembles
46. Ma ana ta nata-riti.	And it no longer wavers.
47. Ana nda hara dois-sa	It suffers greatly
48. Ma ana nda kurudo-sa.	And endures painfully.
49. Huna, ana nara no'uk	Because its progeny are many
50. Ma boan nara heta.	And its creatures are numerous.

Cyclones are a recurrent feature of life on Rote and the historical record attests to severe damage that has occurred, at intervals, on the island. Cyclones, represented as the anger and fury of the sea, feature regularly in ritual language recitations. Some of the opening lines in Hendrik's recitation, *Suti Sai ma Bina Liu*: 'Suti from the Sea and Bina from the Ocean' (Fox 2016, p. 378 ff.) alludes to this fearsome anger of the sea:

> Te sanggu sai na eda   Then a storm arises in the sea
> Ma tuli liun na eno…   And a cyclone makes its way in the ocean…

Given his succinctness, Hendrik only alludes to this anger. Other versions of this same chant make more explicit the heavenly origin of this cyclonic storm.[2] Thus, for example, a version of this chant from the domain of Termanu sets out the details of the episode that occurs at a feast in the depths of the Sea at which visitors from the Heavens are shamed, thus causing the Heavens to erupt in anger (Fox 2016: p. 33 ff.):

> Lain manakoasa   The Heavens who have power
> Ma Poin manakila.   The Heights who see overall.
> Boe ma Lain nggenggele   The Heavens rage
> Ma Poin namanasa.   And Heights grow angry.
> De sangu nala liun dale   A storm strikes the ocean's depths
> Ma luli nala sain dale.   A cyclone strikes the sea's depths.

It is worth noting that this poem, in its concision, offers a template for many possible ritual usages. Its first two lines refer to 'Cyclone Areca' and 'Storm Coconut'. Since the areca and coconut palms *(pua//no)* are female icons, these two lines suggest the possibility of its use in a ritual involving a woman. Other usages are open to speculation. On Rote today, however, there are fewer such ritual occasions because Christian rituals predominate and limit the use of traditional modes of performance. Poems like those offered by Hendrik Foeh and by other master poets are recitations without ritual context. They display traditional knowledge and are still acknowledged as 'words of the ancestors.' They are regarded as revealing knowledge of the past but are no longer needed for the life-giving rituals of the life cycle.

---

[2] According to Rotenese narrative traditions, the Heavens and Seas are in intimate contact with one another. The Sun and Moon rule the Heavens while Shark and Crocodile rule the Seas.

4 Postscript

On the 3rd and 4th of April 2021, a severe tropical cyclone struck Kupang at the western tip of Timor and went on to devastate parts of the island of Rote. Named *Seroja,* this cyclone was one in an historical pattern of recurrent cyclone activity in the region. Preparedness, however, was limited and this led to local efforts to improve awareness of such cyclones.

As a contribution to these efforts, I sent a copy of Hendrik Foeh's *Pua Rulis//No Sanggu* with my translation to a couple of Rotenese graduates of the ANU based in Kupang who were able to use the poem as an example of 'traditional local knowledge' in a campaign to raise awareness and prepare for similar disasters in the future. In an internet-connected postcolonial world, Hendrik's composition could thus be communicated more widely and was able to take on new significance. It offers a message of resilience and recovery from the destruction of cyclones.

References

Fox, J.J. 1971. Sister's child as plant: metaphors in an idiom of consanguinity. In *Rethinking kinship and marriage,* Eds. R. Needham, 219–52. London: Tavistock.

Fox, J.J. 1996. The Austronesian botanic idiom. In *Plants. Indonesian heritage encyclopedia vol. 4,* Eds. T. Whitten and J. Whitten, 66–67. Singapore: Archipelago Press.

Fox, J.J. 2014. *Explorations in semantic parallelism.* Canberra: Australian National University Press.

Fox, J.J. 2016. *Master poets, ritual masters. The art of oral composition among the Rotenese of Eastern Indonesia.* Canberra: Australian National University Press.

Fox, J.J. 2022. Form and formulae in Rotenese oral poetry. In *Weathered words,* 221–242. Eds. Frog and W. Lamb. Cambridge: Harvard University Press.

Schlehe, J. 2013. Concepts of Asia, the West and the Self in contemporary Indonesia. An anthropological account. *South East Asia Research* 21(3): 497–515.

Schlehe, J. 2017. Contesting Javanese traditions. The popularisation of rituals between religion and tourism. *Indonesia and the Malay World* 45(131): 3–23.

Schlehe, J. 2019. Cosmopolitanism, pluralism and self-orientalisation in the modern mystical world of Java. *Asian Journal of Social Science* 47: 364–386.

Regulation of Muslim Marriage in Indonesia: Political Challenges Across the Public/Private Divide

Kathryn Robinson

1 Introduction

The regulation of marriage—in particular women's marital rights—has been a key focus of political contention for Indonesian women activists since the colonial period (the Netherlands East Indies). Demands for a secular marriage law that would ensure women's rights emerged in Indonesia at the turn of the twentieth century, alongside other turn-of-the-century constructs—ideas that emerged out of the French Revolution, such as egalitarianism and individual rights. Such discourses spread in Europe alongside nationalism as political ideals (Williams 1983, pp. 1–8, 164, 218). Central to marriage debates in what is now the Republic of Indonesia, have been arguments about religion and law; whether the regulation and legitimation of marriage should be a matter for the state and forms of secular deliberation or whether its management should reside with religious authorities using modes of Islamic reasoning based in the *fikhi* (Islamic jurisprudence; Islamic norms influencing everyday life) (Millie 2017). How have these debates emerged; how are they impacted by changing forms of public discourse associated with regime changes; and what have been their real-world consequences in relation to women's political and civic rights?

Marriage (the English term and its translations) appears to be a readily understood construct, deployed in everyday discourse—but this 'label' encompasses a wide range of personal, social, cultural, political and religious understandings. The terms for 'marriage' 'in an English–Indonesian dictionary' are *perkawinan*,

K. Robinson (✉)
College of Asia and the Pacific, Australian National University, Canberra, Australien
E-Mail: kathryn.robinson@anu.edu.au

which has connotations of heterosexual coupling, and *pernikahan* for which the root word is *nikah,* the marriage contract (Echolls and Shadily 1976, p. 373). The cosmopolitan spread of enlightenment ideals of individual rights and marriage as the outcome of a romantic attachment between two individuals has resulted in marriage becoming 'a *zone* of cultural debate, an arena where other types, forms and domains of culture are encountering, interrogating and contesting each other in new and unexpected ways' (Appadurai and Breckenridge 1988, p. 6)

Across the Indonesian Archipelago, customary forms of the institution that we recognise or acknowledge as 'marriage' are varied, constituent of differing forms of gendered power (Robinson 2009a). Further, the Indonesian history recounted here illustrates that rights in marriage, and debates and struggles over such rights, are key elements of gender contention, as well as essential to the exercise of gendered power and the construction of gendered subjects. In the case of Indonesia, secular women's groups have demanded that the state extend its reach into family relationships; in particular that the gender-discriminatory provisions of Islamic family law be replaced by secular, state regulations that reflect a modern sensibility of gender equity (Robinson 2006).

Judith Schlehe and Jürgen Rüland organised a path-breaking symposium on reconciling research approaches in the social sciences and area studies (Southeast Asia). This 2012 meeting occasioned vigorous and sometimes fiery discussion between practitioners of different social science disciplines concerning ways of knowing, forms of evidence and modes of research for Southeast Asian Studies. My own contribution to the symposium and the resulting volume (Robinson 2014) argued for the application of a gender relations approach in understanding gendered power and women's lives in Southeast Asia. The structural analysis offered by a gender relations approach is productive in revealing the specific forms of gendered power in the diverse societies of Southeast Asia: Gender relations are imbricated in the exercise of power in all social relations: in institutional structures of politics and economics, in symbolism and ideology, and in the formation of social attachments (Robinson 2014, p. 107).

Leading gender relations scholar R. W. Connell states: "Gender is the structure of social relations that centers on the reproductive arena [i.e. sexual reproduction] and the set of practices [...] that bring reproductive distinctions between bodies into social processes" (2002, p. 10).

I deploy this approach in this chapter. The forms of social relations grouped under the term 'marriage' are quintessentially about managing reproduction (both biological and social). 'The reproductive arena is not fixed, it can be re-shaped by social processes. Indeed it is constantly being reshaped' (Connell 2002, p. 52).

In Indonesia, as in many places, the institution of 'marriage' is central to social reproduction and in particular the reproduction of gender relations.

The organisation and regulation of marriage is a facet of the societal execution of power. It is no accident or mystery that political demands for marriage reform have been at the heart of the Indonesian women's movement since the early twentieth century. The kinds of reforms sought have been in step with institutional arrangements for the exercise of power (from colony to nation); shifts in forms of political rule (between democracy and authoritarianism); and accompanying swings in political ideologies (such as secular and religious). Relations between men and women, most notably reproduced in the institutional arrangements around marriage, are quintessentially part of these power shifts (Robinson 2009a). As a critical site of reproduction of gender relations, scrutinising marriage is central to understanding gender contestation in relation to the power of the modern state.

2   Marriage: Private Worlds and Publics

In the modern world, marriage is a key institution of personal/private life. But in its contemporary forms it is most usually enacted under terms and conditions regulated by states. Marriage has become a bridge between the 'private' spaces of family/personal life and the public (political) world. Formally regulated institution(s) of marriage prescribe ways of relating personal life to the public sphere by determining who can marry or divorce; who has rights over children and property; and who benefits from the welfare state and tax entitlements. These and similar aspects relate to marital status and household composition. In Indonesia, for example, the 1974 Marriage Law formally established men as household heads (Robinson 2006).

The institutions and constituent practices recognised as 'marriage' in both customary and formal legal spheres show differences across societies and nations and are constituent of differing forms of gendered power. Nonetheless, marriage has been 'naturalised,' afforded ontological status, in public debate about rights, responsibilities and relationships. This was made very evident in the last decades on a global level in public debate, often contentious, about legalising same-sex marriage. For example, Australian government ministers opposed to an ultimately successful proposal to legalise same-sex marriage opined that marriage is an institution that has existed for a millennia in a single form, 'a union between a man and a woman,' evoking a definition that had only been inserted into Australia's marriage law in 2004 (Robinson 2015). Debates on this issue are emerging, but reflect a similar valorising of heteronormativity (Yulius 2015). The ontological status afforded the institutional practices of 'marriage' underscore their determinant role in gender orders, in forms of gendered difference and gendered power.

2.1 Anthropological Concepts of Marriage

Marriage has been a key focus of anthropological studies of societies. The study of kinship and affinity and the social groupings formed through these processes, have been central to anthropological conceptualisation of 'non-western' societies and to theorising social regulation, in early- to mid-twentieth-century anthropology (Fox 1967, p. 21 f.). The publication of Claude Levi-Strauss's Les Structures élémentaires de la parenté (The Elementary Structures of Kinship) in 1949 particularly spotlighted the issue of marriage, which he argued is largely about recruitment to kinship groups (Fox 1967, p. 23).

In their ethnographic accounts, anthropologists have invariably identified an institution that they gloss as 'marriage.' Can marriage be regarded as a universal social institution; can we arrive at a universal construct?

While all historical and existing human societies have established practices for the ordering of sexual expression and child rearing, the actual arrangements are many and varied. They do not always take the form of a heterosexual conjugal pair, a relationship between a man and a woman in the nuclear family.

Kathleen Gough (1959), for example, studied the 'limiting case' of the group-polyandrous Nayar, of Kerala in India, whose sexual practices, gender roles and reproductive 'norms' challenged the taken-for-granted ideas of marriage and the regulation of sexuality and reproduction. According to Nayar custom, women lived in their birth families with their brothers, who were also guardians of their children: the nuclear family was 'nowhere to be seen.' The women could take as many as twelve lovers from men of an appropriate affinal group who are 'lawful' sexual partners and the children thus conceived were legitimate children, members of their mothers' kin groups; the offspring who provided the continuation of the clan. Gough defined marriage as a customary transaction that established the legitimacy of newborn children as acceptable members of society.

Leading kinship scholar, Ward Goodenough (1970) argued that marriage at heart is a transaction, concerning contractual rights over a woman's sexuality. Reviewing these debates, Roger Keesing determined that in the corpus of anthropology, the term 'marriage' refers to: "An institutionalised form of relationship in which sexual relationships and parentage legitimately take place" (1981, p. 514).

Further, it is 'characteristically not a relationship between individuals but a contract between groups' that 'entails a transfer or flow of rights' [emphasis in original] (p. 252) (such as sexuality, offspring or property). While this institution typically regulates rights to sexual access for men, the Nayar case illustrates that these are not always exercised directly or exclusively. Most anthropological definitions include the interpersonal matter of sexual relations and the 'public' recognition of the social place of individuals.

That is, arrangements regulating sexual relations or parentage need not be monogamous, or even heteronormative, to be 'marriage' as Keesing defines it. But the social arrangements that are recognised as 'marriage' cross culturally always link sexual relations, social and biological reproduction and social order; connect the 'personal' or individual self, sexuality, emotions and identity. More than being confined to the personal or 'private,' these arrangements belong in the public world of social order and customary norms. Moreover, 'marriage,' or more accurately social institutions that can be recognised as marriage are always subject to changes and variation, spatially and over time.[1]

"There is literally nothing about marriage that anyone can imagine that has not in fact taken place, whether prescribed, proscribed or optional. All these variations seemed quite natural to those who lived them." (Barnard 1972, p. 272)

2.2 The History of Marriage in the West: Capitalism, Property and Personal Relations

In the European cultural tradition, the version of marriage as we now know it is a relatively recent phenomenon. Marriage contracts emerged as a way of securing property and inheritance. For the 'lower classes,' marriage was a matter of consent. In the sixteenth and seventeenth centuries, the churches became increasingly involved in regulating marriage, and the now common form emerged in the Church of England's Book of Common Prayer in 1549. In the case of Australia, the Marriage Act of 1961 was altered as recently as 2004 to include the definition: 'Marriage means the union of a man and a woman to the exclusion of all others, voluntarily entered into for life.' Prior to the 2004 revision, the Act did not include a definition of marriage, relying on common law (that is, customary practice)—although marriages were registered by the state which also

---

[1] This anthropological definition highlights what marriage equality proponents are arguing for: the formal institutionalisation of the sexual relationships same-sex couples enter into, and the legitimisation of their rights to be parents.

regulated divorce. In modern capitalist societies, marriage has been analysed as a cornerstone of personal life (Barnard 1972; Zaretsky 1976), and portrayed as the 'haven in a heartless world' (Lasch 1977).

3   Forms of Marriage in the Indonesian Archipelago

There are variations in customary cultural practices regarding 'mate selection' and formal social acknowledgment of unions (and offspring) across the archipelago. And it can be observed that distinctive customary practices of kinship relations, descent and marriage are fundamental to the acknowledged differences between cultural groups, often used for the expressions of identity (Robinson 2009a). Key issues are how spouse selection occurs, how the negotiation take place and to which social group the offspring belong.

Marriage as an institutionalised practice was about relations between groups, histories of alliances, or binding people in bilateral kin networks. The contract establishes not only the conjugal pair but also extends connectedness through affines. Rituals surrounding marriage publicly stage these relations; and in many places marriages express forms of political power.

For example, among the Bugis of South Sulawesi, the Bugis term *siala* which can be glossed in English as 'marriage' means 'to take each other,' referring to the alliance between the families of the conjugal pair. The arrangement of marriage could cement relations with the expanding group of bilateral kin ('bringing people back in') through a preference for cousin marriage, or it could be about expanding affinal relations to secure a kinship group's social influence and power (Idrus 2004). The negotiation of marriages and their public celebrations were the principle public rituals of the society. Millar (1989) terms them 'rituals of social location.' Negotiations over bride wealth but also bride price and cost and size of the public feasting provided public affirmation of the relative social status of groups of kin and their affines. Staging such rituals was the principal way in which the most high status families expressed and validated their power (Robinson 1998).

In Java, divorce rates have customarily been high and it has been the practice for children to stay with the mother (who often returned to her parents' home). On remarriage, the new husband accepts his responsibilities for his wife's children. This kind of 'matrifocality,' where mothers and their children are the fundamental enduring units, is not unique to Java. Indeed, it has been argued to be a form of female power by feminist anthropologists (see, for example, Tanner 1974).

But a key common characteristic across the archipelago, is that marriage is a doxic practice that was crucial to the passage of the individual from childhood to adulthood. *Marital unions* in most societies of the Indonesian Archipelago have primarily not taken the form of an intimate relationship between individuals but a contract between groups. There are variations on the details of how this rite of passage is negotiated and performed, but forms of familial control over choices of spouse and the solemnisation of unions has been common, only being eroded in the twentieth century (Robinson 1998; Jones 2010). While for the individual these customary forms of marriage were important for the social achievement of adulthood and parenthood, marriage was not seen as the cornerstone of personal life as it has come to be in modern capitalist societies (Barnard 1972; Zaretsky 1976; Lasch 1977), and it has not until recently been a reflexive process, a manifestation of individual choice and life purpose.

4   Islam and Marriage

Islam expanded through the archipelago from around the fifteenth century onwards. The integration of Islamic rituals and beliefs with customary practices around life cycle events was a key way in which Islam became imbedded in local cultures. In many communities in Eastern Indonesia, for example, initial conversion was often associated with the marriage of a local woman to a Muslim migrant or sojourner (Robinson 2020, p. 5).

The Islamic marriage contract, the *akad nikah,* performed by a religious authority is a contract between the groom and the bride's guardian, and witnessed by as few as two people. This formal marriage practice was grafted onto existing rituals that socially legitimated marriage, commonly a public feast at which the bride and groom sit side by side *(duduk bersanding)* in front of assembled guests, who are offered feasting, speeches and entertainment. This is the social moment of recognition of their union; the important juncture when the marriage is authorised/legitimised by custom *(adat),* not religion.

When I first undertook fieldwork in Sorowako, South Sulawesi, in the late 1970s, the *akad nikah* was a simple religious ceremony enacted by the religious authority (the *imam*), between the groom and the bride's *wali* (guardian), witnessed by family members and in the eyes of God.[2] Nowadays, as in many places across the archipelago, the *akad nikah* is enacted in front of a roomful of guests,

---

[2] This may have been influenced by Darul Islam.

witnessed by a broader audience—indeed a public occasion. In addition, nowadays, if the *akad nikah* it is not immediately followed by the *resepsi* and the *duduk bersanding* (described above) it is followed by its own festive communal meal.

Marriage as an institution, among the Islamic peoples of the archipelago, can be analytically understood as combining Islam as a key element, and *adat* (custom)—although salafi and other groups influenced by Saudi Islamic constructs propose radical 'cleansing' of Islam of such customary practices (see for example 'Alimi 2014). Customary marriage practices, as kinship-based forms of power, were in mutual accommodation with religious precepts (*fikhi*). The regulations contained in *adat* in regard to issues such as marital property, or rights in children, were elided into the marital practices of Muslim communities. There were creative responses to the protection of rights, especially women's rights, assumed to be matters of the Islamic *fikhi* such as men's rights to unconditional divorce and polygyny (*poligami*), the latter practice at variance with the customary rights and roles of women (Robinson 2006). I will expand on this below.

For Muslim peoples of the archipelago, until recently there has apparently been little reflexivity about the bounds of Islam and those of cultural practice. For example, Yasir 'Alimi (2014) recounts a story of a couple who had undertaken an Islamic marriage contract in front of an *imam,* within a novel Islamic sect but had not had a ceremony witnessed by the community. They were very anxious that they were not in fact properly married.

Until today, after over a century of state intervention into the regulation of Islamic marriage (discussed below) there remains a lack of clarity or even lack of consensus about the limits of state and religious authority in regard to marriage in many parts of the archipelago. This is evident in the continuing use of the services of Islamic celebrants who are not registered by the state to perform marriage services—the so-called *imam liar,* or 'wild *imam*'—who provide marriage and divorce certificates (Idrus 2009) in some parts of the archipelago.

5 Regulation of Marriage in the Netherlands East Indies

The Dutch East India company slowly spread its reach over the archipelago beginning in the seventeenth century; and from the beginning of the twentieth century the Netherlands Government exercised authority over what is now Indonesia (the colony of Netherlands East Indies, NEI). The colonial government passed laws which regulated marriage for Europeans, so called 'Foreign Orientals' and Christians, reflecting modern sensibilities about marriage regulation in the public sphere (Robinson 2006). But in common with many colonial regimes controlling Muslim populations, the colonial power did not regulate marriage and family for 'natives' (Martinez 2004). For the majority Muslim population of the archipelago family law—including marriage (as well as polygyny), divorce and inheritance—was regulated within communities, by 'custom' which encompassed the institutions of Islam and local religious authorities, which in some regions included religious courts form the late nineteenth century.

Marriage in the NEI was acknowledged as being conducted by the *penghulu* or some other local officiant. The official Indonesian dictionary, *Kamus Besar Bahasa Indonesia* (Large dictionary of Indonesian), defines *penghulu* as a '*kepala*' (head) and elaborates that it can refer to a head of custom; head of Islamic affairs in a district or city; an advisor on religious matters to the religious court(s); or serve as a synonym for *kadi* (judge in a religious court) (Departmen Pendidikan dan Kebudayaan dan Balai Pustaka 1998, p. 748, my translation).

In the colonial period elite women began to challenge the uncodified nature of the Islamic law and demanded that the NEI colonial government enact clear regulations on marriage divorce and inheritance. Islamic leaders resisted any involvement of state law/courts and they argued for the ongoing role of *fikhi* in regulating marriage.

5.1 Demands for Marriage Reform in the Indonesian Archipelago

From the late nineteenth century onwards modernist ideas and sensibilities originating in Europe were circulating in the NEI, especially among young 'natives' who had begun to enjoy the right to a western education. Before the nationalist movement 'firmed up' in the early twentieth century, native intellectuals and Dutch officials were voicing ideas about the rights of colonial subjects. A strong voice that emerged in this field was that of a young Javanese woman, R. A. Kartini, whose colonial official (*priyayi*)[3] father enabled her to be educated in Dutch—thus envisioning the possibility of her taking her place as the wife of a native-born colonial official (Robinson 2019a, p. 133). In her teenage years she

---

[3] This is the term used for a class of officials of Javanese customary courts who were recruited as officials in the colonial bureaucracy.

was taken from school to be 'imprisoned' (*dipingit*) at home, while awaiting the fate of a woman of her class—an arranged marriage to a man of similar status.

Paradoxically, while secluded at home, she read widely and also developed pen-pal correspondences with a number of Dutch women, including the Dutch feminist Stella Zeehandelaar. Kartini was a keen reader of novels and perhaps from this she developed a strong sense of self-fashioning and the reflexivity of a sense of private life (Watson 2000). In her letters she critiques the young marriage practices of her class—especially polygyny—and dreamed of a love marriage, of a marriage as a personal relationship. She expressed disgust at polygyny that was a common practice in her social class and milieu. Kartini, in her writings and life, exemplifies the complexity of marriage as a social institution that encompasses the personal and private; the social and collective; and the public and the regulatory.

In the end her actions followed the doxic practices of her social milieu, rather than her expressed aspirations for self-determination. She agreed to her father's choice of husband; she became the principal spouse of a widower of similar rank who already had several minor wives (Watson 2000). Apparently, self-realisation through marriage did not eventuate—she committed to following her father's wishes—and dutifully accepted where her social relations and responsibilities lay. Her correspondence and posthumously published writings provide a window into the changes occurring at this very significant historical moment of colonial transformation of the structures of state power and the ways in which these were ramified through gendered relations. Her aspirations and vision of women's equality have influenced generations of Indonesian women (Robinson 1987, 2019a).

5.2 Nationalist Women and Demands for Marriage Law Reform: Civic Rights versus Religious Regulation of Marriage

Demands for marriage reform, for the passage of a marriage law that would override the regulation of marriage by religious officials and courts, was a key demand of the Indonesian women's movements in the colonial period. In the early part of the twentieth century, several organisations supporting women's rights came into being in the Netherlands East Indies. The politicised women's groups that were part of the early-twentieth-century nationalist movement saw improvements in women's rights, notably in regard to marriage, divorce and inheritance as essential for improving women's welfare (Robinson 2006).

They advocated for the replacement of what they saw as the anti-egalitarian provisions of Islamic family law by a secular legal regimen that limited male prerogatives and protected women's rights. Public debates about religion and law manifested in demands by women's organisations in the first decades of the twentieth century that the state extend its grasp into the private domain of the family. That is, they were demanding reform based on a concept of civic rights for women that challenged the normative regulation of marriage according to religious precepts (Robinson 2006).

Principal issues of concern were child marriage; forced marriage; forms of polygyny which did not meet the requirements of Muslim law (for example, based on lust); and arbitrary divorce and failure to pay alimony beyond the *iddah* period (the minimum waiting period for women to remarry following divorce which resulted in failure to support children). Polygyny in particular aroused disgust in many of these women, just as it had in the nineteenth-century figure Kartini. Women felt threatened by 'successive polygamy' in which men discarded wives and even abandoned children in order to remarry.

As stated above, age at marriage, especially child marriage, was also a contentious issue. Islamic law provides no stipulated minimum age, and girls could be married with the consent of their male *wali-mujbir* (coercive guardian) regardless of their own will. (This continues to be a key issue of women's rights campaigning today and will be discussed below).

Nearly thirty of the nationalist women's groups came together for the first national women's congress held in 1928. Secular nationalist organisations all had women's sections, who asserted that improvements in rights for women were linked to the broader goals of the nationalist movement: women's rights as citizens were a cornerstone of a modern nation. The congress debated issues of polygyny, forced and underage marriage and women's rights in *talak* (repudiation). Siti Sundari, a nationalist figure who edited the magazine *Wanito Sworo* (Women's voice), reported that she had received letters from women complaining about polygamy and arbitrary repudiation.

She told the 1928 congress, 'Polygamy, child marriages, repudiation and divorces are unlimited in number [...] When a woman's independence disappears in marriage [...] it signifies the failure of the emancipation of our people' (cited in Robinson 2006, p. 28). The necessity and right of the state to intervene in Muslim marriage was contentious. Ali Sastroamijoyo, a future prime minister addressed the 1928 women's congress and argued that Muslims had the 'right to marry without the intermediary of a government official, provided that all the conditions of the Islamic law (*fikhi*) were fulfilled' (cited in Robinson 2006, p. 34). The congress carried a motion that the government require the officiant/celebrant (*penghulu*) to explain the meaning of the *talik* (divorce) following the formalisation of the marriage contract *(akad nikah)*. In 1932 the colonial government took a first step towards state regulation of Muslim marriage, setting in place a requirement that the *talik* be explained to the *wali* at the conclusion of the marriage.

After the 1928 congress, women's organisations came together in national conferences on a regular basis, but it was many years before they again came to a consensus on marriage reform. Islamic clerics opposed state interference in what they saw as a religious domain, but women activists saw the clerics' stance as protecting male prerogatives and so it was difficult for Islamic and secular women's organisations to reach consensus on the necessity and desirability of government intervention in marriage. The issue grumbled on and a compromise finally emerged at the 1935 Congress, a decision to set up a Commission to Investigate Marriage Law which was required to report back to the congress (Robinson 2006).

At issue on these debates were the civic rights of women versus the religious regulation of marriage. It was a fundamental challenge to the understanding of marriage and how it reflected 'normative' gender relations. The activist nationalist women were seeking state protection of women's rights in regard to: legal restriction of polygamy inheritance, divorce (repudiation), common property, alimony, regulation of marriage age (anti-child marriage), and marriage without consent (forced marriage).

The public debates concerning women's marriage rights held in the women's congresses and constituent women's organisations marked a shift in focus from the religious to the secular sphere in the politics of marriage reform. Advocates of change argued for the regulation of marriage in secular law (that is, the intrusion of state into the 'private' affairs of the household which were the provenance of custom and religion). Their opponents emphasised the regulation of marriage in accord with the *fikhi* in particular arguing for *poligami* (i.e. polygyny) as a religious right. At stake was a new relationship between religion (in particular Islam) and the state in regard to women's rights, as well as the sphere of authority of religious leaders. Although the colonial state had struck a first blow in the state regulation of Muslim marriage, this matter was unresolved on the eve of independence. This marked a significant shift in gender power but also power in general; and prefigured later developments in independent Indonesia in which the polyphony of forms of gender regimes came to be dominated by a monolithic state discourse of gender that hinged on state regulation of marriage and households and reproduction.

6 Regulation of Marriage in the Independent Republic (post 1950)

The struggle for a unified secular marriage law lost momentum after independence. In the Soekarno period (1950–1960s), Indonesia's founding fathers, by and large, left the regulation of marriage and family life to authorities in the religious, non-state domain. Hence the regulation of marriage and family life was largely exercised in the private domain, with customs such as *duduk bersanding* defining the role of a wider public in normative marriage. In the case of Muslim marriage (that is for the majority of Indonesians), the religious courts were the public authority in terms of divorce and inheritance and they remained outside the national legal system and under the authority of the Ministry of Religious Affairs (Robinson 2006). But the agenda to improve women's rights by imposing secular regulation of marriage and divorce in the public state domain did not go away.

6.1 New Order (1966–1998)

A marriage law that instantiated the role of the state in regulating marriage was finally enacted in 1974, several years after Soeharto assumed power. The law apparently responded to some of the women's movement's demands for marriage: setting a minimum age for marriage (for both males and females); and formalising state registration of marriage. The secular marriage law did establish some state protection of women's rights in divorce *(talik)* in that men had to obtain the wife's approval before taking a new spouse; and made it illegal to marry young women without their consent. Men's rights to polygynous marriage was restricted in that they were required to furnish proof of the first wife's consent, and show they were able to support more than one household. Regulation of divorce and *poligami*[4] still fell to the authority of Islamic courts. However, they were required to make judgments regarding divorce and polygamy not just in terms of the *fikhi* and modes of religious reasoning but also in terms of clauses in the new law that afforded some protection of women's rights.

But the passage of a secular marriage law was not a manifestation of a surge in the power of women vis-a-vis men, in spite of its adopting some of the reforms long called for by women activists. The law defined men as household heads,

---

[4] In Indonesia, the term *poligami* refers to polygyny, the taking of multiple wives. It does not encompass polyandy (the taking of multiple husbands).

and this legal narrative endorsed a powerful fiction that women are secondary to men in nuclear households (Robinson 2009b). This is a formal instantiation of the 'patriarchal dividend,' 'the advantage to men as a group from maintaining an unequal gender order' (Connell 2002, p. 142). All men benefit from the states co-optation of gendered power in its expression and exercise of power (Robinson 2014). Women were incorporated into state corporatist organisations as mothers and wives, as 'citizen mothers.' The government's interest in marriage reform was linked to its massive family planning campaign where, for example, setting a minimum age for marriage supported its goal of lower fertility. In a further drift away from religious authority in family matters, the New Order was intolerant of polygamy and further circumscribed the rights of civil servants to take second wives with a presidential instruction that required civil servants to seek the permission of their office superior, as well as their wives (as required by the law) (Robinson 2009a, p. 85 f.).

In 1994, the New Order further shifted the balance between secular and religious authority; religious courts were brought under the umbrella of the state courts. The compilation of Islamic law that accompanied this process of formalisation codified the everyday practices that had grown up in judgments of the Islamic courts across the archipelago (Bowen 2003). These reflected the ways in which Islamic law and practices had accommodated to the varied forms of local practices, for example, in regard to common property rights (Robinson 2006).

6.2 Reformasi Era

The legal regulation of marriage and state protection of women's rights is not a settled matter in Indonesia. Following the fall of the New Order, the political euphoria of Reformasi (1998), with its political catch cry of *pemberdayaan* (empowerment), opened up 'democratic space' for many previously suppressed issues. Women's rights activists reopened the question of women's marriage rights demanding stronger state regulation of Muslim marriage. They called for a revision of the Soeharto-era marriage law, including re-opening the demand to outlaw polygamy as being inconsistent with the equal status of men and women in Indonesia's constitution; and to revisit the age of marriage, especially for girls, due to concerns about child marriage. Siti Musdah Mulia, an Islamic scholar, produced a 'counter legal draft' from inside the Ministry of Religious Affairs.

But some men also saw the opening up of the political space of Reformasi as a chance to make counter moves to express their demands for marriage prerogatives that they saw as being provided by Islam. Polygamy, while allowed, had been restricted under the 1974 Marriage Law. One very public political campaign was organised by restaurant owner Puspo Wardoyo; he formed the organisation Poligami Indonesia and organised '*poligami* awards' to publicly praise wealthy polygamists. He famously declared that if all men who were *mampu* (wealthy) took an extra wife this would solve the 'problem' of women migrating overseas to work. He promoted *poligami* in his chain of restaurants serving *poligami* juice and other similarly named menu items. His public events were subjected to protests by women. And while he achieved a lot of publicity and public discussion, he did not achieve mainstream political support or have success in his legal challenge.

A more significant shift in the locus of the debate took place in 2007 when a case was brought by M. Insa to the Constitutional Court, an institution that had been established in 2003 as part of the democratising political reforms in Reformasi. He argued that *poligami* was a religious right for him as a Muslim and the legal restriction in the secular marriage law was unconstitutional as it took away this right (Butt 2010). This court case was an attempt to challenge the state (secular) law on the basis of religious reasoning. It was unsuccessful, but it perhaps marked a shift to the longstanding discourse of marriage reform that had always been argued from the perspective of secular, citizenship rights. Arguments from an Islamic perspective had largely been put forward prior to the enactment of the 1975 law. This shift in the locus of the struggles over gender are related to the novel forms of political debate allowed by Reformasi and its new institutions, which enabled a shift (back) to the legitimacy of Islam as a political force. This shift has been associated with a renewed purportedly Islamic discourse in regards to gender relations and gender regimes.

7 The Contemporary Debate: Child Marriage

In 2015 child advocacy groups turned to the Constitutional Court seeking a judicial review of the age of marriage stipulated in the 1975 Marriage Law.[5] They were keen to strengthen the provisions for girls in the marriage law, arguing that the minimum age of marriage, sixteen for girls, should be raised to eighteen, to 'harmonise' with the 2002 law on child protection (No 23/2002) which used the definition from the Convention on Rights of Child, which Indonesia had ratified in 1990.

---

[5] This issue has emerged in Islamic publics since the increase in Islamic education, piety as an aspect of middle-class identity.

In rejecting the proposed change to the minimum age at marriage, the Constitutional Court used a novel form of legal reasoning in this 'secular' legal forum: the judges turned to Islamic processes of deliberation, in considering a submission by the Majelis Ulama Indonesia- Indonesian Islamic Scholars Council (MUI) that gave textual exegesis in relation to minimum age at marriage/child marriage even though the case was being heard under the civil code. Under Islamic law there is no stipulated minimum age of marriage and girls can be married with the consent of their male *wali-mujbir* regardless of their own consent or otherwise.[6] The Court accepted a narrow religious argument from *kiyai* (MUI) on the biological basis of *baliq* (adulthood) and rejected the argument to lift the legal age of marriage.

8 New Modes of Legal Reasoning in the Secular-Religious Public Sphere

Advocates for women's rights in Indonesia have historically relied on secular processes of public deliberation to provide a conceptual umbrella for securing gender equality. But at the current historical moment, where Islamist groups are crystalising as a political force, they are also turning to modes of Islamic reasoning.[7] This turn away from secular modes is surprising and has strengthened conservative Muslim voices in the public and political realm (Butt 2010). Islamic leaders, the state and the Constitutional Court in Indonesia—as well as both religious and secular women's organisations—debate over women's rights with opinions divided between religion and secular modes.

In April 2017, women's groups associated with Nahdalatul Ulama staged a Kongres Ulama Perempuan (Congress of women Islamic scholars) to explore the role of women as religious leaders and women's authoritative voices in in relation to the *fikhi*. Working groups at the congress focused on a number of issues, including child marriage. I was invited to attend a workshop on marriage. Hosted by activists from the children and women's rights group, Rumah KitaB, a principal aim was to discuss forms of Islamic reasoning that countered the MUI argument put to the Constitutional Court concerning age at marriage (Robinson 2019b).

---

[6] Usually referred to as *wali* (guardian) this appears to be the principle context in which Indonesian Muslim women experience male guardianship. This issue caused some confusion at the path-breaking Indonesian Congress of Women Ulama, see Robinson 2017, and below in this article.

[7] Robinson (2008) discusses Islamic feminism in Indonesia and the championing of women's rights as quintessentially Islamic values.

Young male *kiyai* presented arguments, concerning concepts of *baliqua*, or adulthood and how it might be determined; child marriage as *maksiat* (vice/sin); and challenging interpretations of the Al-Quran/*hadits* used to validate child marriage: e.g., the case of the Prophet Muhammad marrying Aisyah when she was a child, perhaps nine years old.

From exegesis of contesting *hadits,* they discussed the difference between *baliq* as biology (menstruation) and *aqil baliq* (adulthood) as sociological; and *rusyd* (adulthood) encompassing biological and psychological aspects, including the development of rationality. The outcome was a *fatwa* passed by the final plenary of the Congress based on scriptural arguments for a legal challenge: to counter the (narrowly based) opinion accepted by the court, to argue for a minimum age of marriage for girls of eighteen. A second *fatwa* proclaimed that violence against women *(kekerasan seksual),* including within marriage, is *haram* (forbidden to Islam). A third *fatwa* argued that environmental destruction is *haram* as it can trigger social and economic burdens on women and children (Robinson 2017).

In terms of Islam and women's rights, there was an interesting moment in the opening international seminar, when a speaker from Saudi Arabia, Hatoon al-Fassi, mentioned the Saudi women's campaign, 'I am my own *wali.*' A bewildered Indonesian women asked for clarification from the floor: for Indonesian woman the *'wali'* is relevant to the *akad nikah* (marriage contract) but has little place in other life decisions, indicating that Muslim marriage is a key area of contestation over women's rights. But the kind of inequality implied by women's subjection to the will of the *wali* in all aspects of life did not resonate with the experience of the pious women attending the congress.

9 Conclusion: Marriage, Gender Relations, Private and Publics, Secular and Religious Reasoning

Marriage in Indonesia is increasingly no longer a socially, culturally, religiously, legally and politically regulated practice that is an aspect of inter-family, intergroup relations, to an expression of adult personhood. The move to free-choice marriage has been a significant shift in gender relations over the last four decades. For contemporary Indonesians exercising free-choice marriage is a form of reflexive practice, of self-expression. Changes in marriage regulations are key aspects of shifting gender regimes, and of the relative power of men and women.

When Islam was excluded from the public (secular) sphere of law making, women marriage-reform activists appealed to the secular regimens of politics (colonial period, New Order) to intervene on the exclusive right of religious authorities to regulate marriage, divorce, and other family matters. The New Order implemented marriage law reforms, but in ways that supported its own gender regime, in particular the naturalisation of the authority of the father in the household (Robinson 2009a).

The regulation of marriage is a significant point in the relation between religion and the state. Reforms since independence have meant it is jointly controlled by religion (Islam) and by the state. Women have demanded the intrusion of the state into the private affairs of marriage and the family, but these arguments have been resisted by Muslim individuals, scholars, and some political groups. It becomes evident from my description that a public fight about the limits of religious and of state authority, and, with them, the questions of gender relations lie at the heart of power. Post-Reformasi, there has been increasing legitimation of Islamic public discourse, especially in the court challenges to provisions of the marriage law. Muslim women's groups have responded by claiming authority in the Islamic public sphere.

Women's marriage rights are no longer mainly debated in the secular sphere, and well-educated Muslim women are now claiming a space in the public sphere of Islamic authority, relying on Islamic reasoning to argue for gender equity and women's rights. They seek to influence public policy, both secular and religious.

References

Alimi, Y. 2014. Islam as drama. Wedding rites and the theatricality of Islam in South Sulawesi. *The Asia Pacific Journal of Anthropology* 15(3): 265–85. https://doi.org/10.1080/14442213.2014.915875.

Appadurai, A., and C. Breckenridge. 1988. Why public culture? *Public Culture* 1(1): 5–9. https://doi.org/10.1215/08992363-1-1-5.

Barnard, J. 1972. *The future of marriage.* New Haven, CT: Yale University Press.

Bowen, J. 2003. *Islam, law and equality in Indonesia.* Cambridge: Cambridge University Press.

Butt, S. 2010. Islam, the state and the constitutional court in Indonesia. *Washington International Law Journal* 19(2): 279–301.

Connell, R.W. 2002. *Gender.* Cambridge: Polity Press.

Departmen Pendidikan dan Kebudayaan, and B. Pustaka. 1998. *Kamus Besar Bahasa Indonesia.* Jakarta: Balai Pustaka.

Echolls, J.M., and H. Shadily. 1976. *Kamus Inggris Indonesia.* Ithaca, NY: Cornell University Press.

Fox, R. 1967. *Kinship and marriage.* Harmondsworth: Penguin Books.

Goodenough, W. 1970. *Description and comparison in cultural anthropology*. Chicago: Aldine Publishing Co.
Gough, K. 1959. The Nayars and the definition of marriage. *The Journal of the Royal Anthropological Institute* 89(1): 23–34.
Idrus, N. I. 2004. Behind the notion of *Siala*: Marriage, *Adat* and Islam among the Bugis in South Sulawesi. *Intersections: Gender, History and Culture in the Asian Context* 10. http://intersections.anu.edu.au/issue10/idrus.html. Accessed: 3 March 2022.
Idrus, N. I. 2009. 'Its the matter of a piece of paper.' Between legitimation and legalisation of marriage and divorce in Bugis society. *Intersections: Gender, History and Culture in the Asian Context* 19. http://intersections.anu.edu.au/issue19/idrus.htm. Accessed: 3 March 2022.
Jones, G. W. 2010. *Changing marriage patterns in Asia*. Asia Research Institute Working Paper Series No 131, Singapore: Asia Research Institute. https://doi.org/10.2139/ssrn.1716533.
Keesing, R. 1981. *Cultural anthropology. A contemporary perspective*. New York, NY: Holt, Rinehart and Winston.
Lasch, C. 1977. *Haven in a heartless world. The family besieged*. New York, NY: Basic Books Inc.
Lévi-Strauss, C. 1949. *Les structures élémentaires de la parenté*. Boston, MA: Beacon Press.
Martinez, P. 2004. Islam, constitutional democracy and the civil state in Malaysia. In *Civil Society in Southeast Asia*, Ed. L.H. Guan, 27–53. Singapore: ISEAS Publishing.
Millar, S. 1989. *Bugis weddings. Rituals of social location*. Berkeley, CA: University of California Centre for South and Southeast Asian Studies.
Millie, J. 2017. *Hearing Allah's Call. Preaching and performing in Indonesian Islam*. Ithaca, NY: Cornell University Press.
Robinson, K. 1987. What price equality? Kartini's vision and the position of women in Indonesia. *Mankind* 17(2): 104–13. https://doi.org/10.1111/j.1835-9310.1987.tb01284.x.
Robinson, K. 1988. Love and sex in an Indonesian mining town. In *Gender and Power in Affluent Asia*, Eds. K. Sen and M. Stivens, 63–86. London: Routledge.
Robinson, K. 2006. Muslim women's political struggle for marriage law reform in contemporary Indonesia. In *Mixed blessings. Laws, religion and women's rights in the Asia-Pacific Region*, Eds. A. Whiting and C. Evans, 183–210. Leiden: Brill.
Robinson, K. 2008. Islamic cosmopolitics, human rights and anti-violence strategies in Indonesia. In *Anthropology and the new cosmopolitanism. Feminist, vernacular and rooted perspectives*, Ed. P. Werbner, 111–135. Oxford: Berg.
Robinson, K. 2009a. *Gender, Islam and Democracy in Indonesia*. London: Routledge.
Robinson, K. 2009b. Islam, gender and politics in Indonesia. In *Women in Asia, vol. 1. Women and political power*, Eds. L. Edwards and M. Roces, 292–306. London: Routledge.
Robinson, K. 2014. What does a gender relations approach bring to Southeast Asian Studies? In *Methodology and research practice in Southeast Asian studies*. Eds. M. Huotari, J. Rüland and J. Schlehe, 107–127. Basingstoke; Houndsmill; Hampshire; New York: Palgrave Macmillan.
Robinson, K. 2015. Marriage equality. What will the neighbours think? *SBS*. https://www.sbs.com.au/news/article/marriage-equality-what-will-the-neighbours-think/5blazny1d. Accessed: 28 February 2022.

Robinson, K. 2017. Female Ulama voice a vision for Indonesia's future. *New mandala: New perspectives on Southeast Asia.* https://www.newmandala.org/female-ulama-voice-vision-indonesias-future/. Accessed 3: March 2022.

Robinson, K. 2019a. Call me Kartini? Kartini as a floating signifier in Indonesian history. In *Appropriating Kartini. Colonial, national and transnational memories of an Indonesian icon,* Eds. P. Bijl and G.V.S. Chin, 131–156. Singapore: Institute of Southeast Asian Studies (ISEAS) Publishing.

Robinson, K. 2019b. Rumah KitaB and the campaign against child marriage. *Rumah KitaB.* https://rumahkitab.com/tag/kupi/. Accessed: 3 March 2022.

Robinson, K. 2020. Introduction. In *Mosques and Imams. Everyday Islam in Eastern Indonesia,* Ed. K. Robinson, 1–23. Singapore: National University of Singapore Press.

Tanner, N. 1974. Matrifocality in Indonesia and Africa and among Black Americans. In *Woman, culture, and society,* Eds. M.Z. Rosaldo and L. Lamphere, 129–156. Stanford, CA: Stanford University Press.

Watson, C. W. 2000. *Of self and nation. Autobiography and the representation of modern Indonesia.* Honolulu, HI: University of Hawai'i Press.

Williams, R. 1983. *Keywords. A vocabulary of culture and society.* London: Flamingo.

Yulius, H. 2015. Same-sex marriage in Indonesia. *Indonesia at Melbourne.* https://indonesiaatmelbourne.unimelb.edu.au/same-sex-marriage-in-indonesia/. Accessed: 27 February 2022.

Zaretsky, E. 1976. *Capitalism, the family and personal life.* New York, NY: Harper and Row.

Indonesian Selfie Tourism Abroad and at Home: Creating Images of a Cosmopolitan Self

Mirjam Lücking und Nuki Mayasari

1 Introduction

The challenges and opportunities of multiculturalism, trans-culturalism and cosmopolitanism in our globalized world are recurring themes in Judith Schlehe's numerous research projects. Among others, her research on cultural theme parks like Taman Mini, a park with miniature replicas of Indonesian attractions, such as architecture (e.g. Schlehe 2017a), on *kirab budaya*, a cultural parade in Yogyakarta (Schlehe 2017b), and on paranormal practitioners in Java (Schlehe 2019) reveals the ways in which representations of culture function in concert with economic and political interests. As an example, in Taman Mini Indonesia's ethnic diversity is mainly represented in rather essentializing stereotypes and separate from one another. Yet, since the beginning of the *reformasi* period, the democratization period since the end of the Suharto dictatorship, there have also been new directions of representation that have the potential to inspire thinking of 'relatedness and entanglement of culture, of the complexities of cultural crossings' (Schlehe 2017a, p. 87).

Another example of pluralist cultural representation can be found in spiritual experts like healers, who are known as paranormal practitioners in Indonesia.

M. Lücking (✉)
Martin Buber Society of Fellows, The Hebrew University of Jerusalem, Jerusalem, Israel
E-Mail: mirjam.luecking@mail.huji.ac.il

N. Mayasari
Yogyakarta, Indonesia
E-Mail: nuki.mayasari@gmail.com

© Der/die Autor(en), exklusiv lizenziert an Springer Fachmedien Wiesbaden GmbH, ein Teil von Springer Nature 2023
M. Lücking et al. (Hrsg.), *In Tandem—Pathways towards a Postcolonial Anthropology | Im Tandem – Wege zu einer postkolonialen Ethnologie*,
https://doi.org/10.1007/978-3-658-38673-3_12

These spiritual entrepreneurs refer to a plurality of religious and ethnic cultural markers in their outward appearance and overall performance. They practise 'an assemblage of tradition and modernity, locality and translocality, religion and mysticism, spirituality and business, and global esotericism and popular psychology' (Schlehe 2019, p. 364). They self-orientalise, but simultaneously, they promote cosmopolitan ideas in regard to the inclusivity of various cultural and religious traditions.

Based on these observations, Schlehe indicates opportunities for popular cultural representations in business and entertainment that allow room for complexities, nuances and trans-cultural encounters. In Indonesia, the processes of post-colonial nation-building challenge innovative pluralist and cosmopolitan visions, but in fact, Indonesia could become an inspiring global role model in this regard (Schlehe 2017a, p. 79).

In relation to these observations and considerations, the article at hand presents examples of what we call 'Indonesian selfie tourism', seeking to discuss the ways in which the creation of images of a cosmopolitan self inspires socio-cultural plurality, intercultural encounters, and inclusion.

When we speak of cosmopolitanism, we refer to the concept of vernacular cosmopolitanism (Bhabha 2004; Werbner 2006) as connectedness to other places in the world, tolerance for other cultures and peoples, and appreciation of cultural plurality that stem from everyday experiences, including migratory experiences, and not only from elitist travel. In reference to Schlehe (2017, p. 382), we consider whether other-than-human entities and forces are included in peoples' acknowledgement of cultural diversity and multiple centres of the world.

Knowledge about global cultural diversity can evolve from travel and therefore tourism is an interesting field of study in this regard. In this article, we discuss two very different forms of tourism: domestic tourism to local selfie parks and international religious tourism. These two examples have in common that the creation of self-portraits, or selfies, is important to the tourists. In reference to the colloquial emic term, *'wisata selfie',* we speak of 'selfie tourism'.

Similar to the cultural theme parks studied by Schlehe, in recent years, several new parks have opened their gates to visitors in Indonesia under the label *'wisata selfie'*—selfie tourism. These parks are often located outside big cities and consist of installations that serve as backgrounds for photos. Such installations are multifarious and creative, ranging from artistic sculptures to miniatures of famous national and international landmarks like the Eiffel Tower. Quite often the parks include nature, either through locations near rice fields, beaches, rivers or forests, or through planted flower fields and artificially constructed lakes. Some parks are professionalized with personnel and fixed entrance fees, while others are more informal and sometimes temporary set-ups to take selfies, asking for voluntary donations.

However, selfie tourism does not only happen in such parks that are specifically designated for the creation of photos. Selfie tourism has also become part of other forms of Indonesian tourism like guided religious package tours, which are a common way to travel domestically and internationally. An example of such package tours are Muslim and Christian pilgrimages to Israel and Palestine. When asking Jerusalemite tourist guides what is important when guiding Indonesian pilgrims to the city's holy sites, one of the most frequent answers is 'managing time' because Indonesians and other Asian tourists need a significant amount of 'selfie-time', referring to time in which the group members pose for photographs. Thus, in addition to ritual aspects of the journey, Indonesians need time to take photos, or, as one of the pilgrims put it himself: 'If I haven't taken a picture, it's like I haven't been here'.

The selfie becomes proof of presence and an aesthetic performance. For instance, as a sign of having completed the prestigious pilgrimage to Mecca, many Indonesian hajj returnees put posters on their houses, showing themselves in front of the Kaaba, Islam's holiest site. These 'Mecca selfies' are in fact photoshopped collages, made on the computer. A continuation of this tradition is found on social media platforms where people portray themselves as cosmopolitan travellers, even if the pictures originate from places close by like the above-mentioned selfie parks. Selfies are published on personal online social media platforms. Such online documentation connects pilgrims to their social lives in the home context. In the case of international travel, in particular religious travel, the images carry a notion of connectedness to the world or cosmopolitanism, and they mark affiliation with a social class that can afford international travel.

A comparative look at pilgrimage selfies and domestic selfie tourism reveals the interreferential creation of cosmopolitan self-portraits, including the repetition or imitation of well-known poses and backgrounds, and the social dimensions of taking photos. After all, most selfies in Indonesia are in fact, *'wefies',* showing a group of people and not only one individual (cf. Jones 2017). It also shows how the accessibility of portraits of a cosmopolitan self has changed through new media and technologies. Furthermore, representations of being connected to international destinations are a way of claiming one's place in a postcolonial world. Indonesians take part in filling international (religious) centres with life and define how such places are represented online.

The material that we present and analyse here stems from our individual and collaborative research. We first met in 2008, more than 14 years ago, during a student tandem research collaboration between Universitas Gadjah Mada and the University of Freiburg, which had been initiated by Judith Schlehe. Ever since, we have continued collaborating on various projects and our ongoing research discussions are still inspired by the Freiburg-Yogyakarta model of tandem and team research, consciously reflecting on our research positionalities and combining our different perspectives (see Schlehe and Hidayah 2014). The analysis of selfie tourism is based on the following three elements: 1) Nuki Mayasari's long-term experience and observations as a social media influencer who runs the highly popular Instagram profile @pesonaimogiri, which has more than 50,000 followers and features images from the Indonesian province Yogyakarta, including images from selfie parks; 2) on Mirjam Lücking's research with Indonesian Mecca and Jerusalem pilgrims that was conducted in 2013 and 2014 in Indonesia and since October 2017 in and around Jerusalem; and 3) on our joint selfie park visits and discussions that took place in August 2018. Before we present the observations from research with pilgrims and park visitors, we provide some theoretical thoughts on self-portraits and changing technologies.

Portraits of the Self
Research on the history of portraits of the self, lays open how accessibility to self-portraits has changed with changing technologies (see Ullrich 2019, p. 11 ff.). This change of technologies has led from painted portraits to black-white photographs made with box cameras, to pictures from smaller and more mobile cameras, to coloured photographs and instant polaroid prints, to developed photographs and slides from personal travel cameras and, eventually, to digital images taken by various sorts of cameras and mobile phone cameras. With the change of technologies, the relation between the maker of portraits and the object of portraits has changed too. While painters and photographers used to be artists and experts, today everybody can take a photo and the digital images are more easily editable. The so-called 'selfie' has changed the relationship between the portrayer and the portrayed most radically because a selfie is a picture of oneself that is taken by oneself.

The art historian Wolfgang Ullrich (2019, p. 6) argues that this means that the taker of the selfie takes a picture of a picture. Firstly, a person poses for a selfie—this is the first picture or position in which the person wants to photograph him or herself—and secondly, the person takes a picture of this pose—creating a picture of a picture. The selfie taker holds the camera in front of her- or himself, not looking through the lens or through the screen but looking at the screen like looking into a mirror. The painter of a self-portrait sits in front of the canvas, in the same position in which he or she would sit when painting another person. The painted self-portrait is painted with reference to memories, imaginations, mirrors or previous pictures. The digital selfie is taken on the spur of the moment and with the smartphone showing a reflection of oneself, giving the portrayed person a chance to adjust the pose before taking the picture, deleting it and taking another one.

The gesture of holding the phone like a mirror in front of oneself is obviously one of the reasons that selfies have been widely associated with narcissism. Selfie takers look at the image of themselves on their phone like Narcissus at his reflection in the water. The fact that selfies are reflections of oneself also means that they are often mirror-inverted, which becomes obvious when the selfie includes text. In Indonesia the selfie-stick, an extension of the arm that enables a wider angle for the photograph, is called *TongSis,* which is an abbreviation for *tongkat narsis,* the 'narcissistic stick'. This term hints at the humoristic self-reflexion of Indonesians' love of selfies. This self-irony also accompanies the taking and distribution of portraits from selfie parks, where everyone ultimately knows that the images are taken in front of installations and yet they are aesthetically appealing and convey a feeling of prestige. In this way, they are also a humoristic reference to the prestige of tourism and travel, which can happen at home without a big budget.

Unlike artwork, especially abstract and surrealist artwork, photography is deemed to represent the actual reality (Frosch 2019, p. 28). This actuality is a crucial dimension of taking and sharing selfies via online social media (Lobinger and Brantner 2015), which are often images sharing one's current situation. This can happen in everyday situations, documenting one's tiredness on a long working day or a coincidental meeting with a friend and it can be a proof-image, sharing one's location at a certain spot.

However, the feeling that photographs represent the actual reality is misleading. The editing of photographs—especially in the digital age—allows multiple possibilities for making changes to what is portrayed. Therefore, selfies and other online images are neither only truth nor fake. They are images of images, repetitions of previous images and reflections of the self. This means that selfies reveal how the selfie-taker wants to represent him- or herself in a more or less conscious performance. The way that selfies often show part of the arm of the photographer is an obvious example of the fact that photographs capture the photographed objects from a certain angle and are thus a subjective interpretation of reality. In this regard selfies are a performative act, contributing to a persons' self-representation and social identity.

Moreover, for their users, selfies are an important means of everyday communication (Lobinger and Brantner 2015, p. 1849) and the act of taking the picture is an experience in itself. In literature on digital selfies, it is argued that taking a picture of oneself and sharing it via online social media is related to interests in prestige and power (Weiser 2015). For the examples at hand, we relate this claim to the prestige of travelling in Indonesian society as the selfie parks often imitate travel destinations from abroad and have themselves become domestic travel destinations. Furthermore, we also consider that beyond questions of power and prestige, social media activities have become culturally important in everyday lives based on repetition or imitation. Ullrich (2019, p. 12) and Frosch (2019, p. 14) emphasize the relevance of imitation and repetition in social media activities, arguing that selfies and static online images are a paradox within the processual nature of social media activities. While on the one hand, images and stories are constantly changing, selfies and screenshots relate to previous stories and represent the stillness of a certain moment, imagination or feeling. In Indonesia, this continuity is rooted in experiences of representing meaningful travel, such as pilgrimage.

2 Pilgrimage Portraits

Relating to the well-known text 'Image and Pilgrimage in Christian Culture' by Victor and Edith Turner (1978), Simon Coleman and John Eade (2004, p. 2) argue that the acts of representation and movement, in a physical and spiritual sense, in pilgrimage are a dilemma since the images cannot grasp the movement and transformation, which is an essential feature of pilgrimage. And yet the experience of religious mobility becomes meaningful through well-known images of pilgrimage. In Indonesia one of these well-known images is that of Mecca returnees, combining various elements of social prestige: a certain wealth (to afford the travel), knowledge and spirituality. Even today, and probably now more than ever, the pilgrimage to Mecca is a sign of material and spiritual success and those who have accomplished it return with an increased social status.

The first time I was introduced to Indonesians' images of Mecca was in 2013 when I started research on the question of how Indonesians see the Arab World (Lücking 2020). A young *hajj* returnee illustrated her account of the *hajj* to Mecca by swiping through the pictures she had taken with her phone. Later I learned how important pictures are in the context of the *hajj*: pictures that pilgrims take before their departure, pictures that they print and physically carry to certain places in Mecca and Medina, pictures they take during the pilgrimage and the pictures that they show after their return—some of them photoshopped posters showing themselves in front of the Kaaba, as until recently it was forbidden to take cameras into the Holy Mosque and therefore 'Mecca Selfies' are usually photoshopped collages.[1]

The practice of entrusting *hajj* candidates with letters and photographs before their departure is related to the belief that the physical presence of the images and names of aspiring *hajj* candidates will support the realization of their dreams to do the *hajj*. 'When my picture has made it to Mecca, I will hopefully follow soon', one interlocutor explained. This is related to the custom of *hajat* prayers (intercessory prayers) that pilgrims perform in Mecca, not only for those who aspire to do the *hajj* but also for health, love and success. Thus there is a belief in the physical quality of pictures, which can serve as vessels for blessings or conveyers of one's own (future) presence.

Pictures are highly relevant upon return from Mecca as well. Large posters show photoshopped images of Mecca returnees with the Kaaba in the background. In order to create these images, the pilgrims dress up in white, with accessories from Saudi Arabia, such as a chequered headdress for men, to show their changed prestigious status.

The pre- and post-pilgrimage activities and images localize the pilgrimage experiences and support the Turnerian re-structuring into local social hierarchies. Indonesians' pilgrimages to Mecca become meaningful in the local context through resembling (photoshopped) pictures that every Indonesian pilgrim brings home. This corresponds with Ullrich's (2019, p. 12) and Frosch's (2019, p. 14) claims that communication through visuals is based on repetition. While the travel is the processual part of the ritual, the image stands still, representing the social structuring. Similarly, selfies in the world of online communication are a stable marker in a dialogic sphere.

The example of Mecca returnees shows that this is not a new phenomenon. Decorations on the houses of Mecca returnees that include images of the pilgrims have a long tradition in the Muslim world. While in Indonesia's rural areas, printed images and photoshopped selfies that are put up in front of the houses of pilgrimage returnees are widespread, members of Indonesia's urban middle classes share images more instantly and digitally on social media platforms like

---

[1] 'Real' Mecca Selfies (not the photoshopped ones) are a controversial issue in this context. Numerous newspaper articles report clerics' disapproval of taking selfies in front of the most sacred site in Islam. Obviously, opinions differ here. What some see as the 'ultimate selfie', for which they are willing to pay brokers who smuggle their cameras/phones inside the Holy Mosque in Mecca, others see as Westernization of Mecca—as the authors of the book 'Ketika Mecca menjadi Las Vegas' ('When Mecca becomes Las Vegas', Kusuma 2014) argue.

Facebook, Twitter, TikTok and Instagram.[2] Their peers who see the pictures might sit using their phones in traffic jams in Jakarta and would not walk by a poster in front of someone's house. It is probably also due to the conditions of urban life that many Indonesians establish spirituality and social relationships online (see Slama 2017).

While the hajj to Mecca is an obligatory pilgrimage for Muslims who can afford the journey, other travels are voluntary but in Indonesia they are widely considered as recommended according to Shafi'i Islamic law, such as the minor pilgrimage to Mecca, the *umrah* (see Mayasari 2014), the pilgrimage or *ziarah* (visitation) to al-Aqsa mosque in Jerusalem (see Lücking 2019) and other religious package tours, which are advertised as *wisata halal* ('halal tourism') for the Muslim market or *wisata rohani* ('spiritual tourism') for the Christian market. Several Christian research participants describe so-called Holy Land Pilgrimage to Jerusalem and Bethlehem as equivalent to their Muslim compatriots' hajj. Moreover, these religious travels feature prominently in popular media like contemporary prose, cinema and TV series (see for example 'Haji Backpaker', Rifki 2014).

Coming back to the argument of repetitious images, this means that the creation, imitation and repetition of certain images happens within social change in Indonesian society and is influenced by the travel industry, the government and the media. However, a repetition of motifs can be contested. Pilgrimage travels to Jerusalem are an obvious example of this because of political controversies.

While pilgrimage to Jerusalem started to become widespread among Indonesia's Christian minority in the 1980s, today it is also relevant in the Muslim market. Muslim travel agents and pilgrims refer to a hadith by Al-Bukhari, which says that the Prophet Muhammad commanded his followers to visit three mosques: the Holy Mosque containing the Kaaba in Mecca (*al-masğid al-ḥarām*), the Prophet's Mosque in Medina (*al-masğid an-nabawī*), and the 'farthest mosque', which is considered to be Al-Aqsa Mosque in Jerusalem (Lücking 2019, p. 204). Moreover, they claim that Muslim tourism to Jerusalem is a way of showing solidarity to Palestinian people and fostering Muslim presence in Jerusalem (Lücking 2019, p. 197). This political subtext marks the field of images of Jerusalem as particularly contested.

Ideas of taking sides and showing solidarity with either Israel or Palestine are also prominent in travel agencies' advertisements. According to their Muslim or

---

[2] Indonesia is the nation with the third largest number of Facebook users, the fourth largest number of Twitter users, and the twelfth largest number of LinkedIn users (Yuswohady and Gani 2015).

Christian customers, travel agencies can create an image of Jerusalem as the occupied capital of Palestine or as the Holy City and home to God's chosen people (the Jewish people) and the capital of Israel. The competitive aspect in Muslim and Christian images of Jerusalem does not only concern the status of the city, as capital of Palestine or Israel, but also Muslim-Christian relations and internal frictions within Indonesia's Muslim and Christian communities. As an example, a female travel agent from Jakarta recounted that some of her closest friends had 'unfriended' her on Facebook when they saw that she had started organizing pilgrimages to Al-Aqsa Mosque because they supported the boycott of Israel and would not visit Jerusalem if it meant accepting an Israeli visa. Therefore, this travel agent was particularly keen on showing her solidarity with Palestine, among other things through numerous solidarity selfies with Palestinians whom she met on her travels, with the Palestinian flag and in front of Al-Aqsa Mosque, adding captions like 'Jerusalem is Ours' or 'Jerusalem, the eternal capital of Palestine'.

This example shows that Indonesians' online pilgrimage documentation is subject to the online and offline reactions of others. In this case, selfies are not only proof of pilgrimage presence—like the posters on the houses of Mecca returnees—but also a form of presence in online spaces and interaction with an online community, where a selfie can be seen as political statement.

Accordingly, a dialogic and processual nature shapes the experience of creating images while the images themselves are rather static and repetitive. Selfies and other images or 'stories' (in Instagram slang) are shared instantly on social media platforms. Pilgrims see sacred spaces through the lenses of their smart phones and with a homeward perspective, thinking about their friends' and followers' reactions.

In some cases, the visual documentation is professionalized. Selfies are complemented with videos and other photographs. In certain places in Jerusalem professional photographers offer photo documentation services, like a photographer on the Via Dolorosa who rents out wooden crosses to Christian pilgrimage groups who want to enact the way of the cross. The photographer takes pictures throughout the walk along the Via Dolorosa and offers them for purchase.

Apart from performing and transcending pilgrimage experiences beyond the spatial and temporal context of the pilgrimage, taking pictures is an event. What appears obvious in the case of images of Jerusalem—the contestation of images, doubts about their originality and competition over them—is more subtle in the everyday practices of taking and sharing selfies. Here, the experiential value of going on a selfie excursion is more obvious.

3 Everyday Selfie Tourism

In domestic selfie parks the creation of portraits of a cosmopolitan self is accessible without a big budget. The following scene from our joint visit to a selfie park in August 2018 gives an idea of the experience in an Indonesian selfie park:

> A short motorcycle ride brings us out of the bustling activities of Yogyakarta city into the green oasis of Selopamioro village in Imogiri, a rural area on the outskirts of Yogyakarta. We park our motorcycles next to a goat shed in front of a private house. Laundry is drying on a clothing line and residents sit in front of the house, greeting us in a friendly manner. To the side of the house, we find the entrance to the selfie park, which is the purpose of our visit. The entrance is a temporary bridge that leads down to the dried basin of the Oyo River. During dry summertime, the water debit in the riverbed is low and most of its basin is completely dried up. Therefore, a Village Based Tourism Community *(Kelompok Sadar Wisata)* decorates the basin as a seasonal park. The community consists of locals who aim at developing tourism in each village and is supervised by the village government. There is no entrance fee, just a donation box located to the side of the entrance gate and further donation boxes down in the riverbed at every so-called *spot selfie*, or selfie spot, which are marked spots on which the taker of a selfie positions her-/himself, defining a certain angle to capture the stunning nature of the river valley or a special decoration or model of famous landmarks. After traversing the gate and passing through a greenish-toned clear summer water flow, we can see numerous *spot selfie* that are beautifully arranged on top of a marble-like stone river basin. These include a water bike, a bench with a fire-place decoration, a replica of the Tugu Pal Putih, a famous landmark which in original can be found in one of the busiest areas in the city of Yogyakarta, and a massive stone with a white door-like decoration. We stroll around, take photos, chat with other visitors when they ask if we can assist them by taking their photo and get to talk with one of the park's creators, a local resident who is delighted about the money and life that the park has brought to the village.

Parks like the one described here have become popular entertainment destinations for Indonesians from all walks of life. Some decorations refer to nature and travel—the bikes and fireplace possibly refer to the Netherlands, the former colonizer of today's Indonesia—and easily identifiable landmarks, like miniature replicas of the Tugu monument. Their creation can be seen as part of a more general endeavour to establish community-based tourism in Indonesia, where the village community is encouraged to use the idyllic village environment for touristic purposes (see Ell 2019). A visit does not take much preparation, the parks are easily reachable from urban areas and visiting is not expensive. There visitors can take pictures of themselves in front of imitations of famous landmarks from Indonesia and Europe, or in front of the scenery with local nature or creations of foreign-looking nature, like flower fields. Regarding European landmarks, one finds many references to the Netherlands, like the above-mentioned bicycles, 'Dutch tulip fields', or windmills as well-known symbols of the Netherlands. The Eiffel Tower is probably one of the most popular miniature installations, but characteristic red British telephone booths, Viennese boats, or Japanese cherry blossom trees are also common. Most installations refer either to Europe, in particular the Netherlands, or Indonesia. One of the most famous Indonesian selfie parks is the European village-themed amusement park Devoyage in Bogor, which is highly professionalized, with an entrance fee of 40,000 Rupiah (2.5 €).

Without having to board an airplane, cross borders or immerse oneself in the busyness of touristic areas, visitors can take selfies in front of European and Indonesian scenery. The parks thereby transfer the experience of something special, like a touristic journey, into everyday life, they de-centre domestic and international centres though replications and people's photographed interactions with these places. Going on a trip to a selfie park is an entertaining activity and when the aesthetic selfies are shared on online social media, individuals receive social recognition through likes and comments from their friends and followers even if they have not actually visited the foreign places, because their photos are beautiful, funny or creative.

The phenomenon of selfie parks struck us with regard to the similarities in the creation of selfies and investment in them but also because they foreground the experience and in fact a new sense of presence in a rural area that only comes to be acknowledged due to aspirations regarding online presence. Even though it seems like everybody has equal access to online communication, the hierarchical structure of park creators and owners, social media influencers or travel influencers does affect the form, content and proliferation of images. Travel influencers can be distinguished into two types: those who have thousands of followers due to *instegramable* picture posts and who are usually called *'selebgram'*, which is an abbreviation of 'Instagram celebrity', and travel information accounts. The latter is the type of account I (Mayasari) run under the name @pesonaimogiri. It operates by posting travel photos or videos and reposting any content that is made by other creators. Images from selfie tourism are popular on @pesonaimogiri and the experience of running this Instagram profile has led to acquaintances among selfie park owners, village communities and *selebgram*. These acquaintances reveal that for the local community, selfie tourism entails actual economic profits and for selfie-takers the photos entail social prestige. In the following, we describe the required characteristics for a profitable selfie.

As we described in the introductory scene, village communities in Yogyakarta have built selfie parks as attractions for domestic tourism. A selfie park is worth visiting when the pictures one can take there have value on Instagram, which means that they are worth posting, commenting on and sharing. Visitors refer to the 'parks' selfie spots as *'instagramable'*. This term has become a label to evaluate suitability for being posted on Instagram and gaining attention there. Attention on Instagram is measured through the number of people who see, like, comment and share the image. Usually, selfie park visitors come in groups, sometimes wearing photo-appropriate make-up and chic apparel, such as fashionable sunglasses, special headscarves or a hat. Thus a handful of accessories are needed as photo props related to images of prestige among *selebgram*, or *selebgram* wannabes, who will take several poses. Sometimes they will wear fancy sunglasses, then take them off, apply more make-up, put on a shawl, and take another picture. Most female visitors tend to pose with their face facing the camera. Male travel *selebgram*, or female *selebgram* who are less self-confident about their appearance usually don't emphasize their faces or turn them away from the camera, gazing into the distance. They will take hundreds of pictures at a time. Oftentimes, they will ask the park's crew or visitors from other groups for help taking their picture. In this regard, the hunt for good selfies opens up a new sense of presence and interaction.

The so called *selebgram*—the Instagram celebrity—will then edit the picture, sometimes using autumn-like colour effects. Mostly, selfie park visitors use the smartphone apps Light Room or Snapseed Photo Editor, which can be easily operated on android phones. For those who tend to be photographed from afar, bright coloured apparel is a must. Usually they opt for red, fuchsia, orange, or yellow. Those who are not *selebgram* normally adopt the first concept by using make-up and good apparel for female, or branded apparel for male park visitors. This means that being good-looking is imperative for the creation of images of prestige among female *selebgram* imitators while male *selebgram* imitators tend to represent themselves as wealthy. These selfies are performances of middle-class identity, portraits of a self that can afford make-up and expensive clothing. At the same time, they represent the notion of travel and exploration through the parks' selfie spots with nature and landmarks.

Professional *selebgram* will collaborate with Instagram photographers. Sometimes, the collaboration expands, including make-up artists, gown rental, and even local designers. Moreover, the parks and other touristic places where photo or video taking takes place have Instagram accounts to which the selfies are tagged.[3] Consequently, everyone involved gets a credit written in the photo or video

---

[3] See for instance the Instagram account of Devoyage https://www.instagram.com/accounts/login/?next=/devoyagebogor/.

caption. Like for Mecca selfies and Jerusalem selfies, the social capital of a selfie depends on peoples' social networks and peers' reactions.

As long as the object is good enough to be captured in an edited photo with full make-up, with models wearing casual, travel-like apparel, the place will soon be visited by more people. Based on what I (Mayasari) learned while managing @pesonaimogiri, any place with unique objects that is good enough to be captured and posted on an Instagram feed or story section will be visited by an increased number of people shortly after it is posted. It doesn't have to be a brand new touristic place. Sometimes, it needs to be only a beautiful bench located at the side of a rice field. This can include the visitation of traditional pilgrimage sites, such as Imogiri, the royal graveyard of the Sultan's court, where people usually come to pray but nowadays also to take photos (see Fig. 1).

The aim of taking pictures makes people travel and get to know these places in Indonesia's rural areas. This supports peoples' pride in Indonesian nature and heritage and offers income opportunities for local communities. Nevertheless, internationality, a flair for travel and cosmopolitanism are also best-sellers.

Fig. 1 Visiting the royal graveyard in Imogiri to take photos (Mayasari, April 2022)

Especially popular are places which look as if they were somewhere outside of Yogyakarta. With descriptions such as 'this is our version of Ubud'[4] or 'have you visited Jogja's version of the Sierra Nevada?' followers will soon engage with the post, hop on their motorcycles and ride out of the city to explore the location. Since everyone knows that the location is not abroad but in Indonesia, these captions create humoristic self-confidence about living in a place that is worth being photographed. Thus the replications of foreign attractions are not mere copies but self-confident interpretations of what actually comprises a place worth visiting.

Urban social media users leave the reality of their mobile phone screens and explore a reality outside of their immediate surroundings. Even if this happens within the designed environment of the parks, there is a new form of interaction between people from urban and rural areas—at least during the processual anti-structure of being on the 'selfie-pilgrimage', if one compares the park visits to ritual processes during pilgrimage as theorized by Turner. Even though, for selfie park visitors, the transformation of their social status takes longer than a one-time pilgrimage. For *selebgram,* the social status parameters lie within 'engagement rates' and the number of followers. So, if the selfie park photos boost both parameters, then they increase the *selebgram's* social status, at least digitally.

Like in the case of Mecca selfies and images of Jerusalem, repetition and competition between different parks and selfie-takers shape this communication through images. The creation of selfies does not happen out of the blue. It is an interreferential endeavour in which people relate to previous images and narratives: they imitate, improve and extend them, presenting an image that speaks to their audience in a way that will be understandable but also gradually experimenting with new content.

Through their Instagram posts, selfie takers present favourable images of themselves and imitate a middle-class lifestyle of traveling and exploring the world. The make-up, clothing and overall design of the image, including the background scenery, which is created by the parks and the editing process, create images that are prestigious. Like Mecca and Jerusalem selfies, the everyday visits to selfie parks relate to previous park visitors' photos and are quests in search of the aesthetic. For people who are not a *selebgram,* their followers are an audience of friends, relatives, neighbours, classmates and colleagues. Usually, most of their followers are people they know in the offline world.

---

[4] Ubud is a town in the interior of Bali Island, known for its beautiful nature with rice terraces, temples and cultural attractions.

However, the images do not only entail social and symbolic capital for those who are portrayed in the selfies but also for the network of people behind successful Instagram images. For every *instagramable* photo posted on Instagram, several stakeholders get some benefit. *Selebgram* and travel influencers will benefit from increased engagement on the online platform, which is useful for gaining income from advertisements. For those working as influencers, finding nearby *instagramable* objects is an economic move. Highly engaging content can be produced using limited resources. Consequently, for those who want to be a *selebgram* imitator without really monetizing their Instagram account, finding a nearby *instagramable* object is still a gem. Beautiful yet varied themes of vacation-like photos or videos can be gained in no time.

For professional travel *selebgram*, the audience comprises thousands of followers and businesses that may use their services for brand promotion, usually called 'endorsement'. *Selebgram* with better content will get a higher endorsement rate. However, it takes time for an influencer to gain decent monetization. Influencers/*selebgrams* need to post at least one content a day and in order to keep up with the target, influencers need to visit easily reachable places that can offers large numbers of *instagramable* pictures or videos and the competition is harsh. If successful, a wide range of industries, such as local restaurants, tour and travel agencies, hotels, make-up vendors, local watchmakers, clothing and apparel labels and outlets, or even health supplements may use their services. For instance, through my (Mayasari) Instagram account, I have received endorsements from Spotify, OPPO and Xiaomi (a Chinese mobile phone brand) through an endorsement manager.

Furthermore, Kelompok Sadar Wisata, the village association which runs the above-described park, will also gain benefits in the form of potential income from the popularity of their *instagramable* objects when more visitors come to the parks and donate or pay entrance fees. The creation of village associations, like Kelompok Sadar Wisata, which was formed in order to reduce unemployment in villages, has been successful, or has at least created another stream of income through tourism even if the selfie parks are small and improvised, generating only little income (see Fig. 2).

4 Conclusion: Images of a Cosmopolitan Self

Selfie tourism might be frowned upon because of its narcissistic self-centredness. However, like Schlehe's examples of popular cultural representations among paranormal practitioners at cultural parades and in theme parks, our research similarly

Fig. 2 Small selfie park at the beach in Parangtritis (Lücking, August 2019)

shows that the creation of cosmopolitan self-portraits can go beyond essentializations, be reflexive and become an opportunity for encounters, inclusion and more nuanced representations of culture. The reflexivity is often humoristic, like the description of the selfie-stick, *TongkatNarsis,* or imitations of successful *selebgram.*

Despite notions of representing elitist cosmopolitanism as global travellers, the example of domestic selfie tourism shows that the boundaries between the upper- and lower-middle classes can be blurred, and that vernacular cosmopolitanism is created in everyday experiences. Thereby the prestige of images of the self is no longer limited to those who can afford to travel to special places. In this regard selfies that are produced with a smaller budget are not merely imitations or repetitions of selfies from international tourism, as argued by Ullrich (2019, p. 12) and Frosch (2019, p. 14) for online images in general, but they can be seen as a creative comment on travel selfies, promoting local travel destinations.

Strikingly, there are no religious landmarks in selfie parks, only worldly ones. Why this is the case needs yet to be researched. A first assumption from our observations is that playful engagement has its limits when it comes to sacred sites, where the originality of the place appears to be important. Therefore, our juxtaposition in this article is complementary rather than comparative. Selfie park images do not refer to Mecca or Jerusalem selfies but in both cases the social meanings of the selfies, of taking photos together and being aware of peers' reactions, are similar. A selfie is validated through the gaze of peers and therefore it must be analysed beyond what is being portrayed. This confirms Jones' (2017) observation that selfies are embedded in social relationships, making them useful for communication and not only representation. The relational mediation process is especially obvious in the online sharing of images. To a certain extent, the mediation is dialogic. Everyone who has a phone and internet access can participate in creating and sharing images, even though there are trends toward professionalization and there are hierarchies defining favourable images, as the success of *selebgrams* and imitations of their style show. Yet the success of *selebgrams* is also an example of how people can experience upward social mobility through popular aesthetic performances and without any formal education in this field.

Instead of religious sites, selfie parks feature local Indonesian attractions, in particular nature, and European, in particular Dutch, landmarks. Popular references to the Netherlands indicate Indonesian peoples' complex and ambivalent relationship with the former colonizer. Despite the colonial exploitation of Indonesia, the image of the Netherlands in Indonesia is not entirely negative. In fact, Dutch themes in selfie parks are popular and people are proud to take photos in front of windmills and tulip fields, maybe even with a whitening-skin filter for their selfies. The Netherlands remains an important reference point for Western modernity within multiple global and local reference points. The ability to make certain Dutch landmarks one's own in Indonesian selfie parks can be seen as a humoristic postcolonial sense of connectedness to Dutch culture and ambivalent engagement with foreignness.

Another difference between Mecca and Jerusalem pilgrims and selfie park visitors is the role of their mobility. Different from the extraordinary character of a pilgrimage ritual, a visit to a selfie park can be brief, spontaneous, and casual even if the Instagram selfie pages are known as travel accounts and the parks show imitations of famous travel destinations. Nevertheless, our examples reveal similarities in the blurring of social boundaries while traveling and also restructuring through visual representations. The blurring of boundaries applies, for instance, to encounters between rural and urban populations in the parks and to encounters between Muslim and Christian Indonesian pilgrims in the Middle East.

For the question of presence, this means that pilgrims and selfie park visitors are simultaneously present at the site they visit and in their online community where the selfies are shared. After all, taking a selfie means turning one's back on the site. Does this symbolic turn toward the camera and away from the site reflect a changing sense of presence? Our observations certainly show that selfies are a sign of presence within an online community and a manifestation of social presence in one's peer group.

The importance of peers' reactions to these images shows that the cosmopolitanism in the selfies is rooted and vernacular. Indonesians refer to multiple centres in the world, but they are also focused on their immediate social reality. This corresponds with Schlehe's (2019, p. 381) conclusion about cultural 'hybridisation and pragmatic harmonisation' among paranormal practitioners. Even though some selfies, like Jerusalem selfies, are contested, there is an overall tendency to combine a multitude of places and cultural representations in selfie tourism—the more the better.

In her research on cultural parades in Yogyakarta, Schlehe (2017b) found that economic reasons can legitimize popular local religious rituals and make them acceptable in an increasingly Islamised environment. In local selfie parks the added representation of global and local landmarks and young peoples' fun activities are apparently similarly harmless in the eyes of Indonesian society. Moreover, they promote romantic images of Indonesian nature and village life at a time where urban middle-class lifestyles appear to be the most aspired to. Thus vernacular cosmopolitanism includes rural areas and nature.

The belief in the power of images—as vessels for blessings in the case of pilgrimage and as a source of income in domestic pilgrimage tourism—provokes the question of whether people acknowledge other-than-human entities in their selfie tourism, as observed by Schlehe for paranormal practitioners' relations to the supernatural (2019, p. 382). In our research we saw that selfie-takers treat an image as an entity in itself—not as a mere representation of actual reality but as something that is real in itself and functions especially within online communication. Whether one can go as far as to claim that images and online mechanisms, like algorithms, have agency in themselves remains a question for further research and discussion.

References

Bhabha, H. K. 2004. *The location of culture*. London: Routledge.

Coleman, S., and J. Eade, Eds. 2004. *Reframing pilgrimage. Cultures in motion.* London: Routledge.

Ell, A. 2019. *Wissenstransfer im Community Based Tourism. Eine Feldstudie in der Region Yogyakarta, Indonesien.* Baden-Baden: Tectum.

Frosch, P. 2019. *Screenshots. Racheengel der Fotografie.* Berlin: Wagenbach.

Jones, C. 2017. Circulating modesty. The gendered afterlives of networked images. In *Piety, celebrity, sociality. A forum on Islam and social media in Southeast Asia.* https://americanethnologist.org/features/collections/piety-celebrity-sociality/circulating-modesty. Accessed: 11 April 2022.

Kusuma, M. T., Ed. 2014. *Ketika Makkah Menjadi Seperti Las Vegas. Agama, Politik, Dan Ideologi.* Jakarta: PT Gramedia Pustaka Utama.

Lobinger, K., and C. Brantner. 2015. In the eye of the beholder. Subjective views on the authenticity of selfies. *International Journal of Communication* 9: 1848–60.

Lücking, M. 2019. Travelling with the idea of taking sides. Indonesian pilgrimages to Jerusalem. *Bijdragen tot de Taal-, Land- en Volkenkunde/Journal of the Humanities and Social Sciences of Southeast Asia* 175 (2): 196–224.

Lücking, M. 2020. *Indonesians and their Arab world. Guided mobility among labor migrants and Mecca pilgrims.* Ithaca: Cornell University Press.

Mayasari, N. 2014. *Recharging faith. The practice of multiple umrah trips among the middle class in Yogyakarta.* Unpublished M.A. Thesis. Yogyakarta: Gadjah Mada University.

Rifki, D. 2014. *Haji backpacker.* Jakarta: Falcon Picture.

Schlehe, J. 2017a. Staging multiculturalism in theme parks. Re-imagining post-reformasi Indonesia In *Wisdom. Local wisdom, global solutions,* Ed. W. Nuryanti, 78–89. Yogyakarta: Gadjah Mada University Press.

Schlehe, J. 2017b. Contesting Javanese traditions. The popularization of rituals between religion and tourism. *Indonesia and the Malay World* 45 (131): 3–23.

Schlehe, J. 2019. Cosmopolitanism, pluralism and self-orientalisation in the modern mystical world of Java. *Asian Journal of Social Science* 47 (3): 364–386.

Schlehe, J., and S. Hidayah. 2014. Transcultural ethnography. Reciprocity in Indonesian-German tandem research. In *Methodology and research practice in Southeast Asian studies,* Eds. M. Huotari, J. Rüland, and J. Schlehe, 253–272. Basingstoke: Palgrave Macmillan.

Slama, M. 2017. A subtle economy of time. Social media and the transformation of Indonesia's Islamic preacher economy. *Economic Anthropology* 4 (1): 94–106.

Turner, E., and V. Turner. 1978. *Image and pilgrimage in Christian culture.* New York: Columbia University Press

Ullrich, W. 2019. *Selfies. Die Rückkehr des öffentlichen Lebens.* Berlin: Wagenbach.

Weiser, E. 2015. #Me. Narcissism and its facets as predictors of selfie-posting frequency. *Personality and Individual Differences* 86: 477–481.

Werbner, P. 2006. Vernacular cosmopolitanism. *Theory, Culture & Society* 23 (2–3): 496–98.

Yuswohady and Gani, K. E. 2015. *Depalan wajah kelas menengah.* Jakarta: Gramedia.

Globalization, Migration, and Representation

Imagining Together: The Social Dimension of Imagination

Till Förster

1 Introduction: Imagination as Social Practice

Imagination is a fundamental part of human agency. It is performed from day to day. Without imagining what we aim at, without imagining a possible future, we would not act at all. However, imagination is not always practiced in the same way. To some degree, it is performed habitually, but there is always an element of the unfamiliar in it because we cannot fully predict the future – even if we know from experience what is possible and what is not. How we, as individuals or as members of a social milieu, imagine is related to many different factors: the historical situation, our own personal experience, others' images around us, as well as material or cultural constraints that we have to face when we imagine. There are additionally various stimuli for imagining. For instance, imagining may represent an escape from a depressing present; it may also be a joyful projection of our wishes and desires into the future. Imagination can be extremely powerful, as it can motivate revolutions as well as the rejection of worldly affairs. There is no social life that is completely void of imagination – but imagination is not simply there. It is a creative social practice.

The relevance of imagination is recognised widely in the social sciences. It would be difficult to work on politics without taking political imagination into account (e g. Comaroff and Comaroff 1999). Groups within a society are subject to and of social imagination, for instance the youth (e.g. Durham 2000). Religious

---

T. Förster (✉)
Ethnologisches Seminar, Universität Basel, Basel, Schweiz
E-Mail: till.foerster@unibas.ch

imagination is seen as one of the driving forces of change in Africa (e.g. Fernandez 1982). Imagination is also a part of aesthetics and the arts. Even society as a coherent entity is imagined by the people who think of themselves as its members.[1] Not least, ethnography and social description are seen as the product of anthropological or sociological imagination (Willis 2000; Mills 2000).

Imagination does not unfold in the solitary world of the individual, rather it relies on an "interworld"[2] of the social, on how humans as social actors agree, negotiate, reciprocate or bargain over shared meaning. Obviously, imagination is a basic constituent of social agency (Emirbayer and Mische 1998). Imagining together has immediate relevance in postcolonial times as it fosters the reciprocal understanding of "self" and "other". However, despite its wide use in the social sciences and its significance for social theory, imagination has not received the same attention as other basic terms, such as domination, conflict, and structure, to name a few.[3] This essay addresses this gap from an anthropological perspective. It aims at conceptualising imagination by analysing and comparing three short case studies from Africa. Based on this comparison, I argue that imagination is best theorised as a social practice that generates images.

From an anthropological viewpoint, this involves basic questions about the social. Neither the practice of imagining nor the mental images it creates are directly accessible. Yet the actors indeed engage in such processes, producing their own images and sharing mental ones. First, this raises epistemological questions: How is collective imagination possible? How can an individual share and experience the mental images of "others"? How are collective images created in the first place? Second, it challenges comparative anthropological methodologies. How can researchers access such processes? What do they compare if neither the process nor the subjects of imagination are visible – which is not necessarily always the case, but often so?

I will argue that collective images – images shared by a group or a society – are generated by social practice, a practice I call imagination. Researchers can access imagination and the practice of imagining by participating in and observing these practices. As a social practice, imagination brings different individual images and intentions together and thereby produces an imaginary entity that goes beyond the mere sum of its individual idiosyncrasies. Social images are not

---

[1] For societies in general, see Castoriadis 1987, for nation states, see Anderson 1991, for anthropology as imaginative practice, see Bloch 2016; Koukouti und Malafouris 2020.

[2] Crossley 1996, p. 4, translating Husserl's "Zwischenwelt" into English.

[3] A notable exception is McLean and Coleman 2007. Kearney (1988, 1998) provides overviews from a transdisciplinary perspective.

only shared; they have a distinct form that builds upon the social practice through which they emerge.

2 A Clarification: Image and Representation

It is important to note at the outset what this paper is not about: the realist and monadic misunderstanding of imagination. In the past, imagination was often thought of as the capacity to envision a stable content within the mind, thereby making it a constituent of subjectivity. As the projective dimension of individual agency, it offered a space for the actors' idiosyncratic wishes, hopes and dreams, alienating them from everyday reality. Imagination in this sense was often defined as what the actors consciously think of as "not real" (e.g. Sartre 1972).

Such an understanding of imagination encompasses several shortcomings. For example, it relates imagination to the problem of solipsism because it reduces the imagination of others to the consciousness one may have of them – to "my" subjectivity, as it were. Derived from this first point, it conceives imagination as both individual and individualising. It would be very difficult to capture the social dimensions and societal effects of imagination within such a framework, e.g. in political and religious imagining. For instance, why would anybody follow a charismatic leader if his vision of how the social world should look like is immediately framed as "unreal" or "unrealistic"?

Deviating from this strand of thinking, recent approaches emphasise more so the discursive character of imagination (e.g. Kearney 1998) – a presupposition that avoids the former shortcomings because it situates imagination among the intersubjectivity of the actors (as opposed to their monadic subjectivity). Conceptualising imagination as a discursive process leads, however, to other difficulties. A widespread critique is that the presumption of fluid processes and unstable mental images constitutes a culture-bound, typical post-modern way of thinking. While (post)modern cosmopolitans who have adopted this way of thinking appreciate that fluidity, others may seek stable images and hence engage in other ways of imagining – ways that generate more predictable, reliable images. The implicit question is whether there are different forms of imagination – a question that calls for an empirical answer. Anthropology hence has to combine theoretical reflection and empirical enquiry if it wants to advance a conceptualisation of collective imagination.

Before looking at imagining as social practice, I will briefly address the possible subject of the following process: What is an image? Since visual culture and visual studies emerged as interdisciplinary fields[4], the concept of "image" has been the subject of numerous debates that revolve around the use of language and how words may refer to visual experience. English-speaking scholars have a different view of the field than, for instance, scholars working in German (e.g. Boehm 1994). While English has two words for what I will preliminarily call image and picture, German and other languages address the same scope of meaning by one word only, namely "Bild". Of course, there are other words, but they do not cover the same semantic fields as image and picture. "Bildwissenschaft"[5], the German term that would more or less correspond to visual studies in English, has other connotations, too. Language and discursive practices affect theoretical reflections on picture and image.

However, there is a parallel between the debates in English and German: Though no longer a neglected subject in the humanities, picture, image and "Bild" are still undertheorised in *social* theory – this despite their pivotal role in imagination and social agency. Preliminarily defined as the products of imagination, shared images of how the social should look like often guide collective action. They shape the understanding of the social and turn mere impression into social facts.

Before developing a social understanding of what an image is, I will forward an elementary definition. It goes back to W.J.T. Mitchell's picture theory (Mitchell 1986, 1994), but it also echoes common sense understandings of how humans think and how we situate ourselves within a shared life-world. For analytical reasons, Mitchell (1994) claims, "it is useful to play upon distinctions between the two terms [picture and image]: the difference between a constructed concrete object […] and the virtual, phenomenal appearance that it provides for a beholder" (4 and *passim*). To some extent, Mitchell picks up the common distinction of image as a mental representation of a picture as its material counterpart. According to both his and common sense notions of image, one can distinguish between something that one perceives as an object in the material world and how one thinks of it, i.e., the image that one has in mind. Most would not deny that the two overlap, but rather that they are two distinct objects – one "real", the other "imagined". In Mitchell's understanding, the two relate to each other, but they have a different ontological status.[6] This conceptualisation would reduce image

---

[4] See Dikovitskaya 2005; Mirzoeff 2014; Sturken und Cartwright 2001.

[5] Literally "science of images", often translated as "image studies".

[6] Mitchell posited that "imagination […] create[s] much of our world out of the dialogue between verbal and pictorial representations" (Mitchell 1986, p. 46). But this dialogue was situated at the level of meaning and representation while the sensory experience only underpinned it.

either to the "unreal", as in Sartre's understanding, or to a mental representation of a real object.

In contrast, "Bild", the German equivalent to picture *and* image, is usually understood as an artefact that aims at reproducing a semantic content. Though one could argue that this way of putting it simply reverses Mitchell's argument, the material and the mental side are thought of as one. One may perceive this as an imprecise way of thinking, but the problem goes deeper. First, it would be difficult to deny that actors may engage in different ways of seeing the same object and that they may have differing ideas of what they envision in their mind.[7] In Mitchell's framework, one could understand "image" as a mental (re)presentation of something that could also be visible as a material object, possibly even as a "picture". Images in this sense would *relate* to what one perceives in the real world – but their form would not solely be a mirror of a material picture. Of course, humans use their minds to produce images that then affect how we perceive real things. Pictures as "real" objects are therefore difficult to separate from imagined objects. Besides the epistemological consequences that such views entail, they also point to problems in social theory because these images are not mere products of the individual – they are social facts, which leads back to the question of social practice (Gilbert 1992).

Second, one would also not deny that humans might have images of things in mind that do *not* have a material underpinning. In colloquial English, such images are often called "ideas". The idea of society as an entity is perhaps the broadest of these. Unable to experience society as a whole in all its aspects and dimensions, humans as social actors would need some sort of imaginary unit for society (or the nation, Anderson 1991) in order to be able to refer to it in their daily social practice. In an extreme version of this view, Castoriadis (1987) says that the social imaginary is forced upon all members of society when they are socialised. Imagination in his understanding is a violent process that is never fully completed, as it is constantly met with the resistance of the individual.

From an anthropological perspective, both views are problematic. The first still struggles with the distinction of "real" vs. "unreal". It circumvents the question of what the objects of imagination are: Are they things that could have existed in the natural life-world? Or could they exist at least as objects of sensory experience – though not as entities, as the second view would claim? If the latter holds true, social actors would constitute them as mental objects and make them as real as images in their own right – not as images that represent or mirror something "out

---

[7] See Mary Douglas' work on dirt perceived as "things in the wrong place" (Douglas 1966).

there". The second view has no convincing answer to the question of how and why social actors can share an imagined object.

3 Images as Intentional Objects

To overcome the Cartesian as well as the monadic misunderstandings of imagination of object vs. mind as real vs. unreal, I conceptualise images as intentional objects. An image is an intentional state about something that comes into being through this very intentionality, that is, how actors relate to it. A house, or any other object, for that matter, is seen in a particular way only through one's intentional relationship to it. We would recognise a social order as an entity only because of our intentionality. Whether images are related to a material or another kind of object is a secondary question. More important is that images as intentional objects are objects *for* somebody (Crane 2001, p. 342), that is, for the actors who constitute them. Because intentionality presumes a relation to a shared life-world, images are embedded in the intersubjectivity of social life. Collective imagination means lending images the status of ordinary life-worldly objects – objects that would be accepted as "real" by most social actors.

Social life is filled with such intentional objects. Besides society itself, "tradition", "community", "the nation" and "the state" belong to this group. It is impossible to experience them as entities, so the actors need to have images of them in mind. Though the literature on such images is quite dispersed and heterogeneous[8], it confirms my point: images as intentional objects are indispensable. The actors need them to maintain their agency and to situate themselves in their social life-world. One could reverse that argument and argue that a social order presumes the existence of shared images that are continuously generated by social practice – else there would be no space for social agency.

4 Bringing Images to Light: Divination

To illustrate my argument, my first example deals with individuals who create and shape images of the social through direct, unmediated exchange. I will look at the emergence of images by focusing on interactions that, in the beginning, are an exclusive exchange between two or perhaps three persons. These actors create

---

[8] A few examples: on "tradition" see Hobsbawm und Ranger 1983; on "the nation" Anderson 1991; on "community" Hayden 2007; on "the state" Migdal 2001.

images that then go through the test of time and the social environment they live in. At times, the images are accepted and confirmed by "others"; at other times, they are rejected and do not stand the test, depending on how "others" perceive and value them. What is important is that they start with an interaction between a limited number of actors who create a particular image of their social environment. These images are not the outcome of individual phantasy; they always have a social source.

To clarify this relationship between the production of images and the social, I will first look at a strictly framed genre of imagination: divination. My example comes from West Africa[9], in particular from the savannahs of the Western Sudan region, but very similar forms of divination exist in many other parts of Africa (de Boeck and Devisch 1994; Devisch 1985; Jackson 1978; LaGamma 2000; Peek 1991; Turner 1975; Werbner 1973) and, to a lesser degree, also in other continents (e.g. Winkelman and Peek 2004; Tedlock 2006; Curry ed. 2010). In an African context, it is important to distinguish divination from prophecy (Jules-Rosette 1978). Divination does not aim at predicting the future, as interpretations based on the Latin root of the word *divinare* – "to foretell, prophesy, forebode," – would suggest (Langer and Lutz 1999). Divination in Africa rather provides interpretations for problems that arose in the past and that affect the lives of the clients in the present.[10] It helps the clients of the diviner to make sense of an unclear situation and thus to re-establish their agency. Agency in such situations has to build upon three dimensions: the actors' habits, their judgment of the situation and their imagination (Emirbayer and Mische 1998).

In mainstream anthropology, this practice is usually interpreted in a rationalist or functionalist way. Divination is generally conceived as a method to judge a situation through a consideration of incomplete evidence (Curry 2010). It covers a gap in the clients' knowledge of the situation, of which they do not know enough to come to a reasonable judgement. Divination is thought of as a technique that generates apparently positive knowledge to empower those who seek advice and to re-integrate them in the everyday *durée* of social practice.[11]

---

[9] The data presented in the following paragraphs is based on field research conducted for my PhD dissertation in the 1970s and 1980s among the Senufo in Côte d'Ivoire (Förster 1985).

[10] E.g. Ndembu divination: "The diviner's insight is retrospective, [...] he discloses what has happened, and does not foretell future events" (Turner 1975, p. 209, more precisely Zeitlyn 2012).

[11] Such mainstream explanations of divination reproduce Evans-Pritchard's classic argument (Evans-Pritchard 1937): All human practice is rational, only the basis of knowledge is different.

In a somewhat contradictory move, these anthropological analyses highlight rational choice in a situation where it is not possible. Such interpretations are misleading. First, they ignore the basics of human agency. They implicitly posit that human acts always rely on a rational judgment of a particular situation. These approaches "[…] rationalise divination after the fact, totally removing it from the realm of intentionally effective action" (Tedlock 2010, p. 195, also Tedlock 2006). Second, they underestimate the capacity to act habitually under the postulate that things and situations remain as they were.[12] Actors may deal with such situations by sticking to everyday assumptions and typifying it as "normal". Though this might be inappropriate from another's perspective, it still sustains their agency. Third, mainstream anthropological interpretations of divination largely overlook that social practice may be based on the actors' capacity to imagine a situation – which is not a mere substitute to "objective" knowledge. Through its projectivity, imagining can become a social fact that, to some degree, *creates* a situation.

From an emic point of view, most actors will want to consult a diviner because they understand their problems as deeply embedded in social life: most often the social is what deserves an explanation. Diviners and their clients know that such problems can be profound, complex and open to multiple interpretations – just as social life itself. Neither the diviner nor the clients assume that divination will instantly provide the one and only possible interpretation.[13] The problems that lead to the consultation of a diviner can be banal, for instance a quarrel with one's neighbour, but also very serious, such as the death of a relative.

Diviners of the Senufo in the West African savannah apply several techniques.[14] Most often, they use a collection of tiny divinatory objects, cowry snails, or sand. Trivial everyday problems are addressed in short séances where the diviners cast the objects, the cowries or the sand across the floor in front of them. Ordinary clients say that serious problems are not easy to clarify and therefore call for more than one opinion. Diviners, they claim, may have access to other "truths" and would therefore provide different interpretations of their clients' problems. Many people seeking an explanation for complex problems thus consult

---

[12] See Alfred Schütz two basic life-worldly idealisations of "and so on and so forth" and "I can do it again" (Schütz 1967, pp. 76 f., 135–138).

[13] The relationship between diviner and client is well covered in Jackson's work on the Kuranko (Jackson 1978).

[14] Fieldwork was conducted among the Senufo in Northern Côte d'Ivoire between 1979 and 1985 (Förster 1985). Similar divinatory techniques are widespread in Africa, see Eglash 1997; Fortes 1966; Grillo 1992; Mendonsa 1982; Paulme 1937; Suthers 1987; Zeitlyn 2012; for overviews see Peek 1991; van Beek und Peek 2013.

more than one diviner. These séances are more elaborate and longer than an ordinary consultation, which seldom lasts longer than 20 to 30 min.

A divination séance either takes place in the diviner's house or in a small circular hut in the compound. The place is usually somewhat hidden. Outsiders may notice the people sitting there, but they would neither be able to watch what they are doing nor would they understand their words. Divination cabins offer space for only two, sometimes three sitting individuals: the diviner, the client and possibly a witness that the client may want present to listen to what is said. Séances start with an appeal to the beings of the wilderness, or "bush spirits" in colloquial English. The diviner needs their assistance "to see" the client's problem. As diviners are considered to be "blind", it is not them who speak but the beings of the wilderness speak through them.[15] Their presence is a precondition for a successful divination séance. The diviner calls them by playing a musical instrument, either a rattle or a bridge-harp.[16] The beings then guide the movements of the diviner and will answer his questions.

Each diviner owns a personal collection of divination objects, which consists of all sorts of objects as long as they are small enough to be used in the cabin. They loosely refer to everyday life in a typical village or town: the bone of a fowl may stand for the animal itself, but also for a good meal; a pen for schools and schooling; a knob for doors and houses; a small piece of rag for costumes; cowry shells for money, and so forth. Small replicas often represent bigger objects. Tiny iron reproductions of hoes are part of almost every collection, as are little depictions of animals cast in brass. The objects are, however, not symbols in a narrow sense. Their meaning is not fixed. It is determined during the divination séance only.

Senufo divination is a skilful process of questions and answers.[17] They see-saw between the beings, the diviner, and the client. Diviner and client sit opposite of each other on the ground so that the two legs touch each other. Clients do not speak until the diviner has identified their social problem. The diviner is expected to prove his competence by specifying the client's problem through the help of the beings from the wilderness alone.

---

[15] Diviners can be male or female. Women may become diviners because they inherit this position and occupation from a deceased relative. Men cannot succeed diviners in their lineages; they become diviners only after having gone through an existential crisis, e.g. a serious illness or a mental affliction (Turner 1968).

[16] Female diviners usually have rattles, while male diviners may play bridge-harps in addition to the rattles.

[17] A comprehensive account of Senufo divination séances is published in Förster 1985.

The séance starts when the diviner casts his collections of objects onto the floor between his splayed legs. The diviner then tries to discover an eye-catching configuration, say for example replicas of agricultural tools forming a cluster or a "disturbing" element such as a flask of nail polish in the middle of agricultural tools. He looks for a pattern that could catch his or the client's attention, presuming that this configuration is a message sent by the beings of the wilderness. For instance, he may observe that a screw is lying next to a miniature doorknob, which might hint at "a problem of construction", perhaps a quarrel over support during the building of a house. If the diviner works with cowry shells only, geometric patterns will be the only signs to interpret (Fig. 1).

Such patterns do not always appear, but if they do, they are often interpreted as a strong sign that brings elements of the client's life to his attention. Patterns establish a relationship between elements that might, in the course of the séance, reveal the cause of the client's problems. If a pattern has not become visible, the diviner may re-arrange the objects slightly, making evident what only he was able "to see".

Fig. 1 A diviner arranges cowry shells in front of his client. The figuration relates events and things of the life of those who are affected by all sorts of misfortune or confusion (Nafoun, Nov 12, 2013)

A pattern of objects is often only a tentative hint at what might lie behind the client's problems. Holding the client's hand in his, the diviner then starts to ask a series of questions, beginning with simple ones and then becoming more and more precise as the séance unfolds. For instance, the first steps may aim at identifying the setting in which the problems arose: "Is it a thing of the compound?" The beings will answer each question by directing the two hands. The answer is a "yes" when the hands clap on the client's thigh. If it is "no", the beings from the wilderness will dismissively wave the hands. If they would need to know more, they will search with the two hands in the air. The skill of a good diviner is mainly to base each question on the proceeding ones in a way that neither entirely eliminates a possible cause nor simply asserts it. The interaction between the diviner and the client is extremely subtle; slowly moving the client's hand in his, the first may insinuate a possible cause while carefully paying attention to the other's hand support or reluctance to follow his movement, signalling approval or resistance. The latter listens in a similarly careful manner to what the diviner asks and how the beings guiding his hand answer it.[18]

There are critical junctures in the process, for instance when the diviner touches on something that is potentially dangerous or so essential to his client's life that he cannot move on without having a clear and definite answer. Such junctures may lead to a break in the sequence of questions and answers. Diviners then leave the room and tell the clients to talk directly to the beings of the wilderness who would later tell him, the diviner, what is at stake. The act of stepping out of the divination cabin and urging the client to speak directly to the spirits can be dramatic. Some diviners change their voice and only whisper while others do not say a word and use gestures to move out silently. When they come back, they will ask the client and the being of the wilderness whether they have come to terms. The beings may then lead the two hands into the collection of objects on the ground and pick out one that is of special relevance.

The client will indirectly confirm or reject this particular juncture. This act, which is seen by most as crucial to divination, recognises a hitherto unknown link between an element of the client's life-world and his problem. It is the first step towards a new, meaningful figuration. In the course of a divination séance, such critical junctures may occur several times, but not too often. Some clients could perhaps suspect that the diviner is actively searching for such dramatic moments merely to impress his clientele. The entire procedure is a subtle and watchful interaction but never hilarious. The actors do not play – they are serious about the

---

[18] See also the film on divination among the Tswapong directed by Richard Werbner (2005).

problems they address and claim not to stage a performance for others. Witnesses are sometimes invited by the client to testify that the séance was unbiased.

Once such a critical juncture has been trespassed, the diviner may proceed more quickly and introduce a few additional elements, completing the figuration and the image that was about to emerge. He may relate the small replica of a hoe to a pencil lying next to it and state that a pupil of the compound is no longer willing to work in the communal field, thus causing a dispute between others about "free-riders". Finally, clients are invited to say a word about the outcome of the séance and whether they are satisfied. If so, the séance is declared closed, and if not, the entire process can start again. Finally, the diviner would wrap up what has been said and done by all parties.

What surfaces in the final part is a broader presentation of the client's problems. By linking certain elements of the client's life-world to his or her problems, the diviner provides a meaningful interpretation and helps the clients "to see" what has happened, as the Senufo would put it. The work of the beings of the wilderness, which are behind the diviner's acts, is characterised by them as cɛlɛ, "to sort out", "to pick out" or as "to separate and gather" – an accurate description of what a divination séance does: It creates a meaningful image of a social problem by bringing different and seemingly contradictory life-worldly elements together into one figuration. This new figuration works through the links that it creates. It generates sense through figurative thinking, not through mere ascriptions of meaning based on an already existing worldview.

Divination as a practice creates images that can and do serve as intentional objects – material as well as mental objects that the actors can relate to, that make sense to them and re-establish an important dimension of their agency. The object is the social life-world itself. By making the social meaningful, divination enables the actors to imagine their present situation as a coherent entity. Clients usually make use of such images after divination. They articulate them in public and claim that this view is an appropriate depiction of their problem. They may then face other opinions, other images of what has "really" happened, and sometimes, they adapt the image they developed during divination accordingly. In this wider interaction, images of such social problems are re-arranged, and after some time, a more stable one may emerge. But from the client's point of view, it starts with divination and the interpretation that it provided. By creating a new image of the social, the actors regain their agency. It helps them to overcome irritating and disturbing matters that previously did not make sense, and it also enables them to articulate their own views accordingly.[19]

5 Spreading the Image: A Regional Charismatic Movement

My second example looks at a case of expanding collective imagination, a charismatic movement. In the past, such social movements emerged repeatedly in the West African savannah. The bigger, revolutionary movements often had an Islamic background, as, for instance, the *jihad* of al-Hajj Umar Tal in the middle of the nineteenth century (Robinson 1985; Robinson and Triaud 1997). Smaller, regional movements incorporated many local religious beliefs and practices, but also elements of Islamic faith and later Christianity. In the West African savannah, charismatic movements were initiated by economic, social and political crises. As regional cults (Werbner 1977), they spread rapidly over wide areas and rocked older institutions as well as the administration of the colonial and postcolonial state. For instance, the movement of Massa in the late 1940s and 1950s was related to the end of forced labour in French colonies – for many peasants a sign of the weakness of the colonial state (Royer 1999).

From a local perspective, the early 1990s resembled the late 1940s. The independent state of Côte d'Ivoire was in crisis. Many peasants experienced the decline of raw commodity prices in the 1980s more directly than townspeople who were engaged in trade or who even received a regular income. The political situation was in disarray, too. Félix Houphouët-Boigny, founding father of the nation and at the time first and only President of Côte d'Ivoire, was in his 90s and barely able to direct the economic development of the country. The fact that he had to accept multi-party elections and a rival candidate for the presidency in 1990 was seen by many as a sign of weakness – as was the case with the abandonment of forced labour by the French in 1946. The historical situation bore many parallels to the last years of colonialism.

What distinguished the 1990s from the days of decolonisation was the growing insecurity. Hold-ups and deadly attacks on travellers were a daily occurrence. Imposter policemen controlled drivers, harassed them and eventually killed those who refused to hand over their cars and trucks while real policemen tried to squeeze out money from everyone whom they could get hold of. Nobody knew

---

[19] When this meaning reproduces a conventional worldview, it may link the social world back to the habitual practices that the actors are familiar with.

who was who, as a then-popular saying went (Förster 2002). The social world was showing signs of disintegration. Spaces beyond the immediate control of the administration reverted to the largely acephalous social order of the nineteenth century, now on the premises of the post-colony. Urban neighbourhoods, towns and villages organised night watches, and a growing number started to set up roadblocks at overland roads, many fortified by barricades. Youth associations and self-defence organisations emerged.

It was a historical moment that, many said, called for an answer. That answer was, in rural areas but also in many urban neighbourhoods, a creature called *kondoro*. In 1992, news of its cult spread extremely rapidly throughout the entire region.[20] In remote villages, the inhabitants were ignorant of the cult's origin. However, they knew about not-too-distant villages where *kondoro* had done "good things" – things that fitted well to their life-world such as witch hunts and respect for elders and ancestors. Its internal organisation as well as the dissemination of its message followed long-established patterns.[21]

Kondoro was a movement that adopted and adapted many religious elements from its regional predecessors. Very much like the older cult of Massa, it spread through the establishment of local shrines in which a substance from the place where *kondoro* was founded or from one of its subsidiary shrines was inserted. Before the erection of a new shrine, the members of *kondoro* examined carefully whether the conditions for a shrine were fulfilled. They did not actively promote the cult. Rather, they insisted that the request for a new shrine had to come from the villages where it would be needed – else the inhabitants "would not be ready". The followers of *kondoro* were strict about the conditions. They expected a delegation of elders who had a say in village affairs.

A cone made of sun-dried mud was the centre of the shrine. In and onto it, the members inserted parts of sacrificed animals such as horns, paws, hooves, bones, and porcupine spines. A thatched roof upon which other signs of power were fixed covered the cone. Rags of wrappers were displayed as remnants of successful witch-hunts – cloth that had been taken from witches when they were identified and found guilty of having acted against the community.

Unlike its predecessors, *kondoro* was, however, much more a social movement of its day. Though there was no leader who would claim divine rights to teach and ordain the misguided, the movement staged its extraordinary authority in charismatic ways: The members were visibly different from ordinary men. When

---

[20] On *kondoro*'s history until 1996 see Förster 1997, p. 515–526.

[21] Fieldwork was conducted between 1991 and 1996 in Northern Côte d'Ivoire, in particular on the erection of a *kondoro* shrine in Nafoun in December 1992 and January 1993.

addressing issues of *kondoro,* they often spoke in a pitched voice, made very short sentences that resembled more commandments than ordinary speech. They had to wear a special costume, a locally woven shirt and trouser dyed in the sap of red bark.

When talking to the envoys of a neighbourhood or a village that asked for the erection of a shrine, the adepts of *kondoro* did not argue – they baldly stated what the community had to do. Strict requirements had to be fulfilled before the emissaries of *kondoro* would come, inspect the community and search for a place where the shrine could be built. These requirements rotated around three contemporary social problems: individualisation, consumerism, and social cohesion. They articulated the malcontents of modernity and how they should be overcome (Comaroff and Comaroff 1993). In local discourse, the followers of *kondoro* spoke of the three problems in terms of communal cooperation, fieldwork, mutual aid and reciprocity – while the shortcomings of modern life were diagnosed as selfishness and greed, disrespect and disdainfulness, theft and blackmailing.

The commandments of *kondoro* were first communicated to village envoys, who then had to report whether their communities were actually "working the field" – a metaphor referring to the hard but honest life of peasants and to the social as a field of activity. Every lineage or family had to send an envoy to make sure that the entire community supported and welcomed the new cult. Usually, the envoys needed to come back twice or more often to demonstrate that their delegation finally included representatives of all groups, including Muslims and Christians. Only then would the adepts of *kondoro* start to investigate whether the conditions for a shrine were fulfilled.

What *kondoro* stipulated was not enunciated in words only. The community had to perform the social practice that would bring an end to the troubles they were experiencing. Over the weeks that preceded the erection of a shrine, adepts of the movement came to the village, gave orders and controlled whether their commands were being executed. The villages had to set up communal stocks of food, firewood, and money – the basics of ordinary life. Several procedures were adopted: On an individual basis, every man and woman had to contribute a certain amount of staple food, for instance a bowl of groundnuts for women or five paddies of rice for each man. The stocks were kept in the compound of the headman, but followers of *kondoro* monitored them.

More important and impressive were the contributions raised through communal work. Whenever adepts visited the community, they held speeches announcing what the community had to do next to facilitate the arrival of *kondoro*. While the first addressed individual contributions, they later urged the inhabitants to work together. The women were called to fish together. Each compound should send at least one woman to participate. The men were sent hunting, and again, all compounds were to be represented. Fish and game should be handed over to the adepts of *kondoro* who would dry the catch and the meat and stock it in the headman's court. The queues were much longer than anything the villagers had seen before. When the women came back from the river, they sang about how they, after years of discord, had finally found themselves belonging to one united community. Neither jealousy nor disdain would ever divide them again. The beat of the song coordinated the movement of their bodies when they were marching into the compound of the headman to deliver their catch.

On the next occasion, lineages that had not made themselves visible were fined, and on the third visit, the adepts were satisfied that, apparently, all compounds were participating in the communal works, this time assisting with the clearing of roads for men and of the market for women. In the evening, the participants were praising the experience of having worked together as one. During the day, those who worked on the roads asked every passer-by to join them. They said that one should form a single queue and start helping them. The metaphor of forming a queue for helping each other referred again to the coordination of bodily movements (in general Bücher 1899; Csordas 1994).

Several months later, when the adepts of *kondoro* had witnessed the efforts of the community to change their everyday life, the shrine was formally installed. By participating in the collective works, the community had developed a different image of their own social world. The ills of society were refuted by the real, lived experience of an alternative, of a fair and balanced social order that was possible despite all the obstacles and malcontents of modernity. Unlike divination, imagination was a collective act, not one between two actors in a small, secluded space. Whether that image would last longer was, however, another question that did not surface at the time.

6 Between the Worlds: Greener Pastures as Collective Imagination

My third case shows how imagination unfolds in a global figuration of actors. It looks at how Africans in their home country perceive and conceive their relatives and friends in the diaspora, and how Africans living in Europe see and think of their fellow countrymen back home. Over the past two decades, the accelerated pace of globalisation has affected their relationship profoundly. Social relations across spaces that were once barriers between different life-worlds have become everyday realities: Since about the turn of the millennium, the diffusion of mobile phones (Bruijn et al. 2009; Etzo and Collender 2010), the easy, instant transfer of money and comparatively cheap air fares have altered the character of transnational migration to an unanticipated degree.[22]

In African history, mobility had always been an answer to crises, no matter what had caused them: war and violence, environmental change or catastrophes. Today, migration is often an option out of a depressing economic situation and lacking perspectives for comparatively well-educated young people. If not caused by war, migration towards the global North is often a phenomenon of the lower middle classes.[23] Cameroon may serve as an example. Entire families often contribute to travel expenses and send the most promising younger relatives across the Mediterranean, presuming that they have a fair chance in a world where an industrious life could lead to wealth and social status.

These images of the North, in particular of advanced European and North American countries, are cast into a biblical idiom. Cameroon is a devastated land where patrimonial ties decide whether one will become a *débrouillard* – a jobless fellow who will spend his life by muddling-through – or a respected man who is able to feed his family. Europe and North America are the "Greener Pastures" of the bible where the shepherd will lead innocent sheep that walk "through the valley of the shadow of death".[24]

This imagery rephrases the Old Testament. The path to greener pastures is a hardship, a time of suffering and loneliness (Förster 2009). One has to be smart to deal with countless obstacles along the way, whether these be civil servants who ask for extra bribes for the delivery of a passport, Nigerian traders who sell false passports in the back rooms of their shops, or even policemen trying to seize that passport. The passage to the capital and the airport is but the first step. Far greater is the challenge to cross the sea and to get access to European soil.

Obtaining a visa is a privilege. One may try to consult the embassy of a European country, arrive there before sunrise and queue in the hot sun for half of the day – just to learn that one will not get beyond the guard. One may spend weeks, if not months, waiting for the right occasion to gain access to the lobby where one may or may not receive application forms for the visa. To fill out the forms, one may need professional advice, someone who knows the "right"

---

[22] Overviews from an anthropological perspective by Hannerz 2003; Baba 2013. Albrow (1996) argues that this change produces a new quality of the social at large. Giddens (1990) and others believe that it radicalises modernity only.

[23] Young men of these social strata often have a good education but lack the social capital that they would need to get access to an appropriate employment in their home country.

[24] Psalm 23. On the image of greener pastures in Africa see Adepoju und van der Wiel 2010; Poeze 2010.

answers. Or one needs to camouflage their origins if one carries a passport bought from a counterfeiter. Adopting another accent might be an obligation to make that identification paper more plausible.

Countless stories about the final barrier circulate in Cameroonian cities. Arduous ordeals come, the migrant is told, when one wants to enter Europe. It is the moment when a man must be brave and clever. He must confront police and customs that will apply the strictest scrutiny to bar the long road to success and wealth. Women may have to appeal, perhaps to flirt with the officers. They will need other skills, but they may fail as well. The stakes are high: Failing at this last barrier means wasting the money of the family, deceiving one's relatives, becoming a loser who will be doomed to a mediocre life in the overcrowded neighbourhoods of an African city. Cameroonian English has a word for the new middle passage: bush falling. It is an image in itself. The passage to the wealthy North is seen as the wilderness that a man or, less often, a woman must trespass to master his or her life. The bush is the rogue space beyond the horizons of one's own life-world, beyond the familiarity of home. Behind it, when one eventually reaches greener pastures, lays the Promised Land. It is a world where the migrant can easily make money, find a decent job, build a patrimonial network, and finally come back as an adult, as a respected personality. Those are the expectations back home; the ideal trajectory of a bush faller.

Migrants often know better. Those who have gone through all the hardships of the passage to Europe know that the suffering does not necessarily end when one has finally reached that Promised Land. They have their own stories to tell – stories that feed into a counter imagery to what is called Greener Pastures back home. One may be arrested if the police realises that the man on the photo does not resemble the man carrying the passport. One may spend many months, sometimes years awaiting trial and deportation.

Living in a Parisian *banlieue* without papers means working for little and without any social security. Exploitation is the fate of illegal migrants. Salaries hardly suffice to cover daily expenses – and yet, they are expected to send something home. Women may be worse off, sometimes selling their bodies because there is no other way to eke out a living. It is easy to become an illegal migrant – even if the arrival was legal. One may violate the law if one has a short-term visa and simply "extends" it while seeking an employment. For many bush fallers, the real challenge comes where their friends and relatives do not expect it.

Those who stayed back home will try to reach out to the bush fallers. They will call them more or less regularly (Tazanu 2012; Frei 2013). But they only "beep" them – they let the phone ring once or twice and hang up; telling the migrants that they should call back. Bush fallers say that Cameroonians back home assume that everybody living in the diaspora can easily afford international calls while they believe that they are poor and penniless. Another way of reaching out to migrants is the Internet. One may send them mails and pictures to make migrants aware of the misery back home: photos of wounded limbs or of arms and legs in bandages that show how unlucky they are and how badly they need support. The gap between here and there is a dominant trope. These acts are often subtle, but they reconfirm the image of the migrant as someone who has made it to greener pastures, who has the means that Cameroonians do not have in their home country.

The image of the affluent bush faller in "Whiteman Kontri" is so powerful that migrants are hardly able to satisfy the expectations of their country fellows. They face repeated demands to send remittances, to cover the expenses for accidents and illnesses, for school fees, and much else. Whenever they come home, they need to bring back all sorts of gifts and also cash. They are asked to settle the economic woes of close and distant kin, of investing in all kinds of business. Many of them have only the cloth that they wear when they fly back to Europe. They will eventually feel like zombies, sucked dry by their own relatives, writes Francis Nyamnjoh (2005), himself a migrant living abroad. They have fallen victim to Nyongo, a secret craft to destroy or kill others and use their bodies to work for those who master it (Nyamnjoh 2005, p. 242).

The flip side of the coin is what Cameroonians tend to call "the European disease" (compare Schlehe 2013). Bush fallers, they say, tend to become as selfish as Europeans. They look after themselves but no longer take care of those who had made their journey to greener pastures possible. Migrants do not call back, suspecting that they are cheated when they are asked for contributions to an investment back in Cameroon. They do not even speak the language they learned as infants anymore, quickly adopting a British or an American accent. Worse is that they develop a tendency to live alone: They are not amused when they learn that a sibling will visit them, and they even show signs of dissent when they are asked to support them, to help them take roots in the greener pastures.

This is the flipside of the Greener Pastures. Those who had sent the migrants abroad expect and claim a return on the investment. Others who happen to know a bush faller will appeal to his feelings as a Cameroonian who is proud of his country and his fellow citizens, who must know about the desperate state of the economy that calls for support from wherever better-off people might live. Spaces of dependency and spaces of engagement are intertwined. The image of Greener Pastures mirrors a social figuration that links bush fallers and Cameroonians across continents. As an image, Europe is a signifier of wealth and success, but also of isolation, superficiality, and eventually social decay.

7 Intersubjective Creativity

These three case studies show that it would be a gross misunderstanding to assume that imagination leads to a finite realm of images that are secluded in a private world. Imagination is neither solipsistic phantasy nor mere imaginary – though the latter may be one of its outcomes. Evidently, imagination links actors to the world. It is an elementary social practice: "self" and "other" both participate in the process of imagining. All cases described above rely on a transposition of thoughts and feelings between a person or group of people. This imaginative transposition is a thoroughly social practice (Crossley 1996, p. 68).

During the divination séance, the clients re-examine the situation that they confront with the help of the diviner. The image of that situation is not simply revealed to one or the other actor; they create it through their interaction. The collective work requested by the adepts of *kondoro* is an experience that the participants inevitably share, and one they have to produce themselves by participating in these acts. The migrants may understand greener pastures in a different way than their relatives in Cameroon, but the imagination of greener pastures on both sides is the outcome of their interaction. The relationship may be flawed, but it exists and ties the actors to each other.

Any analysis of imagination as social practice thus has to explore its intersubjective character first. Imagining in this sense generates shared or collective intentionality. To understand how it does so and what that means for a theory of imagination, I will reflect briefly on how an anthropological understanding of collective intentionality differs from a philosophical one. In his brilliant book on imagining, Edward Casey (2000, p. 38 ff.) distinguishes an "act phase" from an "object phase" of imagination. During the act phase, the "mind directs itself onto and absorbs itself in a specific content" (Casey 2000, p. 38). From a social anthropological perspective, however, it is unclear why a mind should direct *itself* onto a particular content. Anthropologists would rather posit that such an orientation, and hence intentionality, is always embedded in the structures of relevance that the actors have to face when they situate themselves in the life-world (e.g. Schutz and Luckmann 1980, 1984). They would also claim that intentionality has a sensory and bodily dimension, and that merely mental intentionality is more the exception than the rule. Structures of relevance as well as sensory and bodily experience have a social dimension, as other actors are always a constituent part of the life-world.

If the emergence of collective intentionality is not thought of as restricted to acts of consciousness only, Casey's "act phase" of imagination is, reframed as social practice, a possible way to approach my initial question, namely how

Imagining Together: The Social Dimension of Imagination 251

intersubjectivity informs imagination. To examine different ways of imagining, I will first look at the time-space continuum in which its intersubjectivity unfolds. Secondly, I will examine the specific character of intersubjectivity in these settings. Thirdly, I will look at what imagination as intersubjective practice achieves for the social life-world.

The most striking feature of the first case, divination, is its secluded character. Though it can be practiced at any time, it is separated from the everyday in time and in space. The séance has a beginning and end. Both are clearly marked by verbal statements and by the bodily gestures of both diviner and client. They interact in a quiet, almost isolated place. Their words are no longer heard. The setting of their interaction temporarily *suspends* the relevance of the everyday lifeworld around them, but it does not isolate diviner and client. Indeed, the existence of absent "others" is still recognised.

The suspension of the everyday social world opens a space where diviner and client can freely re-arrange the meaning of the situation that has become problematic. The two do so by depicturing that situation as a figuration of material objects. This act has two dimensions: First, it makes an image of condensed experience visible and enables diviner and client to literally *re-position* one or the other element, represented by divinatory objects. Second, by making it visible, the picture endows the image with an *aesthetic quality* that a merely mental act may not have. One could argue that figurative thinking is translated into visible acts.

By working at these two levels, divination involves an element of reflection. Moving the elements back and forth, trying one or the other figuration is an act of balancing, of weighing. The clients adopt an aloof look upon the situation and their place in it. Whether that works in the end depends, of course, on the clients and their ability "to see", as the diviners would say. The process starts with sensory perception, but the longer a divination séance takes, the more the diviner is likely to weave his questions into bits and pieces of a longer narrative, which transforms the picture on the ground more and more into an image. Though the image is not rooted in the narrative, it is enhanced and advanced by it. By engaging with the diviner, by taking or shifting one or the other object, by answering subtly the mumbled questions of the diviner, and by being slowly sucked into the unfolding narrative, the clients situate themselves within the image that unfolds during the séance.

New images can change the world. The clients will leave the divination hut with a new or altered image of the problematic situation they face. At this stage, it is still open whether that image will be widely shared. Intersubjective creativity is instigated by the interaction of diviner and client, but it is not limited to the séance itself; it continues after the diviner has done his work. The clients may find the new image convincing, but they may encounter the resistance of others who may find the image less convincing or simply a wrong account of what that social problem "really" is.[25] The image is tested and subjected to the criticism of others when the clients articulate it in public. They may find one or the other detail less or more convincing. They may also see the overall image in another way and introduce additional elements, thus shaping it in all senses of the term.

The second case, the *kondoro* movement, shows another form of collective imagining. Intersubjectivity emerges through bodily experience when actors participate in the same activities. By participating in the same acts, they orient their attention consciously or unconsciously towards the same content.[26] Such social practice has a long history among peasant societies of the West African savannahs – a history that *kondoro* built on. By urging the new followers to engage in collective acts and practices, they also urge them to share their bodily and sensory experience. Walking together to the river, fishing together, and sharing the catch are all acts of collective intentionality (Gilbert 1990).

Here, the time-space continuum is enrooted in the horizon of the local social world. No barrier, physical or social, separates men or women from the others in their community – on the contrary, all participants shall and should be visible. The *kondoro* movement targets collective action, and both its imagery and the image that it generates are meant to be inclusive. The long queue of men or women walking to the wilderness or to the river will make those who are reluctant to join aware that they are the outsiders, and as such, they will not match the image of the community as one.

Kondoro is a double-sided social movement. It cuts through the social – it unites and simultaneously divides it if someone does not join in. It does not tolerate the cautious weighing and sorting that is so typical for divination as a social process. The adepts of the movement poorly communicate their expectations and insufficiently make the actors aware of their goals. These goals are part of the discursive formation rotating around the political crisis and social disintegration, but as normative objectives, they are not discussed and are thus exempt from criticism. Very much as charismatic leaders would, the adepts of *kondoro* tell new followers to take it or leave it – literally, the substance representing the spirit of *kondoro*.

---

[25] It is often very much the beginning of a much broader social drama, as Turner would have said (Turner 1975; cf. de Boeck and Devisch 1994).

[26] Csordas relates intersubjectivity directly to intercorporeality (Csordas 2008, also 1993).

The movement stipulates preconditions, not the new followers and their community. The urge to participate is authoritarian, and it implies that the actors will consciously join in the prescribed activities. They know that they are engaging in a collective practice requiring the participation of all if it is to work as promised. The pressure on individuals as well as kin groups is enormous: There is an obligation to participate, and the society at large is attributed a right to rebuke those who are reluctant to join.

The emerging collective intentionality, the "we-sentiment", has its roots in this framework of sharing a collective experience. The participants mutually rely on each other. Fishing in a stream requires that one group of women chases the fish in the bow nets held by another group of women. Neither men nor women could work together without committing themselves to the communal task.[27] Unlike divination, *kondoro* does not aim at conscious reflection. Though some may talk about their affection for the idea of an undivided society – the image the movement disseminates through its acts – most participants neither express it nor do they comment on the feelings of "others". The imaginative process is embedded in irreducible embodiment and empathetic sharing.

The scale of this form of imagination is wider than in the first case. It embraces entire communities and links them through the regional network that the movement creates by disseminating the substance of *kondoro* in local shrines. While divinatory processes with their uncertainties of balancing and weighing need to be framed as intimate interactions that are only subsequently submitted to the public, charismatic imagining is an inclusive and open process. The participants may have hidden agendas, perhaps strategies to participate only to demonstrate conformity and pretend to agree. But sharing the bodily experience with others might overwhelm them, too. It does not matter much as long as they make their commitment public by participating in the activities of *kondoro*. As an image, undivided society is created through participatory social practice. The image is tested when it is practiced – and not in retrospect, as in divinatory processes. This also sets spatial limits. Imagination building on participation is bound to social spaces of unmediated sociality.

However, imagination is not bound to intimate spaces or direct encounters; it can stretch across entire continents, as the last case shows. The image of distant Greener Pastures in Europe or North America is created through the interaction of people living in different worlds. As a social fact, the production of Greener Pastures requires the regular use of media that link the actors on both sides of the

---

[27] This example shows that the theoretical views of Gilbert (1990), Alonso (2009) and Roth (2004) are not exclusive: obligation and public commitment can work together.

Atlantic or the Mediterranean. Through media, they participate to some extent in the lives of their relatives and friends in Cameroon or in the diaspora. Physical distance is still important, but it is now related to the media: For instance, the actors cannot verify what they hear on the phone or see on the screen. The media provoke suspicion.

Whether the arm under the bandage is really broken is something the older brother living abroad cannot verify. The picture is sent as proof that one needs money, but the indexicality of photos is no longer taken for granted in that "other" world. And who knows whether the relatives "over there" are really as occupied as they claim? Nonetheless, the phone and the Internet keep the "others" within reach. They still contribute to the reproduction of what the Greener Pastures are.

Receiving aid confirms the image of Greener Pastures and of the wealth of migrants "over there", as well as the image of their accessibility. Not receiving any support will not affect the image as long as there are others who come back with cars, stereos, TV sets, computers, and, of course, a bag of money. It is a vicious circle: The more the migrants try to meet the expectations, the more is expected of them when they come home. If a migrant deceives, he must be a stupid man who has not made it over there where life is easy. He must be a lazy man, a loser who was unable to pick up the money lying on the streets. Or, alternatively, he is contaminated by the "European Disease" – a liar who hides his wealth because he does not want to share.

Repatriates know this because they are constantly reminded of their families' expectations when they read their messages or talk to them. They would do a lot not to come back empty handed. Some even borrow money to buy gifts to demonstrate that they are "winners" who have cultivated the Greener Pastures well. Thus, they re-confirm the image that their friends and relatives have shared during their absence. They participate in the collective imagination of Greener Pastures as much as those whose views they silently defy.

This form of imagination is not only different in scale; it has a different character. It does not generate one consistent image of its subject; instead, it produces an image with two faces. One is the promised land of the Greener Pastures, the "other" is the life of a bush faller and its intricacies. The two faces are, however, of the same coin. In this case, imagination does not lead to shared intentionality as in the case of the charismatic movement. What it produces are entangled views that necessitate their counterparts – very much as the figuration of actors across the continents.

Imagining remains, however, a social practice in which different actors have to participate to produce the multifaceted image of Greener Pastures. It generates a collective imagery, but not a shared image. Shared intentionality in a strong sense presupposes that the actors experience the worldly possibilities as an object world that "others" will experience more or less the same way. Collective intentionality in a weak sense is a merely summative relationship to an object. My third case belongs to this type. The imagery is composed of elements that may vary or take on a different meaning on both sides of the coin, though they are sustained by the same process. The image in its multiple facets remains an intentional object, as the actors will still relate to it – though in different ways. It informs their agencies in Cameroon as well as in Europe and North America.

8 Anthropological Dimensions of Imagination

Comparing the three cases above leads back to the initial questions. There are different ways of imagining, some easily accessible while "others" are hidden and barely surface in everyday life. There are also different ways of sharing the images that imagination creates. However, some commonalities surface in all examples.

First, the three cases show several ways of imagining: Divination is a process whereby skilful figurative work generates a visible picture and then a figure of thought, an image that the participants can accept and that is eventually examined, perhaps even debated by others. The emphatic shared intentionality of the charismatic movement is an entirely different and direct, bodily way of imagining. It immediately reaches out to everybody. Conversely, the mediated imagination that produces the image of Greener Pastures is dispersed over time and space. The difference hints at how the various actors joined in the given process. An anthropological approach hence has to compare the processes of imagining, not only the images that it produces.

Second, images generate a shared interpretation of the social. They may do so for entire societies, for large groups or for a few people only. In each case, they are always based on social practice. Sometimes, this practice leads to a bifurcation of the image into a diverging, even contradictory imagery. More often, however, the images are coherent and bring order to life-worldly elements that were incomprehensible until then. This figuration is seldom one purely of thought; it is made visible in various ways.

Finally, by projecting that figuration on the social, imagination instigates shared agency. Shared images motivate the actors for collective action as, for instance, against an oppressor or against rules and regulations that, according to the interpretation provided by that image, inhibit the wellbeing of all. Shared intentions to change social reality grow out of joint intentional acts, as they are embedded in the social practice that also generates shared images. Through engaging in the particular kind of social practice that imagination is, individuals form a plural subject. They are no longer a sum of individuals that have the same images in mind, but become in a strong sense one collective actor.

References

Adepoju, A., and A. van der Wiel. 2010. *Seeking greener pastures abroad.* Ibadan; Nigeria: Safari Books.
Albrow, M. 1996. *The global age.* Cambridge: Polity Press.
Alonso, F. 2009. Shared intention, reliance, and interpersonal obligation. *Ethics* 119(3): 444–475.
Anderson, B. 1991. *Imagined communities.* London: Verso.
Baba, M., Ed. 2013. Migration policy and its ground truths. Special issue, *International Migration* 51(2).
van Beek, W., and P. M. Peek, Eds. 2013. *Reviewing reality.* Hamburg, Germany: Lit-Verlag.
Bloch, M. 2016. Imagination from the outside and from the inside. *Current Anthropology* 57(13): 80–87.
de Boeck, P., and R. Devisch. 1994. Ndembu, Luunda and Yaka divination compared. *Journal of Religion in Africa* 22(2): 98–128.
Boehm, G., Ed. 1994. *Was ist ein Bild?* München, Germany: Fink.
Bücher, K. 1899. *Arbeit und Rhythmus.* Leipzig, Germany: Teubner.
Casey, E. 2000. *Imagining. A phenomenological study.* Bloomington, IN: Indiana University Press.
Castoriadis, C. 1987. *The imaginary institution of society.* Cambridge: Polity Press.
Comaroff, J., and J. Comaroff, Eds. 1993. *Modernity and its malcontents.* Chicago: University of Chicago Press.
Comaroff, J., and J. Comaroff. 1999. *Civil society and the political imagination in Africa.* Chicago: University of Chicago Press.
Crane, T. 2001. Intentional objects. *Ratio* 14(4): 336–349.
Crossley, N. 1996. *Intersubjectivity.* London: Sage.
Csordas, T. 1993. Somatic modes of attention. *Cultural Anthropology* 8(2): 135–156.
Csordas, T., Ed. 1994. *Embodiment and experience.* Cambridge: Cambridge University Press.
Csordas, T. 2008. Intersubjectivity and intercorporeality. *Subjectivity* 22: 110–121.
Curry, P., Ed. 2010. *Divination.* Farnham: Ashgate.
Curry, P. 2010. Embodiment, alterity and agency in divination. In *Divination*, Ed. P. Curry, 85–118. London: Ashgate.
De Bruijn, M., F. B. Nyamnjoh, and I. Brinkman, Eds. 2009. *Mobile phones. The new talking drums of everyday Africa.* Buea, Cameroon: Langaa.
Devisch, R. 1985. Perspectives of divination in contemporary sub-Saharan Africa. In *Theoretical explorations in African religion*, Eds. W. van Binsbergen and M. Schoffeleers, 50–83. London: Kegan Paul.
Dikovitskaya, M. 2005. *Visual culture.* Cambridge, MA: The MIT Press.

Douglas, M. 1966. *Purity and danger.* London: Routledge.
Durham, D. 2000. Youth and the social imagination in Africa. Introduction to parts 1 and 2. Special issue, *Anthropological Quarterly* 73(3): 113–120.
Eglash, R. 1997. Bamana sand divination. *American Anthropologist* 99(1): 112–122.
Emirbayer, M., and A. Mische. 1998. What is agency? *American Journal of Sociology* 103(4): 962–1023.
Etzo, S., and G. Collender. 2010. The mobile phone 'revolution' in Africa. *African Affairs* 109 (437): 659–668.
Evans-Pritchard, E. 1937. *Witchcraft, oracles and magic among the Azande.* Oxford: Clarendon.
Fernandez, J. 1982. *Bwiti. An ethnography of the religious imagination in Africa.* Princeton, NJ: Princeton University Press.
Fortes, M. 1966. Religious premisses and logical technique in divinatory ritual, in: *Philosophical Transactions of the Royal Society B*, 251: 409–422.
Frei, B. 2013. *Sociality revisited? The use of the internet and mobile phones in urban Cameroon.* Bamenda, Cameroon: Langaa.
Förster, T. 1985. *Divination bei den Kafibele-Senufo.* Berlin: Reimer.
Förster, T. 1997. *Zerrissene Entfaltung.* Köln: Köppe.
Förster, T. 2002. «On ne sait plus qui est qui». Öffentlichkeit zwischen Dorf, Stadt und Staat. *Paideuma* 48: 101–123.
Förster, T. 2009. Greener pastures. In *Europa und Afrika,* Ed. G. Kreis, 59–78. Basel, Switzerland: Schwabe.
Giddens, A. 1990. *The consequences of modernity.* Stanford, CA: Stanford University Press.
Gilbert, M. 1990. Walking together. *Midwest Studies in Philosophy* 15(1): 1–14.
Gilbert, M. 1992. *On social facts.* Princeton, NJ: Princeton University Press.
Grillo, L. K. 1992. Dogon divination as an ethic of nature. *Journal of Religious Ethics* 20(2): 309–330.
Hannerz, U. 2003. *Transnational connections.* London: Routledge.
Hayden, R. M. 2007. Moral vision and impaired insight. *Current Anthropology* 48(1): 105–131.
Hobsbawm, E., and T. Ranger, Eds. 1983. *The invention of tradition.* Cambridge: Cambridge University Press.
Jackson, M. 1978. An approach to Kuranko divination. *Human Relations* 31(2): 117–138.
Jules-Rosette, B. 1978. The veil of objectivity. *American Anthropologist* 80(3): 549–570.
Kearney, R. 1988. *The wake of imagination.* Minneapolis, MN: University of Minnesota Press.
Kearney, R. 1998. *Poetics of imagining.* Edinburgh, UK: Edinburgh University Press.
Koukouti, M. D., and L. Malafouris. 2020. Material imagination. In *The Cambridge handbook of the imagination,* Ed. Anna Abraham, 30–46. Cambridge: Cambridge University Press.
LaGamma, A., Ed. 2000. *Art and oracle.* New York: Metropolitan Museum of Art.
Langer, A., and A. Lutz, Eds. 1999. *Orakel.* Zürich, Switzerland: Museum Rietberg.
McLean, S., and S. Coleman, Eds. 2007. Engaging imagination. Anthropological explorations in creativity. Special issue, *Irish Journal of Anthropology* 10(2).
Mendonsa, E. L. 1982. *The politics of divination.* Berkeley, CA: University of California Press.

Migdal, J. 2001. *State in society.* Cambridge: Cambridge University Press.
Mills, W. C. 2000. *The sociological imagination.* Oxford: Oxford University Press.
Mirzoeff, N. 2014. *How to see the world.* London: Pelican.
Mitchell, W. J. T. 1986. *Iconology.* Chicago: University of Chicago Press.
Mitchell, W. J. T. 1994. *Picture theory.* Chicago: University of Chicago Press.
Nyamnjoh, F. 2005. Images of Nyongo amongst Bamenda grassfielders in Whiteman Kontri. *Citizenship Studies* 9(3): 241–269.
Paulme, D. 1937. La divination par les chacals chez les Dogons de Sanga. *Journal de la Société des Africanistes* 7(1): 1–14.
Peek, P. M., Ed. 1991. *African divination systems.* Bloomington, IN: Indiana University Press.
Poeze, M. 2010. *In search of greener pastures?* African Studies Collection, 27. Leiden, Netherlands: African Studies Centre.
Robinson, D. 1985. *The holy war of Umar Tal.* Oxford: Oxford University Press.
Robinson, D., and J.-L. Triaud, Eds. 1997. *Le temps des marabouts. Itinéraires et stratégies islamiques en Afrique occidentale française vers 1880–1960.* Paris: Karthala.
Roth, A. S. 2004. Shared agency and contralateral commitments. *The Philosophical Review* 113(3): 359–410.
Royer, P. 1999. Le Massa et l'eau de Moussa. Cultes régionaux, «traditions» locales et sorcellerie en Afrique de l'Ouest. *Cahiers d'Etudes Africaines* 154(39): 337–366.
Sartre, J.-P. 1972. *The psychology of imagination.* London: Methuen.
Schlehe, J. 2013. Re-imagining 'the West' and performing 'Indonesian modernities'. Muslims, Christians and "paranormal" practitioners. *Zeitschrift für Ethnologie* 138(1): 3–21.
Schutz, A. 1967. *The phenomenology of the social world.* Evanston, IL: Northwestern University Press.
Schutz, A., and T. Luckmann. 1980, 1989. *The structures of the life-world.* 2 vols. Evanston, IL: Northwestern University Press.
Schütz, A. and T. Luckmann 1984: Strukturen der Lebenswelt. Konstanz: UVK Verlagsgesellschaft.
Suthers, E. 1987. Perception, knowledge, and divination in Djimini society, Ivory Coast. (PhD diss.) University of Virginia.
Sturken, M., and L. Cartwright. 2001. *Practices of looking.* Oxford: Oxford University Press.
Tazanu, P. 2012. *Being available and reachable.* Bamenda, Cameroon: Langaa.
Tedlock, B. 2006. Toward a theory of divinatory practice. *Anthropology of Consciousness* 17(2): 62–77.
Tedlock, B. 2010. Divination as a way of knowing. *Folklore* 112(2): 189–197.
Turner, V. 1968. *The drums of affliction.* Oxford: Clarendon.
Turner, V. 1975. *Revelation and divination in Ndembu ritual.* Ithaca, NY: Cornell University Press.
Werbner, R. 1973. The superabundance of understanding. *American Anthropologist* 75(5): 1414–1440.
Werbner, R., Ed. 1977. *Regional cults.* London: Tavistock.
Werbner, R. 2005. *Séance reflections.* (Film) London: Royal Anthropological Institute.
Willis, P. 2000. *The ethnographic imagination.* Cambridge: Polity Press.
Winkelman, M., and P. M. Peek, Eds. 2004. *Divination and healing.* Tucson, AZ: University of Arizona Press.
Zeitlyn, D. 2012. Divinatory logics. *Current Anthropology* 53(5): 525–546.

A Javanese Conversation with Central Asia on Transitive Matters

Philipp Schröder

1 Introduction

In my contribution to Judith Schlehe's 'Festschrift', I would like to bring into conversation her work on Indonesia with the Anthropology of Central Asia (which is my field of interest). Until rather recently, these two regions might indeed have been regarded as 'worlds apart', and to insinuate that something fruitful could emerge from pursuing any association between them would have led to raised eyebrows rather than laudation.

But ever since Chinese President Xi Jinping announced his country's 'One Belt One Road' (OBOR) initiative in 2013, Central Asia and Southeast Asia have been tied together in an unprecedented way through China and what glamorously presents itself as history's largest-scale ambition at economic infrastructure integration by sea and land. That circumstance, equally new as controversial, might have been sufficient for relating Central Asia and Indonesia along some of the themes that have been important for Judith Schlehe, such as cosmopolitanism and modernity (Schlehe et al. 2013; Schlehe 2019), or the environment and postcolonial politics (Schlehe 2010; Schlehe and Yulianto 2020). And, admittedly, this was my original proposition for what I could write about in this volume. But while acquainting myself more closely with Schlehe's writing, I realized that there were parallels and contrasts with more historical and ethnographic substance to be explored for an Indonesian-Central Asian conversation than the fresh and third-party mediated one brought about by the OBOR initiative.

P. Schröder (✉)
Nazarbayev University, Astana, Kazakhstan

In the following pages, I will take up three such threads for a conversation. My starting point is Schlehe's single encounter with Central Asia, where in 1999/2000 she examined the nexus of shamanism and tourism in Mongolia. I will suggest that this brief regional digression, which occurred at about the middle of her career, created a relevant academic impulse that Schlehe carried over to her 'home turf' in Indonesia, particularly in regard to her subsequent work on 'paranormal practitioners'. From there onwards, two segments will outline how Schlehe's post-millennial contributions resonate quite well with anthropological debates on Central Asia. This includes the commercialization and politics of spirituality and Islam, as well as the significance of public spectacle for the performance and experience of nation building. In conclusion, I will argue that an emphasis on 'the hybrid' and 'the transitive' could be regarded as the key thread in Schlehe's conceptual positioning—one that might even have been inspired by precisely those Javanese viewpoints that she always so carefully sought to capture.

2 A Consequential Digression to Central Asia?

When situating Judith Schlehe's body of work within the anthropology of Central Asia, there is one obvious tie and many subtler ones. I will elaborate on the latter in the segments following this one. The obvious tie concerns Schlehe's brief encounter with shamanism in Mongolia, which in the more encompassing definition of the region is part of Central Asia, and until the late 1980 s was closely aligned with the Soviet Union. Schlehe's research there was based on two rather short field visits that covered about five months between 1999 and 2000 (Schlehe and Weber 2001; Schlehe 2005). Her findings identify a 'revitalization' of shamanic practice that evolved after a decades-long socialist ban of public spirituality. In itself, this is very much in line with other academic contributions on that region and around the turn of the new millennium. Caroline Humphrey (1999, p. 10), for example, noted for Ulan-Ude, the capital of the neighbouring Republic Buryatia in Russia's Far East: '[…] it seems that people enjoy the shamans' magical incidents of destabilization of Soviet and Buddhist contexts (the school, the hospital, the monastery) and their re-vitalization as sites of spiritual vigour'.

Unlike this rather historical observation, which emphasizes a newly 'occultized locale' (ibid., p. 10) in the post-atheist urban domain, Schlehe's attention was focused on the blending of revitalized shamanism with an emergent, future-oriented tourism industry. Examining the performances of spiritual experts during organized events and their reception by a (paying) audience of international guests and locals, she captured both affective and pragmatic dimensions of trance and other rituals, such as when shamans and worshippers join to circulate a stone heap and contribute their sacrifices of milk, vodka or something else during an *ovoo* ceremony in order to secure the protection of local spirits for travellers from near or far

Judith Schlehe also pointed to an apparent commercialization of tradition and cultural identity, which even then extended beyond the national borders of Mongolia and into cyberspace. For her, this was particularly embodied by a young woman called Saraangerel, who had a Buryat mother and a German father, who was born in the USA and first came to Mongolia as an adult, and since then had emerged as a controversial yet tech- and marketing-savvy shaman. 'Like no one else', remarked Schlehe and her co-author, this female shaman would be 'capable of forging connections: new and old Buryat-Mongolian bodies of thought with Western curiosity and a global "New Age"-desire, own experiencing with theoretical abstraction, material interest with missionary intention' (Schlehe & Weber 2001, p. 112).

Much later, and referring to Pentecostalist minorities in Muslim Kyrgyzstan, Mathijs Pelkmans (2017) pointed to the 'fragility of conviction' in religious landscapes that are characterized by a convergence of epistemological and existential uncertainty. If knowledge about religion is as unstable as the conditions of securing a livelihood, he states, then spiritual leaders are confronted with the paradoxical, quasi-impossible task to somehow make the miraculous mundane in order to maintain their followers' enchantment and loyalty. Certainly, this might be more relevant if the unit of analysis is an established local community, as in Pelkman's case, and not a rotating client base of in- or external tourists, as in Schlehe's.

Still, one could argue that this digression to the central part of Asia was consequential for Schlehe's later work back in Indonesia. While previously Schlehe had been concerned (in her habilitation thesis) with female water spirits, particularly Ratu Kidul, the goddess of the southern Java sea (Schlehe 1998), after Mongolia this evolved into a prolonged interest in 'paranormal practitioners'. One could argue, following Schlehe's definition, that these are not so far removed from the Mongolian shamans: 'the paranormal or supranatural are a contemporary reconfiguration of *dukun* or mystical-spiritual experts and traditional healers' (Schlehe 2012, p. 95).

As the very next segment will show, the commonalities between those experts mediating access to the transcendental world in Central and Southeast Asia extend further and into the domain of spiritual economies, where their attractiveness and success critically hinge on the skilful association of established 'cultural values' with entrepreneurial talent. Yet what we can already take away now, and what maybe Schlehe took with her from the ethnographic detour to Central Asia, is a refined sense of how not only spirituality but also other convictions or ideologies, such as 'modernity' or the 'East and the West', are entwined with commerce and the politics of nation building in contexts that are in a fragile, uncertain or transitory state.

3   The Commercialization and Politics of Spirituality

Around the turn of the millennium many ethnographic observers across the globe, but also those focusing on Indonesia and Central Asia, detected an advancing 'religionization' in public life, in lines of conflict and capitalist formations. Within that emergent field, Schlehe decided not to follow the trend of solely attending to any of Indonesia's six officially recognized religions, which are Islam, Protestantism, Catholicism, Hinduism, Buddhism and Confucianism. Instead, she aspired to 'de-exoticize' the outlier phenomenon of 'paranormal practitioners' in order to follow their specific situatedness between religion, economy, politics and healing. In Schlehe's reading of their spiritual economy, these paranormal practitioners do not oppose or only adjust to 'modernity', but actively co-create it by 'smoothly' and 'tolerantly' associating Muslim belief with 'local, Javanese, mystical-magical perceptions' (Schlehe 2012, p. 100). In their business model, claims Schlehe, profitability rests on the credible assurance that money-making is not the paranormal practitioners' primary objective, although they are making a living, some even a fortune, from their practice.

Material ambivalences aside, paranormal practitioners are attractive to their clientele, which spreads from the thin layer of local elites to the many less privileged, because their offer is individualized and transactional, i.e. directed at matters of affluence, influence, affection and health, while equally this relatedness to clients is personalized and meaningful in cultural and religious terms.

Ethnographic insights from Central Asia reveal quite similar syncretistic constellations, there embodied by those referred to, for example, as *bakshi* (spiritual healers) or *közü achyktar* (literally those with 'opened eyes', meaning clairvoyants). But I can also draw from my own fieldwork in southern Kyrgyzstan to illustrate some of the spiritual quandary that might emerge for someone seeking the services of such paranormal practitioners.

In 2015, Dinara and Murat, a Kyrgyz couple from the city of Osh, were desperate: three years into their marriage, their wish for children remained unfulfilled and social pressure from their parents and wider kin was mounting. Not yet ready to try medical fertility treatments, they decided, in their words, 'to try it the traditional way'. This meant that they arranged for an appointment with Rahman, a local healer of the finest reputation, who was also regularly consulted by Dinara's mother. Dinara and Murat allowed me to tag along when they embarked on the two-hour car ride to Rahman's dusty settlement, suitably referred to as 'Snake Village'. Upon arrival, cars were already lined up on both sides of the road next to Rahman's house. Inside, the courtyard was overcrowded with clients, some of whom apparently had been waiting for hours regardless of the excruciating August heat. When it was Dinara's and Murat's turn, Rahman first inquired orally about 'their issue'. He then felt their palms and pulses, diagnosing that Dinara was fine, but Murat would somehow 'be blocked'. He then calmed them down assuring them that they would have children eventually if they remained 'patient' and 'faithful'. Rahman also prepared a *tumar* for them to keep, an amulet with an excerpt from the Qur'an. For non-spiritual treatment, he advised Murat to eat two quail eggs a day in the coming months and Rahman's helper quickly jotted down the mobile number of a local farmer who would offer these 'for the best price and highest quality'. Following a 'voluntary donation' of about € 15, Dinara and Murat left Rahman's compound. During the car ride home, the couple was evidently relieved that 'nothing is wrong with us', and they appreciated Rahman's approach, which they considered 'pragmatic' and tailored to their currently most pressing need. But at the same time, they articulated an inner dilemma about how they, as 'truly believing Muslims', should handle advice from a source which the *imam* of their local mosque regularly decried as prolonging an 'un-Islamic', pagan heritage (see also Rasanayagam 2011).

This vignette about Dinara and Murat very much resembles one that Schlehe recounted from fieldwork in Java conducted around the same time, when she joined a long-time friend for a visit to a local paranormal practitioner. In light of what she attested had been a recently 'growing Islamisation' in Indonesia, Schlehe emphasized her friend's pragmatism and pluralistic open-mindedness, similar to that of Dinara and Murat, which did not prevent her friend from consulting a paranormal practitioner to treat her illness. But even more so, Schlehe found noteworthy that local paranormal practitioners apparently considered it necessary, at least more than before, to adopt self-protective measures, such as not giving traditional offerings of flowers or incense (*sesajen*), in order to pass as a 'proper' healer even for Muslims of a stricter, 'modernist' persuasion (Schlehe 2019, p. 374).

Returning to Central Asia, the case of Dinara and Murat encapsulates that the post-Soviet 'religious question' continues to critically be about the handling of Islam's societal re-appearance and multivocality. Before, during more than six decades of state-enacted scientific atheism, much about 'being a Muslim' was relegated to the hidden, private domain, and the ability of local believers and scholars to forge ties regionally and with the global *umma* was decisively restricted. The 1990s then brought not only a surging interest in Islamic ritual, knowledge and morality, but also revealed a widespread desire for orientation about how a 'proper' Muslim would act and what she or he ought to believe in (Privratsky 2001; McBrien 2017).

One key line of contestation separated 'traditional' Islam, a localized form of cultural-ethnic spirituality that was largely oral and customary (Khalid 2007), from newly incoming and 'reformist' notions, such as 'Saudi-style Salafi Islam' (Biard 2015), which emphasized supranational connectivity, was strongly script-oriented and propagated social conservatism. And although the vast majority of such 'newly pious' citizens were found to have no associated political agenda (McBrien 2009), states across post-Soviet Central Asia were opposed to what they portrayed as 'foreign', anti-secular and thus potentially 'extremist' movements, from Wahhabism to Hizb ut-Tahrir or Tablighi Jamaat (Hann and Pelkmans 2009). Instead, governments aspired to incorporate the 'harmless', traditional-cultural and moderate Islam into their post-Soviet nation building efforts (Rasanayagam 2014). For example, Maria Louw notes that political elites in Bukhara, as elsewhere across Uzbekistan, have attempted 'to co-opt the concept of "Muslimness" and the sacred places which embody "Muslimness" within the ideology of national independence' (2006, p. 336).

Quite fittingly, the politics of representation have also been a recurrent theme in Schlehe's work. And, as it turns out, the paranormal practitioners offer suitable insights not only for refining our understanding of Javanese spiritual economies, but also to reflect on the (earthly) shaping of cultural identities and the senses of self-situatedness within a globalized world. Following contemporary re-imaginations and reflections on 'the West' across different communities of believers in Indonesia, Schlehe found paranormal practitioners to be avid proponents of universalism who foregrounded the mutual aspects of humankind and also claimed to appreciate Western logic and technology. At the same time, the paranormal practitioners were not shy to point out an 'Eastern superiority' in spiritual capacities over the West's appropriative materialism and its over-reliance on only the rational 'half [of] a brain' (Schlehe et al. 2013, p. 17). Regardless of the 'auto-orientalization' and 'self-mystification' that is evident in such a viewpoint, the paranormal practitioners' cosmopolitan, integrative version insightfully contrasts with other 'Indonesian modernities', particularly the dualistic one offered by the (minority position of a) rather fundamentalist Islam that is fashioned as a morally preferable, non-compatible alternative to a decaying West (Schlehe 2013).

Schlehe's joint research with Eva Nisa on Indonesian (alumni) students of Cairo's al-Azhar University provides this segment's final thread of conversation with Central Asia. We learn from these young Indonesians that the 'middle way' between Islamism and secularism that they were taught in Egypt neatly aligns with the concept of *"Islam Nusantara'* ('Archipelagic Islam'), which was presidentially endorsed in 2015 and describes an Indonesian 'friendly, anti-radical, inclusive, tolerant Islam full of politeness' (Schlehe & Nisa 2016, p. 7).

This again is very much reminiscent of the idealized socio-spiritual contract that most Central Asian governments would wish to enter into with their majority Muslim citizenry. Schlehe and her co-author refer to Afifuddin Muhajir's (2015) summary of *Islam Nusantara*'s understanding and practice 'as an effect of the dialectics between written Islamic law and local realities and cultures'. For the elements of moderacy and national heritage reflected in that citation, one could thus probably assume that most present-day political elites across Muslim Central Asia would not oppose having 'the archipelago' replaced by 'Kyrgyzstan', 'Uzbekistan' or another post-Soviet neighbouring state in that region.

4 The Prism of Public Spectacle

Schlehe's way of approaching spirituality in its commercial and political entanglements offered a first entry point for an ethnographic conversation involving Indonesia and Central Asia. Let me for a brief moment situate this in a more historical, geopolitical dimension.

While Indonesia's Suharto regime (1967–1998) officially declared a position of neutrality during the Cold War, its de facto relations with the Soviet Union remained hesitant at best and during certain periods were unmistakably antagonistic (Horn 1975). This poor state of affairs was also indicated by the fact that President Suharto's first visit to Moscow only occurred in 1989, more than two decades after his accession to power and only two years prior to the Soviet Union's 1991 dissolution. Much more than it did for the communist world, Indonesia aspired to align with 'the West' (including Japan and South Korea), which was a position also guided by the intention to attract more substantial foreign aid and investment.

Still, when reading about the ideological underpinnings and some of the quotidian realities of Suharto's self-coined 'New Order' society in Schlehe's work and others, one can point to a set of characteristics that the Indonesia of this era shared with the Soviet Union. Among these, notes Kramer (2003, p. 22), were 'a highly centralized government', 'an immense and sprawling territory consisting of ethnically concentrated regions', and 'a multitude of languages [...] [and] [...] groups with strong ethnic identities'. In consequence, Indonesia and the Soviet Union could be argued to have encountered some similar challenges after their respective 1990 s regime changes: the resignation of Suharto from power in 1998 was followed by the so-called 'Reform era', whereas the signing of the 'Belavezha Accords' in 1991 de facto sealed the dissolution of the Union of Soviet Socialist Republics (USSR).

In the aftermath of these landmark events, Indonesia remained a unitary nation state, but aspired to internal adjustments towards more 'democratisation, decentralisation and regional autonomy' (Schlehe 2011b, p. 157). In contrast, the post-Soviet era created fully independent nation states, which even more profoundly altered the demographic, territorial, economic and political profiles of these new entities. But all distinctions notwithstanding, the inescapable task during both the post-Suharto and the post-Soviet transformation was to fill major ideological voids left by the 'New Order' and 'communism', and to reinvent their strategies for nation building. Schlehe's diagnosis of the *Reformasi* era in Indonesia is thus also applicable to the situation in post-Soviet Central Asia: 'in the present post-authoritarian period of transition, a vigorous renegotiation of national identity, cultural identifications, social relations and belonging is occurring' (Schlehe 2013, p. 498). One viable avenue to access such renegotiations would be to carefully chronicle local self-positionings vis-à-vis 'the West'. As mentioned above, Schlehe employed exactly such an approach in order to identify shifting orientations in Indonesia which lead beyond the polarity of Orient and Occident and reference to still "other" imagined centres of the world located in the Global South and East.

But Schlehe has proposed yet another ethnographic prism that allows us to approach the intricacies of collective representation and performance: the public arena and spectacle.

One of her sites was 'Taman Mini Indonesia Indah' ('Beautiful Indonesia in Miniature'), a cultural theme park in Jakarta dating back to the Suharto era. From Schlehe's (2011b) insights into this park's past, we learn that the New Order slogan of 'unity in diversity' translated into an essentializing and exoticizing display of regional material cultures and customs; and that is not very much unlike how the Soviet slogan about 'the friendship of peoples' rested on continuous efforts at social engineering that institutionalized primordial imaginaries of delimitable ethno-territorial communities (Hirsch 2005; Slezkine 1994).

Moving towards the present, Schlehe emphasizes that after *Reformasi* a Chinese cultural park and a Confucian temple were erected in the miniature park, which in itself would be a remarkable 'revitalization' given that the Suharto regime had suppressed Chinese cultural expression and outlawed Confucianism. But despite such 'innovation', reflects Schlehe, the park's visitors are restricted in their learning experience due to the still-static representation of Indonesian ethnic and religious traditions, a potentially entertaining but decidedly undifferentiated 'staging of the past' (Schlehe and Uike-Bormann 2010). Furthermore, she remarks that such carefully orchestrated relationality between "self" and "other" would be detached from the multiplex, fluid and transgressional exchanges across cultural boundaries that were a quotidian reality (and for which 'transculturality' would thus be a well-suited concept; Schlehe 2011, p. 152).

Similarly, Laura Adam's (2010) approach to Uzbekistan as a 'spectacular state' points to the continuity of Soviet cultural essentializations and their intention to legitimize political rule. Her ethnographic insights on public mass parades, which are supposed to celebrate post-Soviet 'Independence Day' and the pre-Soviet heritage of *Nawruz* (spring equinox), document a mere shift in ideological content, from communism to nationalism, whereas their symbolic choreography still follows the well-established script of an 'Olympics-style' blend between Uzbek traditional values and the elite's internationalist agenda. Much in line with Schlehe's observation on the 'Indonesia in Miniature' park, Adams detects that these 'official' performances have become critically dissociated from the quotidian experience of most Uzbekistani citizens, which in her case meant that the parades were more and more perceived as a tedious, unconvincing cliché upheld by an underperforming state.

This appears to be quite different in the case of another Central Asian spectacle: the 'World Nomad Games' that were hosted in Kyrgyzstan in 2014, 2016 and 2018. Mathijs Pelkmans (forthcoming) presents these games, which feature disciplines such as eagle hunting, archery, wrestling, and horse racing, as an attractively crafted event that caters not only to the orientalizing expectations of global visitors to feel a 'wild', cultural authenticity; but also fulfils a Kyrgyz desire for uniqueness and de-marginalization, which is achieved by presenting 'their traditions' to the world and by performing 'incomparably' well (i.e. with Kyrgyzstan clearly leading in the medal standings).

Back in Indonesia, Schlehe turned to the popular destination of *Bukit Kasih,* the 'Hill of Love', in order to reveal that such a disconnected mode of side-by-side representation is not confined to the ethnic or regional domain, but may also extend into the spiritual one. Situated in a remarkable landscape in North Sulawesi, the 'Hill of Love' assembles a Catholic and a Protestant church, a

Buddhist and a Hindu temple and a mosque. It is confined to remaining a 'multi-religious' site propagating harmonious co-existence because believers usually visit only their own house of worship without being much stimulated to engage in any form of 'trans-religious' experience or collectivity (Schlehe 2014a, p. 297).

A contrasting case is provided by *kirab budaya,* a 'cultural parade' held annually in a historic area of Yogyakarta featuring colourful costumes and artistic performances, but also Muslim prayer and the ritual purification of a sacred spring connected to ancient kings. Here, Schlehe's ethnographic exploration illustrates that such syncretic, (re-)invented religious spectacle, especially if it is harmlessly directed at popularizing tradition and attracting tourists, may ensure that local spiritual rituals are acceptable in an 'increasingly Islamised context'. More generally speaking, it may also present a non-confrontational way to transgress 'contested borders between horizons and worldviews' (Schlehe 2017, p. 20).

5 Conclusion: A Javanese Perspective?

Beginning from her single encounter with Central Asia more than two decades ago, this chapter has attempted to engage in an ethnographic conversation between this region and Schlehe's 'home turf' in Indonesia. And while I could not cover Schlehe's academic oeuvre in its entirety, hopefully some select threads worth pursuing have been taken up. One concerns the commercialization and politics of religious persuasion, in particular the niche (left) for syncretic, vernacular spiritualities and modes of self-positioning in times of an advancing script-oriented Islam in Indonesia as in Central Asia. The other concerns the value of attending to public performances and spectacles for situating post-regime (Suharto and Soviet) efforts at collective identity making and nation building.

In this brief conclusion, my aspiration is not to revisit these segments in detail. Rather, I want to suggest that a synopsis, understood as the exercise of 'seeing everything together', would allow us to identify an even more fundamental thread, and thereby a truly key one, that binds together most of Schlehe's contributions. Unavoidably, maybe, this emerges as a matter of perspective and its epistemic consequences. Let me provide some illustrations for this.

In an edited volume entitled 'In-between cultures, in-between genders', Schlehe (2000) explored romantic relations involving European female tourists and their Indonesian partners as potentially creating innovative 'interstices' that facilitate a (indispensable) post-colonial, post-orientalist attitude in a globalizing world. For a follow-up contribution, Schlehe associates this topic with the notion of 'transdifference', which acknowledges the efficacy of prevalent binaries—such as Orient-Occident, male-female or inside-outside—but equally aspires to be receptive to any 'temporary de-construction' and 'novel re-construction' of these basic classifications, with European-Indonesian romantic encounters serving as an example (Schlehe 2011a, p. 190). As part of another volume, on 'Religion, Tradition and the Popular', Schlehe revisited the practice of paranormal practitioners in Indonesia, arguing that they achieve a position of 'ambiguity and in-betweenness' by avoiding taking sides in a contemporary climate of Islamization and religious fundamentalism, which would also equip them with the potential 'to undermine exclusiveness' and 'to overcome boundaries between knowledge systems and social groups by translating between diverse traditions' (2014b, p. 199).

When added to what has been more intensively debated before in this contribution, from these accentuations on 'interstices', 'transdifference' or 'translations' emerges a perspective in Schlehe's writing which attends to those situated in-between and seeking niches; which is relational by examining their fluid exchanges across boundaries; and which, in consequence, is conceptually oriented towards 'the hybrid' and 'the trans-', with the latter referring to its literal meaning of 'carrying across' (Stephan-Emmrich and Schröder 2018, p. 49).

Nowhere could I find captured what, in my view, makes up the essence of Schlehe's anthropological perspective more pointedly than in the following remark, which takes us back to the 'Beautiful Indonesia in Miniature' park, and picks up on the 'promising direction' of the celebration of the 'Chinese New Year (*Imlek*)' in 2010 that brought together a diverse group of spiritual practitioners from all over Indonesia: 'If there were', writes Schlehe, 'more of this kind of inclusive representation and if visitors were stimulated to think not just of cultural differences but also of relatedness and entanglement of cultures, of the complexities of cultural crossings, of ways to blur and overcome boundaries and of new promising and interesting mixtures, then there could be vivid, creative exploration and exchange instead of a fixation on folkloristic, commodified categories' (Schlehe 2011b, p. 167).

Without any allusion to exoticism or orientalization, as this would violate the core of Schlehe's anthropological identity, there was one instance that got me thinking about how much her emphasis on the hybrid and transitive might have been inspired by those very same emic viewpoints that she so carefully seeks to represent. It occurred when reading Schlehe's ethnographic account on local, transcendental interpretations of the 2006 Yogyakarta earthquake and other recent natural catastrophes. For what was likely meant as a mere side note to provide further context, Schlehe referred to 'traditional Javanese culture' as not being organized according to mutually exclusive opposites, e.g. between the traditional and the modern. Instead, and here comes into view a noteworthy parallel to Schlehe's own conceptual perspective, the Javanese worldview was historically characterized by its inclination to 'adopt new elements and to harmoniously integrate these into the already established' (Schlehe 2008, p. 228).

Regardless of whether or not this observation might suffice to speak of a distinctly 'Javanese' vantage point, the least it does, in my reading, is to elucidate a final constitutive angle of Schlehe's ethnographic perspective: that is, the experiential one of the personal, intimate (transcultural) encounter, which is embracing, uplifting and programmatic, and which also appears to have been the one that Schlehe found hugely joyful and worth pursuing.

Reference

Adams, L. L. 2010. *The spectacular state. Culture and national identity in Uzbekistan*. Durham: Duke University Press.

Biard, A. 2015. Power, "Original" Islam, and the reactivation of a religious utopia in Kara-Suu, Kyrgyzstan. *Central Asian Affairs* 2(4): 347–366. https://doi.org/10.1163/22142290-00204002.

Hann, C., and M. Pelkmans. 2009. Realigning religion and power in Central Asia. Islam, nation-state and (post)socialism. *Europe-Asia Studies* 61(9): 1517–1541. https://doi.org/10.1080/09668130903209111.

Hirsch, F. 2005. *Empire of nations. Ethnographic knowledge and the making of the Soviet Union*. Ithaca: Cornell University Press.

Horn, R. C. 1975. Soviet influence in Southeast Asia. Opportunities and obstacles. *Asian Survey* 15(8): 656–671. https://doi.org/10.2307/2643383.

Humphrey, C. 1999. Shamans in the city. *Anthropology Today*, 15(3): 3–10. https://doi.org/10.2307/2678275.

Khalid, A. 2007. *Islam after Communism. Religion and politics in Central Asia*. Berkeley: University of California Press.

Kramer, M. 2003. Introduction. *Journal of Cold War Studies* 5(4 (Special Issue: The Collapse of the Soviet Union (Part 2): 3–42.

Louw, M. 2006. Pursuing "Muslimness". Shrines as sites for moralities in the making in post-Soviet Bukhara. *Central Asian Survey* 25(3): 319–339.

McBrien, J. 2009. Mukadas's struggle. Veils and modernity in Kyrgyzstan. *Journal of the Royal Anthropological Institute* 15(1): 127–144.

McBrien, J. 2017. *From belonging to belief. Modern secularisms and the construction of religion in Kyrgyzstan*. Pittsburgh, Pa: University of Pittsburgh Press (Central Eurasia in context series).

Muhajir, A. KH. 2015. Meneguhkan Islam Nusantara untuk Peradaban Indonesia dan Dunia. In *Islam Nusantara. Dari Ushûl Fiqh Hingga Paham Kebangsaan*, Eds. A. Sahal and A. Munawir, 61–68. Bandung: Mizan.

Pelkmans, M. 2017. *Fragile conviction. Changing ideological landscapes in urban Kyrgyzstan.* Ithaca: Cornell University Press.

Pelkmans, M. Forthcoming. Recognizing uniqueness. On (not) comparing the world nomad games. In *How people compare*, Eds. M. Pelkmans and H. Walker. Routledge.

Privratsky, B. G. 2001. *Muslim Turkistan. Kazak religion and collective memory.* Richmond Surrey: Curzon Press.

Rasanayagam, J. 2011. *Islam in post-Soviet Uzbekistan. The morality of experience.* Cambridge; New York: Cambridge University Press.

Rasanayagam, J. 2014. The politics of culture and the space for Islam. Soviet and post-Soviet imaginaries in Uzbekistan. *Central Asian Survey* 33(1): 1–14. https://doi.org/10.1080/02634937.2014.882619.

Schlehe, J. 1998. *Ratu Kidul, die Meereskönigin des Südens. Geisterpolitik im javanischen Alltag.* Berlin: Dietrich Reimer.

Schlehe, J. 2000. Reiseromanzen. Beziehungsstrukturen zwischen westlichen Frauen und indonesischen Männern. In *Zwischen den Kulturen—zwischen den Geschlechtern. Kulturkontakte und Genderkonstrukte*, Ed. J. Schlehe, 125–141. Münster: Waxmann.

Schlehe, J. 2005. Shamanism in Mongolia and in New Age movements. In *Central Asia on display. Proceedings of the VII. Conference of the European Society for Central Asian Studies*, Eds. C. Rasuly-Paleczek and J. Katschnig, 283–295. Münster: LIT.

Schlehe, J. 2008. Religion, Natur und die aktuelle Deutung von Naturkatastrophen auf Java. In *Religion und die Modernität von Tradition in Asien. Neukonfigurationen von Götter-, Geister- und Menschenwelten*, Eds. B. Rehbein and J. Schlehe, 207–234. Münster: LIT.

Schlehe, J. 2010. Die Zukunft von Natur und Politik im chinesischen Jahr des Tigers. In *Spiegel und Prisma. Ethnologie zwischen postkolonialer Politik und Deutung der eigenen Gesellschaft*, Eds. D. Schulz and J. Seebode, 326–340. Hamburg: Argument Verlag.

Schlehe, J 2011a. Äußere und innere Grenzen. Genderkonstruktionen und die Rede vom Geld in transnationalen Liebesbeziehungen. In *Border Crossings. Grenzverschiebungen und Grenzüberschreitungen in einer globalisierten Welt*, Ed. S. Randeria, 179–194. Zürich vdf-Hochschulverlag.

Schlehe, J 2011b. Cultural politics of representation in contemporary Indonesia. *European Journal of East Asian Studies* 10(2): 149–167. https://doi.org/10.1163/156805811X616093.

Schlehe, J. 2012. Moderne Paranormale als spirituelle UnternehmerInnen in Indonesien?. *ASIEN. The German Journal of Contemporary Asia* 123: 95–111.

Schlehe, J. 2013. Concepts of Asia, the West and the Self in contemporary Indonesia. An anthropological account. *South East Asia Research* 21(3): 497–515.

Schlehe, J. 2014a. Bukit Kasih, the hill of love. Multireligiosity for pleasure. In *Dynamics of religion in Southeast Asia*, Ed. V. Cottowik, 281–298. Amsterdam University Press. https://doi.org/10.1515/9789048516278-015.

Schlehe, J. 2014b. Translating traditions and transcendence. Popularized religiosity and the paranormals' position in Indonesian society. In *Religion, tradition and the popular. Transcultural views from Asia and Europe*, Eds. J. Schlehe and E. Sandkühler, 185–201. Bielefeld: transcript.

Schlehe, J. 2017. Contesting Javanese traditions. The popularisation of rituals between religion and tourism. *Indonesia and the Malay World* 45(131): 3–23. https://doi.org/10.1080/13639811.2016.1219494.

Schlehe, J. 2019. Cosmopolitanism, pluralism and self-orientalisation in the modern mystical world of Java. *Asian Journal of Social Science* 47(3): 364–386. https://doi.org/10.1163/15685314-04703005.

Schlehe, J., M. V. Nertz, and V. I. Yulianto. 2013. Re-imagining "the West" and performing "Indonesian modernities". Muslims, Christians and "paranormal" practitioners. *Zeitschrift für Ethnologie* 138(1): 3–21.

Schlehe, J., and E.F. Nisa. 2016. The meanings of moderate Islam in Indonesia. Alignments and dealignments of Azharites. *Southeast Asian Studies at the University of Freiburg* (Occasional Paper No 31).

Schlehe, J., and M. Uike-Bormann. 2010. Staging the past in cultural theme parks. Representations of self and other in Asia and Europe. In *Staging the past: Themed environments in transcultural perspectives*, Eds. J. Schlehe et al., 57–91. Bielefeld: transcript Verlag. https://doi.org/10.14361/transcript.9783839414811.

Schlehe, J., and H. Weber. 2001. Schamanismus und Tourismus in der Mongolei. *Zeitschrift für Ethnologie* 126(1): 93–116.

Schlehe, J., and V. I. Yulianto. 2020. An anthropology of waste. Morality and social mobilisation in Java. *Indonesia and the Malay World* 48(140): 40–59. https://doi.org/10.1080/13639811.2019.1654225.

Slezkine, Y. 1994. The USSR as a communal apartment, or how a socialist state promoted ethnic pluralism. *Slavic Review* 53(2): 414–452.

Stephan-Emmrich, M. and P. Schröder, Eds. 2018. *Mobilities, boundaries, and travelling ideas. Rethinking translocality beyond Central Asia and the Caucasus*. Cambridge, UK: Open Book Publishers.

Faszination tsantsa? Interkulturelle Perspektiven auf die Schrumpfkopfpraxis bei den Shuar

Anna Meiser

1 Einführung: Der *tsantsa* – mehr als ein Objekt der Orientalisierung

Bereits in der Einleitung zu seiner Monographie *Leben und Sterben in Amazonien* macht Philippe Descola unmissverständlich deutlich, welcher Untersuchungsgegenstand ihn nicht zu den Achuar und Shuar ins ecuadorianische Amazonasgebiet geführt habe und welche Problemstellung er auf den folgenden Seiten daher bewusst ausklammere: nämlich die des *tsantsa*, wie der geschrumpfte Kopf des getöteten Feindes in der Sprachfamilie der Aénts Chicham[1] genannt wird. „Man wird kaum glauben, wenn ich sage", hält der Lévi-Strauss-Schüler fest, „daß nicht irgendeine von den Schrumpfköpfen ausgehende Faszination mich zu den Jívaro geführt hat" (Descola 1996, S. 26). Seit Descolas ausgedehntem Feldforschungsaufenthalt in den 1970er Jahren sind über vierzig Jahre vergangen. Doch der Faszination und der Debatte rund um den *tsantsa*, um seinen Umgang in den musealen Sammlungen im europäischen und US-amerikanischen Raum

---

[1] Auf der Tagung *Yápankam' – Las Voces de la Investigación en la Alta Amazonía Ecuatoriana* im ecuadorianischen Sevilla Don Bosco im April 2018 haben intellektuelle und politische Führer der Shuar sowie mehrere WissenschaftlerInnen der „Jívaro" bzw. „Jíbaro"-Forschung beschlossen, auf eben dieses Xenonym zu verzichten und nunmehr den Terminus *Aénts Chicham* anstatt „Jívaro"/„Jíbaro" zu verwenden – in Bezug sowohl auf die Nennung der Ethnie als auch der Sprachgruppe (Deshoullière und Utitiaj Paati 2019).

A. Meiser (✉)
Institut für Interkulturelle Kommunikation, Ludwig-Maximilians-Universität München, München, Deutschland
E-Mail: anna.meiser@ikk.lmu.de

sowie um die kulturellen Bedeutungen für die Achuar und vor allem Shuar tat dies keinen Abbruch. Erst 2020 entschied die Museumsdirektorin des Pitt Rivers Museum in Oxford, Laura Van Broekhoven, die *tsantsas,* die spätestens seit 1936 zur Sammlung gehören, aus der Ausstellung zu nehmen: „Many think of these objects as bizarre, gruesome, barbaric, a 'freak' show. The practice of headhunting, instead of being better understood, is misunderstood entirely. The Shuar communities do not want to be represented in these stereotypical ways", so Van Broekhoven bereits ein Jahr vor diesem Entschluss (Bailey 2019, online). Die gezeigten Schrumpfköpfe hätten eher interkulturelles Missverstehen und negative Stereotype begünstigt, denn eine tiefergehende Auseinandersetzung mit der Shuar-Kultur gefördert. So waren die *tsantsas* in einer Vitrine mit der Beschriftung „Treatment of Dead Enemies" ausgestellt, zusammen mit Schädeln der Naga aus Assam und der Ilongot aus den Philippinen. Diese Vitrine war in unmittelbarer Nähe zu einer anderen platziert worden, welche wiederum den Titel „Treatment of Dead" trug. Sie zeigte Objekte naher und freundschaftlich verbundener Toten – und war damit ein Gegenpol zu jener Vitrine, welche sich auf den Umgang mit getöteten Feinden konzentrierte (Peers 2011, S. 7 f.).

Ein Jahr nach der Entscheidung in Oxford entschloss sich auch das Historische und Völkerkundemuseum St. Gallen, in ähnlicher Weise zu handeln (Becker 2021, online). Die erst im Jahr 2010 erworbenen sechs *tsantsas* werden nicht mehr ausgestellt. Freilich war bereits die Anschaffung von einem enormen und ambivalenten Echo begleitet gewesen – sodass man sich fragen kann, warum es für diesen Schritt der Museumsleitung elf Jahre gebraucht hat. Schon damals kommentierte die Appenzeller Zeitung: „Wieso kauft ein Völkerkundemuseum heute [2010] sechs Schrumpfköpfe? […] Grusel lockt Volk ins Völkerkundemuseum. Denn die Leute wollen sich gruseln" (zit. nach Schlothauer 2011, S. 56). Im Schweizer Radio DRS wiederum mahnte eine Ethnologin an, dass die Schrumpfköpfe, welche im Zentrum der Ausstellung stünden, das Klischee des „primitiven Wilden", „brutalen kaltblütigen Killers" und „Kannibalen" nährten. Das Museum in St. Gallen stehe in der Verantwortung, keine Vorurteile gegenüber den Shuar zu erzeugen (zit. nach Schlothauer 2011, S. 57).

Den Argumenten und Bedenken der beiden Ethnologinnen aus Großbritannien und der Schweiz ist zweifelsohne recht zu geben: Die scheinbar bewusst in Szene gesetzte Darstellung der indigenen Objekte in den Ausstellungen schürt die Sensationslust des europäischen Publikums und exotisiert im gleichen Zuge die Kultur der Shuar sowie ihre Mitglieder selbst. Was erstaunlicherweise im Zuge der Debatten rund um die museale Repräsentation der *tsantsas* jedoch kaum Erwähnung findet und nicht weitergedacht wurde, ist die Frage nach der kulturellen Biographie der Objekte – nach der Geschichte ihrer kulturellen Bedeutung, den möglichen Reinterpretationen und Refunktionalisierungen, welche die Schrumpfköpfe seitens der Achuar und Shuar erfahren haben. Die Diskussion um die Ausstellung der menschlichen Überreste in Form von *tsantsas* in den genannten europäischen Museen ist insofern eng geführt und einseitig, als sie einerseits die Schrumpfköpfe als kulturelles Symbol einer ausschließlich vergangenen Epoche versteht; der *tsantsa* ist ein Relikt vergangener Zeiten und repräsentiert eine Ethnie, deren „Gleichzeitigkeit" mit unserer gegenwärtigen Lebenswelt im Sinne Johannes Fabians negiert wird (Fabian 1983, S. 35). Andererseits nimmt die Diskussion um das Für und vor allem das Wider der gezeigten Objekte vorwiegend deren Wirkung auf das europäische Publikum und damit dessen Perspektive in den Blick; den Stimmen der Shuar und Achuar gibt sie hingegen keinen Raum. So möchte der vorliegende Artikel die interkulturellen Zuschreibungen und die soziokulturellen Praktiken aufzeigen, die die Achuar und zuvorderst die Shuar in rezenten Jahren mit dem *tsantsa* verbinden. Hieran schließt sich die Fragestellung an, auf welche Weise die Shuar mit diesen Zuschreibungen umgehen und wie sie selbst den Schrumpfkopf als ethnokulturelles Symbol einzusetzen wissen. Auf diese Weise werde ich aufzeigen, inwieweit das Faszinosum *tsantsa* – jenseits aller schauerlichen Perzeptionen und stereotypisierenden Imaginationen, die es zu evozieren vermag – dennoch ein für die Ethnologie erkenntnisreicher und faszinierender Gegenstand der Analyse sein kann. Diese berücksichtigt Ansätze, Diskurse und Auseinandersetzungen, die auch in Judith Schlehes Forschungsfeldern und zahlreichen Publikationen zentral geworden sind und unter anderem globale Dynamiken aus der Sicht lokaler AkteurInnen in postkolonialen Kontexten beleuchten und erklären. So beschäftigt sich Schlehe in mehreren ihrer Arbeiten mit inter- und transkulturellen Beziehungen, sich wechselseitig bedingenden Repräsentationsformen und -praktiken des kulturell „Eigenen" und „Fremden", der Wieder-Erfindung lokaler Traditionen und kollektiver Identitäten sowie der Popularisierung von kulturellen Phänomenen und Praktiken (vgl. etwa Schlehe 2009; 2011; 2013; Schlehe et al. 2013; Schlehe und Sandkühler 2014). Dementsprechend sucht der vorliegende Beitrag, die gegenwärtige Bedeutung des *tsantsa* für die Shuar zu erörtern, indem in der Conclusio einige der oben ausgewählten Problemstellungen in den Fokus der ethnologischen Betrachtung genommen werden.

Nach den oben skizzierten Perzeptionen und Debatten rund um den *tantsa* im europäischen Raum soll im Folgenden der Blick in das ecuadorianische Amazonasgebiet gerichtet werden: Ich werde einen kurzen Einblick in die wichtigsten ethnologischen Erklärungsversuche zur Schrumpfkopfpraxis bei den Shuar geben und einige Fakten darlegen, die Relevanz und Kontexte derselben deutlich machen (Abschn. 2). Im Weiteren gilt es, anhand von drei einschlägigen Beispielen aufzeigen, mit welchen Perspektiven die Shuar heute auf den *tsantsa* blicken; dabei werde ich erörtern, inwieweit letztere damit lokale Antworten auf globale Zuschreibungen des *tsantsa* geben (Abschn. 3). In der Conclusio (Abschn. 4) sollen zentrale Argumentationslinien des Beitrags nochmals hervorgehoben und die Anknüpfungspunkte zu Judith Schlehes Arbeiten verdeutlicht werden.

2 Die Shuar und der *tsantsa*: Ethnologische Fakten und Erklärungsversuche

Gleich bei meinem ersten Aufenthalt in Ecuador vor über zwanzig Jahren – der noch nicht von studentischen, gar wissenschaftlichen Interessen geleitet war – bin ich dem Phänomen *tsantsa* begegnet: Einer der Söhne meiner Shuar-Gastfamilie ist bis heute Lehrer an der Sekundarschule „Unidad Educativa Comunitaria Intercultural Bilingüe ‚Tsantsa'" im Ort Tsurakú (Provinz Pastaza), die praktisch ausschließlich indigene SchülerInnen ausbildet und mehrheitlich Shuar-LehrerInnen beschäftigt. Während meiner Reise im Jahr 2001 konnte ich diese besuchen und wurde dabei auch über Name und Logo der Schule aufgeklärt: So sind auf dem ovalförmigen Schulwappen, dessen Autor wohl ein Schüler der Bildungseinrichtung war, in der Mitte ein aufgeschlagenes Buch mit Schreibfeder zu erkennen, im oberen Bereich ein Mikroskop mit der Unterschrift „Ciencia" (Wissenschaft), im unteren ein Computer mit dem Schriftzug „Tecnología" (Technologie), links ein Sportler sowie der Titel „Deportes" (Sport) – und rechts: die Skizze eines Schrumpfkopfes, versehen mit der Bezeichnung „Cultura" (Kultur) (vgl. Facebook-Auftritt der Unidad Educativa Tsantsa, online). Auf einem Banner der Schule ist dieselbe *tsantsa*-Darstellung zweimal prominent abgebildet, unter dem Namen der Schule prangt zudem der Leitsatz: „Impulsando una educación con identidad propia"[2] (vgl. Homepage der Unidad Educativa Tsantsa, online).

Für die Angehörigen der Unidad Educativa wie auch die BewohnerInnen von Tsurakú ist der *tsantsa* ein Sinnbild des Alltagsgeschehens wie auch Symbol der kulturellen Identität; sie begegnen ihm einerseits in der geregelten, unaufgeregten Routine des individuellen Schulbesuchs und verstehen ihn andererseits als Bekenntnis zu einem kollektiven Selbstverständnis, welches aus spezifischen soziokulturellen Traditionen und Praktiken schöpft. Sowohl der Schule in Tsurakú als auch den Museen in Europa dient der *tsantsa* der kulturellen Repräsentation der Shuar, wenn auch in zweifach unterschiedlicher Weise: Die museale

---

[2] Übersetzung ins Deutsche: „Anstoß zu einer Bildung mit eigener Identität".

Ausstellung der Schrumpfköpfe ist, wie sollte es auch anders sein, ein Akt der Fremdrepräsentation – die Setzung des *tsantsa* als Identitätsmarker hingegen Ausdruck shuar'scher Selbstzuschreibung. Für die LehrerInnen und SchülerInnen der Unidad Educativa sind sie zudem positiv verstandene Embleme der eigenen Ethnie, während die Schrumpfköpfe in den Museen, so zeigen es die oben zitierten Kommentare, als negativ belegte, die Shuar im besten Fall exotisierende kulturelle Artefakte wahrgenommen werden.

Dementsprechend schreibt auch Michael Harner in seiner Monographie *The Jívaro – People of the Sacred Waterfalls,* die immer noch als eines der Standardwerke zur Ethnologie der Aénts Chicham gilt (erstmals 1972 erschienen):

> Tales of their fierceness became part of the folklore of Latin America, and their warlike reputation spread in the late nineteenth and early twentieth centuries when Jívaro 'shrunken head' trophies, *tsantsa,* found their way to the markets of exotica in the Western world. (Harner 1984, S. 1)

Den Stoff für die Legende vom kriegerischen Volk hatten frühe ethnologische Schriften gewissenhaft mitgesponnen (vgl. etwa Karsten 1935, S. 259; Stirling 1938, S. 41), aber auch Michael Harner selbst leitet – nur wenige Zeilen über der zitierten Formulierung – sein Werk ein mit der Aussage, dass die einzige indigene Ethnie auf dem lateinamerikanischen Kontinent, die der spanischen Eroberung – und auch der kriegerischen Expansion seitens der Inka – getrotzt hätte, die Shuar gewesen seien (Harner 1984, S. 1, 17; Mader und Sharup' 1993, S. 112). Es ist eine Attribution, die neben der der „Schrumpfkopfmacher"[3] den wissenschaftlichen Diskurs über die Shuar lange geprägt hat.[4]

Die Shuar zählen rund 148.800 Mitglieder und siedeln vorwiegend in den südöstlichen Amazonasprovinzen des Landes (Pastaza, Morona Santiago, Zamora Chinchipe) (vgl. Territorio Indígena y Gobernanza, online); die linguistisch und kulturell verwandten Achuar leben traditionell im ecuadorianisch-peruanischen Grenzraum, wobei eine deutliche Mehrheit im nordöstlichen Peru ansässig ist.[5]

---

[3] Dieser Titel, allerdings mit einem Fragezeichen versehen, trägt der Katalog der von Mark Münzel konzipierten und im Frankfurter Museum für Völkerkunde im Jahr 1977 gezeigten Ausstellung (Münzel 1977).

[4] Auch vereinzelte Publikationen von Missionaren trugen dazu bei, die Wahrnehmung der Shuar als kriegerische Schrumpfkopfjäger zu festigen; vgl. etwa die 2002 erschienene Monographie von Frank und Marie Drown: *Mission to the Headhunters – How God's Forgiveness Transformed Tribal Enemies.*

[5] Die Bevölkerungszahl der Achuar beträgt ca. 7000 Personen (vgl. Territorio Indígena y Gobernanza, online).

Sowohl die Shuar als auch die Achuar sind politisch in verschiedenen Föderationen organisiert; dabei sticht die 1964 gegründete *Federación Interprovincial de Centros Shuar* (FICSH) hervor, denn sie gilt als eine der ersten indigenen Organisationen in Südamerika mit Vorbildcharakter für die gesamte indigene Bewegung Ecuadors und mit beachtlichen Erfolgen in Fragen der Sicherung von kollektiven Landtiteln sowie der Etablierung eines bilingualen interkulturellen Bildungssystem (Juncosa Blasco 2020, S. 214 ff.; Meiser 2013, S. 80 ff.; Neumann 1994, S. 90). Während der landesweiten, von der indigenen Bewegung angeführten und schlussendlich erfolgreichen[6] Proteste im Herbst 2019, die sich gegen die Beendigung der staatlichen Kraftstoffsubventionen richteten, waren auch die Shuar in der ecuadorianischen Presse präsent. Die Fotos aus der Hauptstadt Quito, welche unter anderem den medialen Diskurs bestimmten, zeigten sie einmal mehr in martialischer Haltung und mit Lanzen abgebildet – obgleich in denselben Artikeln die interviewten Indigenen die Friedfertigkeit ihres Protests betonten (vgl. auch Meiser [2023]). Doch Berichte wie die über die „Hunderte[n] indigene[n] Krieger aus Amazonien", wie etwa das Nachrichtenportal *elmostrador* titelte (11.10.19), perpetuieren das Narrativ von einer kämpferischen und widerständigen Ethnie, zu dessen augenfälligstem Symbol der *tsantsa* wurde.

Tatsächlich war die Herstellung eines Schrumpfkopfes bis etwa in die 1950er Jahre hinein üblicherweise mit einer gewaltvollen und kriegerischen Auseinandersetzung verbunden, die den Mord eines befeindeten Gegners nach sich gezogen hatte – wobei ein solcher Feind gewöhnlich ebenfalls ein Shuar oder ein Achuar war. Denn bis dahin siedelten die Shuar, im Gegensatz zu vielen anderen ethnischen Gruppen in Amazonien, nicht im Dorfverband, sondern in der erweiterten polygynen Kernfamilie (Harner 1984, S. 41). Dieser Siedlungsform folgend, existierte bis zur Gründung von Dorfverbänden mit dem Ziel der Sicherung von kollektiven Landtiteln in der Mitte des 20. Jahrhunderts auch kein ausgeprägtes kollektives Shuar-Bewusstsein (Neumann 1994, S. 111 f., 117). Anders als bei vielen Ethnien Amazoniens ging das „Wir-Gefühl" zumeist nicht über die jeweils eigene Hausgemeinschaft hinaus, was auch Philippe Descola zu der Formulierung verleitete, dass „bei ihnen [den Shuar] […] laufend blutige Konflikte zwischen den nächsten Nachbarn und Verwandten ausgetragen" wurden, wobei der französische Ethnologe sich gar des Hobbes'schen Ausdrucks vom „Krieg

---

[6] Knapp zwei Wochen nach Beginn der Demonstrationen, Straßensperrungen und Streiks sowie der zeitweiligen Verlegung des Regierungssitzes von Quito nach Guayaquil hob der damalige Staatspräsident Lenín Moreno das Dekret 883, welches die staatliche Subvention von Benzin beenden sollte, wieder auf. An dieser Entscheidung, die gleichbedeutend mit dem Ende aller Proteste war, war der wichtigste indigene Dachverband des Landes, die CONAIE (*Confederación de Nacionalidades Indígenas del Ecuador),* maßgeblich beteiligt.

aller gegen alle" bedient, um die damaligen sozialen Beziehungen unter den Shuar zu beschreiben (Descola 1996, S. 29). Grund für die dauernden Fehden war die fehlende Vorstellung eines ohne Fremdeinwirken herbeigeführten natürlichen Todes. Unabhängig davon, ob jemand im Kampf, an einer Krankheit gestorben oder etwa von einer Giftschlange gebissen worden war, galt der Tod einer jeden Person in vielen Fällen als intendiert[7], weshalb sie von ihrer Familie gerächt und die (vermeintlich) Verantwortlichen ausfindig gemacht werden mussten; sehr häufig wurden Schamanen belangt, denen vorgeworfen wurde, mittels ihrer Magie den Tod der nahestehenden Person verursacht zu haben (Harner 1984, S. 52 f.; Taylor 1996, S. 202 f.). Wurde nun im Zuge einer solchen tödlichen Rache der männliche Gegner besiegt, wurde ihm in den meisten Fällen der Kopf abgeschlagen und dieser in einem mehrtätigen Verfahren derart präpariert, dass er beträchtlich zusammenschrumpfte, ohne dass jedoch die Gesichtszüge des getöteten Kriegers verloren gingen. War der *tsantsa* fertig, schloss sich ein Fest an, das von Descola als „einigermaßen rätselhaft" beschrieben, in mehrere Zyklen aufgeteilt war und sich über etliche Monate, insgesamt rund zwei Jahre, erstreckte (Descola 1996, S. 288 ff.; vgl. außerdem Fausto 2012, S. 258 f.; Harner 1984, S. 187 ff.; Münzel 1977, S. 228 ff.; Taylor 1993, S. 671 f.). Rätselhaft und bis heute nicht eindeutig geklärt ist auch die Frage, warum die Shuar überhaupt Schrumpfköpfe herstellten. Auf zumindest drei Erklärungsversuche soll an dieser Stelle in aller Kürze eingegangen werden:[8] Elke Mader und Richard Gippelhausen begründen die Transformation der erbeuteten Kopftrophäen in geschrumpfte *tsantsas* mit der spirituellen Dimension des Krieges, der zufolge es das Ziel war, die Kraft des getöteten Feindes auf den erfolgreichen Kämpfer und seine eigene Gruppe zu übertragen (Mader und Gippelhauser 2000, S. 63). Münzel führt an, dass der Schrumpfkopf aufgrund der von ihm ausgehenden Kraft auch bei Krankenriten Verwendung fand; des Weiteren beging der erfolgreiche Schrumpfkopfjäger mit seiner Trophäe um den Hals die Felder, da dies deren Fruchtbarkeit fördern sollte (Münzel 1977, S. 228). Michael Harner argumentiert, dass die Herstellung des *tsantsa* dazu gedient habe, die Wirkkraft der Racheseele *musiak* zu bändigen, die im Kopf des Getöteten verortet sei und von dort zu entweichen suche, um Vergeltung zu üben (Harner 1984, S. 143 ff.). Aus diesem Grund musste das abgeschlagene Haupt entsprechend präpariert und dessen sämtliche Öffnungen, vor allem Mund und Augen, zugenäht werden, um das Entkommen

---

[7] Eine Ausnahme bildeten etwa „Krankheiten des weißen Mannes" wie Keuchhusten, Masern, Erkältungen, Durchfall (Harner 1984, S. 152 f.).
[8] Für eine prägnante und kurze Zusammenfassung möglicher Erklärungsversuche: vgl. Ruberstein 2004, S. 17.

musiaks zu vereiteln und Schaden von dem glorreichen Kämpfer sowie Besitzer des *tsantsa* abzuwenden (Münzel 1977, S. 228; vgl. auch Boster 2003, S. 157; Descola 1996, S. 288). Ein zum Katholizismus konvertierter Shuar erklärte mir, dass die Schrumpfkopfpraxis sowie die damit verbundenen kriegerischen und tödlichen Auseinandersetzungen zwar eindeutig „sündhaft" seien, aber die Herstellung des *tsantsa* als ein Versuch verstanden werden müsse, die Spirale der Rache und der Gewalt zu durchbrechen. Letztlich rette der Schrumpfkopf und die darin besänftigte Racheseele *musiak* das Leben anderer (Interview mit P.T. am 09.12.09). Dieser Gedanke, durch die Anfertigung von *tsantsas* Leben zu bewahren bzw. neues zu gewinnen, will überleiten zum dritten, in der Ethnologie diskutierten Ansatz: So zeichnen sich für Carlos Fausto und David Rodgers amazonische Gesellschaften weniger dadurch aus, materielle Güter zu mehren, sondern neue Menschen zu produzieren; darin sehen sie den Sinn des *tsantsa*-Rituals (Fausto und Rodgers 1999, S. 934, S. 947 ff.; Fausto 2012, S. 258 f.). Mit dieser Argumentation knüpft Fausto an die Ausführungen von Anne-Christine Taylor an, die darlegt, dass das *tsantsa*-Ritual letztlich der Produktion von neuem Leben diene: Denn für die Shuar war die mögliche Anzahl menschlicher Individuen begrenzt. So sollte durch die Herstellung des *tsantsa* die Identität des Getöteten gleichsam eingefangen und der eigenen Gruppe zugeführt werden. Auf diese Weise versinnbildlicht der *tsantsa* des einstigen Feindes die Inkorporierung eines zusätzlichen Individuums in die Gruppe des Siegers und damit die Aneignung und Sicherung von neuem Leben, welches als begrenzte Ressource gilt (Taylor 1993, S. 659, 671 ff.). Meines Erachtens stehen diese drei Erklärungsansätze in keinem notwendigen Widerspruch zueinander; so ist letztlich allen gemein, dass durch die Herstellung des *tsantsa* Macht, wenn nicht sogar Leben potenziert wird – so verfremdend diese Deutung auch wirken mag, wenn man aus einer Außenperspektive im *tsantsa* zuallererst ein Emblem des Todes und der Gewalt erkennen will.

3 Der *tsantsa* heute: Produkt transnationaler und interkultureller Beziehungen

In den 1960er Jahren verbot die ecuadorianische Regierung die Herstellung von Schrumpfköpfen, auch wenn in manchen weit abgelegenen Regionen bis in die 1980er Jahre hinein indigene Köpfe zu *tsantsas* verarbeitet wurden. Bereits zuvor hatten die kriegerischen Auseinandersetzungen unter den Aénts Chicham mit dem Einfluss der christlichen Mission und der damit verbundenen Gründung von

Shuar-Dörfern sowie der allgemeinen Präsenz des Staates allmählich abgenommen (Taylor 1993, S. 657, 670; Wasserstrom 2016, S. 512). Dass vereinzelt doch neue Schrumpfköpfe auftauchten und es mancherorts zu Kopfjagden kam, war zumeist dem Interesse von individuellen LiebhaberInnen und Museen aus Europa und Nordamerika geschuldet, welches gegen Ende des 19. Jahrhunderts eingesetzt hatte und unaufhörlich gestiegen war (Rubenstein 2007, S. 359). So sollte mit dem Erlass des ecuadorianischen Staates aus den 1960er Jahren nicht nur den immer seltener gewordenen Fehden unter den Shuar Einhalt geboten werden; er galt in gleicher Weise dem mittlerweile florierenden internationalen Souvenirhandel mit Schrumpfköpfen, den man auf diese Weise einzudämmen suchte. „Das Interesse der Weißen an den gruseligen Objekten war bald größer als die Kriegslust der Indianer: Die Anzahl der Köpfe reichte nicht. Händler gruben Leichen aus und übergaben die Köpfe indianischen Fachleuten zur Präparierung, schließlich trieben sie die Jíbaro sogar zur Kopfjagd auf Bestellung", konstatiert Mark Münzel (Münzel 1977, S. 248). Im Zuge der Interaktion mit der nicht-indigenen Welt wurde der Schrumpfkopf für die Shuar damit auch zu einem Tauschobjekt, das mit „westlicher" Technik, vor allem in Form von Schusswaffen, oder mit direkten Geldzahlungen beglichen wurde. Eine solche Transaktion stattete die einzelnen Indigenen zwar nicht mit neuem Leben, aber mit Mitteln aus, die die eigene Machtposition zu stärken vermochten.

Immer wieder bezeugen kurze Ausführungen von EthnologInnen, dass der Handel mit Schrumpfköpfen auch bis weit in die zweite Hälfte des vergangenen Jahrhunderts andauerte. So berichtet Elke Mader in einem 1994 publizierten Artikel von massiven Vorwürfen gegen den damaligen Präsidenten der oben erwähnten politischen Organisation FICSH, der beschuldigt worden sei, Shuar und Achuar getötet und enthauptet zu haben, um *tsantsas* herzustellen, die er für einen hohen Preis US-amerikanischen Interessenten verkauft habe (Mader 1994). Steven Rubenstein verweist in seinem Artikel auf einen Interviewpartner, der als Shuar am Cenépa-Krieg (1995) zwischen Ecuador und dem benachbarten Peru teilgenommen hatte, der durch Streitigkeiten über den Grenzverlauf entlang des Amazonaszuflusses Río Cenepa ausgelöst worden war. In den Militäreinheiten beider Länder wurden Shuar und Achuar eingesetzt, deren Siedlungsgebiet sich sowohl auf ecuadorianischem als auch auf peruanischem Territorium erstreckt. So standen sich an den Frontlinien eines binationalen Krieges Shuar und Achuar erneut einander gegenüber. Der Veteran erzählte Rubenstein, dass ein Freund mehrere *tsantsas* aus den Köpfen getöteter peruanischer Soldaten hergestellt habe (Rubenstein 2007, S. 370; vgl. auch Beitrag von El Mundo am 13.12.09).

Auch mich selbst hatte keine „von den Schrumpfköpfen ausgehende Faszination" zu den Aénts Chicham geführt, um die in der Einleitung zitierte

Formulierung Descolas erneut zu bemühen. Dennoch wurde ich mehr als einmal während meiner Forschungsaufenthalte unfreiwillig mit der oben dargelegten, durch die Einbettung dieses kulturellen Artefakts in den internationalen Handel gewandelten Bedeutung des *tsantsa* konfrontiert. Im Dezember 2009 begleitete ich einen katholischen Shuar-Priester zu einem Gottesdienst in eine mehrheitlich von Shuar bewohnte Gemeinde, die unweit des Ortes Méndez (Provinz Morona Santiago) gelegen war. Ich kam zum ersten Mal in dieses Dorf und so wurde ich zum Ende der Messfeier darum gebeten, mich vorzustellen. Ich sagte einige wenige Sätze zu meiner Person und skizzierte kurz mein Forschungsprojekt, das sich mit dem Einfluss der katholischen und evangelikalen Mission unter den Achuar und Shuar auseinandersetzte. Ich hatte die Sätze gesprochen, doch die Blicke der Anwesenden drückten Anspannung und Skepsis aus, der Kirchenraum war von einem nach meiner Wahrnehmung angestrengten Schweigen erfüllt. Ich wandte mich fragend an den Priester, der mir bedeutete, dass ich außerdem klarstellen müsse, mit der sogenannten „Schrumpfkopf-Mafia" bzw. „Mafia der Kopfabschneider" („mafia de tsantsa" bzw. „mafia de cortecabezas") nichts zu tun zu haben. Ich kehrte zurück zur Mitte des Kirchenschiffs, sprach erneut zu der versammelten Gemeinde und formulierte mechanisch, dass ich nicht dieser Gruppe von Kriminellen angehörte, die durch die verschiedenen Shuar-Dörfer fuhr, um potentielle Opfer zu identifizieren, deren geschrumpfter Kopf die internationale Nachfrage an *tsantsas* bedienen sollte. Es täte mir unermesslich leid für all diejenigen, die vermutlich in den letzten Monaten von eben dieser „Schrumpfkopf-Mafia" ermordet worden seien und ich schämte mich zutiefst für die jüngst begangenen Verbrechen, die von „weißen" Menschen verantwortet seien, auch wenn sie selbst nicht die unmittelbaren TäterInnen waren. Der befreundete Shuar-Priester beschloss meine kurze Ansprache, indem er gegenüber den anwesenden Frauen, Kindern und Männern für die Wahrhaftigkeit meiner Worte bürgte. Wir versammelten uns alle zum Abendessen, das ich eher schweigsam zu mir nahm; meine Gedanken kreisten einerseits um die große Sorge und Unsicherheit, die viele Shuar angesichts der jüngsten Gewalttaten in ihrer Region erleben mussten, und andererseits um die vermeintlich neue Rollenzuschreibung, von der ich aufgrund der Eingliederung des Schrumpfkopfes in ein transnationales, interkulturelles Beziehungsnetzwerk erfahren hatte (Feldtagebuchnotizen vom 11.12.09). Bereits einige Tage vor meinem Besuch in jener Gemeinde hatte man in den regionalen wie nationalen Zeitungen etliche Artikel über die Festnahme von mehreren Shuar lesen können, die als Mitglieder der sogenannten „Schrumpfkopf-Mafia" seit etwa 2005 in der Region agierten und für den Tod von mehreren geköpften Frauen[9] sowie für den Verkauf ihrer *tsantsas* verantwortlich gemacht wurden (vgl. etwa HOY vom 08.12.09). Damit komme ich zu meinen drei kurzen Beispielskizzen, mit denen ich aufzeigen möchte, auf welche Weise die Shuar jene globalen und nicht-indigenen Attributionen, die der *tsantsa* erhalten hat, interpretieren und welche neuen Bedeutungszuschreibungen sie ihrem kulturellen Artefakt damit verleihen.

3.1 Die „neuen" Schrumpfkopfjäger

Die im Dezember 2009 von der ecuadorianischen Polizei vier verhafteten Shuar-Männer hätten, so die mediale Berichterstattung, aus finanziellen Motiven gehandelt. Die Schätzungen zur Summe, die ihnen für einen präparierten *tsantsa* gezahlt worden sei, gehen in den vier- bis unteren sechsstelligen US-Dollar-Bereich – ein Betrag, der für viele Menschen in der Region einen scheinbaren Ausweg aus einem prekären Leben verheißen würde (vgl. El Mundo vom 13.12.09). Unter den Shuar gingen die Debatten, welche die Ereignisse rund um die Gefangennahme der Verdächtigen begleiteten, vor allem in drei Richtungen: Zum einen bewirkten die Gewalttaten der „Schrumpfkopf-Mafia" Aggression und Misstrauen unter und gegenüber den Shuar. Obgleich der Vorwurf der Komplizenschaft auch „weiße" Menschen traf, waren es zunächst die Shuar selbst, die nunmehr sehr schnell in den Verdacht gerieten, mit der „mafia de corte-cabezas" zu paktieren. Zum anderen bedeutete die Kopfjagd aus Habsucht und zum Zwecke der Veräußerung von *tsantsas* einen radikalen Bruch mit der gleichsam traditionell-spirituellen Dimension der Schrumpfkopfpraxis; sie produzierte nicht mehr neues Leben für die eigene Gruppe – um etwa die Argumentation von Anne-Christine Taylor aufzugreifen –, sondern reduzierte dieses und schwächte so die Gemeinschaft. Schließlich evozierte die neue Schrumpfkopfpraxis, an der indigene wie nicht-indigene AkteurInnen beteiligt sind, denkbar negative Fremdbilder über letztere. So formulierte mir gegenüber ein Shuar und politischer Aktivist: „Das ist schlecht, dass sie, also die Shuar, wieder auf Kopfjagd gehen. Jetzt sind wir wieder für viele ‚die Wilden'. Aber noch schlechter sind die Weißen, die Geld dafür geben und die *tsantsas* sammeln. Sie sind die

---

[9] Der Grund für die mehrheitliche Ermordung von indigenen Frauen war ihre zumeist lange Haartracht. Zwar tragen noch viele Achuar-Männer zumindest schulterlanges Haar, aber nur noch sehr weniger Shuar-Männer. Doch nur ein *tsantsa* mit langen Haaren hatte wohl die Chance, von internationalen KäuferInnen als „authentischer" Schrumpfkopf eines Shuar-Kriegers aus der ersten Hälfte des 20. Jahrhunderts anerkannt zu werden (vgl. Online-Beitrag von El Mundo am 13.12.09).

wahren Barbaren" (Interview mit H.P. am 08.12.09). Es sind „die Weißen", die zu Schrumpfkopfjägern geworden sind, die Gewalt und Tod säen und die Menschen untereinander entzweien. Die Imaginationen rund um den *tsantsa*, die den Shuar zu ihrer zweifelhaften Berühmtheit in der „westlichen" Welt verholfen haben, beginnen wieder zu wirken – aber dieses Mal bleiben sie nicht auf die Shuar fokussiert: Mein Gesprächspartner H. P. übernimmt jene Jahrhunderte alten, von Europa und den USA aus generierten Imaginationen zu den Shuar, richtet sie aber neu aus und projiziert sie zurück auf die „Alte Welt". Denn die heutigen Schrumpfkopfjäger – die neuen Barbaren und Wilden – sind die „Weißen" selbst. So wird die Orientalisierung der Shuar durch die Weißen gewissermaßen zur Okzidentalisierung der Weißen durch die Shuar.

3.2 Der tsantsa in der Kirche

Der katholische Shuar-Diakon P. T. schließt sich dem oben zitierten Urteil an, hinterleuchtet aber zusätzlich und auf doppelte Weise den veränderten, entfremdeten Kontext der Schrumpfkopfpraxis: „Früher haben sie [die Shuar] nicht deswegen *tsantsas* hergestellt, um zu töten oder um Geld zu verdienen. Sie haben deswegen *tsantsas* gemacht, um die Fehden zu beenden", hält der Diakon fest und konnotiert den *tsantsa* damit ungewöhnlich positiv. Und er präzisiert dann auf ebenso ungewohnte Weise: „Das *tsantsa*-Ritual sollte neue Kraft und Frieden bringen. So wie Jesus das Böse besiegt und Frieden gestiftet hat" (Interview mit P.T. am 09.12.09). In dem Zitat prangert der katholische Shuar nicht allein das Vorgehen der Schrumpfkopf-Mafia an, er kritisiert die veränderten Umstände, unter denen *tsantsas* gegenwärtig angefertigt werden: Es gehe allein ums Töten und Geldverdienen. Der *tsantsa* diene nicht mehr seinem ursprünglichen Zweck, den der Diakon mit „neuer Kraft" und „Frieden" verbindet. Und um dem Gesagten gleichsam besonderen Nachdruck zu verleihen, setzt er die Schrumpfkopfpraxis mit dem Sinn und Zweck der im Evangelium postulierten Botschaft in Beziehung: Der *tsantsa* wird zum biblischen Friedensbringer und das *tsantsa*-Ritual dadurch legitimiert. Deshalb verwundert es auch nicht, wenn sich in der Shuar-Kirche, in der mein Interviewpartner zum Zeitpunkt der Feldforschung tätig war, ein Gemälde findet, welches neben einem Kreuz auf der linken Seite auch einen Schrumpfkopf zeigt (vgl. rote Umrandung, Abb. 1). Das in der Mitte abgebildete Schwein verweist auf ein während des *tsantsa*-Rituals geschlachtetes Schwein, welches je nach Quelle *iíkmak* bzw. *imiak* genannt wird und die Funktion eines Sühneopfers innehabe (Descola 1996, S. 289 f.; Pellizzaro und Náwech 2005[2],

Abb. 1
Tsantsa-Darstellung auf einem Gemälde der katholischen Kirche San Papru. (Sucía, Ecuador, Foto und Markierung: A. M.)

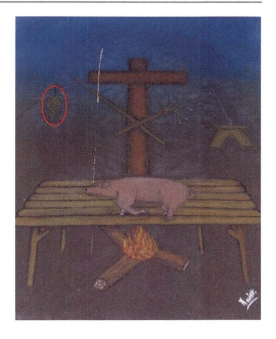

S. 172 f.); in der katholischen Shuar-Theologie wird die Rolle des Schweines *iík-mak* bzw. *imiak* mit der des christlichen „Lamm Gottes" verglichen.[10] Auch der katholische Diakon verändert in seiner Aussage den Kontext der Schrumpfkopfpraxis; er interpretiert sie vor seinem christlichen Hintergrund neu und kommt dabei meines Erachtens einer der drei vorgestellten traditionellen kulturellen Bedeutungen des *tsantsa*-Rituals doch relativ nahe, nämlich der Ermöglichung neuen Lebens.

3.3   tsantsa und Iwia: Sinnbilder der Nie-Eroberten

Dies gilt nicht in derselben Weise beim dritten Beispiel, das den kulturellen Bedeutungswandel des *tsantsa* für die Shuar aufzeigen will. Auch hier erfährt der Schrumpfkopf in seiner Zuschreibung eine eher positive Konnotation, die ihn aber

---

[10] Zur weiteren Darlegung und Diskussion der Re-Kontextualisierung und Re-Interpretation von kulturellen indigenen Symbolen und Riten, der Kosmologie sowie Mythologie der Shuar durch indigene KonvertitInnen und christliche MissionarInnen siehe: Meiser 2013.

zweifellos wieder in den Kontext der Gewalt rücken lässt. „In unserer Geschichte wurden wir Shuar niemals von den Spaniern erobert. Unsere Vorfahren haben uns erzählt, dass die Krieger der Shuar den Spaniern ihre Köpfe abschlugen und sie zu *tsantsas,* zu Kriegstrophäen, verarbeiteten", stellt der Shuar G. T. zunächst fest, bevor er fortfährt: „In der Vergangenheit, seit wir auf der Erde existieren, haben wir die Dämonen des Regenwaldes vernichtet und wir haben keine Angst, vor nichts und vor niemandem" (Interview mit G.T. am 06.01.06).

Für den Shuar ist der *tsantsa* augenscheinlich zum Sinnbild dieses Jahrhunderte langen und erfolgreichen Widerstands geworden; damit bedient er sich freilich eines eigentlich ambivalenten Narrativs über die Shuar, welches von nicht-indigenen AutorInnen, unter ihnen Ethnologen, zumindest mit-erzählt wurde (vgl. die Ausführungen in Absch. 2). Doch in seiner Aussage ist der *tsantsa* Ausdruck des ethnischen Stolzes der Shuar und weniger Symbol ihrer diffamierenden Repräsentation durch die nicht-indigene „westliche" Welt. Denn G. T. kehrt gerade die negative konnotierte Imagination des „wilden" Shuar um in eine positive Deutung des „Nie Eroberten"; er macht sich die Fremdzuschreibung zu Eigen. Damit ist er nicht allein; in ähnlicher Weise nutzt sie der ecuadorianische Staat: 1981 wurde die militärische Elitetruppe „Iwia" installiert, der ausschließlich Indigene aus dem ecuadorianischen Oriente, in der großen Mehrheit Shuar, angehörten (Uvidia Cañizares 2017, S. 17). Iwia ist der Name eines menschenfressenden Riesen der Shuar-Mythologie, welcher letztlich durch den mythischen Helden Etsa unschädlich gemacht wird. Seit der siegreichen Zurückschlagung des peruanischen Heeres im oben erwähnten Cenepa-Krieg genießt die Elitetruppe in der ecuadorianischen Gesellschaft hohes Ansehen, so dass das Motiv des „Nie eroberten" Shuar die Attribution des „wilden Shuar" zunehmend überdeckt hat (vgl. auch Meiser [2023]). Dass in dieser Auseinandersetzung auch erneut Schrumpfköpfe hergestellt worden sein sollen, hat den nunmehr ambivalent bis positiven Diskurs über die Eliteeinheit eher noch bestärkt. Ähnlich wie die einst negative Konnotation des Menschenfressers Iwia durch die Erfolgsgeschichte des gleichnamigen Bataillons eine veränderte und von der ecuadorianischen Gesellschaft mitgetragene positive Zuschreibung erfahren hat, haben die Shuar – hier beispielhaft G. T. – die einst stereotype Fremdzuschreibung umgedeutet und zu einem Identitätsmarker der eigenen Ethnie gemacht. G. T.'s Formulierung mag auch erklären, warum auf dem Schulwappen der Unidad Educativa Comunitaria Intercultural Bilingüe in Tsurakú ein *tsantsa* abgebildet ist.

4 Conclusion: Der *tsantsa* als hybrides Objekt

Die oben dargestellten Beispiele wollen freilich nicht nur aufgezeigt haben, dass der Schrumpfkopf nach wie vor ein prominentes und dabei auch ambivalentes kulturelles Artefakt sowohl in der Shuar- als auch der ecuadorianischen Gesellschaft ist. Vielmehr wird er mit sich wandelnden, da interkulturellen Bedeutungszuschreibungen versehen.[11] Im folgenden Abschnitt möchte ich zusammenfassend darlegen, inwieweit der *tsantsa* als „hybrides" Objekt ebenso postkoloniale Prozesse versinnbildlicht. Im Weiteren geht es mir darum aufzuzeigen, auf welche Weise die ethnologische Auseinandersetzung mit den vorab skizzierten Shuar-Diskursen zum Schrumpfkopf das allgemeine Potential des Faches verdeutlicht – wobei ich auf Forschungsfragen und Ansätze von Judith Schlehe zurückgreifen werde.

Für Steven Rubenstein ist das Wesen des *tsantsa* „hybride" (Rubenstein 2007, S. 359). Schrumpfköpfe seien zum einen menschliche Überreste – das Produkt eines Mordes –, zum anderen ein sozial konstruiertes, kulturelles Artefakt. Auf diese Weise transzendiere der *tsantsa* die festgelegten Dichotomien von Natur und Gesellschaft, von Vergangenheit und Gegenwart, von Lokalem und Globalem. Der *tsantsa* unterläuft, wie ich zudem meine, die scheinbaren Gegensätze von musealer Kuriosität und gängiger Alltagspraxis sowie von einer eindeutig negativen oder positiven Zuschreibung. In seiner Argumentation knüpft Rubenstein an das Konzept des „Quasi-Objektes" in Bruno Latours Werk *Wir sind nie modern gewesen* (Latour 2008, S. 70 ff.) an: physikalische Prozesse, kulturelle Praktiken und glokale soziale Diskurse machten den *tsantsa* zu dem, was er ist und bedingten so seine symbolische Wirkkraft. Diese haben aus einer kulturellen Praxis durch die Exotisierung und Skandalisierung „der Weißen" einen kulturellen Identitätsmarker der Shuar gemacht.

Arjun Appadurai hat das Bewusstsein dafür geschärft, dass in einer global vernetzten Welt nicht nur territoriale Grenzen durchlässig, sondern ideelle Landschaften, „ideoscapes", neu geschaffen werden (Appadurai 2008[8], S. 33 ff.). So ist etwa Amazonien nicht nur ein geographisch lokalisierbarer Raum; die Landschaft Amazoniens trägt auch die Umrisse unserer Imaginationen und Bilder. „Wer moderne Berichte über Amazonas-Indianer in manchen Massenmedien

---

[11] Ich selbst wurde das letzte Mal im Sommer 2012 mit der Schrumpfkopf-Mafia konfrontiert, als mich auf den Straßen der Provinzhauptstadt Macas ein fremder Mann ansprach und fragte, ob ich Interesse an einem *tsantsa* hätte; in diesem Fall könne man gerne ins Geschäft kommen. Ich verneinte und meldete den Fall anonym den Behörden. Seit einigen Jahren sind mir keine weiteren Gewalttaten in der Region bekannt geworden, von denen vermutet wird, dass sie durch Mitglieder der so genannten Schrumpfkopf-Mafia begangenen wurden.

liest", konstatierte denn auch Mark Münzel, „gewinnt den Eindruck, daß der Orientkomplex sich heute vom Orient nach Südamerika verlagert hat" (Münzel 1977, S. 51 f.). Der *tsantsa* ist hierfür ein anschauliches Beispiel: Er ist physisches Objekt und zugleich Sinnbild unserer Attributionen zu Amazonien und seinen Bewohnern. Gleichwohl sind diese imaginierten Räume und Zuschreibungen weder starr noch fix; sie werden in einer globalen Welt interkulturell verhandelt. Denn Imaginationen, formuliert Appadurai, prägten nicht nur unsere Vorstellungswelt, sondern zögen auch konkrete soziale Praktiken nach sich (Appadurai 2008[8], S. 31): Zum einen offenbart sich das in der mörderischen Konsequenz der Exotisierung des Schrumpfkopfs durch die „weißen" Souvenirjäger. Zum anderen wirkt etwa das Wissen der Shuar um die Ausstellung eines *tsantsa* in europäischen und US-amerikanischen Museen auf die Bedeutung zurück, die sie ihnen selbst zuschreiben. Die in diesem Beitrag vorgestellten Shuar antworten in ihren Imaginationen und in ihrer sozialen Praxis auf die verschiedenen, teils negativen Konnotationen um den *tsantsa;* sie eignen sich die fremden Imaginationen kreativ an und gestalten die ideelle Landschaft Amazoniens mit (vgl. auch Rubenstein 2007, S. 377). In dieser ist der Schrumpfkopf Symbol eines kollektiven ethnischen Selbstbewusstseins geworden und steht für eine kulturelle Tradition, die sich positiv von Praktiken der „weißen" Welt abheben will. Gleichzeitig gilt es festzuhalten, dass die Attributionen, die der Schrumpfkopf erfährt, von den Shuar unterschiedlich und daher auch kontrovers interpretiert sowie diskutiert werden; das führt nicht nur zu den im Beitrag beispielhaft dargelegten Diskursen und Praktiken, sondern auch zu einer Verdrängung und Verharmlosung des *tsantsa*-Phänomens in eine kulturelle Vergangenheit hinein, ohne sonderliche Bedeutung für die gegenwärtigen Aénts Chicham. In diesem Fall behält der Schrumpfkopf seine negative Konnotation bei und bleibt Sinnbild für eine augenscheinliche Wildheit und kriegerische Brutalität der Shuar, die nicht mehr Teil der gewandelten kulturellen Praxis der Shuar ist bzw. sein will (vgl. etwa Buitron und Deshoulliere 2019, S. 184; Rubenstein 2004, S. 18).

In Homi Bhabhas Argumentation schaffen interkulturelle Prozesse hybride Handlungsräume, in denen koloniale Asymmetrien unterlaufen und koloniale Diskurse – etwa der zum *tsantsa* – hinterfragt werden (Bhabha 2007, S. 150). Dieser hybride oder „dritte Raum", wie Bhabha es formuliert (Bhabha 2007: S. 55 ff.), ermöglicht die subversive Handlungsmacht indigener AkteurInnen: Der heutige indigene Umgang mit der Schrumpfkopfpraxis zeigt, dass die Shuar sich den kolonialen, orientalistischen Imaginationen durchaus entziehen können beziehungsweise diese für sich positiv reinterpretieren.

Die ethnologische Auseinandersetzung mit dem *tsantsa* ist zunächst eine Mikrostudie, fokussiert auf ein einzelnes kulturelles Artefakt in den Weiten Amazoniens; doch sie verdeutlicht die verschiedentlichen Beziehungen der Shuar nicht nur zu ihrer indigenen, sondern auch zur nicht-indigenen und globalen Mit-Welt. Diese werden in den musealen Ausstellungen – zumindest so, wie sie in den oben aufgeführten Zitaten kommentiert werden – nicht thematisiert, worin aus meiner Sicht die genannte Engführung und Einseitigkeit in der Repräsentation der Schrumpfköpfe besteht (vgl. Kap. 1.). Judith Schlehe analysiert in ähnlicher Weise in ihren Studien zu indonesischen Themen- bzw. Kulturparks, in denen die kulturelle Vielfalt des Inselstaates dargestellt werden soll, dass die verschiedenen Ethnien nicht nur essentialisierend, stereotypisierend sowie dekontextualisierend beschrieben werden. Es fehlten darüber hinaus Verweise auf mögliche Interessensunterschiede sowie Konflikte innerhalb der jeweiligen ethnischen Gruppe, gänzlich ausgelassen würden interkulturelle Kulturtransfers und Aneignungen, die die Kulturen Indonesiens im Zuge von weitläufigen Migrationsprozessen und transregionalen Interaktionen erfahren haben (Schlehe 2011, S. 156). Diese glokalen Relationen und Vernetzungen, die auch den Bedeutungszuschreibungen des *tsantsa* zugrunde liegen, sollen mithilfe von ausgewählten Argumentationen von Judith Schlehe zum Abschluss dieses Beitrags resümierend zusammengeführt werden:

Zum einen postuliert Schlehe, den inhärenten Dualismus, den solche Ansätze wie der des Orientalismus, Okzidentalismus oder auch Eurozentrismus in sich tragen, kritisch zu hinterfragen und stattdessen den Fokus auf verschiedene Perspektiven und interpretative Zugänge, die „zwischen den Kulturen" entstehen, zu legen (Schlehe 2013, S. 501). Das hybride Verständnis des *tsantsa* ermöglicht es, den Diskurs über den Schrumpfkopf nicht allein als eine dichotome Spielart des Orientalismus oder, wie in 3.1 dargestellt, eines Okzidentalismus zu lesen. Vielmehr handelt es sich um ein Ineinandergreifen wechselseitiger Zuschreibungen, die einander voraussetzen und aus dem *tsantsa* eben ein interkulturelles Symbol machen, das heutzutage nur aufgrund dieser Aushandlung „zwischen den Kulturen" seine Wirkkraft und soziale Praktiken entfalten kann. Zugleich drücken sich in den verschiedenen oben skizzierten Attributionen des Schrumpfkopfes auch unterschiedliche Imaginationen der „westlichen" Welt aus, die wiederum auch ein multiples Selbstverständnis der Shuar beschreiben – etwa das der moralisch "besseren" Schrumpfkopfjäger oder der "Nie-Eroberten"[12] (vgl. Schlehe et al. 2013, S. 6). Judith Schlehe und Evamaria Sandkühler verweisen zudem darauf, dass lokale Traditionen unter bestimmten Umständen als Gegen-Bewegungen zu globalen Diskursen und "westlichen" Formen des indigenen Otherings zu verstehen sind (Schlehe und Sandkühler 2014, S. 13). Die Hybridität des *tsantsa* und seine interkulturelle Re-Interpretation bedingen, dass er als kulturelle Praxis unter den Shuar quasi neu erfunden wird – in Antwort auf den Schrumpfkopf-Diskurs in der euroamerikanischen Welt. Diese gegenwärtigen Bedeutungszuschreibungen machen den Schrumpfkopf nicht nur zu einem negativ belegten Sinnbild in musealen Repräsentationen, sondern eben auch zu einem populären Symbol sowie kulturellem Emblem, welches sich auf Schulwappen und anderen Shuar-Logos findet und Ausdruck eines stolzen ethnischen Identitätsbewusstseins sein will. So wählte etwa ein Shuar für das eigene Profilbild auf Facebook die Darstellung eines Kriegers mit einem *tsantsa;* darunter schrieb er: "puro Shuar" – "ganz Shuar".

Literatur

Appadurai, A. 2008^8. *Modernity at large. Cultural dimensions of globalization.* Minneapolis [u. a.]: University of Minnesota Press.
Bhabha, Homi K. 2007. *Die Verortung der Kultur.* Tübingen: Stauffenburg Verlag.
Boster, James S. 2003. Blood feud and table manners. A Neo-Hobbesian approach to Jivaroan warfare. *Antropologica* 99–100: 153–164.
Buitro, N. und G. Deshoulliere. 2019. The Shuar writing boom: Cultural experts and the creation of a 'scholarly tradition'. *Tipití – Journal of the Society for the Anthropology of Lowland South America* 16(2): 175–194.
Descola, P. 1996. *Leben und Sterben in Amazonien. Bei den Jívaro-Indianern.* Stuttgart: Klett-Cotta.
Deshoullière, G. und S. Utitiaj Paati. 2019. Acerca de la declaración sobre el cambio de nombre del conjunto Jívaro. *Journal de la Société des Américanistes* 105(2): 167–179.
Drown, F. und M. Drown. 2002. *Mission to the headhunters. How god's forgiveness transformed tribal enemies.* Ross-shire: Christian Focus Publications Ltd.
Fabian, J. 1983. *Time and the other. How anthropology makes its object.* New York: Columbia University Press.
Fausto, C. 2012. *Warfare and shamanism in Amazonia.* New York [u. a.]: Cambridge University Press.

---

[12] In ähnlicher Weise argumentieren Schlehe et al. (2013) in Bezug auf den indonesischen Kontext: Unterschiedliche Imaginationen "des Westens" führen zu mannigfachen Vorstellungen über das eigene indonesische "Selbst".

Fausto, C. und D. Rodgers. 1999. Of enemies and pets. Warfare and shamanism in Amazonia. *American Ethnologist* 26(4): 933–956.

Harner, M. 1984. *The Jívaro. People of the sacred waterfalls.* Berkeley [u. a.]: University of California Press.

Juncosa Blasco, J. 2020. *Civilizaciones en disputa. Educación y evangelización en el territorio Shuar.* Quito: Universidad Andina Simón Bolívar, Sede Ecuador [u. a.]

Karsten, R. 1935. *The head-hunters of Western Amazonas. The life and culture of the Jibaro Indians of Eastern Ecuador and Peru.* Helsingfors: Helsingfors Centraltryckeriet.

Latour, B. 2008. *Wir sind nie modern gewesen. Versuch einer symmetrischen Anthropologie.* Frankfurt am Main: Suhrkamp.

Mader, E. 1994. Deviance, conflict and power in Shuar-Achuar society. *Theoretical Anthropology* 0(2): [ohne Seitenangaben].

Mader, E. und R. Gippelhauser. 2000. Power and kinship in Shuar and Achuar society. In *Dividends of kinship meanings and uses of social relatedness,* Hrsg. Peter P. Schweitzer, 61–91. London [u. a.]: Routledge.

Mader, E. und F. Sharup'. 1993. Strategien gegen Ausgrenzung und Assimilierung. Die Föderation der Shuar und Achuar im ekuadorianischen Amazonasgebiet". In *Kultur, Identität und Macht. Ethnologische Beiträge zu einem Dialog der Kulturen,* Hrsg. Thomas Filitz, Andre Gingrich, Rasuly-Paleczek, 109–122. Frankfurt am Main: Verlag für Interkulturelle Kommunikation.

Meiser, A. 2013. *„Ich trinke aus zwei Flüssen". Zur Logik transkultureller Prozesse bei christlichen Achuar und Shuar im oberen Amazonien.* Stuttgart: Kohlhammer.

Meiser, A. [2023]. Etsa und Iwia in Kirche und Kaserne. Amazonische Mythen als interkulturelle Kontaktzone. In *Urwälder Lateinamerikas. Lebenswelten, Kontaktzonen, fragile Biotope,* Hrsg. Sergej Gordon, Miriam Lay Brander. Berlin Neofelis Verlag.

Münzel, M. 1977. *Schrumpfkopf-Macher? Jíbaro-Indianer in Südamerika [Roter Faden zur Ausstellung 4].* Frankfurt am Main: Museum für Völkerkunde.

Neumann, S. 1994. *„Sólo unidos somos fuertes". Entstehung und Festigung ethnischpolitischer Organisationen im Tiefland von Ecuador am Beispiel der „Federación de Centros Shuar".* Bonn: Holos Verlag.

Peers, L. 2011. *Shrunken heads.* Oxford: University of Oxford.

Pellizzaro, S. und F.O. Náwech. 2005². *Chicham diccionario Shuar-Castellano.* Quito: Abya Yala.

Rubenstein, S. L. 2004. Shuar migrants and shrunken heads, face to face in a New York Museum. *Anthropology Today* 20(3): 15–18.

Rubenstein, S. L. 2007. Circulation, accumulation, and the power of Shuar shrunken heads. *Current Anthropology* 22(3): 357–399.

Schlehe, I. 2009. Zur Inszenierung nationaler, lokaler und religiöser Identität in indonesischen Kulturparks. In *Form, Macht, Differenz. Motive und Felder ethnologischen Forschens,* Hrsg. Elfriede Hermann, Karin Klenke, Michael Dickhardt, 165–179. Universitätsverlag Göttingen.

Schlehe, I. 2011. Cultural politics of representation in contemporary Indonesia. *European Journal of East Asian Studies* 10: 149–167.

Schlehe, I. 2013. Concepts of Asia, the West and the Self in contemporary Indonesia. An anthropological account. *South East Asia Research* 21(3): 497–515.

Schlehe, J., M. V. Nertz und V.I. Yulianto. 2013. Re-imagining 'the West' and performing 'Indonesian Modernities'. Muslims, Christians and paranormal practitioners. *Zeitschrift für Ethnologie* 138: 3–22.

Schlehe, J. und E. Sandkühler. 2014. Introduction. Religion, tradition and the popular in Asia and Europe. In *Religion, tradition and the popular. Transcultural views from Asia and Europe,* Hrsg. Judith Schlehe, Evamaria Sandkühler, 7–25. Bielefeld: Transcript.

Schlothauer, A. 2011. Tatort Sankt Gallen 2010. Von schreibenden Schweizer Schrumpfköpfen und sauren Gurken. *Kunst & Kontext* 2: 54–57.

Stirling, M. W. 1938. *Historical and ethnographical material on the Jivaro Indians.* Washington: U.S. Government Print. Office.

Taylor, A. 1993. Remembering to forget. Identity, mourning and memory among the Jívaro. *Man. New Series* 28(4): 653–678.

Taylor, A. 1996. The soul's body and its states. An Amazonian perspective on the nature of being human. *The Journal of the Royal Anthropological Institute* 2(2): 201–215

Uvidia C. und S. Miryam. 2017. *El conflicto del Alto Cenepa de 1995 y sus repercusiones en el aspecto social del Ecuador.* Quito: Universidad Central del Ecuador [Online-Publikation: http://www.dspace.uce.edu.ec/handle/25000/11425].

Wasserstrom, R. 2016. Waorani warfare on the Ecuadorian frontier. *The Journal of Latin American and Carribbean Anthropology* 21(3): 497–516.

Internetquellen (Zeitungsartikel & Websites)

Bailey, M. 06.03.19. Oxford museum rethinks famed display of shrunken heads. In *Art Newspaper*, https://www.theartnewspaper.com/2019/03/06/oxford-museum-rethinks-famed-display-of-shrunken-heads [22.03.22].

Becker, K. 21.09.21. Moorleichen und Mumien im Museum zeigen – geht das noch? In *Radio SRF 2 – Kultur, Kontext,* https://www.srf.ch/kultur/gesellschaft-religion/ausgestellte-tote-moorleichen-und-mumien-im-museum-zeigen-geht-das-noch [22.03.22].

CAREI. 08.12.09. Población pide linchar a implicados en asesinatos, http://careitv.blogspot.com/2009/12/poblacion-pide-linchar-implicados-en.html [22.03.22].

elmostrador. 11.10.19. Cientos de guerreros indígenas de la Amazonía se unen a protestas en Quito, https://www.elmostrador.cl/dia/2019/10/11/cientos-de-guerreros-indigenas-de-la-amazonia-se-unen-a-protestas-en-quito/ [15.03.22].

El Mundo/Samuel Mayo. 13.12.09. Con los úlitmos "Reductores de cabezas" del mundo, https://www.elmundo.es/suplementos/cronica/2009/738/1260658804.html [16.03.22].

Territorio Indígena y Gobernanza: https://www.territorioindigenaygobernanza.com/web/ecu_06/ [11.08.22].

Unidad Educativa Tsantsa: https://uetsantsa.com/ [07.03.22].

Unidad Educativa Tsantsa – Facebook: https://www.facebook.com/tsantsa.unidadeducativa.9 [02.09.22].

Whom to Remember? An Outsider Perspective on the (Un)Making of Social Memory of the Holocaust through Stolpersteine in Freiburg, Germany

Vissia Ita Yulianto

1 Introduction

Today, the German and global narrative of the Holocaust refers to the genocide of approximately 6 million Jewish people by the German Nazi regime between 1933 and 1945. This history and memory are reflected in the sheer number of books written about these events in addition to different memorials, exhibitions, TV documentaries and school textbooks. I will contribute to the ongoing discussion of remembrance and reflection, drawing from my extensive ethnographic fieldwork between 2009 and 2017 in Freiburg im Breisgau, Germany. In this city, little attention is paid to the other groups who were as badly treated during the Holocaust as Jewish people. This paper aims to illustrate two things: the making and unmaking of social memory of the holocaust through *Stolperstein,* and the consequences of the massive installation of these decentralized individual memorials.

Freiburg im Breisgau was the first city in south Germany—and the eleventh city in the country—to support the installation of *Stolpersteine*. The first one was

V. I. Yulianto (✉)
Southeast Asian Languages and Cultures, National Chengchi University, Taipei City, Taiwan
E-Mail: vissia_ita@yahoo.com

installed in Freiburg in 2001 by Gunter Demnig,[1] a political artist and creator of the *Stolpersteine,* and was dedicated to Professor Dr. Robert Liefmann[2] of the University of Freiburg. It was laid in front of Liefmann's last address in *Goethestraße* 33, Wiehre, Freiburg. This very first installation, however, was illegal as permission had not been gained from the city administration which at the time was in a period of transition between the former city mayor Rolf Böhme (1982–2001) and Dieter Salomon (2002–2018). By October 2017, when this fieldwork ended, there were 414 *Stolpersteine* laid in Freiburg.

According to my interview with the late Rolf Böhme in July 2017, laying *Stolpersteine* was a private initiative and although it was hotly debated due to different proposals on how best to commemorate victims of the Nazis, the idea gained the approval of the local government as it was seen as part of the government's policy to have a better relationship with the Jewish community. Böhme drew a comparison with the Jewish population between 1925 and 1940, during which time there was a gradual decrease until by 1942 there were no more Jewish people in the city of Freiburg, the result, according to him, of their victimization by the National Socialist regime. Therefore, he emphasized:

> It is politically important to show our attitude and to facilitate reconciliation by supporting the idea of memorialization. I have even written a book about what the government did after the war, to tell the new Germany that it was wrong, that it was terrible and Hitler was an evil man. (Interview with Böhme 2017)

2 Methodology and Data

In this study, different types of interviews were conducted with 40 informants in three different categories determined on the basis of generation, social class and political orientation. They comprise 17 members of older generations from the upper class both inside and outside academia; 2 young, upper class doctoral students; 13 young, middle-lower class students; 1 middle-aged member of the German right wing-party AfD; 1 older generation person who is an ex-SS member; 5 older generation WWII survivors; and 1 young member from the

---

[1] The *Stolpersteine* memorial project is the brainchild of Gunter Demnig, a West German political artist born in 1947. His father was a member of the Condor Legion, the German military unit responsible for the bombing of Guernica during the Spanish civil war (Debus 2007).

[2] For more info on his biography see Meckel 2006, p. 109 ff.

Sinti and Romani group. In some informal interviews, I was accompanied by 'door openers' comprising two Indonesians with German citizenship, while formal interviews—such as with the late Rolf Böhme, Marlis Meckel and academia in the university—that were conducted purely in English were done on my own.

In order gain a broad view, this study applies classical ethnographic methods including observation, participant observation, collecting literature (including grey literature) and different types of interviews, and a multi-sited ethnography recommended by George Marcus (1995). This last method was adopted due to the fact that the study of social phenomena that cannot be accounted for by focusing on a single site must be multi-sited to provide richer empirical data to assist researchers to gain a broader picture of the society under study. In this case, observations began in 2010 in a suburb of Freiburg im Breisgau and in the small town Gengenbach, and then moved and gained data from other crucial sites across different parts of the city of Freiburg until 2013. In order to be more empirically grounded and to fill the missing gaps, research continued in 2017 in Freiburg, a village called Simonswald in Emmendingen, Berlin, and also in Oświęcim (Auschwitz), southern Poland. This multi-sited-ness was fruitful for grasping the complexity of related factors (see Yulianto 2015, p. 70 ff.). These major sites, namely Freiburg, Emmendingen, Berlin and Oświęcim provided a better basis for my research investigation, analysis, and knowledge production.

3 The Embodiment of the *Stolpersteine*

Stolperstein literally means 'stumbling stone', contrasting with the centralized state-sponsored memorials that present state narratives of the Holocaust. Unlike the Memorial for the Murdered Jews of Europe, or in German Denkmal für die ermordeten Juden Europas, which is installed in a 19,000 square meter area in Berlin and consists of 2751 anonymous concrete slabs of differing heights, mounted in symmetrical rows on an uneven surface, the *Stolpersteine* are decentralized mini monuments for individual victims of all targeted groups, sponsored by the public. Informed by many details from the victims' biography, today there are more than 17,000 *Stolpersteine* across Europe, making them the largest decentralized memorial in the world. *Stolpersteine* are small, personalized commemorative stones for each individual victim of the Holocaust. A typical *Stolperstein*, measuring 10×10 cm and made of brass, will inform the public/pedestrians of the last address or workplace, date of birth, place and date of deportation and date and place of death of the individual person/couple/family. Although one may suggest that a mere inscription is not sufficient, the idea of erecting these 'stumbling stones' is that any passer-by may stumble over the stone, bow their head and read the inscription and remember the person and the moment he or she was murdered. As Demnig often states, the idea of this is to bring them back to their neighbourhood. The words *Hier wohnte...* ('Here lived...') are written on most of the plates, emphasizing that the victims of persecution did not just live and work in some anonymous place, but right there where the monument is. The date and place of birth, the date and place of deportation and the date and place of each individual death are compulsory pieces of information, as seen on the images below:

As we can see from the above illustrations, the first stone (Fig. 1) is dedicated to Sofie Bloch who was born in 1898 in Wachenheimer, deported in 1940 to Gurs, and was killed in 1942 in Auschwitz. The second stone (Fig. 2) is for Jessy Mayer, who was born in 1894, fled to Belgium in 1938 and passed away on 5 April 1939. His stumbling stone is installed on the pavement in front of his last address in Salzstraße, Freiburg. Further investigation—that is, not only based on what is written on the stone—tells us that he was a male Jewish banker who ran a private bank in Freiburg named 'Bankhaus Mayer'. He was arrested and then released, but only after paying a substantial fine. On 5 November 1938, he fled via Switzerland to Belgium, where he took his life on 5 April 1939. The bank was liquidated in October 1940. The third illustration (Fig. 3) is an image of several stones inserted into the pavement in Salzstraße 7. They are dedicated to Mayer's family members. Each of them also tells the public about the fate of each individual victim (Fig. 4).

However, as I observed throughout the city of Freiburg, one may also find another type of *Stolperstein*. Of special mention is one *Stolperstein* that has been laid in front of the main gate of the University of Freiburg im Breisgau:

From what is written on the stumbling stone above, the public may learn that the memorial is dedicated to Edmund Husserl, a German philosopher who is well known for the phenomenological approach in academia and beyond. Husserl taught in the University of Freiburg but was suspended from his academic position in 1933 and was prohibited from being involved in any university activity in the same year. Husserl's political rights were revoked. This meant that from then on, he no longer enjoyed any of the rights that the state could give him as a German citizen. Husserl was replaced by his former student and colleague Martin Heidegger, who joined the Nazi party and who was soon elected rector of the University of Freiburg after Husserl's 'retirement'. Husserl died in 1938 aged 79 following an illness and his gravestone—not *Stolperstein*—is located in Günterstal, also in Freiburg.

Fig. 1 A Stolperstein for Sofie Bloch, located on Salzstraße 7, Freiburg. (Photo by VIY)
Here lived Sofie Bloch
Place and date of birth: Wachenheimer, 1898
Taken: 1940 to Gurs
Place and date of death: 1942 in Auschwitz

Fig. 2 A Stolperstein for Jessy Mayer, located on Salzstraße, Freiburg. (Photo by VIY)
Here lived Jessy Mayer
Date and place of Birth: 1894
Date & place of deportation: 1938 in Belgium
Fled to suicide

From this, we may see that through the object agency (or the informative power) of the *Stolpersteine*, people are driven to know more than the stone tells them—in this case, Husserl's political persecution in academia. Although

Fig. 3 Image of several Stolpersteine on Salzstraße 7, Freiburg. (Photo by VIY)

the *Stolperstein* offers relief by making it possible to confront emotionally burdensome and barely comprehensible crimes by reducing complex instances of persecution to simple relationships and by expressing empathy for individual innocent victims (Apel 2014, p. 186), in this particular form, the public may learn not only about the individual victim, but also about the structural and political ideology of German Nazism. For example, Husserl's *Stolperstein* outlines that he was a victim of political 'genocide'. Thus, despite its small size and the apparent ability of these unimposing memorials to make complex relationships manageable (see Apel 2014, p. 186), this mini memorial embodies vast and important historical knowledge.

4 Findings: Public View of the *Stolpersteine* and the Holocaust

The first finding of this study refers to the public's view of the *Stolpersteine* as Holocaust memorials specifically for Jewish victims. Accordingly, responses from the different groups of people and the collective memory of the Holocaust amongst respondents is illustrated below:
As illustrated by the above Fig. 5, when asked if they know the meaning of the *Stolpersteine*, 83 per cent of the 40 informants—all of whom were from the city of Freiburg—replied yes, and 99 per cent of them associated the *Stolpersteine*

Fig. 4 The Stolperstein for Edmund Husserl located in front of the main gate of the University of Freiburg. (Photo by VIY)
Here taught Edmund Husserl
Date of birth: 1859
Date and place of work suspension: 1933
Date of death: 1938

with the commemoration of the Jewish victims of the Holocaust during the Nazi regime in 1933–1945.

In response to questions on their memory of the Holocaust, older generations were able to talk more vibrantly about their memory of the past. A 73-year-old female survivor who lives in Stühlingerstraße in Freiburg voluntarily showed a collection of books which document her memories of life in the early 1930 s. She told me what happened to her Jewish neighbours and that Freiburg was one of the central cities for the Nazi administration. She showed pictures of Kaiser Joseph-straße, Freiburg's main street and the city centre, which were flooded with

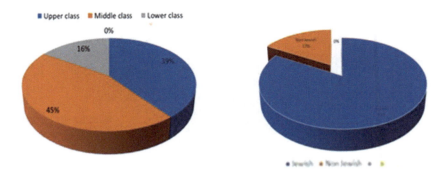

Fig. 5 Shows the visualization of the 40 informants and their response to the Stolpersteine. The left chart shows the informants' sociological category and the right chart illustrates the reception of the Stolpersteine as well as the social memory of the Holocaust in Freiburg. Following Savage et al., the criteria of upper, middle and lower class are not based solely on income but also on educational attainment. (Savage et al. 2013)

people and decorated with Nazi paraphernalia welcoming Adolf Hitler in 1932. A similar experience was shared by an old, retired German policeman who also showed me an item from a newspaper portraying what had happened to Jews in Germany. He said that he and his brothers had buried their ugly memories and remained silent for many years.

Young people in their 20s typically said: 'Sure, where should I start [...] so, under National Socialism [...] anti-Semitism was at its peak. It was extreme, nobody could believe it [...] there was a Holocaust, the killing of six million Jews'. Continuing in this vein, a group of undergraduate students also confidently explained what they knew of the history and mentioned that the *Stolpersteine* are memorials that refer to Jewish victims. One of them added: 'I believe all Germans will understand the Holocaust as the killing of Jews. If you ask any German, I think you will get the same answer'. This viewpoint was shared by a professor based in Munich whom I interviewed in 2018.

Understanding these statements is not difficult as they originate from the everyday lives and common understanding of the German people whom I observed and talked with in the field. The Holocaust is undoubtedly known as the industrial killing of 6,000,000 Jewish people during the National Socialism (NS) era. It is worth noting that none of the people I spoke with at that time indicated any knowledge of other groups who were seen as 'sub-humans' by the Nazis such as Africans, the Romani, the Sinti people, and those the Nazis labelled as 'asocial' or 'unworthy' people, like anyone who was homosexual, deaf, blind, disabled or mentally ill, being targeted for racial cleansing (Rogow 1999, p. 72). The young people with whom I talked did not even know if there is a memorial for Sinti and Romani people. Most notably, a female Romani person in her 30 s whom I was fortunate to talk to in Freiburg was also not aware of the presence of the *Stolpersteine* memorials and the idea behind their installation in Freiburg or Germany at large.

Other non-Jewish victims were omitted too. Young informants did not know of homosexual victims either. Other groups of informants from different social backgrounds and political orientations provided more or less similar answers; that the *Stolpersteine* are dedicated to the Holocaust victims, meaning Jewish people. One difference, however, is that respondents from far-right parties tended not to place much importance on memorialization of the Holocaust or were even Holocaust deniers. Notwithstanding this, for them, the Holocaust also refers to the killing of Jews.

I encountered a very similar response when asking German visitors to Auschwitz—the biggest Nazi concentration/extermination camp—in Poland in 2017, most of whom were young. Hardly any of them mentioned non-Jewish victims.[3] Such straightforward association of the *Stolpersteine* with the Holocaust—understood as the killing of 6,000,0000 Jews—clearly suggests that this knowledge and understanding is deeply and structurally embodied and inherent in contemporary German public history and memory.

5 The Exclusion and Inclusion of the Alleged Reason for Killing in *Stolperstein* Inscriptions

What and who, then, are the unknown and forgotten in the context of the Holocaust, and more specifically in the context of *Stolperstein* memorials? First of all, we should understand that what has been largely unknown is the fact that the first *Stolpersteine*, which were installed in the city of Köln, were laid as memorials for Sinti and Romani victims who comprised the second-largest group of people killed on racial grounds, referred to as Porajmos. The killing of this group, which the Nazis called 'gypsies', followed a similar pattern to the Jewish Holocaust. However, the Romani and Sinti Holocaust has largely been ignored (as seen from my data from Freiburg and Berlin, and the fact that various forms

---

[3] I was greatly unprepared and sickened by what I saw in Oświęcim, Auschwitz. Never in my life have I seen such unbelievable horror.

of anti-gypsyism which remain strong; see Loveland and Popescu 2016; Kende et al. 2021).

The above figure (Fig. 6) is 'only' a pond. It is located in an inner-city park, around 500 m from the national Holocaust Museum, close to the Reichstag building which houses the German parliament *(Bundestag)*. When visiting this memorial in late 2017, I found it to be calm, lined with trees and shrubs. While the people may feel that it is a site of deep inner sadness, a site of pain. According to the memorial's information board, the water symbolizes the tears shed by those who remember what happened or even by those who do not know what happened to 500,000 Sinti and Romani people who were murdered during the Nazi regime. Visitors might remember that under the Nuremberg Laws on race and citizenship, those groups were seen as alien races and a 'final solution' was enacted for racial hygiene to 'tackle' the 'gypsy question': genocide. By the end of WWII in May 1945, as many as 500,000 Sinti and Romani people had perished. Men, women and children were taken away, or murdered in their hometowns, or ghettos, concentration camps or in the gas chambers. Members of the Yeniche or the nomadic traveling people, including the Lalery and other travellers, formed a separate group of victims who were also persecuted as they were perceived as genetic dangers. Thus, we can see that the intention of the genocide of the 'gypsies' by the 'Nazis' methodical and final extermination took a similar pattern to that of the genocide of the Jews. The intention of the Nazi state and its racist ideology was palpably the destruction of those minority groups. There are clear records of the systematic and industrial scale of the Nazi plan to murder Sinti and Romani people in Europe.

Nonetheless, too little is publicly known about non-Jewish victims, despite the fact that there have been many attempts to inform people, see for example a film by Heather A. Connell entitled Forget us Not (2013). This 70-min documentary film is produced to pay tribute to non-Jewish victims of the Holocaust and to show the international public how homosexual men were targeted by the Nazis and how non-Jewish people were also brutally targeted for complete annihilation. However, those non-Jewish victims appear to have been largely ignored or are at least still less known (even unknown entirely) among the inhabitants of Freiburg. This finding underpins previous studies on public memory of the Holocaust (Barsalou and Baxter 2007; Hillebrecht 2014; Pearce 2019). Hillebrecht for example, pointed out that just 2 per cent of these memorials are dedicated to euthanasia victims, which exemplifies their marginal presence in popular commemoration, whether due to disinterest, reluctance, or a lack of awareness (Hillebrecht 2014 in Pearce 2019, p. 119). This means the historical significance of some of the sites

Fig. 6 Memorial for Sinti and Romani people in Berlin (Photo by VIY 2017)

connected with National Socialist euthanasia remains unacknowledged (Pearce 2019, p. 124).

The second important finding of this study is related to the history of why certain individuals were victimized or targeted. Whether to provide information on why those undifferentiated groups were targeted is a subject of debate in Freiburg. Unlike in some other cities in Germany, where one may find information or symbols that inform the public about why certain individuals were killed, such information is not found in Freiburg as the chief organizer of *Stolpersteine* installation in the city, Merlis Meckel, disagrees with Demnig's aim to be as informative as possible by providing contextual information on the mini memorials. Thus 98 per cent of the 400 *Stolpersteine* in the city in 2017 were installed without any public information being made available about the alleged reason why certain individuals were targeted by the regime. When I asked her why she disagreed with Demnig on 3 July 2017, Meckel said:

> Because I don't want to reproduce Nazi *sprache*, that is very clear. You know, we cannot deny that there are still prejudices towards these members of our society, and we want to stop the discrimination against them. If you say it on the stone, this is still discrimination. You come back to Nazi racist ideology. (Interview statement, July 2017)

Accompanied by her husband, she explained that she did not want to use the Nazi categorization of human or Nazi ideology in general and mentioned that it is highly problematic as the stigma around groups targeted by the Nazis has still not dissipated today. For example, she stated that she is an outspoken advocate for LGBT rights and that despite recent advances in Germany, LGBT people are still discriminated against.

Nevertheless, the above answers did not satisfy my curiosity as an outsider to German historiography and as one of today's generation in this increasingly globalized world. I had a long list of questions regarding why the persons whose names were written on the *Stolpersteine* were removed from their homes and sent to certain places and killed. Why was a family comprising a father, mother and children forcibly taken and methodically exterminated in Auschwitz? Why was a whole family of 18 people targeted? Why were very young children taken to Berlin or Bonn? Why were some people taken to Gurs and some others transported and killed in Dachau or at some other concentration camp? Were all of them Jewish, as the people in Freiburg commonly believed? Or was it due to some other reasons related to the people's race, faith, gender, or political or sexual orientation? Those questions echoed powerfully in my head as there was no explanation or contextual information included on the stones regarding why those individuals were dehumanized and persecuted.

The answers to those questions are indeed perplexing and highly contested. Denazification, in this case the removal of all physical symbols and remnants of the Nazi regime, is the immediate, dominant, common and official answer to the question of why the alleged reason for persecution is not inscribed. Older generation people that I talked with try to hide the history of cruelty committed by the Nazi regime and argue that the victims should live without 'criminal' records or the racial and social categories that the Nazis gave them, and that they should have legal protection in Germany, as emotionally explained, for example, by Meckel above. She and her organization strongly oppose the idea of including the alleged reasons for why certain individual was killed as they fear it will perpetuate discrimination (see Meckel 2006). She used the example of homosexual criminalization to illustrate her point. Homosexuality was criminalized throughout the German Empire by Paragraph 175 or Section 175 of the Reich Criminal Code, and this paragraph remained part of German law until 1994 (see Lautmann 1981). As Lautmann reported, homosexual men had lower social status compared to political and Jehovah's witness prisoners. They were more frequently given the most difficult work assignments and they had a lower survival rate both during imprisonment and upon release. Thousands of homosexual men—identified by pink triangles on their prison uniforms—were forced into concentration camps and were subjected to extreme abuse and died there (Lautmann 1981). According to some survivors that I spoke with, homosexual men were seen as criminals as they have intercourse solely for pleasure, not for procreation. An estimated 100,000 gay men were arrested and some were sent to prisons, while between 5000 and 15,000 were sent to concentration camps, with some being forced to wear pink triangles on their uniforms to show that they were homosexuals (see Ridley 2015). Regarding the fact that such information may trigger a multidimensional and multidirectional remembering interconnected with memories of discrimination and the fact that discrimination against gay men is still common in Germany, Meckel, the chief organizer of Freiburg's *Stolperstein* foundation strongly opposed the idea of including the alleged reason why certain individuals were targeted. Thus, we may see how complicated it is to put the ascribed identity of murdered people on those stones, the dilemma of wanting to know more about them but at the same time not wanting to use the categories that the Nazis assigned to people.

However, there are different issues at play here. This is connected to my third finding in this study. I found one *Stolperstein* with a rather different visualization in Freiburg. Surprisingly, none of my informants knew the symbol inscribed at the bottom of the *Stolperstein,* nor its meaning:

This specific stumbling stone (Fig. 7) is located in front of the University church of Freiburg on Bertoldstraße 17. It is of special interest in this paper because this particular mini memorial displays more information than the other common stones installed in Freiburg. In addition to last address, date of birth, place and date of deportation, and date and place of death, the symbol 'T4', is inscribed at the bottom of the plate. By consulting the existing literatures as well as corresponding with Gunter Demnig, I discovered that this symbol tells us that the person named on that specific *Stolperstein* was taken forcibly from his parents and home, deported and murdered in the context of the euthanasia program, which generated 200,000 victims.[4] However, it is interesting to note that none of my informants knew the symbol or its meaning. Nonetheless, while they did not know or really care about it, some of them opposed the idea of inscribing such symbols on the *Stolpersteine*, similar to Marlis Meckel:

---

[4] The brutal genetic experiments by Dr. Mengele included blood transfusion, injecting diseases, castration, mutilation and organ removal. Some 3000 twins were subject to his gruesome medical experiments. In 1945, Mengele escaped to South America and never faced trial. In his study in 1993, Paul Weindling reported that the terms like 'euthanasia' and 'incurable' were euphemistic medicalized camouflage carrying connotations of the relief of the individual suffering from terminal illness while the procedures were in fact painful and violent (1993, p. 543).

If you write down to which group a person belongs, we may risk that people who look at the *Stolperstein* look at it with prejudice, because there are still some prejudices against some of the groups, if not all [...] Some people still hold prejudices against them and don't treat them equally, as they should be. If we write down the reason why they were killed, you may trigger such prejudices [...]. Every life is worth the same [...] Of course, there were more Jews who were killed but they weren't the only ones. There were other groups and even though they were fewer in number it does not make any difference, because every human life is worth the same, and one victim of a certain group is worth as much as other groups and so all are worth saving [...]. They were smaller in number compared to the Jewish victims but to me it doesn't matter because it was still very bad and to me it doesn't matter what group the person belongs to [...] it's bad that they have been killed. I think about the person not the group they belonged to. (Interview statement by a 20-year-old female university student)

The statement above is very sincere and was uttered by a 20-year-old girl who voluntarily attended my academic presentation on the topic in late 2017 at the University of Freiburg. Her statement was her personal perspective and she further said that her knowledge about *Stolpersteine* had begun in her own village in a suburb of Freiburg. She visited a *Stolperstein* for a person whom she later found out was victimized due to his/her mental illness, information that she thought she should not necessarily know. In a similar vein, a 42-year-old lady of her own accord approached me after attending the same presentation and said that 'it is not necessary to inscribe the reason: [...] I don't know, I never think about it, because I knew, I think for my generation they all knew why [...] so it is not important to do that [inscribe the reason why somebody was killed]'. A similar

Fig. 7 Stolperstein for Eugen Heitz (Photo by VIY)

statement was given by a 48-year-old male professor who was very touched and emotional when explaining that 'This memorialization is enough for me [...] I never thought that the background is necessary [...] everyone in my generation is well informed about it [...] it is very scary'. He further stated that the words 'final solution' should not be mentioned either. For him, those words powerfully played on his memories and feelings, leading him to suggest to me that there is no need to add any other information on the *Stolpersteine*.

Likewise, though shrouded with senses of collective guilt, all of the 40 informants who spoke with me, as well as the approximately 35 people who attended my presentation at the University of Freiburg, did not consider the inclusion of the 'alleged' reason or Nazi racial classification, or any contextual information on why those people were murdered as valuable for inclusion on the *Stolpersteine*. For them, the reason why the people were killed is clearly Nazi brutality and ideology.

Yet, directly contrasting with this point of view, one lady in her 70s mentioned that it may become important to provide contextual information about individual victims of the Holocaust on the *Stolpersteine* for the for the next generation. She thought the inclusion of the alleged reason that they were killed may be important for later generations as they do not have shared experiences or shared feelings because they were not there when the genocide was enacted. It must be noted that she came to this idea as a reflection on my experience and perspectives as an outsider.

The narratives described above are understandable but they also create a dilemma. Drawing from the empirical data shown above, we may be tempted to say that all of the narratives support the exclusion of the alleged reason why certain individuals or groups were targeted. However, while the arguments are understandable, the question of how these victims could be better remembered arises. Is it better not to discuss Nazi rationale, their abuse of power and science, and their political reasons, or is it better to be compassionate, to feel and think of the individual victims who had horrible experiences and see them as living beings who were victimized? People must understand this tragedy more completely.

In the context of other targeted groups, for example, it is important to learn and to know the wider context of the persecution of children during the Nazi regime. As Sally Rogow (1999) has written, cloaked in the terminology of Social Darwinism and eugenics, the persecution of children with disabilities was justified on the grounds that they were a threat to the health of the German nation. Thousands of non-Jewish German children were victims of unrelenting persecution and genocide. Children who were blind, deaf, physically disabled or mentally handicapped, orphans, juvenile delinquents and adolescent non-conformists were removed from their homes and communities, isolated in institutions and work camps, and many thousands were murdered in the interest of improving white genetic supremacy (Rogow 1994, p. 71 ff.). In this sense, did my research group know that German university professors, scientists and physicians planned the euthanasia and were handsomely rewarded with generous research grants, university appointments and unlimited authority? Is it well known that the physicians who supervised the killing wards were rewarded with career advancement, university posts and extra bonuses and were able to avoid military service? Is it well known that children in Austria, Poland and other conquered nations did not escape these euthanasia programs?[5] Is it also known that between January 1940 and August 1941, over 70,000 patients were gassed in six purpose-built killing centres in Germany and Austria as part of Operation T4 and that the euthanasia program was an open secret operation until 1941?

This further research was only sparked after the code 'T4', which stands as a reminder of the Nazi implementation of the principles of eugenics, was found on one *Stolperstein* but was clearly not understood. According to a report from Caroline Pearce between 1939 and 1945, approximately 200,000 patients were murdered under the National Socialist euthanasia program in Germany and Austria. For many years, these victims were largely excluded from post-war commemorative culture and they are yet to attain legal equality with the victims of political or racial persecution (Pearce 2019, p. 118). Indeed, the racial law which the Nazis enacted delivered the most racist consequences for all groups in Germany in order to assert the myth of the superiority of the Aryan race. It is said that the racist doctrine of the Nazis targeted all groups of what they saw as *untermenschen* or 'sub-humans', who they regarded as not meeting the biological and metaphysical criteria for being human (see Steizinger 2018, p. 152), including those who were disabled and forced into 'sterilisation programmes'. In her study of these 'unwanted victims', Caroline Pearce recently wrote that the euthanasia program was in fact the first systematic killing under the National Socialist regime as the murders did not take place in the distant death camps in Eastern Europe but on German or Austrian soil (2019, p. 120). Unfortunately, this is hardly known among my research participants in Freiburg as well as in Berlin.

As described throughout this paper, there are many other groups who were categorized by the Nazis as *asocial* or sub-human and were thus victimized, namely the Sinti and Romani, the Lalery, the Slavic population, those of African descent, physically disabled and mentally ill people, political opponents and

---

[5] This question is inspired by Sally Rogow 1999, p. 80 ff.

homosexuals. The persecution of those groups was as systematic and cruel as the genocide of the Jewish people.

6 Conclusion

One of the most important questions about the social memory of the Holocaust in Freiburg relates to how to treat various pieces of information in remembrance. The findings above indicate how the public in Freiburg and Berlin remember and forget who suffered under the horrors of the Holocaust and to what degree. Drawing from the general tendency and strength of the dominant shared memory, this study concludes two things: The first is that the main narrative of the Holocaust in Germany is palpably the industrial killing of Jewish people in Europe by the Nazis. The second is that non-Jewish genocide victims are profoundly overlooked in the social memory of the German public in Freiburg today, 75 years after the Holocaust.[6] This absence of non-Jewish victims, which is shown by the public understanding of the *Stolpersteine* as 'just' another form of Jewish memorial, underscores that the installation of the *Stolpersteine* cements the main narrative of the Holocaust. Not only does this contradict the initial intention of the artist to remember those whom the nation has overlooked, it also shows a long and continuing battle for non-Jewish victims to find public recognition.

If we go back to the central idea that the purpose of the installation of the *Stolpersteine* is to respect each individual victim of the Holocaust with an inclusive approach, we should be reminded of an urgent need to acknowledge and remember all those who fell victim to Nazi persecution, and to understand the political struggle, the structural and political injustice. This requires a broader terrain of understanding of the Holocaust as not only the industrial killing of Jewish people but also of non-Jewish people who were considered sub-humans during the Nazi era. However, broadly speaking, the *Stolpersteine's* inclusive purpose is undermined by the current social memory and/or official history of the Holocaust, leaving non-Jewish victims' suffering largely unnoticed. From my outsider perspective, this is why critical reflection is required on the non-inclusion on the *Stolpersteine* of the reasons that certain groups of people or individuals were targeted. These findings demand a broader understanding and more just understanding of the Holocaust by including those whom the public in Freiburg tend to (subconsciously) marginalize. It is important to note that this perspective does not intend to de-emphasize Jewish victims, but is an effort to respect, address and

---

[6] See Ikhwan et al. 2019 for other (un) making of social memory of a dark past in Asia.

remember all Nazi victims equally. Non-Jewish victims of Nazi genocide should be remembered and regarded just as much as Jewish victims are, and should not be unseen, unknown, or even forgotten.

Acknowledgement This research was hosted by the Department of Socio-Cultural Anthropology, University of Freiburg, and supported by the DAAD's re-invitation program in 2017. I am grateful to them both. I also thank my three anonymous research assistants for their valuable help. I dedicate this work to all of my research participants and to those whom the world has forgotten.

References

Apel, L. 2014. Stumbling blocks in Germany. *Rethinking History* 18(2): 181–194.
Barsalou, J., and V. Baxter. 2007. *The urge to remember. The role of memorials in social reconstruction and transitional justice*. Washington DC: United States Institute of Peace.
Debus, L. 2007. Steine des Anstosses. *Jüdische Zeitung*. www.j-zeit.de/archive/artikel/754.html. Accessed: 29 August 2022.
Forget us not. United States 2013. Director: Connell, H. Displaced Yankee Productions.
Hillebrecht, S. 2014. Das schwierige Erinnern an Opfer der nationalsozialistischen Patientenmorde. *Gedenkstättenrundbrief* 176: 29–38.
Ikhwan, H., V. I. Yulianto, and G. D. Parahita. 2019. The contestation of social memory in the new media. A case study of the 1965 killings in Indonesia. *ASEAS-Austrian Journal of South-East Asian Studies* 12(1): 3–16.
Kende, A., M. Hadarics, S. Bigazzi, M. Boza, J. R. Kunst, N.A. Lantos, B. Lášticová, A. Minescu, M. Pivetti, A. Urbiola.2021. The last acceptable prejudice in Europe? Anti-Gypsyism as the obstacle to Roma inclusion. *Group Processes & Intergroup Relations* 24(3): 388–410.
Loveland, M. T., and D. Popescu. 2016. The Gypsy threat narrative. Explaining anti-Roma attitudes in the European Union. *Humanity & Society* 40(3): 329–352.
Lautmann, R. 1981. The pink triangle. *Journal of Homosexuality* 6(1–2): 141–160.
Meckel, M. 2006. *Den Opfern ihre Namen zurückgeben. Stolpersteine in Freiburg*. Freiburg; Berlin: Rombach.
Marcus, G. E. 1995. Ethnography in/of the world system. The emergence of multi-sited ethnography. *Annual Review of Anthropology* 24: 95–117.
Pearce, C. 2019. Remembering the 'unwanted' victims. Initiatives to memorialize the National Socialist euthanasia program in Germany. *Holocaust Studies* 25 (1–2): 118–140.
Ridley, L. 2015. The Holocaust forgotten victims. *Huffpost*. https://www.huffingtonpost.com.au/2015/01/27/holocaust-non-jewish-victims_n_6555604.html. Accessed: 22 August 2022.
Rogow, S. M. 1999. Child victims in Nazi Germany. *The Journal of Holocaust Education* 8(3): 71–86.

Savage, M., F. Devine, N. Cunningham, M. Taylor, Y. Li, J. Hjellbrekke, B. Le Roux, S. Friedman, A. Miles. 2013. A new model of social class? Findings from the BBC's Great British Class Survey Experiment. *Sociology* 47(2): 219–250.

Steizinger, J. 2018. The significance of dehumanization. Nazi ideology and its psychological consequences. *Politics, Religion & Ideology* 19(2): 139–157.

Weindling, E. 1993. *Health, race and German politics between national unification and Nazism, 1870–1945*. Cambridge: Cambridge University Press.

Yulianto, I. V. 2015. *Reframing modernities in contemporary Indonesia. An ethnographic study of ideas of center and periphery on Sulawesi and Java*. Berlin: Regiospectra.

Riding a Carousel Horse. REDD+ in West Kalimantan

Pujo Semedi und Carolina Astri

1 Introduction

In this article we discuss the REDD+ programme, a global-scale climate governance programme initiated by the UN in 2007, but one that has not successfully been implemented in Indonesia. REDD+ (Reducing Emissions from Deforestation and Forest Degradation) is a programme to provide economic incentive for people who directly use forest resources to protect forests from further destruction so as to ensure that they continue to be capable of absorbing and keeping carbon in the soil. The plus sign after the title was put in place in the aftermath of fierce protests from civil society movements that the programme should not only serve big companies but should also include the interests of local communities (Howell 2014). The programme promises and is expected by many to be one way to tackle deforestation, carbon emissions and the greenhouse effect (Lang 2012). The creation of REDD+ was based on 'the assumption that deforestation was being driven by insufficient pricing of the carbon services of forests and [it] provided a solution that incentivized forest protection' (Astuti and McGregor 2015, p. 2277). The economic assumption regarding the cause of global warming and climate change led to a belief that the problem could be resolved by protecting existing forests from further destruction and by urging people to engage in reforestation through market incentives, by paying countries and people

---

P. Semedi (✉)
Department of Anthropology, Faculty of Cultural Sciences, Gadjah Mada University, Yogyakarta, Indonesia
E-Mail: pujosemedi@ugm.ac.id

C. Astri
WRI Indonesia, Jakarta, Indonesia

to reduce deforestation, improve forest management, conservation and increase carbon stock (Purnomo et al. 2012, p. 75).

At a global scale, REDD+ involves an enormous amount of funds. A decade ago, it was estimated that to keep the programme working on a global scale a fund of US$ 10–30 billion was required annually (Schneider et al. 2009, p. 14). The plan envisaged that funds would mainly be obtained through a carbon trading mechanism in which industrial countries would apply carbon taxes to companies whose production activities emit carbon. It was from this tax that the budget for REDD+, i.e. the incentive for developing countries to protect their forests from deforestation and degradation, would be paid by the developed countries (Phelps, Webb and Agrawal 2010, p. 312). In 2010, the Indonesian government established cooperation with the Norwegian government, which promised to provide a grant of US$ 1 billion for the implementation of REDD+ in Indonesia. Agreements with developed countries and other donor agencies have also been agreed to finance REDD+ (Haugland 2010; ADB 2016; FORCLIME 2017).

REDD + in Indonesia has not proceeded well. The REDD+ programme, which was originally the subject of discussion, has lost its relevance and various analyses have emerged showing that there have been no real steps to reduce carbon emissions through cessation of deforestation and forest degradation in Indonesia (Howell and Bastiansen 2015). Although there has been a downward trend if measured against the level of forest destruction in the previous period, deforestation and forest degradation were still high in 2015–2019 (Enrici and Hubacek 2018, p. 1; Caldecott 2019, p. 215). In 2020 experts began to issue critical statements around the failure of REDD+ in Indonesia (Williams 2020). Eleven years after the agreement was signed, Indonesia surprisingly withdrew from the REDD+ cooperation agreement with Norway (Jong 2021).

The failure of REDD+ implementation in Indonesia has been analysed at the macro level, at the national and international levels, in both economic and political analyses. Angelsen (2017, p. 242) highlighted implementation difficulties at the global and national institutional levels: 'donors eager to spend and recipients unwilling to reform', and Williams (2020, p. 13) revealed 'oligarchic interest in natural resource extraction'. Both factors have been instrumental in forestalling the implementation of REDD+. This article will examine the failure of the REDD+ programme from a micro perspective by reviewing what is happening at the village and district levels. Micro analysis is needed because governance always takes place in relation to a specific location, time and subject. Analysing why and how a governance programme fails at the local level will give us a more grounded insight. While the organization and management of REDD+ programmes take place in the offices of government agencies and NGOs in Jakarta and provincial capitals, the real carbon-saving work is implemented in forests and orchards in villages (Enrici and Hubacek 2018).

There are three ideas that will guide this micro-analysis of REDD+failures. First, Angelsen's (2017) view above needs to be examined in more detail. It would be unwise not to investigate unwillingness to reform among the recipients of REDD+funds. Policy reform involves a calculus of costs and benefits, just like changes in other social aspects do. It is necessary to see whether the funds offered by donors to run the REDD+programme sufficiently cover the programme's costs – including the opportunity cost (cf. Irawan and Tacconi 2009, p. 430). Second, REDD+, which is run according to the PES market mechanism, requires intermediaries (Akiefnawati et. al. 2010; Loft, Thuy and Lutrell 2014, p. 2). In full market exchange, the role of intermediaries is taken by traders at various levels. However, REDD+is a hybrid programme that involves government and civil society movements. In this case the role of intermediaries is taken by government institutions and NGOs/people associations. As a result, funds from donors undergo long administrative and bureaucratic journeys that mean that the programme has been prone to elite capture, with each intermediary seeking to claim the funds for costs, be it rational or irrational, through both legal and illegal ways. By the end of this process, only a small proportion of the donor fund is left for 'the people living in and around the forests' (Milne et. al. 2019, p. 93; Howell 2014; Howell and Bastiansen 2015, p. 4, 13). In other words, people who are actually involved in forest management only receive small incentives from this programme, too small to create a real progress toward the reduction of deforestation and forest degradation. Third, as Scott (1998) and Li (2007) indicate, large-scale social engineering programmes usually become victims of simplification and rendering the complexities of social relations into technical diagrams. Their assessment can be accurate, but the simplified programmes are hardly fit to the target community's pre-existing social structures.

Social engineering programmes, whether introduced by external sources or generated internally, are basically transfers of tasks from one party to another. A successful transfer requires an appropriate structure strong enough to withstand the burden and tension, just like a transfer of water requires a pipe strong enough to accommodate the volume and pressure that is supposed to pass through it. In this regard, it is necessary to check the social structure in the community where REDD+is implemented to ensure that is strong enough to accommodate REDD+(Howson 2017). Social structures facilitates cooperation among community members, but they are also usually ridden with competition, tension and conflict that weaken their capacity to accommodate social engineering programmes aiming to change peoples' practices in certain aspects of their everyday lives.

2 Method

In this article, we discuss REDD+ in Kapuas Hulu District, West Kalimantan, where enthusiasm for the programme lasted only a few years. Long before the programme was launched in 2010, the district head of Kapuas Hulu, A.T. Husin, pledged that his district would become a conservation district by keeping its existing forest from further conversion (Kabupaten Kapuas Hulu 2003; Kalimantan News 2012b). However, in practice the district's forest is not protected as intended by the REDD+ programme, but has instead subjected to continues conversion into oil palm plantations. In 2007 there were 10,446 hectares of oil palm plantations and by 2020 that number had increased ninefold to 93,969 hectares. The ethnographic data for this article was collected mainly in an Iban village of Kupanalu, Upper Ambaloh sub-district of Upper Kapuas (BPS Kapuas Hulu 2016). The Iban are a large Dayak tribe that live in the north of the Upper Kapuas river region and further north across the Indonesian-Malaysian border (King 1976; Wadley 2001; Eilenberg 2011). Traditionally their economic life is supported by swidden cultivation and forest resource use (Dove 1985). Ethnographic data from the village was collected in a four-month fieldwork by Carolina Astri in 2015. Information and data on the wider context of the REDD+ programme in Indonesia was collected by Pujo Semedi through a series of fieldwork in the Lower Kapuas area, the Schwaner-Muller Mountain Range (West Kalimantan and Central Kalimantan) and in Central Sulawesi from 2010 to 2015 (Howell and Bastiansen 2015). Carolina Astri conducted participant observation in everyday village life and in a local NGO (LPM) activities. She conducted interviews on the village's and the area's environmental history, kinship and local political tensions. Pujo Semedi accessed government documents related to the REDD+ programme, obtained library sources and engaged in discussions with REDD+ administrators on the provincial and national levels. The research was conducted in the Global South-North academic collaboration between Universitas Gadjah Mada, the University of Agder and the University of Oslo based on the Student Tandem Research model initiated in 2003 by the Institute of Ethnology, University of Freiburg and the Dept. of Anthropology, Universitas Gadjah Mada (Schlehe and Hidayah 2014).

3 REDD+ in Kapuas Hulu

Kapuas Hulu, a district with an area of 29,842 km², is in the easternmost part of West Kalimantan. Until the late 1990 s this district was known to have the largest area of tropical forest in West Kalimantan, forests that had survived the looting of logging companies during the New Order era. The story is that as soon as the New Order regime of President Suharto came into power in the late 1960 s, tropical forests in Kalimantan and Sumatra were practically ransacked. Logging companies belonging to private entrepreneurs and military backed-business entities were granted licenses to extract the precious wood. The logs were processed in the provinces for further export to Japan, Taiwan and Korea, and the business proceeds were sent to Jakarta, leaving the forest destroyed, local farmers oppressed and local governments disappointed (Barr 1998; Broad 1995; Peluso and Vandergeest 2001). After three decades in power, President Suharto was forced to step down from the presidency and the centralized national policy of the New Order was put to an end (Warman 2016). Responding to decentralization Law No. 22/1999 (reissued as Law No. 32/2004), in 2004 the Kapuas Hulu district government announced that it would be a conservation district, obtaining revenue from PES and forest nature tourism (Gawing 2010, p. 32).

It seemed the idea of a conservation district and the expectation of earning revenues from payment for environmental services was coming closer to reality when in 2013 REDD+ came to Upper Kapuas under the name of the Forests and Climate Change Programme (FORCLIME) funded by the German Society for International Cooperation, GIZ (FORCLIME 2017). The project was managed directly by FORCLIME from the Ministry of Environment and Forestry in Jakarta, who later set up a managing office, the District Programme Management Unit, in Kapuas Hulu. The District Management Unit delegated the task of implementing the programmes to the field managers of demonstration area (DA) #2 in Bunut Hilir district and DA #8 in Ambaloh River district. The field managers led village and hamlet facilitators before the real work of the REDD+ programme was finally implemented by farmers who were organized into PLMH (*Kelompok Masyarakat Pengelola Hutan,* Farmers' Associations for Forest Management). The two clusters (DA #2 and DA #8) covered 29 Dayak villages with 29 PLMH and were to run forest protection activities in the corridor area between two national parks: Danau Sentarum and Betung Kerihun (Enrici and Hubacek 2018, p. 4).

Traditionally, Iban villages were established as longhouses inhabited by several households. Each had its own territory and socio-political governance and were related to other longhouses in a kinship-based confederacy. The longhouses were built along river tributaries that served as transportation access to other longhouses and markets in downriver towns. Pushed by population growth, a need for privacy and the government resettlement project in the early 1970s, many longhouses developed into hamlets with separate houses (Sitohang 2022, p. 24). The hamlets were integrated into the government administration pyramid of hamlets *(dusun),* villages *(desa),* sub-districts *(kecamatan),* and further up to districts *(kabupaten)* and provinces.

REDD+ in Kapuas Hulu can be divided into two activities: technical activities that are beyond the concern and reach of the village community and activities that directly involve PLMH. Technical activities include an inventory of carbon content in forest areas, analysis of high-resolution satellite images, socio-economic baseline surveys, biodiversity baseline surveys and capacity building at district level for Monitoring, Verification and Reporting (MRV). REDD + activities at the village level that are directly related to farmers are more of a repetition of the Community-Based Forest Management programme, which has been implemented by the Ministry of Forestry since the 1980s. This activity includes the establishment of a tree nursery centre, planting tree seedlings on farmer-owned land, introduction of livestock and fish farming, as well as forest patrol activities. This community-level activity cover an area of 735 hectares (7.35 km^2) for tree planting and 4182 hectares (41 km^2) for the forest patrols. In addition to these two activities, there are two other important activities, namely supporting village forests claim to obtain official recognition of the minister of forestry and drafting resolutions for regional conflicts on natural resources (FORCLIME 2017).

The description above shows that REDD+ activities under FORCLIME's control in Kapuas Hulu are not directly related to efforts to prevent deforestation and forest degradation. All activities that are concerned with farming in the forest environment have been practiced by the farmers for generations. With or without REDD+ the farmers would do it on their own initiative and expertise. The area covered by the REDD+ programme is relatively small, only 41 km^2 compared to Kapuas Hulu's total area of 29,842 km^2 (BPS 2017, p. 8), and moreover, by 2020, the Payment of Environmental Service (PES) had not yet taken place.

FORCLIME's funds are spent on activities that FORCLIME itself designs and runs. The FORCLIME funds might appear to be large, but if they were converted into PES as income for the community and local government, the contribution of the REDD+ programme so far in Kapuas Hulu would not be significant at all. The FORCLIME/REDD+ Kapuas Hulu budget in 2017 was 8.7 billion rupiah (8.6 billion was a grant from the German Government). Comparatively, this amount is insignificant compared to the Kapuas Hulu district regional revenues for public spending which was equalled 1707 billion rupiah (FORCLIME 2017; BPS 2017). In 2021 FORCLIME reported that FORCLIME's investment in community forest economic activities resulted in a harvest equalled 15.2 billion rupiah (FORCLIME 2021, p. 38). However, it should be noted that the harvest is the result of the work of farmers, which in practice they do themselves without the help of FORCLIME or any outside parties (Yuliani et. al. 2018, p. 8).

Statements from implementing agencies that the early stages of REDD+ are directed at achieving readiness for full implementation are often used as explanations for the low levels of funds being channelled through this programme and the absence of PES. The explanation is quite reasonable. However, it directly reduced the amount of funds disbursed at the local level, and made it minuscule compared to local government public spending and community funds.

At the district level, the idea of making Kapuas Hulu a conservation district can be seen as the double face of the elites. As a pathway to access PES REDD+, the conservation district concept is built on two existing national parks, as well as forest, peatland and lake areas which the central government has declared as protected zones with a total coverage 1677 km^2 or 56.21 % of the district's total area (Gawing 2010, p. 32; Enrici and Hubacek 2018, p. 3; Fripp and Shantiko 2014, p. 10; Astri 2017, p. 50). This idea of conservation district is basically the capitalization of existing assets which previously did not generate any revenue for local governments. District conservation policies cannot be fully interpreted as totally pro-environmental protection measures among district elites. At the same moment they designated 1677 km^2 of the district area as a conservation zone, these elites also allocated 399 km^2 for oil palm plantations (Gawing 2010, p. 33).

The discussion above shows that REDD+ in Kapuas Hulu is a programme with relatively weak economic incentives and is facilitated by a local government that assumes a double-faced policy, with a doubtful commitment to conservation.

4 Socio-Ecological Structure of Tanambaloh Society

No social engineering programme has never taken place in a tabula rasa community. When the REDD+ programme was brought to Kupanalu, it had to deal with the complexities of the structures and relations that were already in place (Milne et al. 2019, p. 10). Kupanalu village is located on the bank of the Ambaloh River, a northern riverine of the Kapuas River, some 120 km away from Putussibau, the district town. The larger part of the Ambaloh River area is covered by thick secondary forest, with occasional light green swidden fields now growing back to forest. For decades farmers also planted rubber trees in the swidden areas once the rice season was over. In 15 years, the farmers will start to tap the rubber trees to earn cash. Satellite images of the area hardly show any difference between rubber fields and pristine forest because they are usually blended into each other. According to their oral history, the Ambaloh River people, the Tanambaloh, began to occupy the area along the Ambaloh River in the 1870 s when they were led by a chief named Baki Maling Ma Lunsa (in office 1886–1904). A number of studies, however, indicate they have been in the area much longer (King 1985).

The Tanambaloh Iban are a stratified society. They are divided into three major, non-gendered social classes: *samagat, pabiring* and *banua* (King 1985, p. 126; 2001, p. 11). *Samagat* is divided into the three sub-classes of *samagat tutu, raa* and ordinary *samagat*. The social position of *samagat* is quite high, signified by certain symbols such the right to wear an earring made from hornbill ivory, war headgear embellished with the longest tail feathers of the hornbill and *ruai*, a necklace of leopard teeth, ear rings, and clothes with human motifs. The second layer in the stratification is *pabiring,* which is divided into *pabiring dara' samagat – pabiring* with *samagat* blood – and ordinary *pabiring*. It seems *pabiring* are *samagat* that have been downgraded because of exogamy, the marriage of *samagat* with non-*samagat*. The last class is *banua* or *ulun mam,* literally meaning people with manners and obedience. Historically banua are descendants of people from other villages who have stayed in Kupanalu. There is still another class who have faded away to the recess of history, that of *pangkam,* or slaves taken in war or bought from other party. In the past, a slave might be sacrificed for a longhouse building or to accompany a high *samagat* in their journey to the afterlife (King 1985, p. 141). With the adoption of Christianity in the early twentieth century, slavery was erased from the Tanambaloh social stratification and ex slaves were absorbed into the *banua* class (Ukur 1971, pp. 133–174).

Social stratification among the Tanambaloh probably has its roots in the Hindu culture that spread to the upper part of the Kapuas around the early second millennium, but Victor King proposed that it might originate from cultural contact between the populations of Upper Kapuas and those from lower Kapuas who were heavily influenced by Malay tradition from the seventeenth century onward (King 1985, 2001). The *samagat* as the upper class are the holders of the traditional right to lead the community as well as to be the keepers of the realm. In every spot along the Ambaloh River where the Tanambaloh people have built villages and established longhouses, it is always *samagat tutu* that occupy the most honourable position of *indu banua,* head of the people. In the early twentieth century the Ambaloh region was incorporated into the territory of the Sintang Sultanate, while the rest of the Upper Kapuas region was taken as the colonial government's territory. From then on *indu banua* were appointed as officials in the sultanate bureaucracy with the title of *tumenggung* (Sjamsuddin 2014, p. 221).

Economically, the *samagat* are the group with the largest proportion of forest land owners, entitled to loan the land to village members, to open swiddens, or to give the land away to members of other villages (King 1976, p. 325). In Kupanalu around 60 % of the village area belongs to *samagat*. The rest is *tanah parimbaan,* which belongs to *pabiring* and *banua*. They come to own the land by clearing primary forest for swiddens. Next is *tanah kapulungan* which belongs to extended families and is cultivated by family members. Finally, there is *toan adat* which belongs to the village, is managed by *samagat,* and is used by village members. *Banua* in general have limited access to land. When they want to open a swidden field but cannot find a good spot in their own lands because the forest is not mature enough, they can borrow land from *samagat* in return for tribute (King 1985, p. 127). For decades *samagat* have enjoyed their elevated socio-economic status. Their status dictates that they should not work in their rice fields and thus their swiddens are cultivated by villagers of *pangkam* descent (King 1985, p. 127).

The elevated economic status of the *samagat* started to erode in the late 1970 s as economic growth occurred in Sarawak, just across the Malaysian border, which divides the island of Borneo into a Malaysian and an Indonesian part. Ambaloh youths migrated across the border for better earnings and left the *samagat*'s lands unattended. When the youths who migrated to Sarawak returned home and renovated their houses in a modern style, the *samagat* continued to live in dilapidated, aging wooden houses. Actually, a decade prior to this economic reverse, the *samagat's* social status as guardians of the village had been severely dented when they were forced to become involved in the military conflict between Indonesia and Malaysia in the 1960 s (Eilenberg 2011, p. 14336). Many *samagat* were recruited as paramilitary scouts by the Indonesian military forces but their loyalty was often questioned because they had many kin across the border who were also being recruited to the military by Malaysian forces. Apparently this awkward position was exploited by many *pabiring* to free themselves from the *samagat*'s traditional domination, based on an argument that there is no point in *pabiring* obeying and respecting *samagat* who do not have integrity (Astri 2017, p. 44). In the subsequent years of the reformation that brought the New Order to its end in 1998, the *samagat* gave illegal loggers from Sarawak, the Malaysian part of Borneo, access to enter and ransack village forests (Wadley 2006, p. 118; Astri 2017, p. 44). They received substantial payments from the loggers and became rich, but in doing so they destroyed their social honour and legitimacy to lead the community.

In 2011, a conflict between villagers from Belimbis, who lived next to the Betung Kerihun national park, and the park's management provided the *samagat* with a chance to regain their status. After their longhouse was destroyed by fire, Belimbis villagers planned to build a new one and they needed around 600 ebony beams. They went to the forest to get the beams, but the park rangers stopped them. The 800,000 hectare national park was established in 1982 and a large chunk of Ambaloh territory was unilaterally taken for the national park. Usually the official taken over this did not result in tension between the park and the villagers as the national park's presence didn't change the villagers' economic activities. Villagers kept clearing forest areas for swiddens and took timber for building and commerce as they had always done (Obidzinski et al. 2007). It was just when the Belimbis farmers were about to cut down 600 ebony trees in the national park and the park's management refused to give any permission, the open conflict sparked. The local elite came forwward and led villagers to move against the national park's claim and to determinedly reject any regulation that curtailed the farmers' right to utilize forest resources for their tradition. After a string of struggles, from filing a protest to staging a blockade of the national park's office, they won and to some extent the *samagat* regained their honour and charisma as customary leaders of the community (Firdaus and Widawati 2014, p. 52 f.).

The Kupanalu community is undergoing a structural change wherein ordinary citizens seek to challenge the status quo while the elite try to maintain it. This situation is different from several other villages where the local elite can still maintain their integrity and are still respected by the villagers so that their decisions are obeyed by all villagers (Yuliani et al. 2018, p. 8). It is in the context of rural communities that elites experience social fragility such as not being respected by ordinary citizens, when REDD+ arrived in Kupanalu.

5 A Carousel Horse

REDD+ was implemented in Kupanalu by creating a new institution for environmental governance with a structure that follows governance from the district level to farmers in the village: the District Management Unit, Demonstration Activities, Field Managers and PLMH(*Kelompok Masyarakat Pengelola Hutan*, Farmers' Association for Forest Management). Perhaps the REDD + management hoped that the climate governance programme could be effective by imitating the government structure that had proven effective in carrying out public governance. The creation of this new institution was a necessary ad hoc step because using the existing government bureaucracy to achieve REDD + goals could be difficult.

First, the bureaucracy already had its agendas for the forest environment and its own ways of getting things done (Duchelle et al. 2019, p. 12). Second, REDD+ is based on the market initiative of carbon trading. Inserting funds from the private sector into the state budget would require a long bureaucratic process that is normally detested by the private sector. Third, there has been strong demand from civil society movements that REDD+ pay serious attention to the wishes of the people who live in the forest areas. As Signe Howell (2014) aptly pointed out, NGOs on behalf of the people have proclaimed 'No Rights, No REDD'. However, there is a fundamental difference here between the two institutions. The government structure is built on historically and structurally established territorial control and is supported by a strong and reliable state budget. Meanwhile, the REDD+ climate governance structure was founded on an ad hoc programme that had just emerged, with no strong territorial claims and dubious funding support. Even though there is claimed to be a huge REDD+ fund, people have never really seen it, let alone felt its effects (Newell et al. 2013; UNEP 2017).

At the end of the long, semi-bureaucratic REDD+ chain are the village level Farmers' Associations for Forest Management, each consisting of dozens of members Strangely enough, these private sector-funded associations have the traits of *Gemeinschaft*, of intimate communities based on a sentiment grown out of kinship, similarity of religion, place of living and everyday life practices (Tonnies 2002, pp. 33–35). This view expects the social activities of the farmers' association to be driven by moral values of solidarity, mutual help and common good rather than individual economic motives (see Scott 1974). From this perspective it seems that the farmer's associations are ideal social vehicles 'to shape desires and act on actions, setting the conditions so that people would behave as they ought' (Li 2007, p. 231). Yet this ideal should be checked against the real practices that take place among the farmers.

The presence of an REDD+/NGO-sponsored Farmers' Association in Kupanau has created new elite positions in the REDD+ programme and association management: village facilitators, field coordinators and association caretakers. The village facilitator is responsible for leading LPM, while a field coordinator serves as a connecting bridge between LPMs and NGOs in charge of the REDD+ programme.

The association consists of dozens of farmers and has a leader, secretary and treasurer who are tasked with leading the implementation of the association programmes. Higher formal education is not required to fill those positions, as long as the candidates can operate a computer and master basic skills of administration and reporting, as field facilitators and village coordinators are obliged to send monthly reports on activities in their respective units. It is no surprise that the positions are mainly occupied by *samagat*. Out of eight farmer associations in Ambaloh, four were led by field facilitators of *samagat* social background – two associations were commoner-led and the last two were in the traditionally egalitarian Iban villages. Rather than providing space for a new type of democratically elected leadership, the farmers' associations have mainly been co-opted by *samagat* to regain their status as the communities' traditional *primus inter pares*. It is these administrators who regularly receive salaries from the REDD+ programme, while association farmers only receive activity funds and members receive money if they are involved in forest patrol activities (FORCLIME 2017, p. 17). Implementation of the REDD+ programme in Ambaloh has been providing leading positions for, if not has been co-opted by, the traditional village elite who had been experiencing social decline. From the perspective of the district-level REDD+ management, cooperation with the local samagat to run the programme at village level might seem correct, that they are collaborating with the persons who have traditionally led the community.

Beyond leadership is the economic incentive, distributed to the farmers through several programmes. At a closer observation, however, it is clear that the REDD+ programme implemented in Kupanalu through a set of activities have little relevance to forest degradation and deforestation. They are participatory land use planning (PLUP), tree nurseries, tree planting, food crop cultivation, sylvofishery, pig keeping, rattan handicraft and wild honey collection (Astri 2017, p. 63). All were justified as steps to reach REDD+ readiness and as aiming at the creation of new economic activities to prevent farmers from extracting forest resources (Großmann 2018, p. 322).

Participatory Land Use Planning was implemented to solve inter-village border disputes that often occurred in the area. Through this programme it was expected that people would get a clear idea where the territory of their village ended and the territory of the neighbouring village began. There is no report available at this time regarding the extent to which this goal has been achieved. In late 2015 the tree nursery programme started to provide seedlings for various trees that possess economic value such as agar wood (Aquilaria Malaccensis), coffee, rubber, cacao and various forest trees. A total of 751,992 seedlings were prepared in 19 nurseries. Only 60 % survived and were planted within 845 hectares of fields belonging to 1091 farming households (FORCLIME 2017, p. 17).

Community-based forest patrols by members of farmers' associations, that cover an area of 952 hectares in Ambaloh and 3228 hectares in Bunut Hilir sub-district, attracted the interest of some villages youth. The program invested them with a degree of authority and control in the village territory. Apart from ensuring that their territory is not subjected to logging, forest fires or any activities detrimental to forests, during patrols the farmers conduct flora and fauna surveys. They meticulously collect information on the type and population size of important species and include it in the patrol report. Rattan handicrafts, food crop cultivation, fish culture and pig keeping have all been reported as successes and have allowed the association members to produce market commodities without having any negative effect on the forest and therefore preserving the forest's function of absorbing carbon emissions.

In villages along the Ambaloh River and in Bunut Hilir the farmers' associations PLMH are encouraged to write project proposals to obtain funding for their activities. Those that are approved receive IDR 50 million (US$ 5000) of so-called short-term investment per year, with a maximum total amount of IDR 150 million over the following three to five years. According to the FORCLIME 2017 report, in that year 27 associations were receiving the investment, amounting to roughly IDR 1.35 billion in total. In terms of community-based forest patrols, there were 59 patrol teams with 295 members prepared to take up the task of walking in the forest next to their homesteads. A budget of IDR 709 million was allocated for the activity (FORCLIME 2017, p. 23). An impressive amount of roughly IDR 2.1 billion (US$ 200,000), was delivered to farmers in Ambaloh and Bunut Hilir by the REDD+programme in 2017. In 2020 it was claimed that the programme had managed to create IDR 15.2 billion of turnover for the farmers: IDR 13 billion from agroforestry and IDR 0.8 billion from fish culture, while pig and owl keeping produced IDR 0.8 billion (FORCLIME 2020, p. 28). The reduction of carbon emissions was also reported as a success – by the end of 2020 a total of 645.9 tons of carbon had been saved through the programmes above (FORCLIME 2020, p. 13).

The FORCLIME (2017, p. 40) report admitted that there had been some hindrance to the programme's implementation. In practice only a small fraction of the village population actively participated in the programme. Most of the activities were carried out by members of farmers' associations. Other farmers just waited for tree seedlings that were ready for planting because their work schedule was already full of their own farming activities and by other village developmental projects funded by the village development budget and other ministerial budgets. Closer observation reveal deeper problems around the distribution of the REDD+funds.

The budget sent to the community is only 23 % of the IDR 8.7 billion REDD+funds allocated to Kapuas Hulu District (FORCLIME 2017, p. 48). This means that most of the REDD+funds do not reach the people who live in the forest environment. The funds allocated to the community amounted to IDR 1.35

billion, used as group business capital, not farmers' income. Only IDR 709 million of the forest patrol funds are directly received by farmers as patrol wages. This amount is divided between 295 people, or IDR 2.4 million (US$ 240)/person/year or IDR 200,000(US$ 20)/person/month. It is hard to gauge the extent to which an IDR 50 million fund/year could support revenue-generating activities in a farmers' association, considering that Kapuas Hulu is a rather remote area where goods are expensive. The farmers along the Kapuas River considered the IDR 200,000 forest patrol payment as a minimum wage for a day of labour. Less than that is considered an insult. More cynical responses have been given by farmers who took up logging as a second job, like the one Peter Howson (2017, p. 129) met in another REDD+demonstration area 'The forest is for timber, that's all. I don't go walking in the forest for fun. I go to cut wood for my house'.

It is unrealistic to expect that a significant, positive ecological effect can emerge from that investment. According to the district statistics (BPS Kapuas Hulu 2016, p. 61) there are around 1381 hectares of rubber fields along the Ambaloh River, with an average turnover of IDR 5.7 million/hectare/year, or roughly IDR 7.8 billion/year. Compared to this stable revenue, the forest patrol fee and the short-term investment fund are insignificant. The largest portion of this short-term investment is spent on working capital, thus leaving members of LPM without any individual incentive. To the farmers' association leaders this fact seems to be obscure and they were quite sure that the short-term REDD+investment would really make things work: 'The FORCLIME programme will turn unattended fields into a good shape. Indeed, seedlings that we planted just recently have not produced anything. We know there are many positive things from the FORCLIME community empowerment programme. Don't worry, this programme will be alright [...]', a village facilitator convincingly explained.

Next, all REDD+programmes that are related to tree and crop cultivation, fisheries, husbandry and crafts are activities that have been practiced by the farmers for ages. Without REDD+or any other developmental programmes, those activities would still have been there, supporting farmers' needs. To anyone who is familiar with rural Kalimantan, introducing tree planting, pig keeping, and honey collection to Dayak farmers is not much different from teaching a fish to swim. This is why the FORCLIME report is often funny, if not ridiculous, for example 'The pigs are breeding well, some have been sold and slaughtered' (FORCLIME 2017, p. 40). Finally, the claim of REDD+success in saving carbon was probably true – indeed there had been such an amount of carbon that was kept from polluting the air in the Ambaloh River and Bunut Hilir areas in 2020 because of the farmers' tree planting activities in their fields. However, claiming that the saving was because of the REDD+programme is highly questionable.

In neoliberal thought, uneven distribution of revenue is necessary to generate incentives for capital creation (Friedman 2005). But in the case of REDD+ where the larger portion of the funds is absorbed by high level NGOs and other bodies for management and training, lack of funding for village-level activities have made the REDD+ programmes become blunt spearheads. When they are measured against the revenue from forest areas exploitation, economic incentives from REDD+ at village level are just a joke. It is more a carousel horse, moving round under bright lights and blaring merry music while getting nowhere, rather than a real horse to compete against the highly energized horses of oil palm plantation, mining and forest logging.

6 Palm Oil Plantations: New Money, New Structure

Without sufficient funding support from the REDD+ programme, the good intentions behind declaring the Upper Kapuas a conservation district in 2003 have no power to move against the strong current in favour of other types of land use. In the years following the declaration, the quantity of forest converted into palm oil fields accelerated. In 2003 there were 8126 hectares of palm oil fields in Upper Kapuas district. Twelve years later the number had increased tenfold to 86,719 hectares and by 2020 there were 93,396 hectares of oil palm fields belonging to big plantation companies. Data on smallholders' oil palm fields from that year is not available. Most likely this is because the rapid expansion made it difficult for the district office of statistics to record. Apart from palm oil fields, thousands of hectares of forest land have been opened for (primarily) coal mining (Lanting Borneo 2017). All this data indicates that the idea and status of Kapuas Hulu as a conservation district is very dubious.

High productivity levels lead both entrepreneurs and farmers to involve in palm oil cultivation. With a gross turnover of around IDR 1.5 million per hectare per month, in 2010 the palm oil fields in Upper Kapuas represented a IDR 591 billion per year business – almost on par with the district's annual budget. It is no surprise that palm oil stakeholders are keen to keep expanding their fields. By 2015, 36,719 hectares were assigned to palm oil cultivation in Upper Kapuas and according to our estimate the combined turnover of was larger than the district's annual budget of IDR 1.22 trillion. If money represents power, it is obvious who has more power in shaping the Upper Kapuas environment.

The oil palm cultivation wave reached the Ambaloh River region too. In 2005 some farmers sent a request to the district government to clear some forest for rubber fields, but the district head refused the request on the basis that Kapuas

Hulu was officially designated a conservation district. To the villagers' shock, in 2010 a private company, PT Rimba Utara, obtained a permit from the district government to create 9000 hectares of rubber plantation and even managed to change it into a permit to create palm oil fields of the same size (Kalimantan News 2012; Efriani 2012; Astri 2017). Following the Ministry of Agriculture's decree, the plantation would be operated under a partnership scheme, in which 20 % of the fields would be obtained by the company from the government and the remaining 80 % would be contributed by farmers as their share in the company (Kalimantan News 2012). The farmers would then receive dividends on their shares at the end of the company's fiscal year, with the risk they would receive nothing if the company declared a loss. If they preferred, the farmers could take jobs in the plantation company as farm labourers. It is a poor deal for the farmers. In the lower Kapuas area farmers complained that the partnership scheme was worse than the older scheme of nucleus estate, wherein they cultivated their own fields under contract to sell the harvest to a particular company (Li and Semedi 2021, p. 149).

Yet, a number of farmers of *pabiring* background supported the company and established a palm oil farmers' association. In 2008 the association sent a petition to the district head to permit palm oil cultivation in the Ambaloh River region. The *samagat* were against this move as they did not want to lose land and become plantation coolies in their own village (Astri 2017, p. 78). They claimed that the plantation company had tricked farmers into working for their cause. Seeking clarification, the samagat invited the company to a public meeting in the St. Martinus parish meeting hall on 11 March 2012. Hundreds of villagers waited patiently until afternoon, but the representative of the company failed to come. Later the plantation staff mentioned that they were not ready to come face to face with hundreds of agitated farmers. The customary leaders or *samagat* of the Ambaloh River region declared that the company had breached customary law by failing to fulfil a promise and that they should pay a customary fine. The customary leaders asked the district government to annul PT Rimba Utara's operational permit, but the district head refused (Lin 2012). The Ambaloh River farmers' resistance against the plantation company became big news in national mass media in 2012.

Five years have passed since the Ambaloh farmers' refusal, but government statistics clearly show that palm oil cultivation in Upper Kapuas is unstoppable. Some farmers view this development with dismay. Some other farmers, however, look at the development as a manifestation of the message conveyed in the letter sent to the district head in 2008 in which they stated that they are not afraid to adopt a new way of life to 'earn better revenue and prosperity […]'. From their perspective, palm oil cultivation offers a good path to achieve their aspirations, much better than the path offered by the REDD+programme.

The district government's decision in the late 2000s to release 93,000 hectares of forest land for oil palm plantations was perhaps related to the fact that two national parks in the district cover around 1.5 million hectares, which is probably considered sufficient to make Kapuas Hulu a conservation district (Gawing 2010, p. 35). Seen from this perspective, it appears that the district government of Kapuas Hulu and the district elite were planning to get both PES from REDD+ and money from oil palm cultivation as well. When the REDD+PES failed to materialize, they quietly abandoned the idea of the conservation district. Yet their wish to earn money from the REDD+programme did not die altogether. Some oil palm plantation managers and owners are convinced that they also have a right to REDD+benefits because plantation trees also conserve carbon – forgetting that the plantations' existence is fundamentally against the underlying idea of REDD+(Almadani 2013). The discussion in this part shows how the REDD+programme in Kapuas Hulu has been running in opposition to other production activities that are based on conservation of forest lands and in terms of money, the REDD+programme is comparatively insignificant. In 2014, a district government official complained that people in Kapuas Hulu had been tasked by the global community with being mere 'forest watchmen' without being sufficiently rewarded (Equator 2014).

7   Conclusion

The REDD+programme in Kapuas Hulu is still running up to this day under the FORCLIME programme, covering an area which is a mere fraction of the district's total area, no more than 4500 out of 2.98 million hectares. With this level of implementation, it is difficult to say whether REDD+is a successful programme in Indonesia. Moreover, its activities in Kapuas Hulu are mostly economic activities that the farmers have been carrying out for generations. The discussion above also shows that Angelsen's views that relate the ineffectiveness of the REDD–programme to the Indonesian government's reluctance to reform while donor countries are eager to channel funds seems to be incorrect. REDD+funds sent by donor countries are too small to induce a reformative effect in forest management, be that at the government level or in the lives of rural communities. Even local governments that were originally progressive have been forced to adopt more realistic ideas for obtaining local government revenues. They are forced to assume a two-faced policy of simultaneously welcoming REDD+ and

Table 1 Palm oil cultivation, Upper Kapuas 2003–2020 (ha). Source: BPS Kalimantan Barat, 2003–2016, BPS Kapuas Hulu 2003–2020

Year	Estate	Smallholder	Total
2003	5,176	2,950	8,126
2005	5,176	3,018	8,194
2010	29,844	3,018	32,862
2015	85,882	837	86,719
2020	93,396	NA	93,396

also oil palm plantation companies, whose business is totally opposed to the basic concept of REDD+. At the village level, REDD+ management took the logical step of collaborating with traditional village elites, the *samagat*. The REDD+ programme needs people with strong social influence and knowledge of how things get done in the community. With the *samagat*'s support, REDD+ in the Ambaloh River area has a better chance of obtaining villagers' acceptance. The problem is that the traditional elites in Ambaloh and Kapuas Hulu have lost their dominant role in people's everyday lives. The REDD+ programme in Kapuas Hulu has been superimposed on fragile village-level social relations and two-faced district-level economic-political calculations, and is supported by socio-economically insignificant funding (Table 1).

References

Akiefnawati, R., G.B. Villamor, F. Zulfikar, I. Budisetiawan, E. Mulyoutami, and A. Ayat, et al. 2010. Stewardship agreement to reduce emissions from deforestation and degradation (REDD). Case study from Lubuk Beringin's "Hutan Desa", Jambi Province, Sumatra, Indonesia. *The International Forestry Review* 12(4): 349–360.

Almadani, A. 2013. PT.Cipta Usaha Sejati Terapkan Program REDDPlus. Dec. 10 Ekonomi dan Bisnis, Pontianak. http://borneonusantaratime.com/2013/12/pt-cipta-usaha-sejati-terapkan-program-reddplus/. Accessed: 15 June 2022.

Angelsen, A. 2017. REDD+ as result-based aid. General lessons and bilateral agreements of Norway. *Review of Development Economics* 21(2): 237–264.

Asian Development Bank (ADB). 2016. *Proposed administration of Grant Republic of Indonesia. Community-focused investments to address deforestation and forest degradation project*. Metro Manila: ADB 2016.

Astri, C. 2017. *Bangkitnya Elit Lokal. Pengaruh Implementasi REDD+ Terhadap Kuasa Elit Lokal di Embaloh Hulu, Kalimantan Barat*. Master thesis. Yogyakarta: Dept. of Anthropology, Gadjah Mada University.

Astuti, R., and A. McGregor. 2015. Responding to the green economy. How REDD and the One Map Initiative are transforming forest governance in Indonesia. *Third World Quarterly* 36(12): 2273–2293.

Barr, C.M. 1998. Bob Hasan, the rise of Apkindo, and the shifting dynamics of control in Indonesia's timber sector. *Indonesia* 65: 1–36.

BPS Kapuas Hulu. 2016. *Statistik Daerah Kecamatan Embaloh Hilir 2016*. Kapuas Hulu: BPS.

BPS Kapuas Hulu. 2003–2020. *Kabupaten Kapuas Hulu Dalam Angka*. Kapuas Hulu: BPS.

BPS Kalimantan Barat. 2010–2016. *Kalimantan Barat Dalam Angka*. Pontianak: BPS.

Broad, R. 1995. The political economy of natural resources. Case studies of the Indonesian and Philippine forest sectors. *The Journal of Developing Areas* 29(3): 317–340.

Caldecott, J. 2019. The Indonesia–Norway REDD+ Partnership. *Oryx* 53(2): 211–215.

Dove, M.R. 1985. *Swidden agriculture in Indonesia. The subsistence strategies of the Kalimantan Kantu*. New York: Mouton.

Duchelle, A.E., F. Seymour, M. Brockhaus, A. Angelsen, A.M. Larson, M. Moeliono, et al. 2019. *Forest-based climate mitigation. Lessons from REDD+ implementation*. Bogor: CIFOR.

The Economist. Nov. 16, 2017. Sucking up carbon.

Efriani. 2012. *Isu Perkebunan Sawit di Kecamatan Embaloh Hulu Kabupaten Kapuas Hulu – Kalimantan Barat*. https://plus.google.com/106254434270504310951/posts/D3SmfZGF8rL.

Eilenberg, M. 2011. Straddling the border. A marginal history of guerrilla warfare and 'counter-insurgency' in the Indonesian borderlands, 1960s–1970s. *Modern Asian Studies* 45(6): 1423–1463.

Enrici, A.M., and K. Hubacek. 2018. Challenges for REDD+ in Indonesia. A case study of three project sites. *Ecology and Society* 23(2): 1–20.

Equator, A. 2014. Dilema Kabupaten Konservasi. armand-equator.blogspot.co.id. http://armand-equator.blogspot.co.id/2014/10/dilema-kabupaten-konservasi.html. Accessed: 15 July 2022.

Firdaus, A.Y., and E. Widawati. 2014. *Konflik Tenurial dalam Pembangunan KPH. Pembelajaran dari Hasil Penilaian Cepat di KPHP Berau Barat dan KPHP Kapuas Hulu*. Bogor: Working Group on Forest-Land Tenure.

FORCLIME. 2017. *LAPORAN TAHUNAN FORCLIME FC MODULE 2020*. Jakarta: Kementerian Lingkungan Hidup dan Kehutanan, National Programme Management Unit FORCLIME.

FORCLIME. 2020. *LAPORAN SEMESTER I. FORCLIME FC MODULE 2017*. Jakarta: Kementerian Lingkungan Hidup dan Kehutanan, National Programme Management Unit FORCLIME.

Fripp, E., and B. Shantiko. 2014. *Payment for ecosystem services (PES). Assessment of PES potential in Kapuas Hulu*. Working Paper 165. Bogor, Indonesia: CIFOR.

Gawing, L. 2010. *Indah Kabar dari Rupa. Studi mengenai Pemenuhan Hak-hak Masyarakat Adat dalam Kerangka Hukum dan Kelembagaan Pelaksanaan Demonstration Activities REDD di Kabupaten Kapuas Hulu Kalimantan Barat*. Jakarta: Epistema Institute.

Großmann, K. 2018. Conflicting ecologies in a "Failed" Gaharu Nursery programme in Central Kalimantan. *Sojourn: Journal of Social Issues in Southeast Asia* 33(2): 319–340.

Haugland, S. 2010. *UN-REDD regional information exchange meeting.* Jakarta: UN-REDD/UNDP Indonesia.

Howell, S. 2014. 'No RIGHTS – No REDD'. Some implications of a turn towards co-benefits. *Forum for Development Studies* 41(2): 253–272.

Howell, S., and E. Bastiansen. 2015. *REDD+ in Indonesia 2010–2015. Report of a collaborative anthropological research programme.* Oslo: Department of Anthropology, University of Oslo.

Howson, P. 2017. Intimate exclusions from the REDD+ forests of Sungai Lamandau, Indonesia. *Conservation & Society* 15(2): 125–135.

Irawan, S., and L. Tacconi. 2009. Reducing emissions from deforestation and forest degradation (REDD) and decentralized forest management. *The International Forestry Review* 11(4): 427–438.

Jong, H.N. 2021. Indonesia terminates agreement with Norway on $ 1 b REDD+ scheme. *Mongabay,* 10/09/2021. https://news.mongabay.com/2021/09/indonesia-terminates-agreement-with-norway-on-1b-redd-scheme/. Accessed: 15 July 2022.

Kabupaten Kapuas Hulu. 2003. Keputusan Bupati No. 144/2003 tentang Penetapan Kabupaten Kapuas Hulu sebagai Kabupaten Konservasi.

Kabupaten Kapuas Hulu. 2015. Peraturan Daerah Kabupaten Kapuas Hulu No. 20 Tahun 2015 tentang Penetapan Kabupaten Kapuas Hulu sebagai Kabupaten Konservasi.

Kalimantan News. 2012a. PT. Rimba Utara Mencakup Embaloh Hulu Dan Embaloh Hilir. 13 Oktober 2012, Kalimantan News.com. http://www.kalimantan-news.com/berita.php?idb=16473. Accessed: 15 July 2022.

Kalimantan News. 2012b. Disbunhut Gelar Workshop Pengembangan Sistem MRV REDD+ Kabupaten Kapuas Hulu. 11 December 2012, Kalimantan News.com. http://www.kalimantan-news.com/berita.php?idb=17775. Accessed: 15 July 2022.

King, V.T. 1976. Migration, warfare, and culture contact in Borneo. A critique of ecological analysis. *Oceania* 46(4): 306–327.

King, V.T. 1985. Symbols of social differentiation. A comparative investigation of signs, the signified and symbolic meanings in Borneo. *Anthropos* 80(1./3.): 125–152.

King, V.T. 2001. A question of identity. Names, societies, and ethnic groups in interior Kalimantan and Brunei Darussalam. *Sojourn: Journal of Social Issues in Southeast Asia* 16(1): 1–36.

Lang, C. 2012. Interview with Budhi Sayoko, Laksmi Banowati and Rogier Klaver, UN-REDD Indonesia: "REDD+ is quite a promising thing to tackle deforestation".

Li, T.M. 2007. *The will to improve. Governmentality, development, and the practice of politics.* Durham: Duke University Press.

Li, T.M., and P. Semedi. 2021. *Plantation life. Corporate occupation in Indonesia's oil palm zone.* Durham: Duke University Press.

Lin, M. 2012. Kronologis Kasus PT. Rimba Utara vs Masyarakat Adat Dayak Tamambalo dan Iban di Kecamatan Embaloh Hulu-Kabupaten kapuas Hulu. https://id-id.facebook.com/Kecamatan.Embaloh.Hulu/posts/548661655196874. Accessed 15 July 2022.

Loft, L., P.T. Thuy, and C. Luttrell. 2014. *Lessons from payments for ecosystem services for REDD+ benefit-sharing mechanisms.* Bogor: CIFOR 2014.

Milne, S., S. Mahanty, P. To, W. Dressler, P. Kanowski, and M. Thavat. 2019. Learning from 'actually existing' REDD+. A synthesis of ethnographic findings. *Conservation & Society* 17(1): 84–95.

Newell, R.G , W.A. Pizer, and D. Raimi. 2013. Carbon markets 15 years after Kyoto. Lessons learned, new challenges. *The Journal of Economic Perspectives* 27(1): 123–146.

Obidzinski, K., A. Andrianto, and C. Wijaya. 2007. Cross-border timber trade in Indonesia. Critical or overstated problem? Forest governance lessons from Kalimantan. *The International Forestry Review* 9(1): 526–535.

Peluso, N.L., and P. Vandergeest. 2001. Genealogies of the political forest and customary rights in Indonesia, Malaysia, and Thailand. *The Journal of Asian Studies* 60:3761-3812.

Phelps, J., E.L. Webb, and A. Agrawal. 2010. Does REDD+ threaten to recentralize forest governance? *Science, New Series* 328(5976): 312–313.

Purnomo, H., D. Suyamto, L. Abdullah, and R.H. Irawati. 2012. REDD+ actor analysis and political mapping. An Indonesian case study. *The International Forestry Review* 14(1): 74–89.

Schlehe, J. and S. Hidayah. 2014. Transcultural ethnography. Reciprocity in Indonesian-German tandem research. In *Methodology and research practice in Southeast Asian studies*, Eds. M. Huotari, J. Rüland, and J. Schlehe, 253–272. London: Palgrave MacMillan.

Schneider, G., W.L. Thomas, and B. Vitale. 2009. Banking on the environment. Profiting from investment in REDD+. *Natural Resources & Environment* 24(1): 14–17, 24.

Scott, J.C. 1998. *Seeing like a state*. New Haven: Yale University Press.

Sitohang, L.L. 2022. *Cross-border interaction in the context of border-regional development in Kalimantan*. (PhD). Radboud Universiteit, Nijmegen.

Tonnies, F. 2002 (1887). *Community and society*. New York: Dover Publications.

UNEP. 2017. The emissions gap report 2017. A UN environment synthesis report. Nairobi: United Nations Environment Programme (UNEP).

Wadley, R.L. 2001. Trouble on the frontier. Dutch-Brooke relations and Iban rebellion in the West Borneo Borderlands (1841–1886). *Modern Asian Studies* 35(3): 623–644.

Wadley, R.L., 2006. Community cooperatives, 'illegal' logging and regional autonomy in the borderlands of West Kalimantan. In *State, Communities and Forests in Contemporary Borneo*, Ed. Fadzilah Majid Cooke, 111–132. Canberra: ANU Press.

Warman, R. 2016. Decentralization and forestry in the Indonesian archipelago. *South East Asia Research* 24(1): 23–40.

Williams A. 2020. *Reducing emissions from deforestation and forest degradation in a context of nationalist oligarchy. Lessons from Indonesia*. Oslo: Chr. Michelsen Institute.

Yuliani, E.L., E.B.P. de Jong, L. Knippenberg, O. Denny, M.A.S. Bakara, and T. Sunderland. 2018 Keeping the land. Indigenous communities' struggle over land use and sustainable.